D0016140

FIT FOR THE PRESIDENCY?

Fit for the Presidency?

Winners, Losers, What-Ifs, and Also-Rans

SEYMOUR MORRIS JR.

Potomac Books

AN IMPRINT OF THE UNIVERSITY OF NEBRASKA PRESS

Library of Congress Cataloging-in-Publication Data
Names: Morris, Seymour, author.
Title: Fit for the presidency?: winners, losers, what-ifs,
and also-rans / Seymour Morris Jr.
Description: Lincoln: Potomac Books, An imprint
of the University of Nebraska Press, 2017. | Includes
bibliographical references.
Identifiers: LCCN 2016012184
ISBN 9781612348506 (cloth: alk. paper)
ISBN 9781612348872 (epub)
ISBN 9781612348889 (mobi)
ISBN 9781612348896 (pdf)
Subjects: LCSH: Presidential candidates—
United States—History. | Presidential candidates—
United States—Biography. | United States—
Politics and government.
Classification: LCC JK524 .M67 2017 |
DDC 973.09/9—dc23 LC record available at http://
lccn.loc.gov/2016012184

Set in Iowan Old Style by Rachel Gould.

CONTENTS

PREFACE

The story of U.S. presidents begins when they take the oath of office. Yet a key part of their lives took place *before* they reached the pinnacle, when they were candidates. What had they accomplished? What signals were there to suggest their future performance? How impressive were their résumés?

More than almost any other country, the United States has perfected the art of personnel selection. We apply stringent criteria when selecting a leader for a corporation or nonprofit institution: we require a detailed résumé and carefully check personal and professional references, a process known as "due diligence"; when the candidate comes in for an interview we ask difficult, probing questions. We want complete and accurate information, and we want to be objective and make a decision free of personal bias.

Electing a president is not the same as choosing a CEO, yet in many ways the process is comparable to the sorts of hiring decisions made every day by top managers and boards of directors of companies and nonprofits. It therefore seems reasonable to apply the same degree of discipline and analysis to filling elective offices. In *Fit for the Presidency?* I examine résumés and perform due diligence for the office of president just as a professional recruiter would do to fill a company's executive position. How does the candidate measure up on key criteria such as integrity and judgment? What in the candidate's past suggests his potential success or failure as a president? Is there a good fit between the candidate's skills and the needs of the country at the time? Is there anything in his background that he might not want publicized? This examination is in no way invasive or unreasonable. Voters, said John Adams, have "a divine right to the most dreaded and envied kind of knowledge [concerning] the characters and conduct of their rulers."[1]

Important prior positions like governor or secretary of state invite inquiry about what exactly a potential president has accomplished. We once had a presidential candidate with a sterling job history: he had been a state legislator, diplomat, secretary of state, congressman, and senator. Unfortunately he was a man always one step ahead of his résumé—an example of "the Peter Principle" at work.[2] By the time he became president and had to perform serious diplomacy and negotiation in the prelude to the Civil War, James Buchanan fell short. "The road to leadership, as well as to wisdom," says one management consultant, "is to err and to err and to err again but less . . . and never to make the same mistake twice."[3] Good judgment comes from experience, and experience comes from prior bad judgment; this is why experience can be the best teacher. As every executive recruiter knows, one should beware of the star performer who has an unblemished record of success, who has never known failure or disappointment.

In evaluating a candidate for a top position, executive recruiters are careful not to accept prior success at face value but to analyze the types of organizations that have employed him, the reasons for his success, and whether he can translate his success to a different culture and organization. Wendell Willkie, for example, had no political or government experience, but his work as head of an electric utility dealing with regulators and the public qualified him for the presidency because it's very similar to what a president does. George Marshall, even though he spent his entire career in the military and had never run for public office, demonstrated superb strategic thinking and personnel management skills worthy of a president.

. . .

In this book I present the résumés of presidential candidates and all the important information known about them at the time they ran. Would you have voted for this person? Did he demonstrate the qualities we should look for in today's candidates?

In choosing candidates to profile, I sought a reasonable balance of insiders and outsiders, Republicans and Democrats, visionaries and doers, liberals and conservatives, candidates well-known and candidates not well-known. No judgment is meant to be implied by the selection. Avoiding any attempt to label the candidate as one extreme or the other, I have endeavored, eschewing all gossip, legends, and opinions, to simply detail facts and professional character references for which we have hard evidence. If the result is to show a candidate in a better or worse light than is commonly perceived, it is not due to any desire to whitewash or smear him but simply to let the evidence speak for itself and let you draw your own conclusions.

Some of these candidates turned out to be giants of the presidency; others are now largely forgotten; and a few probably should have won—our nation's loss. Five candidates made it to the White House, and ten did not (a few of whom didn't even make it to the nomination, though they were considered top candidates). My examination of each candidate begins with a brief background and a detailed résumé, followed by an assessment of qualifications and a summary rating—outstanding, excellent, fair, or poor—based on the key criteria of accomplishments, intangibles, and judgment and a category named "Overall" that encompasses all the information we have on the man. Each chapter closes with a review of what happened after the election. In almost every case the candidate's future performance could have been predicted (Abraham Lincoln being a major exception).

All high achievers, no matter how impressive, are human beings with quirks and foibles that form an essential part of their potential fitness or nonfitness for high office. A person able to control his passions? Two of our candidates challenged their enemies to a duel. One of them even challenged his father-in-law. (Luckily the older man—who later became president—had more common sense and told him to cool it.) Personable and charming? Another candidate preferred to spend his spare time trout fishing so he could "talk to the fish." When he talked to people, his favorite sound was "uh." Despite his lack of personal charm, he still managed to become president.

How about the candidate who proposed to a fabulously rich but rather plain young lady on their second date? Would you give him an F for being a gold digger, or would you give him an A for being decisive? His name was George Washington.

Almost all the candidates had a deep respect for learning. One man spent ten years as a recluse, reading books. Another graduated from college at age seventeen (and gave the college commencement speech in Latin). At the other extreme are the college dropouts. Two of them became multimillionaires. A third one became a "Top Gun" pilot who flew dangerous rescue missions over the Himalayas and mastered no fewer than 170 different kinds of aircraft—and went on to write the best-selling political treatise since Thomas Paine's *Rights of Man*.

Not all candidates who managed to finish college were academic standouts. One, who majored in a subject called "varsity football," went on to write two best-sellers. Another attended a third-rate college and never studied finance or accounting, but after becoming president he studied the tax code so thoroughly he could talk on an equal level with the chairman of the House Ways and Means Committee. Still another, who barely finished college, spent most of his time in the nation's capital chasing the girls and dancing all night at nightclubs—and creating the Federal Reserve System.

The star, the pride and joy of his parents? One candidate, 100 pounds and 5-foot-8 compared to his famous 240-pound, 6-foot-4 father, was mocked by his despairing mother as "the runt of the litter." He stormed into the White House in one of the biggest landslides in history. The proud father-in-law? Not this president. When his son-in-law challenged him for leadership of the Democratic Party, he withheld his support and prevented the younger man from winning the party's nomination.

Success or failure in business rarely correlates with success or failure in politics. Two of the candidates almost went bankrupt in their early business career. A third proved there are all kinds of interesting ways to make money: his major claim to fame was his design of a new brand of men's underwear overprinted with large red ants, called "Antsy Pants."

Donald Trump? One of our candidates built the largest real estate complex in the world, covering twenty-seven acres of office space. Move aside, Donald. Brilliant lawyer? Samuel Jones Tilden, one of the top lawyers in the country, had his carefully drafted will overturned after his death because he hadn't paid attention to a fundamental rule of estate law. Another brilliant man insisted on writing his own will without consulting anybody and made a colossal foul-up: by promising that his slaves would be freed after his wife died, he practically invited someone to murder her. The only reason it didn't happen is because Martha Washington, fearing for her life after hearing "talk in the [slave] quarters of the good time coming to the ones to be freed after she died," quickly released the slaves on her own.[4]

Many of the candidates were born poor; some tried to appear so. One candidate came from a family that owned the most magnificent plantation in America, yet he won election because the public believed he lived in a log cabin. (His huge home had a closet door hiding the walls of the original cabin.) Another candidate admitted to being born "in a log cabin equipped with a golf course, a pool table, and a swimming pool."[5] Other candidates made no bones about being rich—very rich. One had a summer job as a young boy selling newspapers from the backseat of his parents' chauffeur-driven Rolls-Royce; another was the richest man in the world for men his age (late thirties). One former vice president of the United States accomplished more for humanity than many presidents or Nobel Prize winners do: his patented invention saved the lives of over a hundred million people. He also left his children an estate eventually worth two billion dollars.

On this list of candidates are two governors of the biggest state in the union, a senator, a mayor, three generals (two of them active in politics), a former congressman, two wealthy businessmen, and five cabinet officers. The cabinet officers were widely considered "the best ever" secretary of war, secretary of the treasury, secretary of agriculture, secretary of commerce, and attorney general. Only one of them became president.

. . .

The best predictor of future performance is past accomplishment. People do not suddenly reinvent themselves the moment they step into the Oval Office. In all candidates the signs of potential greatness—along with potential problems—are there if you look close enough. Does a great résumé predict a good president? More often than not it does, when the jobs and accomplishments are significant enough to reveal character, integrity, clarity, persuasiveness, and certain intangibles that define a leader.

Some voters say the presidency is such a unique job that a candidate's past doesn't really matter. This is a rationalization. Lack of qualifications is not a qualification. Nor is popularity or celebrity. Opined the 1872 Republican candidate Horace Greeley: "Fame is a vapor, popularity an accident."[6]

In describing the job of president, Henry Adams, the great nineteenth-century historian, wrote, "The American president resembles the commander of a ship at sea. He must have a helm to grasp, a course to steer, a port to seek."[7] Would you board a ship headed by a captain who had never commanded before? Who has no principles to support his grasp? No vision of where he wants to go? On-the-job training sounds reasonable, except that it is not supported by history. Almost every one of our two-term presidents had a difficult second term. If a candidate needs further seasoning by the time he gets to the White House, it's probably too late. The presidency is a job for which we expect the winner to hit the ground running. He has a hundred days to make a good first impression and four years to show his leadership capabilities so he can win a second term hopefully as good as his first.

So before getting on the boat, check out the résumé—not how famous he is or what he claims he will do, but what he has done already.

Introduction

*What Our Founding Fathers Looked
for in a Potential President*

At the Constitutional Convention, in their deliberations concerning
the newly created office of the presidency, the Founding Fathers
listed only two qualities a president should have: *experience* and
fortitude.[1] In the *Federalist Papers*, James Madison, Alexander
Hamilton, and John Jay describe the ideal candidate as having
experience. (The word appears no fewer than ninety-one times.)[2]
In their view, truths are taught and corroborated by experience.
They speak of "unequivocal" lessons from experience and the
"accumulated experience of ages." "Experience is the parent of
wisdom," declares Hamilton, and Madison is in total agreement:
"Let us consult experience, the guide that ought always to be followed whenever it can be found." In sum, the primary qualification for president is "the best oracle of wisdom": deep experience.[3]

Delegates to the Constitutional Convention defined *fortitude*
as a combination of courage, steadfastness, firmness, trustwor-
thiness, and integrity. Most were thoroughly educated in religion
and the classics and had read St. Thomas Aquinas, the thirteenth-
century Catholic theologian who taught that prudence and justice
are the virtues with which we decide what needs to be done, and
fortitude gives us the strength to do it. A great president would
combine experience with fortitude.

There was a third qualification the Founding Fathers hoped a

What might have been: George Washington VIII.

candidate would meet, though it was never recorded in writing: he mustn't display any desire to become a king. Here they were most fortunate: in the first go-round they had a candidate, a man of experience and fortitude, who had no sons—clearly a sign of divine providence. So they slept well at night, knowing that in creating the presidential office they were not creating a hereditary dynasty. There would be no string of Washingtons to follow.

There had never been a job like the presidency of the United States. All other countries were ruled by kings, queens, emperors, emirs, or other monarchs. Yet there would be no catalogue of presidential qualifications in the U.S. Constitution for the simple reason that "it was impossible to make a complete one," asserted John Dickinson, who went on to say that the job would require "great Talents, Firmness and Abilities"—whatever they may be.[4]

"The first man at the helm," said Benjamin Franklin, "will be a good one. Nobody knows what sort may come afterwards." Everyone in the meeting room of the Constitutional Convention knew who he was talking about; the Convention's chairman,

Gen. George Washington, was sitting at a table in the front, facing everyone. Franklin continued: "The Executive will be always increasing here, as elsewhere, till it ends in a monarchy."[5] Despite objections that they were creating a government that would some day consist "only of an emperor and a few lordlings, surrounded by thousands of blood-suckers and cringing sycophants," the delegates went ahead and ratified the new job position.[6]

In *Federalist 69*, Hamilton insisted there was nothing to worry about: "Executive authority, with few exceptions, is to be vested in a single magistrate. This will scarcely, however, be considered as a point upon which any comparison can be grounded; for if, in this particular, there is to be a resemblance to the king of Great Britain, there is not less a resemblance to the Grand Seignior, to the khan of Tartary, to the Man of the Seven Mountains, or to the governor of New York."[7]

Forget the governor of New York: the job of president eventually became much more akin to the job of grand seignior. During the Civil War Secretary of State William Seward offered this job description: "We elect a king for four years and give him absolute power within certain limits, which after all he can interpret for himself."[8] After World War II the job expanded even more, to "leader of the free world" (though most citizens of the free world never voted for him).

The job description may change over the years, but traits of great leadership do not. Bookshelves groan under the weight of books on leadership and so-called secrets of effective people. What makes a great leader? Intellect, character, charisma, accomplishment, leadership, courage, wisdom, judgment . . . the list goes on and on. It's impossible to list all the traits because we can't know what future challenges the president will face and what particular strengths and skills will be called on. Every decision, every act of leadership takes place in context. The kind of leadership needed in times of crisis or great peril is different from the kind is needed in times of peace and economic prosperity. When choosing a president should we be looking for a rebel or someone who will maintain the present course? Do we go for a "Black

Swan" risk taker, recognizing the possibility of failure, or do look for a more predictable executive? Every choice demands trade-offs.

Leadership is notoriously difficult to define and comes in many shapes and forms, and all great leaders are exceptions to any single rule. But there are certain qualifications we can pretty much agree a president of the United States should have, regardless of his political views. The most obvious one is accomplishment. The candidate should be a repeat high achiever, not a one-shot lucky wonder. Repeated success is a reasonable assurance that he can handle whatever surprise or unforeseen crisis may come his way as president. And his list of achievements (whatever they may be—career, political, financial, overcoming a personal handicap or near-death encounter) should include one that is of the magnitude he is sure to face in the Oval Office. It's the difficult decisions he had better be good at. The easy ones rarely make it all the way to the president's desk; they get solved by others.

A candidate with good judgment possesses the imagination to anticipate emerging issues and address them before they escalate into a crisis. He makes difficult decisions at just the right moment: not too soon, not too late. Just as fear and greed are the enemies of sound investing, they have no place in the presidency. A worthy candidate is not fearful of making a decision lest he be proven wrong, nor is he so greedy for the glory of appearing decisive that he acts without thorough consideration. (A third alternative—doing nothing—can sometimes be the best decision.)

Also important are the intangibles. To overcome the gridlock that characterizes Washington today, it is not enough to exhort others to be bipartisan; a president must demonstrate bipartisanship himself. This requires integrity. The best candidate combines personal humility with intense determination. By being incorruptible and honorable, he gains the respect and admiration of politicians on the other side of the aisle. He communicates his political goals with clarity: he is straightforward when need be and avoids being a flip-flopper. And he loves the give-and-take of politics, building personal relationships, and working with others to cut a deal. He has what is called "a fascination for the process"—an appreciation of the small details one must have in order to do a job well.

In his 1888 book *The American Commonwealth*, the British jurist and later ambassador to the United States James Bryce argued that aside from the heroes of the Revolution, the only president to display stellar qualities was Lincoln. Then Bryce asked a brilliant question: Would we know Lincoln today if he had *not* become president? No, he said. Of the eighteen presidents from James Monroe to Grover Cleveland, there was only one man who would still be remembered if he had never been president: Gen. Ulysses Grant, the war hero and most famous man of the nineteenth century.

"Why are great men not chosen president?" Bryce asked. His answer: "Great men have not often been chosen, first because great men are rare in politics; secondly, because the method of choice does not bring them to the top; thirdly, because they are not, in quiet times, absolutely needed." He went on to explain what a president does and what we should look for:

> A president need not be a man of brilliant intellectual gifts. His main duties are to be prompt and firm in securing the due execution of the laws and maintaining the public peace, careful and upright in the choice of the executive officials of the country. . . . Four-fifths of his work is the same in kind as that which devolves on the chairman of a commercial company or the manager of a railway, the work of choosing good subordinates, seeing that they attend to their business, and taking a sound practical view of such administrative questions as require his decision. Firmness, common cause, and most of all, honesty, an honesty above all suspicion of personal interest, are the qualities which the country chiefly needs in its first magistrate.[9]

More than a century later this is still an accurate statement. The best candidate will bring to the office a record of proven experience and fortitude. He must be strong, as the Founding Fathers noted, lest he become "but the minion of the Senate," yet not abuse his power so that we end up in "a monarchy."[10] He will have demonstrated his strength either by overcoming adversity or by occupying a position of high power responsibly. The candidate will have proven his executive ability and leadership skills and have had experience in politics running for elective office. He will have the confidence borne of success, tempered by modesty and knowing that "no man could be found so far above all the rest in wisdom."[11] He will be a person of action, capable of "vigorous execution."[12] And, not least, he will conduct himself in a manner consistent with the symbolic importance of his office, evoking "dignity and respect."[13]

Impossible to find such a candidate in the current population? Hardly. There were 3.9 million people in the United States in 1789, and 85 percent of them were ineligible to vote (voting being restricted to white males owning property). Today there are over 320 million people, and the great majority can vote. Out of such a vast pool, is it not reasonable to expect great presidents?

Using history as a guide, let us now examine the qualifications of major candidates for our nation's highest office.

1

···

George Washington, 1789

Here is a job description for the newly created position of chief executive of the United States.

Title

President of the United States

Mission

Establish strong central government to overcome the weaknesses of the Articles of Confederation.

Description of Organization

The United States is a small, newly formed country located on the eastern seaboard of a large, unexplored continent. The country consists of a loose confederation of thirteen states (two of which have failed to qualify for voting in this election). It is surrounded by enemies in the north and the west and could be invaded at any moment in the east by a major European power. The population is three million. The economy is in a shambles, and the government treasury is virtually bankrupt. There is no assurance the country will survive.

Specific Job Functions

- Uphold and protect the Constitution of the United States.
- Ensure that the laws are faithfully followed.
- Review laws passed by Congress and veto if desired (subject to congressional override).
- Nominate ambassadors, judges of the Supreme Court, cabinet members, and other senior officials (subject to approval by the Senate).
- Make treaties (subject to two-thirds approval by the Senate).
- Grant pardons.
- Deliver, from time to time, a State of the Union address to Congress.
- Convene Congress on extraordinary occasions.
- Serve as commander-in-chief of the military.

Reporting Relationships

- Candidate shall serve at the pleasure of the American voters.
- Candidate shall respect the prerogatives of the legislature and the judiciary.
- Candidate may be impeached and removed from office by vote of Congress for "high crimes and misdemeanors."

Term

- Four years, with possibility of additional terms (subject to a national election).

Requirements

- Candidate must be at least thirty-five years old.
- Candidate must be a U.S.-born citizen and have resided in the United States for fourteen years.

There are no requirements related to education level, prior accomplishments, or prior experience.

Although not mentioned in Section 2 of the Constitution, the annual salary is $25,000, and housing will be provided in suitable quarters in New York City, along with servants, an elegant carriage, and a stable of horses and a liveryman. A small stipend for personal expenses will be provided, though it is expected that the president himself will pay for the expenses of hiring staff and entertaining dignitaries.

The process of electing our first president began on January 7, when sixty-nine electors were chosen by 38,818 people casting votes out of a population of approximately three million. Ten out of thirteen states are represented in this historic vote: Massachusetts, New Hampshire, Connecticut, New Jersey, Pennsylvania, Delaware, Maryland, Virginia, South Carolina, and Georgia. New York missed out because the state legislature failed to appoint its electors in time, and North Carolina and Rhode Island because they had not yet ratified the Constitution and therefore were not eligible.

Eleven candidates have been nominated for this new position:

- John Adams of Massachusetts, the former minister to Great Britain
- James Armstrong of Georgia
- George Clinton, the governor of New York
- John Hancock, the governor of Massachusetts and a former president of the United States in Congress Assembled under the Articles of Confederation
- Robert Harrison of Maryland
- Samuel Huntington, the governor of Connecticut and the first president under the Articles of Confederation
- Benjamin Lincoln, the lieutenant governor of Massachusetts
- John Milton, the secretary of state of Georgia
- John Rutledge, the former governor of South Carolina
- Edward Telfair, the former governor of Georgia
- George Washington, the recent president of the Constitutional Convention and retired commander in chief of the Continental Army

On February 4 the sixty-nine electors will vote for two of these nominees. The man with the highest number of votes becomes president; the man with the second-highest becomes vice president.

GEORGE WASHINGTON

· ·

6-foot-2, 210 pounds   Home address:
Excellent health   Mount Vernon
Age: fifty-seven   Arlington, Virginia

MISSION STATEMENT

"To extricate my country from the embarrassments in which it
is entangled, through want of credit; and to establish a general
system of policy which if pursued will insure permanent felicity to
the Commonwealth. I think I see a *path* as clear and as direct as a
ray of light, which leads to the attainment of that object. Nothing
but harmony, honesty, industry and frugality are necessary to make
us a great and happy people."[1]

SUMMARY OF QUALIFICATIONS

Over forty years of political, military, and business experience in
positions of increasing leadership.

LEADERSHIP EXPERIENCE

Constitutional Convention, 1787

Represented Virginia as a delegate. By unanimous vote elected
president of the Convention. Supervised proceedings and
mediated disputes to ensure a sensible compromise document for
a national Constitution to replace the Articles of Confederation.
Document ratified by eleven of thirteen states, 1788.

Continental Army, 1775–1783

Commander in chief. Assumed command of undisciplined,
untrained militia in struggle against well-trained British troops
and Hessian mercenaries. Won initial engagements and forced
the British to leave Boston, but lost New York. Using daring and
bold tactics, crossed the Delaware River on Christmas Day 1776

and defeated superior British forces at Trenton and Princeton. Lost battles at Brandywine and Germantown, summer 1777. Spent winter of 1777–78 at Valley Forge, Pennsylvania, where, despite deplorable conditions, managed to maintain morale and avoid any mutinies or mass desertions. Emerged from Valley Forge with a revitalized army and the confidence of France that the American forces could win; French military support forthcoming. Waged an extensive war of attrition over 1,500 miles of territory stretching from the Carolinas to upper New York State. In 1781 defeated Gen. Charles Cornwallis at Yorktown and secured the surrender of British forces. Moved army headquarters to Newburgh, New York, and led effort to rout the British from their remaining strongholds in Savannah, Charleston, Wilmington, and New York. Successfully negotiated with army officers and quelled pending rebellion of soldiers over unpaid back pay. Retired in November 1783, two months after the signing of a peace treaty with Great Britain.

BUSINESS AND PREVIOUS EXPERIENCE

Self-employed, 1783–present, 1752–1775

1. Planter. Took over family plantation and diversified farming activities beyond tobacco to include wheat, oats, corn, alfalfa, and peaches. Developed a dairy, a whiskey mill, three flour mills, and a herring fishery. Unlike most plantation owners, who lost money, succeeded in running Mount Vernon on a break-even basis.
2. Landowner and investor. Acquired and managed almost forty thousand acres of property in Virginia, Pennsylvania, and Ohio. Cofounder and managing partner of several land development companies, all successful and profitable.

Continental Congress, 1774–1775

Delegate from Virginia to the First and Second Continental Congresses in Philadelphia. By unanimous vote elected general and commander in chief of newly authorized Continental Army.

House of Burgesses, Colony of Virginia, 1759–1774

Representative. Gained firsthand experience in legislative government and political affairs.

Militia, Colony of Virginia, 1752–1758

Colonel. Enrolled as a major at age twenty and joined the British in the French and Indian Wars. Promoted to lieutenant colonel, 1754. Forced to surrender Fort Necessity to the French. Engaged the French again in losing campaign of Gen. Edward Braddock, 1755. Awarded $1,500 by the House of Burgesses for gallant services at the Battle of Monongahela. Promoted to colonel and regimental commander responsible for frontier defenses. Resigned from the militia after election to the House of Burgesses.

Culpepper County, Colony of Virginia, 1748–1752

Surveyor. Carried out surveys of land in northern Virginia. Saved $20,000 from earnings over five years and used money to purchase 1,400 acres.

PERSONAL

Born February 16, 1732. Educated at home by private tutors. Started working at age sixteen as a surveyor. Married, one stepchild, two step-grandchildren. Favorite hobbies are dancing, billiards, playing cards, fishing, fox hunting, and theater. Avid reader. President-general of the Society of the Cincinnati, an association of retired army officers. Honorary chancellor, The College of William and Mary. Only man in America awarded honorary degrees from both Harvard and Yale.

Assessment of Qualifications

The candidate for our nation's first president has the appearance and demeanor of a leader. At 6-foot-2 and powerfully built, he towers over people (especially when he stands next to his diminutive 5-foot-tall wife). He is always impeccably well-dressed and has a flair for the dramatic, with his saber, silk sash, and high boots. He is wealthy, sociable, well-liked, and renowned for his lavish dinner parties at Mount Vernon. He is widely respected as a man of upstanding character.

When the electors cast their votes next month, it is widely expected that Washington will emerge as the winner. Everything about this man—his charm, his achievements, his wealth—connotes success. He is respected to an extraordinary degree, almost to the point of adulation; some people go so far as to say he deserves to be king. Says one, "I shall not call it a Miracle if George Washington is seen living in Philadelphia as Emperor of America in a few years."[2]

There is not a man in America who can match his stature. He has been unanimously chosen by his peers for the two highest positions in America (even more powerful than the presidency under the Articles of Confederation): commander in chief of the Continental Army and president of the Constitutional Convention in Philadelphia. This newly created position, president of the United States, will be the most powerful position of all.

WHAT SHOULD WE LOOK FOR IN A PRESIDENT?

Last year's March 5 issue of the *Pennsylvania Gazette* carried an essay titled *"To the* PEOPLE *of* AMERICA*"* by a political writer who goes by the name of "Modestus." Modestus suggests six criteria we should look for in our first president:

1. Has no son "to obtain the succession."
2. Has "already rejected the alluring temptations" of "ambition and opportunity."
3. Has evidenced no "vindictive spirit."
4. Will not abuse his position for the benefit of his friends.

5. Is not a man of extreme wealth nor in love with "ostentatious living."
6. Has "a candid generous temper" and "an observing and reflecting turn of mind."[3]

It is interesting to note that none of these criteria has anything to do with accomplishments or job skills. The emphasis is solely on personality and character, answering the question: Is this a man who can be trusted with power?

In the March 26, 1788, issue of the *Massachusetts Centinel* there appeared another article on presidential criteria, again focusing on personality and character:

> There is a man, in the United States, who must present himself to the consideration of every freeman thereof, as a candidate for the important station of PRESIDENT of the UNITED STATES. He is known: As disinterested—and therefore it is certain that he will not fleece us.
>
> As having voluntarily laid down his former power—and therefore that he will not abuse those he may receive hereafter. As having no son—and therefore not exposing to the danger of a hereditary successor. As being of a most amiable temper—and therefore that he will not be vindictive or persecuting. His character, in short, is a tissue of virtues, and as there are some of our countrymen who doubt the safety of the proposed government, it is happy for us that we have such an approved and faithful citizen to employ in the experiment.[4]

It doesn't take a genius to discern that the writer is referring to George Washington, a man with no sons and who voluntarily gave up his power as general of the army.

The candidate has had illustrious careers as a businessman, a general, and a patriot. In all three he has demonstrated a high degree of vision and rectitude.

Career in Business

While he is best known for his military exploits, Washington has spent the vast bulk of his career in business (thirty years out of forty-one). It therefore behooves us to examine this in detail.

At the early age of sixteen he chose to become a surveyor so he could get first crack at identifying and buying good land. He saved all his wages in order to invest in property; by the time he was twenty-one he had accumulated over 1,400 acres in the lower Shenandoah Valley. Over the next six years he acquired several thousand more acres through marriage and inheritance. (He married one of the richest women in Virginia, and he inherited Mount Vernon and various other properties upon the death of his late half-brother's widow.)

Managing all these properties has been an enormous responsibility. Washington divided Mount Vernon into five farms, each a separate profit center with its own manager, responsible for giving the owner minutely detailed weekly progress reports. Seeing how tobacco exhausted the soil, he became the first Virginia planter to practice crop rotation. Diversifying into wheat, he soon generated record yields of grain. Then, when the wheat trade declined, he started a flour mill to convert his wheat crops into flour; within three years he became the largest flour producer in the colonies. His "Class A" flour was of such good quality that the bags passed through Caribbean ports without inspection when marked "George Washington, Mount Vernon."[5] No other planter in the colonies enjoys such a reputation for the quality of his products.

Further innovations include breeding superior working mules, devising a new plow, and starting a tannery, a weaving loom, and a candle factory. Always on the lookout for new methods and inventions, he was the first planter to use Oliver Evans's milling separator to turn wheat into flour, increasing his flour output tenfold.

This man is always coming up with new ideas. Asked where he got this trait, he points to his life in the wilderness. Coming from a comfortable life growing up on Virginia plantations and then suddenly having to go into the Blue Ridge Mountains, where few men had ventured before, he had to learn to rough it to stay alive. There is a big difference between living on a plantation and having to survive in the woods on your own wits, especially when you're fighting Indians. He learned to handle hardship and to think quickly and think ahead.

GEORGE WASHINGTON, 1789

As is to be expected of a surveyor, he pays close attention to detail. He runs his plantation the way he measured land: every transaction and crop yield is recorded. Ask him a question about the profitability of wheat on the third farm last summer, or the price of flour in Jamaica in March 1784, or the optimum allocation of resources to devote to his new candle business, and he can quickly look it up and tell you the answer (if he doesn't already have it in his head).

It appears that Washington has a difficult time keeping Mount Vernon afloat. It has poor soil, so no matter how much he cuts operating costs or rotates crops, his plantation barely makes money. To generate additional income, he has resumed his original avocation in his spare time: pursuing land investments. Using his vast knowledge of frontier lands, he has put together investment syndicates to acquire substantial property tracts with little money of his own up front. In all these ventures he insists on being personally involved in evaluating the property, designating subdivision rights, and collecting the rental income. Not a single one of his land deals has failed—a tribute to his vision and hard work.

Performance as General of the Continental Army

As a general his record is mixed. His won-lost record before Yorktown was 2-5-1: he won Trenton and Princeton; lost Long Island, Fort Washington, White Plains, Brandywine, and Germantown; and fought to a draw at Monmouth.

At Yorktown the British general Lord Charles Cornwallis had foolishly assembled his troops on a peninsula at a time when he had no backup from the British naval fleet, as most of the ships were in New York shipyards being repaired. When a French armada suddenly appeared on the scene, Washington saw his opportunity and quickly moved in. Cornwallis had no escape. It was a miracle that stunned the world. (When Cornwallis surrendered, the British Army played the song "The World Turned Upside Down.")

Washington is modest in attributing his last-minute success mostly to luck—or, as he gracefully puts it, "the invisible workings of Providence." The war was won, he says, "by a concatenation of causes" never occurring before and "which in all probability at no time, or any Circumstance, will combine again." Pressed further, he points to the perseverance of his officers and soldiers, who made great sacrifices.[6] Fair enough, but what about the determination, cunning, adaptability, and perseverance of the man at the top? Washington was the only general who could have won this war. To his credit he is very low-key about it.

In evaluating a man we look at the magnitude of the challenges he faced. In Washington's case they were momentous: he had a ragtag, inexperienced army facing the most powerful army and navy in the world.

Now being a victorious general is not the same as being a president. History is full of examples of generals who let success go to their head and became tyrants. Four aspects of Washington's military performance should give us comfort:

1. Led a Volunteer Army
Washington was no militarist with a professional army at his disposal. To the contrary, all he had was a collection of state militias, all underpaid and ill fed. Every year many of his soldiers' enlistments would expire, and he would have to train the new volunteers coming in, plus keep them equipped and fed. It was a fractious medley of men he commanded, always squabbling and bickering. Connecticut men mocked the soldiers from Maryland as "ploughboys," who in turn taunted the Connecticut men as "fops" and "dandies." Washington's job as head of this army, said John Adams, required "more serenity of command, a deeper understanding and more courage than fell to the lot of Marlborough to ride in this whirlwind."[7] Through sheer force of will and persuasion Washington managed to keep his ragtag army together and ensured a continuous supply of troops.

2. Had Good Relations with Congress
Washington, a man who spent sixteen years in Virginia's colonial legislature and two terms in the Continental Congress, maintained good political relations with the congressmen he

reported to. Unlike many of them, he understood that more important than capturing territory is capturing the other side's army; it is not necessary to win every battle or defend every city. In letting New York and Philadelphia be occupied by the British, he took a serious political risk and made sure to communicate his strategy to the representatives of the Continental Congress so he could retain their support. (None of them wanted to see their hometown or sea ports left unprotected.) No matter how frustrated he was with the Continental Congress and state legislatures for failing to send enough money and troops, he continued fighting with whatever resources he had. Even during the harsh winter at Valley Forge he maintained his respect for civilian authority.

3. Winning the Peace

Ask Washington what was the biggest challenge he faced during the war, and he will tell you it was the two years after he won at Yorktown. Everyone was celebrating as though the war was over, but the British had yet to sign a treaty. The French navy quickly left for the West Indies; a number of states stopped paying taxes; and many members of Congress went home, often leaving the remaining congressmen unable to do business for lack of a quorum. It was a nightmare: soldiers were owed back pay and threatened to take over Congress. Washington almost single-handedly kept military pressure on the British and persuaded his soldiers not to desert or rebel against Congress. It was his finest performance as a general, at a critical moment when America almost squandered everything it had gained.

Fervent Patriot

Most men of great wealth played it safe and sided with the Loyalists or very quietly with the revolutionaries. Not Washington: by accepting the post of commanding general, he knew that if the British won he would be a marked man, sure to lose everything and be hunted down and hanged from the gibbet (as the British delicately put it, have his "neck lengthened").

In 1781, when Washington was away at war, a British warship came up the Potomac River and stopped at Mount Vernon. Washington's younger brother sent provisions to the British sea captain, who promised not to attack. The moment he heard about it, Washington wrote his brother, "It would have been a less painful circumstance to me to have heard that in consequence of your non-compliance with their request, they had burnt my House, and laid the Plantation in ruins."[8]

This is a man committed to total war. He is driven by a strong sense of patriotic zeal. At the end of the war he voluntarily retired from the military and returned to his plantation. Everyone was amazed, especially King George III, who said it was remarkable that America had such a man, a Cincinnatus.[9] "If he does that [retire to his plantation], he will be the greatest man in the world," said the king.[10]

He is acutely sensitive to appearing greedy for power. Initially he didn't want to participate in the Constitutional Convention (assembled to create a stronger government), lest it look like power-grabbing on his part. Persuaded to attend, he pushed aggressively for serious reform. In a letter to James Madison he wrote, "My wish is, that the Convention may adopt no temporising expedient, but probe the defects of the Constitution to the bottom, and provide radical cures, whether they are agreed to or not."[11]

No halfway measures for this man; he is bold and decisive. Stiff and formal in manner and not given to bombastic words, he commands respect. Some people say leadership fits him like bark fits a tree. Observes Gouverneur Morris in a letter urging him to accept the presidency of the Constitutional Convention, "No Constitution is the same on Paper and in Life. The exercise of authority depends on personal Character. . . . Your cool steady Temper is *indispensably necessary* to give a firm and manly Tone to the new Government."[12]

As president of the Convention Washington guided the proceedings with discretion and firmness. But he did more: after the Convention was over, there remained the messy struggle of getting the Constitution ratified. Once again, to avoid any accusation of power-grabbing Washington stayed away from the ratification debate even though he had presided over the Convention. A smart move.

Washington has a keen understanding of the dynamics of power and leadership that will serve him well should be become president. Asked how a general maintains his leadership, he responded, "Be easy and condescending in your deportment to your officers, but not too familiar, lest you subject yourself to a want of that respect, which is necessary to support a proper command."[13]

EXTRAVAGANT LIFESTYLE

Some people criticize Washington for being ostentatious and extravagant. For a man who values formality and lavish ceremony, he is unusually careful with money. At Mount Vernon his manner of living is actually quite simple: the food is hearty, not exceptional, and there is no heavy drinking. During the Revolutionary War he had his wife visit him; they spent the winter together, with ample food and wine. He rejected a $25,000 annual salary from Congress for his military services—earning him widespread respect—but when the war was over he submitted a bill for out-of-pocket expenses of $449,221 (much of it accounted for by the collapse of the continental currency).[14] After going over all the accounts, the government auditors found that Washington's figures were off by less than one dollar.

HEALTH

Because we need a strong and vigorous president for our new form of government it is vital that our first president not die during his term in office.

Some people are concerned about Washington's age: at fifty-seven he is far older than the average life expectancy of forty-five for males. But this observation is based on a simplistic understanding of life expectancy statistics, which include the high rate of infant mortality. Men at birth may live to only forty-five, but men who make it to age thirty live to around sixty-four. Washington is a very athletic and strong man. There is no reason why he won't live through the entire four-year term—plus another if need be.

Washington has had health problems that probably would have killed a lesser man. When he was nineteen he had a terrible bout with smallpox, and just in the past twenty years he has suffered influenza, tubercular pleurisy, typhoid, dysentery, and malaria. He appears to be in good health now, though he has aged considerably as a result of strain and overwork during the war. He admitted that just before the Constitutional Convention he was "so much afflicted with a rheumatic complaint in his shoulder that at times he could barely raise his hand to his head, or turn over in bed."[15]

His eyesight is failing, and he has to wear glasses (which he refuses to do in public). His dental problems have gotten progressively worse, to the point where he now has only one tooth left and uses false teeth made of hippopotamus ivory (not the more comfortable wooden model). These teeth are so cumbersome that he has to clench his face muscles and keep his jaw shut to prevent them from falling out; hence his frown. This physical handicap is a major inconvenience for a public figure and prevents him from giving a lengthy speech. (Who knows, that might even be a blessing!) Most important of all, the general is suffering from a progressive loss of hearing so that he cannot carry on a normal conversation; therefore most of his conferences will have to be small or even one-on-one discussions. We can only hope his inner circle will include one or two strong-minded people not afraid to give him the kind of contrary advice every president occasionally needs.

PERSONAL INTERVIEW

At one moment in the French and Indian War General Washington said he enjoyed the sound of bullets whistling by—"There was something charming in the sound"—to which King George II allegedly retorted, "He would not say so, if he had been used to hear many."[16] Washington now admits it was a foolish comment, an indiscretion of youth, a mistake he will never make again. When asked about his first election, when he ran for the

Virginia House of Burgesses in 1757, he confesses he won it the good old-fashion way: he provided twenty-eight gallons of rum, fifty gallons of rum punch, thirty-four gallons of wine, forty-six gallons of beer, and two gallons of cider for the 391 voters.[17] However, every victory since then, he maintains, has been won fair and square. Which, of course, doesn't mean he won't do whatever it takes to get people's attention. In 1774, as a delegate to the Continental Congress, he showed up wearing his full military uniform—obviously hinting to his fellow delegates, "Vote for me!" Clearly this is an ambitious man.

His favorite pet is his greyhound dog, named Cornwallis after the defeated British general at the Battle of Yorktown. He takes great pleasure in ordering the dog to do his bidding: "Come here, Cornwallis! Jump! Sit!" Washington is a formal man, but he does have a mischievous sense of humor. His horse is named Nelson, after the great British admiral. The name he called his Ohio Valley land venture when he was raising money from investors? The Dismal Swamp Land Company.

About John Adams he tells an amusing story of a dinner where Adams, who apparently owns forty acres, went on and on for hours about the secrets of good farming, not knowing that the man he was talking to owns forty thousand. They had a wonderful time, said Washington: Adams likes to talk, and he himself likes to listen.[18]

He is a serious student of the theater. His favorite play is Addison's *Cato,* in which the Roman statesman announces, "What pity is it that we can die but once to serve our country." And the most influential book he has ever read? The 1745 English version of the Jesuit book *Rules of Civility and Decent Behavior,* given to him by a traveling tutor when he was fifteen. He read it carefully and had to write out by hand all 110 maxims. He says this exercise shaped his character and conduct for the rest of his life. How so? He must strive to be a model of self-restraint and rectitude and never lose his temper.

He had a difficult childhood: he grew up with no father and a mother he didn't like, had no formal education, and had no

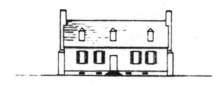

His house *(top)* when he inherited it at twenty-two, *(middle)* when he served in the House of Burgesses, and *(bottom)* how it looks today. This is a man who thinks big.

money when he started out at age sixteen to earn a living. But he was incredibly ambitious and determined to make something of himself. Over the years he has acquired a massive collection of more than nine hundred books, most of which he has read. It is, he says proudly, one of the largest private collections in America.

The man never slows down; he is always trying to improve himself. Even in retirement since 1783 he keeps a busy schedule managing his plantation and writing letters. He subscribes to ten daily newspapers and keeps himself extremely well-informed. His Mount Vernon dinners every night with friends and strangers have provided him with a multitude of observations and insights that make him extremely knowledgeable about public affairs. He doesn't say much, but he asks lots of questions. Because of his military fame his house has become something like a well-visited tavern; in the three years since he came home from the war and then left for the Constitutional Convention, he has had dinner with his wife alone only once. It was on June 30, 1785, he says; that's how easy it is for him to remember.

Knowing so many people and having so many friends will be useful to him in his new position.

HOME LIFE

He is happily married to the former Martha Dandridge Custis, a wealthy widow who owned a plantation called the White House. Washington proposed to her on their second date; she accepted. They have no children of their own; she had two children from her previous marriage, one of them now deceased. Their home is constantly filled with relatives and young children, many of them supported financially by Washington. A very generous man, even when he was away during the war, his instructions to his staff were to maintain the hospitality of Mount Vernon and extend a welcome to whoever showed up at the front door. He directed that should there be general distress caused by the hardships of war, poor persons in the neighborhood should get help from his kitchen or his granaries.

He has a remarkable lack of ego, almost never talking about himself. This austerity makes him a hard man to get to know. To those meeting him for the first time he comes across as stiff and severe. With friends he is warm and friendly. Says the noted businessman and farmer Elkanah Watson, "He soon put me at ease by unbending, in a free and affable conversation. The cautious reserve, which wisdom and policy dictated, was evidently the result of consummate prudence, and not characteristic of his nature."[19]

CONCLUSION

From the time the Revolutionary War began in 1775, General Washington has been the most influential man in America. For his successful service as head of the army and as head of the Constitutional Convention, he has earned the sobriquet "two-time savior of our country."

A man who, as a victorious general, gave up enormous power is a man who can be trusted with even greater power. Throughout the Revolution and the Constitutional Convention he demonstrated that he is a true patriot and not a man out for himself. Being wealthy, he is beholden to no one. Already as a private citizen he has a much nicer house than any presidential mansion the government may come up with. At Mount Vernon he has busts of Alexander the Great, Julius Caesar, Charles XII of Sweden, Frederick the Great, the Duke of Marlborough, and Prince Eugene of Savoy. Does this suggest a man fascinated with military dictators or with patriotic leadership? Everything in Washington's record suggests the latter.

Some fear Washington's fame will go to his head and he will want to serve for life. The Marquis de Lafayette, the French aristocrat who served as a major general in the Continental Army, is certain this will not happen. He quotes a letter written to him by Washington last year: "The Presidency . . . has no enticing charms and no fascinating allurements for me."[20] There is every reason to accept this statement at face value. Likewise Washington told Alexander Hamilton he hopes that "at a convenient and an early period my services might be dispensed with and that I might be permitted once more to retire."[21] The sooner he can return to his beloved Mount Vernon, the better. He is too old to want to make a career of being president. He has no sons to start a monarchy. He will not be corrupted by power because he has had so much of it already.

There is no formal job description for the position Washington has been nominated for, other than a few sentences in the Constitution. It is self-evident, however, that it is a position requiring a grand strategist, a politician, the head of a start-up enterprise— precisely the breadth of skills that makes Washington a good fit. In this first trial it is crucial to fill the position with a man capable of meeting every contingency. Washington, a proven survivor and innovator, is well-suited for an open-ended job.

A second important trait is his vision: he can see the big picture. Back in 1783 when he was retiring from the military to private life, on his own initiative he gave Congress a four-thousand-word "Circular to the States" calling for payment of all state and national debts, establishment of a permanent military force, and the creation of "an indissoluble Union of the States under one Federal Head."[22] This is a man who thinks ahead, who understands that the primary mission of this new office is to unify a nation of thirteen disparate states.

The first president will face the following major tasks:

- Define the duties and role of the president.
- Ensure that Congress adds a Bill of Rights to the Constitution.
- Establish a national currency to replace the local state currencies.
- Set up a taxation mechanism to fund the national government.
- Maintain good relations with England and France.

The United States today may be free and independent, but we are virtually bankrupt, with a huge debt from the Revolutionary War. The euphoria of victory over Britain has long since worn off; already citizens are grumbling that taxes are 10 percent higher than they were during the British occupation. We have already had one internal rebellion (Shays'), and there is the pressing danger a state may try to secede from the nation. Our president must therefore have a firm grasp of military matters should there be war with one of the states. This man should be a doer, a man of action, and not get bogged down in local, petty politics. He should have experience managing money and budgets to ensure a stable currency. As president of the entire country he should be familiar with all four regions: New England, the middle colonies, the southern colonies, and western Appalachia.

We live in tempestuous and dangerous times. We need a conservative president, a recognized leader who promises stability as we endeavor on our "great experiment." While we have concerns about George Washington's elegant lifestyle and the possibility that he will let his enormous popularity go to his head, we feel this possibility is remote given his stature and financial independence. We are confident he can handle adulation, govern with sagacity and circumspection, and brighten the path of our national felicity.

Accomplishments	Intangibles	Judgment	Overall
outstanding	outstanding	outstanding	outstanding

1789

No champagne would be opened on the night of America's first presidential election. It was the middle of winter, February 4, and Congress was not in session. Because of all the snow and ice another two months would go by as congressmen struggled to get back to the nation's temporary capital. Finally, on April 6, there were enough members in New York to constitute a quorum, and the certificates were opened.

As expected, Washington won the vote in the Electoral College, making him the first elected president of any country in the world. Most remarkably he had run against ten opponents, yet not a single one of them got a vote. Four years later he ran for a second term and again was elected unanimously. For a nation that had gone through ten ceremonial presidents of the Continental Congress from 1781 to 1789, his eight years of service provided much-needed stability. Many predicted the new office would work no better than the previous presidency under the Articles of Confederation. Some went so far as to predict Americans would become weary of self-rule and go begging to King George III to take them back into the British Empire.

Imperial and energetic, Washington went to work quickly. A relatively old man, he had impressive stamina and sought men who could keep up with him; as a result his four cabinet officers were young (thirty, thirty-one, thirty-six, and forty-six). In all his presidential appointments he looked for people who were staunchly nationalistic. When he interviewed potential candidates for the Supreme Court, for example, his key question was: What do you think in general terms about the new government and its desired future? Candidates whose answers were pro-state or pro-region were quickly shown the door. Washington wanted no intrastate squabbles; he would be president of a country.

He thought like a politician in choosing his cabinet. Robert Morris was more experienced in finance than Hamilton; John Adams was more experienced in foreign affairs than Jefferson. Yet Washington chose Hamilton and Jefferson for his cabinet because they were the heads of the two great political factions.

He showed no favoritism, going so far as to select for attorney general not James Madison, who helped write the Constitution, but the equally esteemed Edmund Randolph, who refused to sign it. When a close personal friend and a political enemy were under consideration for the same position, Washington selected the enemy. "My friend I receive with cordial welcome to my house and welcome to my heart, but, with all his good qualities, he is not a man of business," Washington explained. "His opponent is, with all his politics so hostile to me, a man of business; my private feelings have nothing to do in this case. I am not George Washington, but President of the United States."[23]

One of his first tasks was to visit every state in New England, then visit all the other states two years later, in those days a very time-consuming undertaking. In contrast to his luxury living at Mount Vernon, the president of the United States traveled with only two secretaries and six servants—no large entourage for him. His trips were important, he said, to establish a personal bond and garner support for the new government. The *Gazette of the United States* agreed, declaring, "The time to pull down, and destroy, is now past." It was time "to build up, strengthen and support" the Constitution.[24]

On his two tours he refused to stay overnight in people's homes lest there be a lot of "George Washington slept here" signs floating around afterward. He was president: nothing must cheapen or demean the presidential office.

He got the Bill of Rights passed in late 1791. He established the authority of his office vis-à-vis the legislature in a meeting with senators who had the temerity to suggest they refer a peace treaty to a committee. A committee? "No bloody way!" he must have said as he stormed out of the room, leaving the senators shocked. Never again would he return to Congress. He would consult with the Senate only after treaties were made—a prerogative of the presidential office that has lasted to this day.

His cabinet meetings were stormy affairs that make today's large gatherings seem positively somnolent. Leading his pro-Federalist forces was the young Turk and his former military chief of staff, the thirty-year-old Alexander Hamilton. Leading the opposition forces of agrarian Republicans was the more diplomatic and experienced Thomas Jefferson, forty-six. It was Washington's job to control disputes and keep the various factions together. This he was able to do, marshaling his enormous popularity and his experience chairing the Constitutional Convention. Though eager to retire after one term, he stayed on for a second term because he knew he was the only person who could maintain unity and harmony among the states. His major task was to get the central government sufficiently established so it could impose unpopular taxes to pay off some of its debts. When he left office in 1796, the new nation had a strong central government, a strong currency, and a strong credit rating for international trade. Most important of all he left behind a country, not a collection of thirteen squabbling republics.

Unlike later presidents who engaged in a flurry of activities to establish their administrations (now known as "the Hundred Days"), Washington never confused boldness with leadership. He, who came to the presidency as the sole proprietor and owner of Mount Vernon, a larger organization than the U.S. Government,[25] had no illusions about presidential power—though he had the power of an emperor. Commented Abigail Adams in an early 1790 letter about Washington, "If he was not really one of the best intentioned men in the world, he might be a very dangerous one."[26] Washington was serving as president only out of a sense of civic duty. His ambition was to put the new government on a sound footing, then get out and retire to his beloved plantation.

Famous for being a general, Washington was actually more a

businessman. He believed no new government could be put on a sound footing unless it had financial security. As a citizen he was fabulously wealthy, considered one of the ten richest men in the America at the time of his death, but his presidency constantly suffered cash-flow problems due to inflation. After the experience of the Continental currency, he determined that America should have a sound currency and strong credit. He directed Hamilton to get the job done. Observes George Schultz, a former Treasury secretary and secretary of state under Ronald Reagan, "Alexander Hamilton redeemed all of the Revolutionary War debt at par value, and he said the 'full faith and credit' of the United States must be inviolate, among other reasons because it will be necessary in a crisis to be able to borrow. And we saw ourselves through the Civil War because we were able to borrow. We saw ourselves able to defeat the Nazis and the Japanese because we were able to borrow."[27] In the twenty-first century excessive government spending makes borrowing difficult; in contrast, in our first two hundred years we were able to pay for two world wars because of our sound currency, inaugurated by a businessman in the White House.

. . .

In what amounts to a one-sentence job description of the presidency, he said, "In every act of my administration, I have sought the happiness of my fellow citizens" by ignoring "personal, local and partial consideration" in favor of the "permanent interests of our country" and the "dictates of my conscience."[28] With a mandate such as he had, he didn't have to worry about popular opinion or what newspaper editors wrote about him.

Though it rarely appears on any executive recruiter's list of criteria, one of the most difficult tasks of any leader is to gauge and maximize his or her available power to achieve objectives. Most leaders do too much or too little. It's a delicate balance, knowing when to push ahead and when to wait. Washington got it right. Like a general fighting a much bigger army, he knew the limits of his power. He moved with caution, careful not to overstep. Whereas a more impatient man might have embarked on aggressive actions to subdue the Indians in the Northwest Territory, resume hostilities with Great Britain, and expand the federal government, Washington relied on diplomacy and compromise to postpone these inevitable conflicts until the nation was better prepared. "With me," he said in his Farewell Address, "a predominant motive has been to endeavor to gain time to our country to settle and mature its yet recent institutions, and to progress without interruption to that degree of strength and consistency, which is necessary to give it, humanely speaking, the command of its own fortunes."[29] It was almost an exact repetition of how he had fought the war: one step at a time, waiting for opportune moments to strike.

He appreciated the symbolic importance of his role. In crafting his Farewell Address, he relied on Madison and Hamilton to get his message down pat, and he ended up producing a masterful document that resonates to this day. Setting forth the tenets of Americans' relations with each other and with the rest of the world, his Farewell Address ranks with the Declaration of Independence and the Gettysburg Address as the most honored of American political discourses. It was read aloud in Congress on February 22 every year until the 1970s.

Washington's sense of perspective applied also to himself. He insisted on fancy living and a presidential carriage to communicate the dignity of the office, but he did not abuse it. As president he had only fourteen household staff—fewer than at Mount Vernon (and paid for out of his own salary). He insisted on formality, but he scorned regal titles. He rejected the architect Pierre L'Enfant's plan for a huge presidential mansion and gardens covering ten acres, insisting it be a fraction of the size.[30] When Adams, presiding over the Senate, proposed that the new executive be known as "His Highness, the President of the United States of America and Protector of their Liberties," Washington retorted that "Mr. President" would do. The only use of his name Washington allowed by during his lifetime was for the new city that would serve as the nation's capital. After he died, however, he became the "god-like Washington," his name appropriated for a state, thirty-three counties, 121 cities and villages, seven mountains, ten lakes, nine colleges, and a national holiday. Outside of the United States his statue adorns city squares in London, Paris, Buenos Aires, Rio de Janeiro, Budapest, and Tokyo.

George Washington is revered throughout the world as our best president. But here in the United States, we give that honor to Lincoln. This disparity says something about ourselves as a nation and what we look for in our leaders.

Unlike Lincoln, who had to fight a civil war while in office, was only narrowly reelected, and then was assassinated, Washington was a demigod during his lifetime. He left office in 1796 widely admired and respected as a conciliator, a leader, a superb administrator, "the father of his country," a man who had saved his country not once, not twice, but three times: as a general, the Constitutional Convention president, and the nation's president.

Yet it was this unusual man, the most aristocratic of our presidents, who made the new constitution and republic work. For the final word on his performance as president, we should probably turn to a man normally expected to be highly critical: Jefferson, the opposition leader. After he had become president himself, Jefferson offered this assessment of his former boss: "He was always in accurate possession of all facts and proceedings in every part of the Union . . . formed a central point for the different branches, preserved a unity of object and action among them . . . and met himself the due responsibility for whatever was done."[31] Other nations, especially Third World nations that have modeled their anticolonialist manifestos after our own Declaration of Independence, respect this. Travel abroad and one sees that it is Washington the doer, the man who was practical, not Lincoln the emancipator, who is revered. Except in London there are no statues of Lincoln outside the United States.

In this country recent history has not been kind to Washington. Unlike Lincoln, who is immortalized in countless photographs and a magnificent statue in Washington DC, our first president is represented by an impersonal obelisk in the nation's capital and by the stern, forbidding figure glaring from several portraits by Gilbert Stuart. Washington and Stuart never liked each other. Allowing his prejudices to affect his perceptions, Stuart exaggerated Washington's dental disfigurement and reddened his cheeks. There is no grandeur, no twinkle in the eye, no humanity in the George Washington of Gilbert Stuart. Compare this with the younger, magnificent general painted by Charles Wilson Peale: a totally different man, not a patrician but a dashing leader.

When Washington relinquished the reins in 1796, the British monarchy was stunned—for the second time. The future William IV of England called him "the greatest man who ever lived," echoing what his father, King George III, had predicted back in 1783: "He will be the greatest man in the world."[32] The father-king spoke of the future ("will be"); the son-king spoke of the past ("who ever lived"). How many people start out as "the greatest" and end up thirteen years later still called "the greatest"?

For the final word on his legacy, let us return to Jefferson, who raised the question most people feared to ask: What will happen after Washington's presidency? Jefferson's answer: "After him inferior characters may perhaps succeed and awaken us to the danger which his merit has led us into."[33]

In 1906 Harvard president Charles W. Eliot gave a series of guest lectures on great American leaders. In trying to explain what made Washington so special, he hit on a point that should resonate with many Americans today, more than a century later. "Washington's mind dealt very little on rights and very much on duties," said Eliot. "For him, patriotism was a duty; good citizenship was a duty." Then came the punch line: "We think more about our rights than our duties. He thought more about his duties than his rights."[34] Today, as Americans squabble over Social Security, medical care, and other entitlements from a government that racks up more and more debts for our grandchildren to pay, is this not a powerful message? Should we not be thinking more about our duties than our rights?

2

....

DeWitt Clinton, 1812

We have a candidate running for president of the United States a man "to the manor born." He hails from one of the three families that control America's biggest and richest state, New York: the Livingstons, the Schuylers, and the Clintons. Were our nation ever to veer toward the wealthy educated aristocracy for a president, a natural choice would be young DeWitt Clinton. Only forty-three years old, he already has a strong record of achievement: first in his class at Columbia (age seventeen), assistant to the governor of New York, state legislator, U.S. senator, mayor of New York. People call him "the Magnus Apollo." He is the son of a Revolutionary War general. More important, he is the favored nephew of the late George Clinton, member of the Continental Congress, president of the 1788 New York Constitutional Convention, governor of New York for two decades, and vice president of the United States for the past seven years under Jefferson and Madison.

Irony of all ironies, with Madison now running for reelection as president, who is his opponent but his vice president's nephew!

It is often said that the only reason America hasn't become a hereditary aristocracy is that George Washington had no sons. Should Clinton win the presidency, such fears may be realized: he has five sons. The Clintons clearly hope to become the preeminent family in America. With this man they have a good chance.

DEWITT CLINTON

Age: forty-three
6-foot-3, 220 pounds
Nickname: the Magnus Apollo

OBJECTIVE: Fifth president of the United States

Mayor of New York, 1803–present

(except for part of 1808–9 and 1810–11)

At age thirty-four took over co-management of city ruled by Common Council appointed by the governor (and by the state legislature after the 1800 victory by the Council of Appointment). Agreed with the Common Council to stop customs fees from going directly to the mayor as personal compensation; henceforth more than half of all fees should go to the city treasury.

Supervised burgeoning growth of our nation's foremost city and former capital. Promoted city planning, public sanitation, public education, and relief for the poor. Established the city's first public school.

Personally acted as chief magistrate; earned reputation as a fair and compassionate judge. Supervised police and took proactive measures to prevent unnecessary riots, fires, and other threats to public safety.

During 1806–11 also served as a New York state senator to ensure proper representation of the city's interests in the state legislature. In 1811 elected lieutenant governor of New York; served that office simultaneously with the office of mayor of New York City.

Founding member of the 1810 Canal Commission; authorized surveys for a potential canal from the Hudson River to Lake Erie.

U.S. Senator, 1801–1803

At age thirty-two elected senator from New York. Gained national recognition for vigorous leadership on immigration and presidential election procedure. Reduced the waiting period for immigrants from fourteen to five years. Introduced legislation leading to the passage of the Twelfth Amendment, separating the voting for president and vice president so as to avoid problems like the imbroglio between Thomas Jefferson and Aaron Burr in 1800. Resigned to accept appointment as mayor of New York.

New York State Senator, 1799–1801

At age thirty appointed to the Council of Appointment. Asserted right of the legislature to name candidates for executive office. Challenged by Governor John Jay and won. Delegate to the New York State Constitutional Convention, 1801.

New York State Assemblyman, 1798

McKesson and Clinton, 1796–1798

Private law practice, specializing in real estate.

Secretary to the Governor of New York, 1790–1795

Hired at age twenty-one by uncle, Governor George Clinton, as his personal secretary. Gained firsthand experience in politics and government affairs. Wrote numerous political essays for newspapers under the pseudonym "A Countryman." Secretary, Board of Regents, Columbia University. Resigned after uncle's temporary retirement from politics.

EDUCATION

Law Offices of Samuel Jones, 1787–1790

Studied law on part-time basis.

Columbia College, M.A. in Natural Sciences 1788

Columbia College, B.A. 1786

Graduated first in class, age seventeen. Gave commencement speech in Latin.

INTELLECTUAL AND CIVIC ACTIVITIES

Philosophy and Politics

Founder of the New York Historical Society (1804) and the
Academy of Fine Arts (1808). Regent, University of New York
(1808–present). President of the Literary and Philosophical Society.
Director of the Humane Society. Member, American Academy of
Arts, Free School Society.

Social and Civic

Member of the Holland Lodge of Freemasons. Elected master in 1793.

Natural Sciences and Archeology

Member of the Linnean Society of London, the Wernerian
Society of Edinburgh, and the Academy of Natural Sciences in
Philadelphia.

PERSONAL

Nephew of George Clinton, the late governor of New York and
vice president of the United States under Thomas Jefferson and
James Madison. Son of James Clinton, a major general in the
Continental Army. Born in small town seventy miles north of New
York City, near the Hudson River; three brothers and three sisters.
Married Maria Franklin in 1796; six children: Charles, James, Dewitt
Jr., George, Franklin, and Mary. Hobbies: collecting rare books,
flowers, and plants. Foreign languages: Latin and Dutch.

Assessment of Qualifications

This is a man so cerebral that his own mother complained it made him too quiet and uncommunicative. He is extremely bright. He has chosen not to be a scholar of books and learning but a politician. He is not naturally fit for such a profession, as he is not outgoing, does not make lots of soft promises, does not solicit bribes or favors. As mayor of the country's largest city for most of the past nine years, he has never taken a dollar for himself from any of the port's customs fees (a major source of income for other politicians). He has instituted a number of major programs to help the indigent and poor. He is truly an aristocrat of the people.

He had the advantage of nepotism, being the nephew of the esteemed George Clinton, who died of a heart attack this past April. As governor of New York for twenty-three years George Clinton was of enormous help in guiding the career of his favorite nephew. He introduced the young man to all the important people in politics, employed him as his personal assistant for five years, steered clients to his law practice, and appointed him to the powerful position of mayor of New York.

Their alliance started when DeWitt was only fifteen. Acting on the advice of his uncle, who claimed it would look better should he decide to go into politics, the young man turned down Princeton in favor of a fledgling college in his home state of New York. What was originally King's College had been closed down during the Revolutionary War. In 1784, under the leadership of Governor Clinton, the state took over the facility, hired professors, and reopened as Columbia College, with the governor as chancellor. DeWitt enrolled in the very first class. One imagines it must have been an intensive education: there were six professors and only six students. That DeWitt graduated at the top of his class is therefore not as impressive as it sounds. More impressive is that he was only seventeen years old when he graduated and could deliver a twenty-minute commencement address in flawless Latin, titled "De Utilatate et Necessitate Studiarum Atrium Liberlium" (Concerning the Usefulness and Necessity of the Eagerness for Free

Conduct). He went on to earn a master's degree at Columbia in natural sciences, specializing in zoology and botany.

During his time as a graduate student he also studied law at Samuel Jones's house, 34 Broadway, while living at his uncle's home on nearby Pearl Street. That his uncle was the governor of New York meant that the young man also got a third education, this one in hands-on politics. New York City being the nation's capital, young DeWitt got to know many of the country's cabinet officers, senators, and congressmen on a first-name basis. Living at the end of the street at the corner of Pearl and Cherry was none other than President George Washington, in a home rented from Walter Franklin, whose daughter Maria is now Mrs. DeWitt Clinton and whose other daughter, Hannah, is married to DeWitt's brother George. It was a small world they all lived in.

Maria brought to the marriage a sizable inheritance, which by law became the property of her husband. By the late 1790s, thanks to his successful law practice, his wife's inheritance, and his speculations in raw land, Clinton owned over a hundred thousand acres. He and his wife have two homes, one in the city and one on Long Island where they spend the summer with their seven children. Their house in the city is like a schoolhouse, "filled with plants, test tubes, curious stones, fossils, and tools and equipment for astronomical and weather experiments."[1]

Clinton is an extremely curious man, with a strong interest in the natural sciences and philosophy. He is a member of numerous scientific societies, such as the Linnean Society of London, the Wernerian Society of Edinburgh, and the Academy of Natural Sciences in Philadelphia. If he hadn't chosen a career in politics, he would have been well-equipped to become a university professor of natural sciences.

He has an orderly mind that prizes efficiency and control. Under his leadership New York has become the only city in America to impose an efficient grid system of streets. A lot of farmers and homeowners had to be displaced to make way for the new streets going straight east-west and north-south, but Clinton prevailed in what obviously was a difficult and ambitious undertaking. It also made him many enemies.

As mayor he demonstrated a mind prolific in civic and philanthropic schemes. In creating a home for the indigent, a home for the deaf and handicapped, and a network of privately funded schools not dependent on the church, Clinton has brought relief to many impoverished citizens. What Benjamin Franklin did for Philadelphia in his generation, DeWitt Clinton has done for the current generation in New York. He is the most imaginative and progressive mayor in America today.

Only a man like Clinton could come up with a project as grandiose as the Erie Canal. As mayor he took a passionate interest in interstate commerce canals and launched a special commission to assess the feasibility of building a canal from the Hudson River all the way to Lake Erie, 363 miles long. Should this project ever get off the ground, it will be the biggest public works project in the world, involving moving a mass of dirt three times the size of the Great Pyramid of Egypt. This man does not think small.

Thomas Jefferson, who certainly has extensive scientific knowledge, says Clinton must be pipe-dreaming; a canal in Virginia, only a few miles long, had already failed, and here is Clinton talking about a canal 300 times bigger! Nobody can say Clinton is not an optimist. He possesses the spirit of the Enlightenment, with unbounded faith in man's capacity to make the world better through the application of scientific rational thinking.

Clinton's intellectual interests go beyond rationalism and natural sciences to include religion and mysticism. He is an officer of the American Bible Society and the Presbyterian Society. He is a member of the Black Friars, the Uranians, and the Masons. As a Freemason he has no hesitation about burying metal plates as if he were a magician promising to make treasures spring from the earth. He has unbridled confidence in himself. On a more sublime level, he is a regent of the University of New York, director of the Humane Society, president of the Literary and Philosophical Society, and founder of both the New-York Historical Society and the Academy of Fine Arts. He is an excellent political writer and has written numerous newspaper articles rebutting the arguments for a strong central government penned by Jay, Hamilton, and Madison in *The Federalist*.

Being such a learned man, Clinton does not attract casual friends. He does not enjoy chatting about trivial topics; he has important things to do, so every moment is precious. Absent-minded and absorbed in lofty contemplations, he is forgetful of people and remembers only the most familiar faces. People who are not his equal often feel awkward around him and humiliated by him. He is a man of passionate views, not afraid to speak out on controversial (dangerous?) topics like the abolition of slavery. He is a risk-taker.

He has a strict code of honor and is quick to engage in a duel rather than try to reach a compromise. He once got into an argument with another gentleman who was offended at being called "a rascal, scoundrel, liar and villain" all in one.[2] ("Rascal" was okay, but not with the other three.) Efforts by friends to mediate an apology failed. Luckily the two men were such poor shots they missed each other. Not content to call it a day, however, Clinton insisted on another round, then another, then another, until he finally hit his opponent (in the leg). Dueling is to be expected of pugnacious personalities, but not of mature men. Should Clinton become president, one hopes that he will show more tolerance. We would not like to see the back lawn of the President's Mansion be used as a dueling ground.

Clinton came to Washington for three weeks last December to seek support for his canal project. According to Silvanus Miller, Clinton "impressed many as an able and formidable man," a worthy heir to his late uncle. One of Madison's supporters, Hugh Nelson of Virginia, says that after meeting Clinton he had "fears for our worthy little James."[3] The 100-pound 5-foot-4 James Madison *should* be worried: the only states he can only count on are the southern ones. Clinton is likely to carry the North and is making a big push to crack the southern barrier and carry Pennsylvania, with its twenty-five electoral votes. If he succeeds he will become our next president.

Madison, the writer of much of our Constitution and *Federalist Papers*, is a brilliant man. So too is Clinton. In fact this is the first presidential election in which two intellectual giants are competing against each other. How we would love to watch them in a debate. This will never happen, of course. Imagine Madison standing next to a man twice his size!

One of the drawbacks of being brilliant is the tendency to over-rationalize. Both candidates find themselves doing intellectual gyrations trying to defend their political positions concerning our war with Great Britain. Madison, who has spent decades since the 1779 Continental Congress mulling over Anglo-American relations and how to make Great Britain respect our new republic, has come up with a novel rationale for war: he says the way to get Britain to stop impressments of our sailors is to invade and occupy Canada. What Canada has to do with America has never been explained, and now America is in a messy war with no end in sight and prospects grim. Does anybody in his right mind expect a nation with 6,000 troops and sixteen vessels to stand up to a mighty empire with 250,000 troops and a 600-ship navy? No wonder Speaker of the House Henry Clay is calling Madison "unfit for the storms of war."[4] We would like to think Mayor Clinton, being a more practical man, is more fit, although his position on the war is even more convoluted than Madison's. In an effort to straddle two different constituencies, the antiwar Federalists and the pro-war Republicans (Madison being the pro-war Republican), Clinton says he would renounce war and avoid it but would support it if it came. That is, he tells the Federalists that he opposes the war and tells the Republicans he will prosecute it more vigorously than Madison and end it quicker. Given his record as mayor of New York, where he impressed everyone with his executive energy and ability to get things done, there is little doubt he will make a better war president than Madison because he will get us out of a war we should never have gotten into in the first place. To declare war without effective means to wage it is irresponsible brinkmanship.

Many suspect that the real reason Madison started this war was to whip up patriotic fervor to ensure his reelection. Madison was renominated on May 18, and just two weeks later he declared war. Since then all everybody talks about is war; everything else has gone by the wayside.

It took the Federalists several months to get their act together and finally meet in mid-September to discuss Clinton as their new leader, and even then there was a squabble. Rufus King declared that Clinton's election "would merely substitute Caesar Borgia for James Madison,"[5] while Harrison Gray Otis said only a man like Clinton could bring them victory. The problem for the Federalists is timing: because there's a war going on nobody wants to hear Clinton's ideas for economic growth and national unity. Nor do they want to hear that it's time to finally get rid of the "Virginia Dynasty" that has monopolized the presidency for eighteen of the past twenty-two years.

Also absent amid the war drums is any discussion of a major constitutional issue: the way we nominate our candidates. Should they continue to be nominated by Congress, or should they be nominated by some form of popular vote? Last month a letter was circulated by a New York committee of correspondence charged with promoting Clinton:

> Another cause urges us more strongly than any other to appeal to you—it is one of principle—it involves a great constitutional question, which is now for the first time brought fairly to the test. The members of Congress have nominated Madison as the next president. This interference in the nomination of a President by a congressional caucus at the seat of government, we conceive to be unwarranted by the constitution—a violation of its spirit, and dangerous to the republic. The state of New York has openly resisted this usurpation, and by the nomination of DeWitt Clinton has brought the question before the American people.[6]

Shortly thereafter the New York legislature called the procedure of congressional nomination of a president "hostile to the spirit of the Constitution, dangerous to the rights of the people, and to the freedom of the electorate."[7] The New York position is that congressional nomination is an infringement of the separation of powers and makes Congress even more of a cozy little club, all-powerful and controlling the presidency. The president is supposed to be independent of Congress, not beholden to it.

Judging from the many articles in the newspapers, Clinton seems to be building popular support. But is he too late? As a dissident Republican seeking to attract a national following, Clinton needed the support of the Federalists, and that could not happen until they held their mid-September caucus. Running against an incumbent—especially in wartime—is hard enough; having to wait until two months before the election makes it extremely difficult to win. There simply isn't enough time.

Clinton's supporters favor him for president for several reasons:

1. The country needs a change. Madison represents the past; Clinton represents the future.

2. The United States needs to alter the way it nominates presidential candidates, especially force Congress to release its iron grip. A victory by Clinton will pave the way for reform.

3. The United States needs a president who can take a fresh look at our mess with Great Britain: either we wage war more vigorously, or we seek whatever face-saving agreement we can get, awkward though it may be.* As the representative of the mercantile state that does most of the country's trading with Great Britain, Clinton is in a good position to deal with this crisis.

   * Former president Jefferson thinks the war will be a piece of cake: "The acquisition of Canada this year, as far as the neighborhood of Quebec, will be a mere matter of marching, and will give us experience for the attack on Halifax, the next and final expulsion of England from the American continent."[8] Jefferson may well be right, but what if he is wrong? It is prudent to ensure that the next president has options.

4. Unlike Madison, who believes the greatest obstacle to democracy is lack of rights, Clinton believes it is lack of prosperity. Clinton brings to the presidential office a thorough grasp of commerce and free trade. The path to prosperity, he says, is

through expansion of the economy and the development of a modern infrastructure.

Under Clinton's vigorous leadership as mayor of New York, the city has prospered. He has proven himself to be a superb administrator of government affairs, and there isn't a whiff of scandal about him. In fact just the opposite. He has taken no salary from his many years on the Canal Committee. An inspection of his real estate portfolio reveals that he never bought property adjoining the canal (which obviously would become a gold mine for him). He is not a rich man; for almost twenty years he has lived on his modest government salary and supported himself by selling off his real estate holdings at an average low price of $1.25 an acre. He does not mix his personal affairs with politics. He is as clean as they come.

Clinton is a visionary mayor who has spearheaded new initiatives in physical infrastructure (streets, sanitation, canals), education, and social reform. He is a progressive-thinking leader. Thanks to him, many thousands of people in New York—especially children—now lead a better life. Were he to become president and expand these programs to a national level, millions would be better off.

He is just the man to get the country out of the critical challenge of the day: our conflict with Great Britain. His provocative comments on the evils of slavery—not necessarily what voters want to hear—also deserve serious attention. He is widely regarded as a learned man of accomplishment and integrity. Like George Washington, he has an austere personality. He will not win a "good old boy" popularity contest, but he will command respect. Because he frequently comes across as arrogant, he rates only "excellent" in the human intangibles, though he possesses exceptional determination and vision. On the important criterion of judgment he is a man potentially ahead of his time. He is a physical giant of a man who thinks just as big.

Accomplishments	Intangibles	Judgment	Overall
outstanding	excellent	outstanding	outstanding

Clinton's enemies "were not tender of his sensibilities."[9] They took full advantage of the inherent contradictions of his pro-war and antiwar exhortations, scornfully proclaiming his "apostasy" and presenting his opinions "in vitiating parallel." In the short time from his nomination in mid-September to early November, Clinton failed to hold on to his lead in Pennsylvania (with its twenty-five electoral votes). His coalition, said the New York *Aurora* newspaper, was "a group more oddly consorted than the assemblage in the ark."[10] Instead of winning 114–103, Clinton lost the election, 128–89. Look at the 1812 election map and the sectional split becomes apparent: 120 of Madison's 128 votes came from states south and west of the Delaware River; 80 of Clinton's 89 electoral votes came from states north and east of the river. It was the Civil War split, almost fifty years ahead of its time (a fact rarely recognized in American history).

There is a reason slaveholding states held the presidency for fifty-eight of America's first seventy years: the infamous Three-Fifths Clause in the Constitution, whereby southern states claimed their nonvoting slaves as three-fifths of a person, thus increasing their electoral votes. Had it not been for that clause, Jefferson would not have won the presidency in 1800.[11] Same for the 1812 election: had it not been for the "votes" of southern slaves who could not vote, DeWitt Clinton would have become president. In this scenario the strong-willed Clinton would have taken steps to unify the economies of the static agrarian South and the expanding mercantile North. The noncompetitiveness of a slave-based economy would have become so apparent that internal change might have occurred and the Civil War might have been averted.

Forced out as mayor after his 1812 defeat, Clinton went on to accomplish even greater things as the driving force behind the Erie Canal. Twice this project had been turned down by President Jefferson as "little short of madness." Such projects get done only by a leader with the tenacity of a madman. During his time out of office Clinton worked full time as a member of the Canal Commission to get the project off the ground. He went to Congress with a proposal backed by a hundred thousand signatures and secured approval of a bill for funding the canal, only to have it vetoed by President Madison. Not to be outdone, Clinton turned to local sources of funding and ran for governor of New York. He won the election and got the New York legislature to plunge ahead and authorize a bond issue with the grandiloquent promise that the canal would "promote agriculture, manufactures and commerce, mitigate the calamities of war, enhance the blessings of peace, consolidate the Union, advance the prosperity and elevate the character of the United States."[12]

Lavish words indeed, but true. George Washington's greatest fear for his new country was that the western states would splinter off from the original thirteen. "The western settlers," he said in 1775, "stand, as it were, upon a pivot. The touch of a feather would turn them any way."[13] At a time when western America had no choice but to use the rivers running through Spanish, French, and Indian territories, the future of the nation would be at risk. It was essential to build canals to unify the new nation and stimulate trade among the states.

Distances in America were made greater because of the lack of roads. It took longer to travel inland from Philadelphia to Pittsburgh than to take a boat to England. Said Gouverneur Morris, coauthor with Madison of the Constitution and a senator from New York with Clinton, "We only crawl along the outer shell of our country. The interior excels the part we inhabit in soil, in climate, in everything. The proudest empire in Europe is but a bauble compared to what America *will* be, *must* be, in the course of two centuries—perhaps of one."[14] New York State, with the Hudson River in the east and Lake Erie in the west, was ideally suited for a canal to provide ready access to the interior of America. Said Clinton, addressing Washington's "touch of a feather," "However serious the fears which have been entertained of a dismemberment of the Union by collisions between the north and the south . . . the most imminent danger lies in another direction. [A] line of separation may be eventually drawn between the Atlantic and the western states, unless they are cemented by a common, an ever acting and powerful interest. One channel, supplying the wants [and] increasing the wealth of each great section of the empire, will form an imperishable cement of connection, and an indissoluble bond of union."[15]

Lofty words by politicians mean nothing without practical implementation. Surveys by the Canal Commission headed by Morris and Clinton found that building a canal through New York State to cement the western states of Illinois, Indiana, and Ohio with the eastern seaboard would be a massive undertaking. It would require thousands of workers to survey, blast, and dig a 363-mile canal, plow through marshes and cut through solid rock, build aqueducts to carry the canal over valleys, and construct over eighty locks to compensate for changes in ground level, which at one point was as high as Niagara Falls. It was a challenge worthy of Ramses II and other Egyptian pharaohs. But in America, where few feats are considered impossible in the hands of a determined visionary, it soon got done.

As governor of New York, Clinton took personal control of the canal project and started construction. Progress at first was slow; many feared the project was far too ambitious and would end up as a huge financial black hole. "Clinton's ditch," newspapers called it. Clinton, a decisive man quick to act and lacking the personal charm typical of most politicians,* was voted out as governor in 1822 for spearheading such a boondoggle. As construction progressed, however, people woke up to the fact that the canal was likely to be a huge success. By 1824, wrote Martha Lamb in *History of the City of New York*, "the fame of DeWitt Clinton had gone to the ends of the earth."[16] Jealous politicians moved in and threw Clinton off the Canal Commission. A big mistake: the public rose up in an outrage at politicians evicting the man who had been the guiding force in getting the canal funded and built, who had never taken any compensation for fourteen years in a project that was now making many people in the state very rich. Even Martin Van Buren, a canny politician and no friend of Clinton's, was outraged. In one of the most profound expressions in presidential politics he screamed at the man who had plotted Clinton's removal, "I hope, Judge, you are now satisfied that there is such a thing in politics as *killing a man too dead!*"[17]

* In his 1846 *History of Political Parties in the State of New York*, Jabez Hammond tells the revealing story of a farmer who sought a pardon for his imprisoned son and got it from Governor Clinton: "The governor was so good as to ask me to breakfast and promptly pardoned my son, but . . . I must say that, although I had seen Gov. Tompkins but twice, and although each time he positively refused to grant me the favor I desired, and Gov. Clinton has granted me that very favor upon the first time of asking, I like Gov. Tompkins better than I like or can like Gov. Clinton—I cannot tell the reason why."[18]

Dead Man Clinton not only got his position back; he won reelection as governor in 1825, just in time to be master of ceremonies at the grand opening of the completed canal. Ever the promoter, and revealing his scientific mind, Clinton arranged for over a hundred cannon to be placed along the entire route; each gun boomed at the sound of the previous one, and so on down the line—from Buffalo to New York and back to Buffalo. (Clinton had proposed that this relay system might provide a way of measuring the speed of sound, but nothing came of it.) On July 4, at the sound of the cannon, the ceremony began. In front of thousands of people lining the canal banks a triumphant Governor Clinton led a grand procession of boats from Lake Erie to Albany, then down the Hudson River ninety miles to the edge of New York Harbor. There he lifted a small wooden barrel and poured water from Lake Erie into the Atlantic Ocean, "the wedding of the waters." Watching the wedding in front-row seats were all the former living presidents: Adams, Jefferson (who must have been embarrassed), Madison, and Monroe. Also present was the defeated 1824 candidate and future president Andrew Jackson. A greater gathering of presidents for a special occasion has never occurred since.

Thus was inaugurated the greatest public works project since the Pyramids. Some called it the Eighth Wonder of the World. Certainly it was the only such wonder ever built by the labor of

The wedding of the waters

free men, not by slaves or forced conscription. The Erie Canal was such an economic success that it recouped its cost in nine years.

In the meantime Clinton was left out in the political wilderness when the man he had backed for president in the 1824 election, Andrew Jackson, lost to John Quincy Adams. Adams offered Clinton the post of minister to England, but Clinton turned it down, hoping Jackson would run again and win in 1828 and make him secretary of state. Fate intervened: in 1827 Clinton's health suddenly declined, and he died the following year, age fifty-seven, just before his good friend Jackson took office.

Today Clinton is long forgotten. Ask Americans who DeWitt Clinton was, and almost everyone will ask if he is related to Bill. (There is no relation.) And the Erie Canal? It is but a shadow of its former self, replaced by railroads and highways.

Clinton was not like other men running for president: he had the vision, drive, and executive ability that many have, but he was also a man of rare high principle pursuing worthy goals. In a speech to the Phi Beta Kappa Society he offered words worth remembering today when we vote for a president:

> Faction and luxury—the love of money and the love of power—were the hydra-headed monsters that destroyed the ancient republics. . . . Pleasure is a shadow, wealth is vanity, and power a pageant; but knowledge is ecstatic in enjoyment, perennial in fame, unlimited in space, and infinite in duration. . . . Good men are too often lethargic and inactive—bad men are generally bold and adventurous. And unless arrested by the vigilant intelligence and virtuous indignation of the community, faction will, in the process of time, contaminate all the sources of public prosperity; a deleterious poison will be infused into the vital principles of the body politic; intrigue, ignorance, and impudence will be the passports to public honors, *and the question will be not whether the man is fit for the office*, but whether the office is fit for the man.[19]

Shortly before his death in 1826 Thomas Jefferson was asked who then alive was "the greatest American"? His answer: DeWitt Clinton.[20] Coming from a man of the rival political party this was quite a compliment. Another president, traveling through Illinois as a circuit lawyer, would often stay in the town of Clinton, named for the man who had built the Erie Canal and done so much to unify the nation. When he won the presidential nomination, Abraham Lincoln was asked whom he most wanted to emulate. He said it was DeWitt Clinton.[21]

3

....

William Henry Harrison, 1840

William Henry Harrison, the loser against the Democrat Martin Van Buren in 1836, is back again seeking the presidency, only this time he is the front-runner. This is not because of anything he's done; it's due to the economic depression of 1837 and the growing unpopularity of Van Buren. "Van Ruin!" the Whigs call him.

A pivotal moment has overtaken this campaign and made it come alive. It occurred when a Democratic columnist took a poke at Harrison: "Give him a barrel of hard cider and a pension of two thousand a year, and our word for it, he will sit the remainder of his days in a log cabin . . . and study moral philosophy."[1] Little did the writer dream when he penned this line "that his taunt would raise such a tornado."[2] The slur launched a thousand articles of newspaper publicity, and overnight the first popular campaign was born, the biggest mass uprising since the days of the Revolution: the emergence of "the log cabin." Here's a rally in Ohio:

> They had come from the hill tops, and had come from the valleys to this grandest of all grand rallies, and the like of that enormous procession of the people never had been seen in the hundred years of Ohio's history or in all the nation's existence. It was an army of banners moving through streets, whose walls were hung with flags, streamers and decorations in honor of a brave old patriot and pioneer,

who had given the best strength and years of his life to protecting the poor men, women and children on the frontiers, and who had settled down in a log cabin to spend his days as a humble farmer at North Bend; and when the people had called upon him in his retiracy to serve them, had been vilified, slandered and traduced by the office-holders and a pensioned press.[3]

Everywhere in the country the Whigs have organized rallies and marching parades of bands, whistles, log cabin floats, coonskins, women waving white handkerchiefs, and songs about "Tippecanoe and Tyler too."

Oh, what has caused this great commotion, 'motion,
'motion, the country through?
It is the ball a rollin' on
For Tippecanoe and Tyler, too
For Tippecanoe and Tyler, too
And with them we'll beat little Van
Van, Van, Van is a used-up man
And with them we'll beat little Van.[4]

Professional politicians are astounded at what's happening, especially since the candidate refuses to say anything specific about key issues or how he will govern. Harrison says this is not important. "A better guarantee for the correct conduct of a Chief Magistrate," he says, "may be found in his character in the course of his former life, than in pledges and opinions given during the pendency of a doubtful context."[5]

WILLIAM HENRY HARRISON

OBJECTIVE: Ninth president of the United States

Self-employed, 1830–present

Won the Whig Party nomination for president in 1836; lost general election to the Democratic Party candidate, Martin Van Buren (170 electoral votes to 73). Managed farm at home in Ohio. Assisted in the writing of a book, *A Memoir of the Public Services of William Henry Harrison.* Currently employed as clerk of local courts of appeals.

U.S. State Department, 1828–1829

Minister to Colombia. Engaged in public debate with Simon Bolivar on need for democracy in Latin America.

U.S. Senate, 1825–1828

Senator from Ohio. Chairman of the Military Affairs Committee. Resigned from the Senate upon appointment as minister to Colombia.

Ohio State Senate, 1819–1821

State senator. Supported programs for building canals and other internal improvements. Led successful movement to improve the state criminal code. Elected by fellow legislators to the U.S. Senate.

U.S. House of Representatives, 1816–1819

Congressman from Ohio. Promoted better pay for servicemen, veterans, and widows and orphans of soldiers. Declined to run for reelection; returned home to manage farm.

Bureau of Indian Affairs, 1815

Commissioner. Negotiated two treaties that added large tracts of land to the United States.

U.S. Army, 1812–1814

Commander of the Army of the Northwest, appointed by President James Madison. Won victories in Indiana and Ohio and recaptured Detroit. Promoted to major-general. Invaded Canada and defeated the British at the Battle of the Thames, one of the two major military victories of the war (along with the Battle of Lake Erie) that ended British domination of Canada and the American Northwest. Resigned from the army in a dispute with the secretary of war; reinstated by Congress in 1817 and awarded a gold medal for military services.

Indiana Territory, 1801–1812

Military governor of vast territory consisting of the future states of Indiana, Illinois, Michigan, and Wisconsin, appointed by President John Adams and reappointed by presidents Jefferson and Madison. Served three consecutive three-year terms. Selected magistrates, civil officers, and all militia officers below the rank of general. Exercised power to confirm grants of lands to individuals having certain equitable claims—with not a single accusation of corruption or favoritism. Divided the territory into political districts. Served as superintendent of Indian affairs. Negotiated thirteen treaties with Indian tribes, opening up sixty million acres for American settlement. Conducted negotiations with Tecumseh concerning lands owned by the Shawnee tribe; defeated the Indians in the Battle of Tippecanoe. Commended by President Madison for "utmost exertions of valor and discipline."[6]

U.S. House of Representatives, 1799–1800

Delegate, elected to represent the Northwest Territory (equivalent to being a representative from a state, except could not vote on legislation). Initiated and secured passage of an act, subsequently named the Harrison Land Act of 1800, helping working-class Americans by allowing them to purchase small tracts on credit. Served on committee dividing the Northwest Territory into two parts: the Ohio Territory and the Indiana Territory.

Northwest Territory, 1798–1799

Secretary and ex-officio lieutenant governor. Served as acting governor during the frequent absences of the governor.

U.S. Army, 1791–1798

Appointed by President George Washington. Learned basic skills in wilderness survival and Indian fighting. Promoted to lieutenant; fought in wars against Indian tribes. Served as aide-de-camp to Gen. Anthony Wayne.

PERSONAL

Born February 9, 1773, the youngest of seven children. Father a signer of the Declaration of Independence. Grew up in Virginia; attended Hampden-Sydney College at age fourteen. Transferred to the University of Pennsylvania to study medicine; gave up studies to enter the U.S. Army at age eighteen. Married Anne Symmes in 1795; ten children (four still living); many grandchildren.

Assessment of Qualifications

In this man, who will be sixty-eight at inauguration, we have a candidate with extensive experience as an army general, congressional delegate, military governor, state senator, congressman, senator, minister to a foreign country, and presidential candidate. Not even George Washington had a list like this!

However, Harrison's last major achievement was his success as a general in the War of 1812, over twenty-five years ago.

Up until the age of forty-two his résumé was outstanding. Since then it has been modest.* To be sure, much of this has to do with the jobs he has had. Being a general and governor gives a man ample opportunity to demonstrate leadership and accomplishment. Being a legislator, ambassador, and private citizen provides fewer opportunities. Over the past seven years, other than running for president, he has pretty much been retired. Not being a member of Congress since 1828, he has no record on such pressing questions of the day as abolition, tariffs, or the central bank. This has worked to his advantage, however, enabling him to sidestep divisive issues and ride on his personal appeal. Indeed some people call his campaign "the great straddle."[7]

> * His campaign biographer, Isaac Jackson, devotes 155 pages to Harrison's life up to 1814 and only twenty-nine pages from 1815 to the present. That's a ratio of 84 percent to 16 percent. In Harrison's own autobiography, coauthored with James Hall, this emphasis on his early career is even more pronounced: 90 percent to 10 percent (279 pages versus 30 pages). Obviously the candidate is more interested in stressing his early career than his recent one. We would prefer that this ratio were reversed.[8]

Harrison originally rose to fame because of his exploits as an Indian fighter and general during the War of 1812, following an enormously successful stint spearheading the expansion and development of the Northwest Territory. Observed President Madison, "General Harrison has done more for his country, with less compensation for it, than any man living."[9] Indeed Harrison is a man to whom the country owes a great debt. It is a debt well remembered by the hundreds of thousands of settlers in the West who now own land thanks to the land reforms he instituted as a military governor.

Though he is a native Virginian "to the manor born," he is a westerner to the core. His supporters describe him as a simple, self-made man born in a log cabin, a man of the common folk. It is a catchy phrase, bearing little truth. Until he was eighteen Harrison probably never knew what a log cabin looked like.

FAMILY BACKGROUND AND THE LOG CABIN

Forget all this hoopla about log cabins; this is a man born with a silver spoon in his mouth. There is not a president, not even Washington, who can match Harrison's background and pedigree. He hails from the elite known as the First Families of Virginia and grew up on a magnificent family plantation, Berkeley. His grandmother was Anne Carter, daughter of the wealthiest man born in America. His mother was Martha Washington's niece. His father was Benjamin Harrison V, inheritor of six plantations and a fifteen-thousand-acre estate, who went on to become one of signers of the Declaration of Independence, a member of the Continental Congress (his roommate in Philadelphia was George Washington), and governor of Virginia. His godfather and uncle was William Byrd, founder of the city of Richmond and builder of Westover, the most magnificent plantation in America. Another uncle was Peyton Randolph, the first president of the Continental Congress. One of his older brothers, Carter Harrison, is now a three-term congressman from Virginia.

When he went away to Philadelphia for medical school he lived in the home of the wealthy Robert Morris, the "financier of the Revolution," who became his legal guardian upon his father's death. When he decided to drop out of college and join the army, who does he go to for a commission but Uncle George? He walks into the President's House and has a talk with Washington, who promptly signs the order on the spot. Years later, when he returned east as a congressional delegate from the Northwest Territory, he got invited to the President's Mansion for dinner several times. The new president, John Adams, was a close friend of his late father from the Continental Congress days. William Henry Harrison is not a man who comes from nowhere.

Yet this massive presidential campaign is full of songs about this humble man who comes from the real America of log cabins. Harrison lives in Ohio in a palatial home that looks like a southern plantation. When asked, "Where's the log cabin?" the general opens a closet door and points inside to the horizontal logs of the left wall. It's the original log cabin where he and his wife began their married life, now covered with plaster to form one of the rooms in the house.

The symbolism is apt: he may live in a log cabin, but it is well-hidden behind the façade of a grand estate covering 2,800 acres. He lives as his father did, a lord of the manor, served by his former slaves. On the land he grows wheat and corn. The income from farming is barely enough to support his large family, so he earns extra money by selling off pieces of his property.

Daniel Webster, in his August 19 speech in Saratoga, New York, had this to say about log cabins and Harrison: "To live in a log cabin is no recommendation of a candidate for the presidency; neither is it any disqualification. It is, however, to be assumed that a man who, by his capacity and industry, has raised himself from a log cabin to eminent station in the country, is of more than ordinary merit. I, sir, have a feeling for log cabins and their inhabitants."[10]

A SELF-MADE MAN

Hardly any of Harrison's wealth comes from his inheritance. Not being the oldest son, he inherited little—just three thousand acres, which he sold to one of his brothers at a cheap price. If he is to make it big, he must make it on his own.

He chose to go west. For a man who is only 5-foot-8 and weighs barely 100 pounds—the runt of the family litter, compared to his father, a 6-foot-4, 250-pound giant—his choice of a career was a gutsy one. Like many undersized men, he compensates with willpower and toughness. Attaching himself to Gen. "Mad Anthony" Wayne, he learned from the master how to be a good fighter and quickly rose through the ranks to become one of the national heroes of the War of 1812. Harrison is a man of the frontier, a risk-taker, an adventurer. He is not a man given to the pomp and circumstance of his boyhood Virginia. As the general leading the Battle of the Thames, he eschewed a military uniform in favor of a fringed calico shirt and a beaver hat with a flamboyant ostrich feather.

He earned the unstinting loyalty of his men. At the Battle of Tippecanoe he was right up at the front line, where a bullet struck his horse in the neck and another bullet passed through the rim of his hat and grazed his head. "The bravest man I ever knew," says Lewis Cass, the former secretary of war and now minister to France.[11] When asked how he managed to gain the loyalty and confidence of his men, Harrison responded, "By treating them with affection and kindness, by always recollecting that they were my fellow-citizens whose feelings I was bound to respect, and by sharing on every occasion the hardships which they were obliged to undergo."[12]

Everyone speaks highly of him. "He combines the charm, easy manners and self-restraint of the Virginia gentleman, with the friendly ruggedness of the frontiersman," says one. "There is not a trace of hauteur in the man."[13] He is personable and friendly, direct and blunt. He is a great storyteller and very facile with amusing one-liners.

Of course one of the pitfalls of being a great storyteller is the propensity to gild the lily. Harrison claims that his victory at the Battle of Tippecanoe was a great achievement, whereas it actually wasn't much of a battle and he had all the advantages. He had twice as many men as the Indians, yet he suffered more casualties than they did. The only reason he won this "draw" is that the Indians didn't come back for more fighting. As is true after any battle with the Indians, whites hear only one side of the story. They heard nothing from the Indian leader Tecumseh, whereas Harrison produced a very lengthy report. Such is "history": what gets recorded on paper by winners eager to boost their reputation.

Harrison freely admits he had far more men at Tippecanoe, but maintains that such superiority was absolutely necessary: "It is an accepted fact that an American could lick two Britishers, three Frenchmen, or four Spaniards." As for "the Indian savages," it was "necessary to out-number them by at least two to one just to achieve a partial victory."[14] As for his other great military victory in the War of 1812, the Battle of the Thames, it was due less to his brilliance than to the sheer incompetence of the opposing British general, who was promptly court-martialed by the British Crown.

Harrison's supporters brag that he never lost a battle. True though this may be, it doesn't say much when one considers his opponents' weaknesses.

GOVERNOR OF THE INDIANA TERRITORY

In contrast to his military career, for twelve years Harrison genuinely shone as administrator, judge, drill sergeant, commander in chief, treaty maker, and empire builder. Exercising martial power, able to do pretty much whatever he wanted, he proved to be a man of superb judgment and administrative ability. But what most stands out is his personal honesty. Possessing power to award land grants, he never made a dime for himself, though he certainly needed the money to support his ten growing children and pay for all the entertaining he had to do as a governor. Just to cover his expenses he had to sell off some of his landholdings. "Many men under like circumstances," says Richard Hildreth in his recent 1839 biography, "would have availed themselves of the facilities for speculation thus afforded."[15] Or opportunities for insider trading or bribery. Not this man.

As governor of the Indiana Territory (1801–12) and commissioner of Indian affairs (1815), Harrison acquired fifty million acres of western land at a cost of under two cents an acre. That's 78,000 square miles. Compared to Jefferson's Louisiana Purchase of 828,000 square miles at four cents an acre—twice as much— Harrison's purchase looks more impressive. However, looks are deceiving. First, the Indians had no choice: if they hadn't accepted the terms, there would have been war. Second, the money for the land was paid in the form of an annual annuity. Had the annuity lasted longer, the cost would have been a lot higher. The reason it remained at two cents per acre is because the treaties were broken and the payments stopped.

Harrison's major achievement as governor was executing the land reforms he had single-handedly pushed through Congress as a delegate in 1800. The original plan proposed by President Washington was to sell plots of four thousand acres. The problem was that such a program—while easy to administer—would only create opportunities for wealthy speculators to buy up the land, subdivide it, and flip small parcels for a hefty profit. The purpose of government land management, argued Harrison, should be to promote rapid settlement by the people actually working the land, not give wealthy people an opportunity to acquire great baronial estates, as the British had done in Virginia and the Dutch in New York. Coming from a man whose family wealth came from huge Virginia land grants, this is unusual and bold democratic thinking.

Harrison's legislation offered small parcels combined with cheap 2 percent credit. Under his vigorous leadership as governor, the new program worked brilliantly in attracting thousands of settlers and creating a thriving economy and a sufficient population to qualify for statehood. Never once was there a whiff of scandal. On no occasion did Harrison pencil himself in for some choice pieces of land or use government power for personal benefit. Considering that in New York, Philadelphia, and Baltimore some of the wealthiest men are customs commissioners of the ports—a veritable gravy train—Harrison's rectitude is all the more remarkable. This man is a pillar of integrity.

Harrison's legislation has been enacted in subsequent territories and is now the prevailing policy in the United States. He has been called the "father of the American land system."[16] It is a sobriquet well-deserved. He has exerted more influence on the westward expansion of America than any president, even Washington or Jefferson.

POLITICAL CAREER AFTER 1815

Harrison has served as a congressman from Ohio, a state senator, a senator from Ohio, and the minister to Colombia, all for very short periods of time. Not mentioned in his résumé is that he has lost two elections: the 1821 election for senator and the 1822 congressional election. In 1828 he was mentioned as a possible running mate with John Quincy Adams.

In 1830, after only six months, he was dismissed as minister to Colombia by his political enemy, the incoming president Andrew Jackson. It was the first thing Jackson did upon taking office. In need of money when he returned to Ohio, Harrison accepted a job as a clerk in the local county courthouse, "a sort of retiring pension," he joked.[17]

His six-month term as minister to Colombia deserves comment. Bolivar never deigned to meet him, so on his way home as a private citizen Harrison sat down and wrote Bolivar a 4,400-word letter that stands today as one of the most profound statements of American principles ever written. It is an eloquent and insightful view of American democracy:

> You alone can save the country from ruin. . . . The strongest of all governments is that which is most free. . . . Unsupported by the people, your authority can be maintained only by the terrors of the sword and the scaffold. And have these ever been successful under similar circumstances? Blood may smother, for a period, but can never extinguish the fire of liberty, which you have contributed so much to kindle in the bosom of every Columbian. . . . There is nothing more corrupting than the exercise of unlimited power. . . . The mere hero of the field, and the successful leader of armies, may for the moment attract attention. But it will be such as is bestowed upon the passing meteor whose blaze is no longer remembered, when it is no longer seen. To be esteemed eminently great, it is necessary to be eminently good. . . . If the fame of our Washington depended on his military achievements, would the common consent of the world allow him the pre-eminence he possesses? The source of his veneration and esteem which are entertained for his character is to be found in his undeviating and exclusive devotedness to the interest his country. . . . General, the course he pursued is open to you, and it depends upon yourself to attain the eminence which he has

reached. . . . The friends of liberty throughout the world, and the people of the United States in particular, are awaiting your decision with intense anxiety.[18]

Bolivar never responded. Instead he released the letter to the public, denouncing it as interference in another country's affairs (while he was making himself a dictator). How unfortunate! This letter shows wisdom and vision worthy of a president of the United States.

CONCLUSION

Nicholas Biddle, the eminent banker, describes Harrison as a candidate "of the past, not of the future." Harrison, he says, should "say not a single word about his principles or his creed, let him say nothing, promise nothing. Let no committee, no convention, no town meeting even extract from him a single word about what he thinks or what he will do."[19] Calling him a candidate "of the past" is unfair. In several ways Harrison is a man of the future:

1. More than being a senator or governor, being a military governor is probably the closest government position to being president. In fact, it is an even more powerful position than the presidency in terms of its total executive power, unhindered by any legislature or judiciary. That William Henry Harrison never abused his extraordinary authority bodes well for a potential president required to "preserve, protect and defend" the Constitution.

2. Harrison is a Virginian whose life in the West has transformed him into an American. He belongs to a cadre of statesmen who entertain views of the government that can be called "national." As we endeavor to strengthen the bonds unifying our states and far-flung territories, this policy is an essential requirement of a potential president.

3. This man will broaden the voter franchise. Wherever he goes, throngs of people clamor to get a glimpse of him and hear him speak. At the Whig rally at the battlefield of Tippecanoe, some sixty thousand people came from miles away by foot and

horseback to see the man touted as "the log cabin candidate," "a child of the Revolution," "the people's candidate."

4. His age could be a problem, though he promises to serve only one term. He is a man of substantial intellectual and physical vigor. We quote from the *Buffalo Journal* at the recent July 20 celebration of the Fort Meigs battle: "Whatever misgivings we had . . . were dissipated after listening to the first few sentences of his address. The trumpet-like tones of his voice rang out as clear at the close as at commencement. . . . We never heard a more effective or appropriate address."[20]

In sum, William Henry Harrison possesses years of experience in high positions, all performed with distinction. It is widely recognized that "no citizen of the United States has ever filled so many civil and military offices . . . and certainly no one has ever been more uniformly successful in discharging the trusts confided in him."[21] He combines the wisdom of age with the idealism and energy of youth. He is a man of probity and totally honest: never once did he seek to profit personally from the land deals under his supervision in the Indiana Territory. He has sound judgment and a solid grasp of democratic principles. He is a first-rate campaigner and will rouse people to come out and vote. An aristocrat as well as a self-made man, he will spearhead the growth of popular democracy. Born into aristocracy, he has chosen to become a self-made man. A westerner as well as an easterner, he is ideally suited to lead the republic as it consolidates its expansion.

Accomplishments	Intangibles	Judgment	Overall
excellent	outstanding	outstanding	excellent

1840

Disaffected citizens who never voted before came to the "log cabin" rallies and caught the election bug. Harrison took to the road and gave stump speeches and attended many receptions so people could see the old general alive and kicking. How dare the Democrats make fun of this vigorous war hero, the man of the humble log cabin! "The Harrison whirlwind," John Quincy Adams called it, envious at the massive outpouring of enthusiasm.[22]

Poor President Martin Van Buren never knew what hit him. "I was drunk down, sung down, and lied down," he moaned. Voters were told their incumbent president walked on Royal Wilton carpets, sat on French tabourets, supped soup à la Reine with gold spoons from a silver tureen, ate pâté de foie gras from silver plates with gold forks, rode in a gilded maroon coach of British make, and slept in a French bedstead. "The royal splendor of a President's palace," thundered Congressman Charles Ogle in a masterpiece of campaign doggerel, "as splendid as that of the Caesars, and as richly adorned as the proudest Asiatic mansion. The garden with its rare plants, shrubs, and parterres in the style of the Royal Garden of England; the East Room and the blue Shepherd Salon garnished with gilt mirrors as big as a barn door, with chains that cost $600 a set."[23]

Voter turnout jumped 40 percent, from 57.2 percent in 1836 to 80.2 percent. Not only was it the biggest increase in voter participation ever; it was one of the biggest electoral landslides in history: a whopping 80 percent, 234 of 294 electoral votes.*

* Other electoral landslides were Washington's two wins, both at 100 percent; Monroe's 99 percent in 1820; and Jefferson's 92 percent in 1804. The only landslides after Harrison were Reagan's 99 percent in 1984, FDR's 98 percent in 1936, and Nixon's 97 percent in 1972.

Harrison was the type of politician who, once he got started campaigning, couldn't stop talking. "He is as tickled with the presidency as is a young woman with a new bonnet," observed one of his friends.[24] Traveling from Ohio to Washington for his inauguration, he gave speeches at every stop. After a visit to the Berkeley Plantation to see his relatives and visit his parents' gravesite, he went to Washington DC. He wrote out a lengthy inauguration speech, which took almost two hours to deliver. Inauguration Day itself was cold and blistery, and Harrison refused to dress warmly, almost as if he were determined to prove his youth and vigor.

If there was ever a president who worked himself to death, it was Harrison. "There never was a president elected who had a more difficult task imposed upon him than General Harrison," said one Whig. "Too much is expected of him."[25] Over the next three weeks, before he came down with pneumonia, he worked around the clock. He attended numerous functions, and kept his door open to anyone who wanted to see him, as he always had back home in Ohio. One stormy day a farmer showed up at the President's House when Harrison was having dinner alone. Upon learning the man had been kept waiting in a cold room, the president rebuked the servant, "Why did you not show the man into the dining room, where it is warm and comfortable?" When the servant mumbled something about the rain-soaked farmer muddying the carpet, Harrison blew up: "Never mind the carpet. The man is one of the people and the carpet and the house, too, belong to the people!"[26]

Harrison interviewed hundreds of office seekers to start his administration as quickly as possible. He picked a strong cabinet, with Daniel Webster as secretary of state, and summoned a special session of Congress to lay out his plans. In a meeting with the imperious Henry Clay, the man he had beaten for the Whig Party nomination, he asserted his authority. When Clay, a man with a high opinion of himself, started hectoring his listener about what needed to be done, Harrison cut him short: "You forget, Mr. Clay, that *I am the president.*"[27]

It was a short-lived presidency, brought about by the medical malpractice of Harrison's doctors, who had no idea what they were doing and tried all kinds of strange medications and drugs that only made the patient worse. After a week of mustard to the stomach, heat to the extremities, cupping (applying a red-hot cup to the skin to suck it in), and numerous quantities of calomel, laudanum, castor oil, rhubarb, snake weed, mercury, and opium, the old man couldn't take it anymore. Precisely one month after taking office, he "paid the debt of nature." In the words of one historian, it was a case of "murder committed in the name of medicine."[28]

"What! Soared the old eagle to die at the Sun?" cried a journalist. "Lies he stiff with spread wings at the goal he has won?"[29]

His wife never made it to Washington, the only first lady never to attend her husband's inauguration nor set foot in the White House. She was back home in Ohio, recovering from a temporary illness. Also missing the opportunity to see the White House was his seven-year-old grandson, Benjamin, living with his parents on a large plot on the corner of William Henry's huge estate. It would be another forty-nine years before Benjamin could walk in the front door like the place belonged to him, himself a newly elected president. With Benjamin Harrison, the longest-lasting dynasty of a prominent American family, 1630–1893, came to an end.

The year 1841 was the first time America had three presidents in one year, a source of delight for trivia buffs. (It happened once again, in 1881).[30]

The vice presidency may be a useless position, but being a heartbeat away from the big prize does have its benefits. Were someone to offer you the job, you probably should take it. Such was the lesson for Henry Clay. Three times he tried to become president, in 1824, 1832, and 1844, only to fail each time. The best chance he had was during the year he didn't run: 1840. Harrison offered him the vice presidency, but Clay never bothered to respond. Such arrogance does not make a man president, certainly not in America. In Latin America it's different. Simon Bolivar, who refused to meet Harrison and made himself a dictator, was revered by the citizens of Latin America as the Great Liberator. Looking at several of the dysfunctional democracies of Latin America today, one wonders: Liberator for what? William Henry Harrison had it right.

4

....

Abraham Lincoln, 1860

The front-runners for the 1860 election are Senator William Seward of New York for the Republicans and Senator Stephen Douglas of Illinois for the Democrats. An intriguing third candidate is an obscure Republican lawyer from Illinois who ran against Douglas for his 1858 Senate seat and lost. Abraham Lincoln actually beat Douglas in the popular vote but lost the election because the Democrats won more legislative seats and the legislature selected the winner.

The population of the country is now twenty-three million, of which almost four million (17 percent) are slaves. Slavery has become the key issue of the day. Seward, an ardent foe of slavery, takes the position that it should be abolished. Douglas argues that citizens of any new U.S. territory should be allowed to decide whether or not to permit slavery in their area. Lincoln takes a middle position, that slavery should not be allowed in the new territories; as for slavery in the South, he is conspicuously silent.

ABRAHAM LINCOLN

Age: fifty-one

6-foot-4, 184 pounds

Married with three sons, ages sixteen, nine, and seven

Nicknames: Abe, the Rail Splitter, the Lone Star of Illinois

Home address

8th and Jackson Street

Springfield, Illinois

OBJECTIVE: Sixteenth president of the United States

FIFTY-WORD STATEMENT OF QUALIFICATIONS: Self-made man from humble background; active in politics for twenty-six years; well-liked by fellow members of the Republican Party; political moderate; respected public speaker able to address the key issues of the day, especially slavery; campaign slogan: "Justice and fairness to all."

LEADERSHIP EXPERIENCE

Candidate for U.S. Senate, 1859

Won Republican nomination; lost to incumbent Stephen Douglas. Waged vigorous campaign virtually single-handedly: no family money, no secretarial staff, no full-time assistants, no designated campaign manager. Conducted seven public debates with Douglas, which captured the attention of a national audience. Stressed the moral issue of slavery as a wrong. Won the popular vote but not enough legislative seats to win the Senate because of the 1850 census, which allocated majority of voting seats to the Democrats.

Candidate for Vice President of the United States, 1856

Came in second out of fifteen candidates for the vice president spot on the Republican Party's first national ticket. Lost to Senator William Dayton of New Jersey, on the "Frémont for President" ticket.

Candidate for U.S. Senate from Illinois, 1855

Switched to the Republican Party; lost the nomination to Lyman Trumbull.

U.S. Congressman, 1848–1849

Elected congressman from Illinois, representing the Whig Party. Became familiar with the horrors of slavery and developed coherent political philosophy on this growing issue. Opposed U.S. invasion of Mexico. Head of 1848 Illinois Whig campaign: delivered many speeches on behalf of Zachary Taylor for president. Upon leaving office, offered position as governor of the Oregon Territory; turned it down to return to Illinois and resume private law practice.

Member, Illinois State Legislature, 1834–1842

Won four successive terms as candidate of the Whig Party. Learned the rudiments of party organization, from distribution of ballots to rounding up the votes. Campaigned for William Henry Harrison for president, 1840.

LEGAL CAREER

Partner in three different two-man law partnerships in Springfield, Illinois, serving numerous clients, large and small, in all matters concerning contracts and litigation. Established reputation as one of the top lawyers in Illinois.

> 1849–present, 1844–1848   **LINCOLN & HERNDON**, senior partner, with William H. Herndon (with time off to serve one term in Congress, 1848–49)
>
> 1841–1844   **LOGAN & LINCOLN**, junior partner, with Stephen T. Logan
>
> 1837–1841   **STUART & LINCOLN**, partnership with John Todd Stuart. In 1839 ran firm as sole proprietorship after Stuart won election to Congress. Dissolved partnership in 1841.

Self-employed, 1831–1837

Worked at numerous odd jobs as carpenter, store clerk, riverboat crewman, soldier, merchant, postmaster, blacksmith, and surveyor.

ABRAHAM LINCOLN, 1860

Notable achievement: election as militia captain in the Black Hawk War. Decided to educate myself in the law and apply my human relations skills to the profession of lawyer and politician.

Personal

Born 1809 in a log cabin in Kentucky, grew up in Indiana; because of family poverty, attended a "blab school" (recite lessons out loud) for less than one year by age fifteen; spent next five years performing manual labor to help struggling father support family; left home and moved to Illinois at age twenty-one. Self-educated. Favorite hobbies: telling stories, solving geometry puzzles, and reading Shakespeare and Robert Burns. Invented and hold patent on device to lift riverboats over shoals.

Assessment of Qualifications

Based on his résumé Lincoln has few qualifications to be president of the United States. He has held no public office for the past ten years; he was a single-term congressman, did not distinguish himself, and would not have been reelected if he had tried. He has never been governor or senator of his state. He has run for the U.S. Senate on two recent occasions and lost both times (to two different people). As a lawyer he has not built up a large firm suggesting administrative or executive management skills; to the contrary, he was content with managing three two-man partnerships, albeit these were successful and able to provide him a modestly comfortable living. He lacks formal education of any kind and has not written any books or developed any significant legal or political positions.

He cites in his résumé as a "notable achievement" his military service in a single skirmish fighting the Black Hawk Indians. Asked about this recently, he freely admits this success "gave me more pleasure than any I have had since."[1] This war-lover is running for president of the United States?

In short, there is little to recommend him for the nation's highest office, especially when that nation is trying to avert war and when a candidate who is highly esteemed and has significant experience is available: William H. Seward, the U.S. senator and former governor of New York. In response to a newspaper request to announce his name for the presidency, Lincoln himself replied, "I do not think myself fit for the presidency."[2] He is not admitting to being unqualified, only that he lacks the obvious credentials.

Lincoln does have the advantage in these tempestuous, divisive times of being a relatively unknown politician, with no political baggage. He is running as an outsider, making a virtue of the fact that his political positions tend to be middle-of-the-road and vague.

LINCOLN AS A LAWYER

While Lincoln is best known for his political activities, he has been a practicing lawyer for twenty-four years, from 1837 to the

ABRAHAM LINCOLN, 1860

present, with time off for a term in Congress. In each of his three small partnerships he has handled an incredible number of cases: 5,600. Allowing for his political campaigning and for time spent traveling all over Illinois by horseback, this works out to be almost a case a day. Obviously the vast bulk of these cases are simple, involving wills, debt collection, and rental contracts that don't pay much (twenty to fifty dollars each). To make a decent living Lincoln has had to generate volume.

He's never been to law school and makes no claim to legal sophistication. He stumbled into the law profession when he met John Stuart as a fellow member of the state legislature in 1836; Stuart invited him to join his law office as an assistant. By reading Sir William Blackstone's *Commentaries on the Laws of England* and helping Stuart with his law cases, Lincoln quickly learned the rudiments of the law and started practicing. He never took the bar exam; under an 1833 Illinois law, he qualified by getting a license from two judges. In his brief 1860 campaign biography he proudly states, "[I] studied with nobody."[3] The man is an energetic and quick learner. He says he never regrets his lack of legal training. When asked for advice by young men considering going into the law, he tells them to train the same way he did back in the 1830s. This is unwise: law in Illinois nowadays, with the growth of large businesses and the railroads, has become far more sophisticated than it was in the days when Springfield was a small farming village.

Lincoln's political friends say he represented only honest clients deserving of justice. This is not true. Like any "hired gun" lawyer, he represented unjust causes and resorted to technical defenses to help win cases. He represented murderers, con men, corrupt railroads—even slaveholders. In what is known as the Matson case he successfully represented a slaveholder seeking to regain custody of a slave woman and four of her children. Asked to explain how he could possibly do this when he claims to be a man who opposes slavery, he gives a convoluted—though undoubtedly legally correct—explanation: that the dispute originated in a state where slavery is protected by the Constitution.

But isn't that what people are arguing about today? What do we do when the Constitution is unclear or imprecise—or morally wrong?

His years as a lawyer sharpened his skills in logical thinking, clear writing, and being able to see the other person's point of view. We draw several conclusions from his legal experience that pertain to his potential success as a president:

He can master an unexpected problem. Going to school and learning is relatively straightforward: you've got a professor telling you what to do and how to do it; just do what he says. Learning on the job can be a lot harder, which is why experience is usually the best teacher. Lincoln had to ask questions, listen carefully to everything, and come up with answers on his own. He is a problem-solver, not a legal specialist. His law practice is broad and has exposed him to all kinds of situations. He is not afraid to take on new cases for which he lacks prior experience. No matter what the problem, he will find a way to master it, as he always has.

He is hands-on and decisive. Managing an enormous volume of small projects requires quick thinking and decisiveness. He is used to being the boss. He is not a perfectionist; he has never had the time or resources to be one.

He has superb people skills. In his last two partnerships his major role was to bring in the business, which is why he spent two hundred days of the year traveling through Illinois on the circuit court. Being a salesman and handling so many clients—obviously this man can handle just about anybody. He is highly regarded by his fellow lawyers on the circuit, even by his opponents. He is a master conciliator.

He has a deep reverence for the law. Like most Whigs, he believes in law and order. In his most famous early speech, given in 1838, he despaired of "the increasing disregard for law," "the growing disposition to . . . the wild and furious passions," and "the worse than savage mobs."[4] This is a man who will do his utmost to preserve and protect the Constitution.

ABRAHAM LINCOLN, 1860

On at least thirty-five public occasions during his political career Lincoln has described himself as "humble." In a speech in 1832 he said, "Every man is said to have his peculiar ambition. Whether it be true or not, I can say for one that I have no other so great as that of being truly esteemed of my fellow men by rendering myself worthy of their esteem."[5] (Note that the word *esteem* appears twice, indicating its importance to him.) Lincoln confided to his close friend Joshua Speed how miserable he was that he had "done nothing to make any human being remember" him should he die. He is incredibly ambitious, says Speed, determined to associate his "name with something that would redound to the interest" of his fellow man.[6]

For a man so ambitious Lincoln is remarkably lacking in the ruthlessness so often found in the world of politics. We cite several examples of his fundamental decency:

- In 1846 when John Hardin broke his promise and ran against Lincoln for Congress, Lincoln refrained from calling Hardin a traitor (as everyone else did) and instead waged a clean campaign, "Turn About Is Fair Play."[7]
- In 1849, returning home as a prominent ex-congressman, he continued to treat his young law associate Billy Herndon as a fifty-fifty partner (unlike his earlier partner, Stephen Logan, who took two-thirds for himself and gave Lincoln the rest).
- In 1855, running for the Republican nomination for U.S. Senator, Lincoln led Lyman Trumbull on the first ballot 45–5, with another candidate having 41 votes. Unable to get more than 47 votes [on] the ensuing ballots and Trumbull's supporter Norman Judd refusing to budge, in order to block the third candidate Lincoln surrendered all his votes to Trumbull, enabling Trumbull to win. Painful though this loss was, Lincoln bore no malice and campaigned vigorously for Trumbull. (Mrs. Lincoln, on the other hand, was so angry she refused to speak to her good friend Mrs. Trumbull, and Lincoln's campaign manager stated that never would he "have consented to the 47 being controlled by the 5").[8]

Such behavior throughout his career has won Lincoln many friends, including both Trumbull and Judd, who returned the favor and assisted him in his 1858 bid for the U.S. Senate. Lincoln is the most popular and well-liked lawyer on the Illinois circuit.

He knows the value of patience, as demonstrated by the way he structured his first campaign for Congress in 1844. Faced with two opponents for the Whig nomination, he conceded to the first candidate on the condition that he serve only one term, then be replaced by the second, and the second person be replaced in turn by a third—the third being Lincoln. It was all very clever and enabled Lincoln to achieve his objective in 1848, albeit later than he wanted. Nobody can say that this man is not a cunning, shrewd politician who thinks ahead.

He understands that a politician cannot be too far ahead of the pack. His views on slavery are not as radical as those of his fellow Republicans William Seward and Salmon Chase, but they are stronger than those of the Democratic candidate Stephen Douglas. Being in the middle has caused many people to claim he is wishy-washy, that he has no principles. This is not a fair charge: Lincoln has taken a strong moral stand on slavery, declaring that it is wrong and should be eliminated in the free states. How to eliminate it in the South is the difficult question. Either it should be eliminated by force—that is, war—or it should be left to die out on its own, being an economically unproductive institution. That Lincoln is trying to work out a solution does not necessarily mean that he has no principles. His recent speech at Cooper Union in New York City is a masterpiece of clear thinking and has established his growing national reputation as an articulate moderate.

Lincoln first ran for public office at the age of twenty-three, only six months after moving to New Salem, Illinois. He failed to win election to the Illinois state legislature, but he did receive 277 of 300 votes cast in his hometown. Obviously he has considerable personal magnetism.

Most prominent politicians rely on assistants to run their campaigns. Not Lincoln: he never had the money to hire people, so he had to do everything himself. When he won election to the state legislature and served four terms, he used his time productively to learn all aspects of political campaigning from the ground up. Nobody is more astute than he at studying the political map, identifying likely segments of friendly voters and figuring out how to appeal to wavering voters. Both in his own campaigns and in campaigns for his party's presidential candidates from 1848 to 1856, he has demonstrated a knack for setting goals and timetables.

In 1856 President James Buchanan offered Lincoln the governorship of the Oregon Territories. Lincoln's friend Joshua Speed urged him to take it, pointing out that he would then be in an excellent position to achieve his dream of running for the U.S. Senate.[9] But Lincoln turned it down, preferring to stay in Illinois. How many politicians would reject such an easy path to the prize? Lincoln did. This suggests a man not afraid of difficult challenges.

Last year he tried again for the Senate but lost. He was not finished, however. His years building the party and losing the party nomination for the 1856 vice presidency had enlarged his political perspective. Observes Joseph Gillespie, "Mr. Lincoln was ambitious but not very aspiring. He was anxious to be in Congress but I think he never aspired to anything higher until the prospect for the Presidency burst upon him."[10]

His strategy for winning the Republican Party nomination is a daring one: to be everybody's second choice. It's a long shot, but it just might work; already he has managed to achieve a stunning coup by getting the party leaders (by one vote, no less) to hold the nominating convention in his home state rather than in the home state of an opponent. His plan is to whip up so much local support that he gets all of Illinois's delegates and wins at least 100 votes in the first ballot—which should be enough to stop the frontrunner, be it William Seward or Edward Bates (Salmon Chase of Ohio and Simon Cameron of Pennsylvania also are potential threats). But these 100+ votes will not represent all of Lincoln's delegates; some are being deliberately held back for later. This is a gamble, because it might not be enough to block the frontrunner, but the plan is to release these additional delegates into the second round to create forward momentum. Assuming the front-runner slips and delegates become concerned he cannot win, they may look for a compromise candidate, especially a candidate from one of the three pivotal states of Illinois, Pennsylvania, and Ohio. The convention being held in Illinois, his home state, gives Lincoln an advantage in trying to wrest the nomination from the front-runner.

CONCLUSION

Lincoln is a deceivingly immodest modest man. No matter how often he touts his humble background—which he does often—and cites his lack of administrative and executive experience as an indicator he is "not fit for the presidency," do not be fooled.[11] This man has a will of iron. He is a master storyteller, using the homespun anecdote to make a point in a way everyone can accept. He is a delight to be with. This will be an invaluable asset for a president trying to control stormy cabinet meetings on slavery and secession. One simply cannot get angry at this man. Does he have the backbone to be an effective president? Even Lincoln himself admits that one of his weaknesses is an inability to say no. He got so panic-stricken he failed to show up for his wedding, leaving the bride at the altar. (A year later he changed his mind and married her.)

Like many self-made men, Lincoln is an incredibly hard worker. During his two years as a congressman he missed only thirteen of 456 roll-call votes. For over twenty years as a lawyer he has spent six months a year traveling the circuit court, hustling for legal business to support his family. He has built up a strong legal reputation for honesty and fairness, so much so that he is frequently designated by the judge of the Eighth Judicial District to preside in his stead when necessary. Obviously Lincoln is highly regarded as a man of sound judgment and rectitude.

At considerable sacrifice to his legal income, he campaigned vigorously for the 1848 and 1852 presidential candidates of his now-defunct Whig Party. He has given over two thousand speeches and made himself an accomplished public speaker. His famous address on slavery at the 1856 Bloomington convention, according to the Illinois state auditor, is "the greatest speech ever made in Illinois and puts Lincoln on the track for the presidency."[12] It led to his being proposed for the 1856 Republican vice presidential spot and made him the acknowledged leader of the new Republican Party in his state. More recent speeches, such as the one at Cooper Union, are brilliant and demonstrate his great intellectual capacity.

As our nation drifts into sectionalism and potential war, we need a leader of proven accomplishment and national stature. Such a man today is William Seward. As the former governor of New York, Seward brings proven executive experience to the job. He is well-known and respected in the South; in fact his closest personal friend in the Senate is Jefferson Davis. He is also immensely feared—a useful trait in a president if the storm warnings of war escalate and we need a deal-maker to get the southern states to accept an ultimatum.

Lincoln is a superb human being singularly lacking in high-level executive experience. His greatest skill is public speaking—a skill much prized in the Senate, a skill that would go to waste were he in the White House. (Presidents rarely give speeches, senators always do.) Lincoln has always said his true ambition in life is to be a senator. His collegiality and ability to get along with people will make him an outstanding legislator. That's where he should be: in the Senate. He will do well there.

Accomplishments	Intangibles	Judgment	Overall
fair	outstanding	excellent	fair

1860

Lincoln executed his 1860 nomination strategy perfectly. After a delay engineered by his supporters, the voting didn't get started until day 3.[13] It would take 233 votes to win. Seward led the first ballot with 173½ votes, followed by Lincoln with 102. In the second ballot Lincoln closed the gap, trailing Seward 184½ to 181. In the third ballot Lincoln clinched the nomination. "I was nominated by a convention that was three-fourths for the other fellow at the start," he ruefully admitted.[14]

In the meantime a group of southern Republicans refused to accept Lincoln's nomination and announced that their candidate would be John Bell, running as an independent. On the other side of the aisle the Democrats nominated Senator Douglas, but the southern members broke away there too and had their own convention to nominate John Breckenridge, the former vice president of the United States.

In a four-way race (Lincoln, Bell, Douglas, and Breckenridge) Lincoln won the election with 180 electoral votes out of 303. Yet he had less than 40 percent of the 4.7 million popular votes and collected not a single electoral vote from ten of the thirteen southern states. Had it not been for the Electoral College and the extraordinary presence of *two* third-party candidates taking votes away from Douglas, Lincoln would not have been elected. Says historian Jay Winik: Lincoln's victory "was in many ways a fluke and nothing more."[15] "His greatest asset," observed the historian Emerson David Fite in 1911, "was obscurity."[16]

. . .

On March 5, 1861, when the newly elected president walked into his office, the very first memo placed in his hands was a letter from the commander of Fort Sumter saying he couldn't hold out without reinforcements. No president has been handed an ultimatum on his very first day, before he even had a cup of coffee. Several days later he got a letter from Gen. Winfield Scott, head of the army, urging immediate evacuation of Fort Sumter. Lincoln equivocated and stalled for time. A month went by, and suddenly Fort Sumter was attacked, catching everyone by surprise.

At that point Lincoln moved fast. Once he made a decision, that was it: there was no wavering, just like the small-town lawyer he was, the master of quick debt collections. He immediately called for seventy-five thousand troops, transferred huge sums into a special bank account for war expenses, suspended civil liberties, and called for a special meeting of Congress—but not, symbolically enough, until July 4. This was the first time a president had declared hostilities without first consulting Congress, as required by the Constitution. Lincoln subsequently justified his rash actions: "Was it possible to lose the nation, and yet preserve the constitution? By general law life and limb *must* be protected; yet often a limb must be amputated to save a life; but a life is never wisely given to save a limb. I felt that measures, otherwise unconstitutional, might become lawful, by becoming indispensable to the preservation of the constitution, through the preservation of the nation."[17] This pattern became Lincoln's presidential management style: to be decisive when circumstances warranted. At the end of one cabinet meeting marked by a lot of heated disagreement, he announced, "Seven nays, one aye; the ayes have it."[18] The president is the boss.

He had no experience managing a war, but as a self-trained lawyer, he determined to teach himself the rudiments of his new trade and to master all the details. He didn't sit in the White House all day and read memos; he walked over to the War Department every morning to read and send telegrams to his generals—the emails of the time. It was like he had his own smartphone. He sent an assistant to the Library of Congress to bring him books on warfare, which he read at night. After several weeks he concluded that the superior forces belonged to the Union, but the Confederates had better generals and greater mobility to shift their troops to particular points. The only way to win this war would be to engage the Confederate forces on many points simultaneously; eventually one or more points would give way and the Confederate forces would find themselves in disarray.[19]

Most people told him to forget it, such a policy was amateurish: the war would be over in a year or two anyway. And what did he know about how to win a war? Did he think he was an authority after reading a couple of books? But the man persisted. He knew he had a lot of learning to do; his rival president, Jefferson Davis, was the former secretary of war of the United States. Somehow he would have to beat him, one man against another, like lawyers in court.

For a president, winning a military war requires more than just hard work; it calls for the ability to figure out what kind of war is being fought and to develop the right policy. A century later Senator Sam Rayburn would say of President Harry Truman that he got many of the small things wrong, but he got the big things right. The same applied to Lincoln. His experience as a litigator taught him that when the other side refuses to listen to reason and you cannot mediate and you have no choice but go to trial, you must go for the jugular and win. Employing his legal skills, he argued that this was a domestic rebellion, not a war between nations. The Confederacy was illegitimate, plain and simple. As the defender of the nation, the president of the United States must seek total victory. More than just capturing enemy territory (the usual objective), more than just capturing the enemy army (the military objective), the United States (the North) must destroy the enemy's government in its entirety (the political objective). Lincoln would pursue nothing less than unconditional surrender, not because he was vindictive but because the war's goal—union—required it.

Barely into his presidency, Lincoln received the most insulting memo ever received by a president. Entitled "Thoughts for the President's Consideration," written by Secretary of State William Seward, it suggested that perhaps Lincoln was not up to the job and that he should delegate many of his responsibilities to his more experienced cabinet members, especially the letter writer, who would be fully prepared to act like an executive. Appalled, Lincoln wrote an angry response—but did not send it. Taking several days to calm down, he met with Seward and let him know in unmistakable terms who was the commander in chief. He also let Seward know how much he needed him. To his credit, Seward swallowed his pride and went on to become Lincoln's strongest supporter. "Executive skill and vigor are rare qualities," Seward later wrote his wife. "The President is the best of us."[20] Such was the beginning of a remarkable relationship between the two men, almost a co-presidency, similar to the relationship between Colonel Edward House and Woodrow Wilson, Harry Hopkins and FDR, and Bobby Kennedy and JFK. It was no coincidence that on the night Lincoln was assassinated four years later, the other man attacked (and almost assassinated) was Seward.

Decision-making generally involves three choices: yes, no, or do nothing. Lincoln recognized this third option. "My policy is to have no policy," he said, referring to his early days steering flat-boats down the treacherous Mississippi River, where he had to zig-zag around floating trees, submerged rocks, and other obstacles, not knowing when he would suddenly have to change course.[21] A boat going straight down the river would quickly sink or be turned over. Lincoln was a pragmatist, not an ideologue; his foremost task was to keep his coalition together and win small victories step-by-step in what would be a long war, just as George Washington had done. "I claim not to have controlled events, but confess plainly that events have controlled me."[22] By being patient, by putting up with innumerable insults and frustrations—especially from his five successive generals, who declined to attack the enemy vigor-ously—he eventually achieved success at the end of 1864.

No question, the man's sense of timing was extraordinary. One of the most insightful compliments about Lincoln was made by a San Francisco newspaper editorialist: "Just the right thing, at the right time, and in the right place."[23] When the Union forces won two battles on the same day—Gettysburg and Vicksburg, on July 4, no less—Lincoln saw an opportunity to finally define what the war was all about. Several weeks later he appeared at Gettysburg, "this hallowed ground," where he gave what may be the greatest speech ever written.

He knew he owed a great debt to former slaves. In his defense of the Militia Act of July 1862 authorizing African American troops, Lincoln announced that emancipation must be an essen-tial part of restoring the Union: "Abandon all the posts now gar-risoned by black men; take 200,000 men from our side and put them in the battlefield or cornfield against us, and we would be compelled to abandon the war in three weeks."[24] But before he could proclaim full emancipation of the slaves, he first had to win the war. And victory was years away and by no means cer-tain. To keep the four border states in the fold,* he issued an Emancipation Proclamation giving freedom to slaves in the South only. Abolitionists in the North were furious that he wasn't doing more. After all, hadn't Lincoln once said, "If slavery is not wrong, nothing is wrong"?[25] Even the pro-emancipation Seward recognized the awkwardness of the situation, writing, "We show our sympathy with slavery by emancipating slaves where we cannot reach them and holding them in bondage where we can set them free."[26] To this Lincoln could only say, "The severest justice may not always be the best policy."[27] He would move ahead one step at a time.

* The border states were Maryland, Delaware, Kentucky, and Missouri. Had Maryland seceded, Washington DC would have been completely surrounded by Confederate territory; had Delaware also seceded, the two states would have nearly doubled the Confederacy's manufacturing capacity.

When victory finally drew near, Lincoln revealed his spirit of forgiveness and welcomed his enemies back into the fold. But it was a battle all the way. When he met with Confederate commissioners in February 1865 and tried to get the rebels to cease their resistance and accept $400 million in return for feeing the slaves, he got nowhere. Even more painful was the reaction back home. His cabinet unanimously rebuffed him. "You are all against me," he despaired.[28] He tried again in early April, going to Richmond to try to persuade the rebel legislature to disband. Getting nowhere, he had to revoke his offer.

At a celebration on the night of April 11 thousands of people gathered in Washington to celebrate victory and hear the president speak. Surely this would be the president's finest hour, his moment of glory. But no, instead of a rousing speech Lincoln gave a long peroration about the difficulties of reconstruction and the knotty problems that lay ahead. It started to rain, and the crowd dribbled away, disappointed and perplexed. Two days later he was dead.

Overnight everything changed. People in shock wondered what might have been if Lincoln had lived to deal with the problems he was attempting to articulate.

Throughout his presidency Lincoln endured constant criticism and abysmal popularity ratings. Yet he persevered and won converts by virtue of patience, dogged tenacity, common sense, and human decency. As military commander in chief, a role he performed brilliantly, he abused his executive power, but he was a man who could be trusted with it. Few people could have predicted this, yet after a month on the job the man who once admitted he could never say no had transformed himself into a strong executive who seized power, made bold decisions, and did not procrastinate when subordinates—especially generals—weren't performing. How to explain this growth? The best answer lies in his unbending character and impeccable integrity. When threatened to the core, Lincoln never got emotional or angry or let depression overtake him. He just kept going, "like a little engine that knew no rest," always in search of a solution, as he had done all his life.[29]

In his style of leadership Lincoln was not the visionary or all-knowing wise man he appears to be in his Washington DC memorial. He made his fair share of mistakes, but he was quick enough to correct them. As a politician he was ready anytime to cut a deal. The most influential editor of the day, James Gordon Bennett of the New York *Herald*, had written years earlier, "The idea that such a man as he should be President of such a country as this is a very ridiculous joke."[30] But Lincoln put Bennett on the list for White House social functions, gave him first crack at hot news from the White House, and offered him the post of minister to France. Bennett declined the post, but needless to say, his views of Lincoln changed considerably.

Many want to be president, but few want to be a politician. Lincoln knew public opinion is fickle. Small steps are more important than principles. Deal with everyone you meet with decency and compassion. Should you win the war, principles will take care of themselves.

. . .

How could a man rated only "fair" as a candidate go on to be so successful a president? It's a question worth pondering every time we go to vote.

How easily we forget: it took only six months for Lincoln to go from ignominy to sainthood, from August 1864 to April 1865. "Lincoln alive," said one historian, "had many detractors; Lincoln, dead, had only extollers."[31] In 1864, when he was striving to be reelected, prospects were bleak. Observed the reporter Richard Henry Dana, author of *Two Years before the Mast*, "The most striking thing is the absence of personal loyalty to the president. It does not exist. He has no admirers, no enthusiastic supporters, none to bet on his head."[32] Nearly every important Republican leader of the day urged him not to run: Salmon Chase, Charles Sumner, Horace Greeley, Thaddeus Stevens, Benjamin Wade, Zachariah Chandler, Orestes Browning, Thurlow Weed. Lincoln won a second term because the election occurred just as Gen. William Tecumseh Sherman and Gen. Philip Sheridan started to win battles and the tide began to turn. He won with only 54 percent of the vote from only half of the country. The historian David Herbert Donald observes, "Fifty-four percent with your enemies not voting is not such an overwhelming vote."[33] Had the election taken place three months earlier, Lincoln would have lost.[34]

Lincoln had his share of good luck, but not because he was in the right place at the right time. He got lucky because he worked hard for it, and the harder he worked, the luckier he got. He won the 1860 nomination because he gambled on a high-risk strategy. He won the Civil War because he figured out what kind of a war it was and what was needed to win it. Most important of all, he had insight. He never confused the issues. He was extremely focused and pushed as hard as he could, but not too hard. In times of crisis, as we know from seeing Winston Churchill in World War II, a leader's strengths at the critical hour can make all the difference. Could this brilliance have been predicted? In part, yes. In times of war, when so much is tangential and unpredictable, anything goes. We can consider ourselves fortunate that a man outstanding in intangible qualities was the man of the hour.

5

....

Jefferson Davis, 1861

Unless a miracle happens, the United States is on the road to war. Nobody should be surprised. The southern states have always warned that if Lincoln were elected, they would secede. Lincoln's victory in the November 1860 election has cemented their resolve. South Carolina seceded in December, Mississippi in early January. By the end of the month five more states had left the Union—Alabama, Florida, Georgia, Louisiana, and Texas—with four others (Virginia, North Carolina, Arkansas, and Tennessee) waiting to see what happens. On February 4, delegates from the seven southern states met in Montgomery, Alabama, to form a new government for a new nation, the Confederate States of America.

Tomorrow, February 9, they will be choosing a provisional president, likely Jefferson Davis of Mississippi, the former U.S. senator and secretary of war.

People in the South generally fall into one of two groups:

- The rabid fire-eaters who favor slavery and secession.
- The moderates who favor slavery but oppose secession.

In between these two groups is Davis, an able man whose name was put up at the 1860 Democratic Convention as a potential candidate for president of the United States. In an 1858 *Harper's Weekly* article he was described as a man one would hardly

call a fire-eater. He is perceived to be extremely able. Yet he is also a strong secessionist. Time and time again he has pronounced strong views about the supremacy of states' rights.

What will Davis do should he be elected president of the Confederacy? Is he the right man for the job? Will he control the madmen, or will he yield to them?

At stake in this election is more than just the Confederacy. Should the Confederacy go to war and win, Davis would become president of the entire United States, the first man to become president via hostile takeover.

JEFFERSON DAVIS

. . . .

Age: fifty-three

6 feet tall, 130 pounds

Fair/good health

Home address:

Briarfield Plantation

Davis Bend, Mississippi

OBJECTIVE: President of the Confederate States of America

PERSONAL STATEMENT: "The post of president of the provisional government is one of great responsibility and difficulty. I have no confidence in my capacity to meet its requirements. I think I could perform the functions of general if the Executive did not cripple me in my operations by acts of commission or omission. . . . I would prefer not to have either place, but in this hour of my country's severest trial will accept any place to which my fellow citizens may assign me."[1]

U.S. Senator, 1857–1861

Returned to U.S. Senate after winning 1856 election. Gained national prominence as moderate in the growing escalation of "national government" versus "states' rights." Earned widespread respect of northern senators, including Simon Cameron and William Seward.

Delegate, 1860 Democratic National Convention. Name placed in nomination for president of the United States by Massachusetts senator Benjamin Butler.

Placed in an untenable situation after election of Abraham Lincoln to the U.S. presidency in November 1860. Nonetheless, as member of the Committee of Thirteen, a last-minute attempt to resolve the differences between the southerners and the northerners, worked assiduously with Senator John Crittenden; all compromises rejected out of hand by Republicans on the committee. After secession of Mississippi, delivered farewell speech and resigned from the Senate in late January. Joined Army of Mississippi; appointed major general of newly formed regiment.

Secretary of War, 1853–1857

Served as favored advisor to President Franklin Pierce. Took over U.S. Army plagued with low morale, high desertion rate, and few reenlistments and turned it around through personal enthusiasm and thorough attention to detail. Instituted numerous reforms to bring the U.S. military up to date:

- Increased size of army almost 50 percent, from 10,415 men to 15,562.
- Acquired modern weapons.
- Identified potential route for building a transcontinental railroad to unify the nation and promote economic development.
- Expanded size of remote frontier forts to strengthen fortifications and create better living conditions for the soldiers assigned to them.
- Awarded pay increases for officers, the first in forty years.
- Created the army's first training manual; added twelve months to the West Point curriculum; sent army officers to Europe to learn latest skills and tools of military warfare.
- Supervised construction of expanded Capitol building and dome.
- Considered by many to be the best secretary of war in the history of the United States; called by the *New York Times* "the autocrat of the cabinet."[2]

Candidate for Governor, 1851

Resigned from U.S. Senate to run for governor of Mississippi. Lost election. Campaigned for Franklin Pierce for president. Upon Pierce's election, was offered a cabinet position; declined offer, at wife's request, in order to remain in Mississippi and manage plantation.

U.S. Senator, 1847–1851

As a war hero, appointed to the Senate to fill vacancy caused by death of incumbent. In 1848 elected by the Mississippi legislature to a full six-year term. Informal advisor to President Zachary Taylor, a member of the opposing party and former father-in-law.

Mexican War, 1846–1847

Appointed colonel of the First Mississippi Volunteers, the only state regiment authorized by the U.S. secretary of war. Served with U.S. Army forces under the command of Gen. Zachary Taylor. Performed with distinction in the battles of Monterey and Buena Vista; badly wounded at Buena Vista; hospitalized for three months, on crutches for two years. Earned widespread praise for fearless leadership under dangerous circumstances; received commendation letter from President James Polk for "distinguished gallantry."

Promoted to brigadier general in February 1847. Turned down the promotion, declaring that it was a violation of states' rights for the national government to appoint officers of a state regiment.

U.S. Congressman, 1845–1846

Representative from Mississippi. Resigned in 1846 to fight in the Mexican War. Before leaving Washington, against the wishes of Gen. Winfield Scott, who favored the old-fashioned flintlock musket, ordered a thousand new percussion rifles for regiment. Rifles worked superbly and are now the standard rifle for the entire U.S. Army, nicknamed "the Mississippi rifle."

Publicly challenged President Polk's announcement that war existed between Mexico and the United States, on the grounds that only Congress has the right to declare war (the president can merely "inform").

EDUCATION AND EARLY LIFE

Enrolled at West Point at age sixteen. Graduated in 1828; class rank 23 out of 33. Served five years in the Northwest Territory, engaged in skirmishes with various Indian tribes. In 1835 promoted to first lieutenant; resigned in order to marry Sarah Knox Taylor. (The bride's father, a general, did not want his daughter to have to endure the life of an army wife.) Wife died of malaria three months later.

Settled in Mississippi after being given 800-acre property by older brother as part of family inheritance. Spent next ten years, 1836–45, building up successful cotton plantation. Used leisure time to amass substantial library of books; read them all. Delegate, 1843 Democratic State Convention and 1844 Democratic National Convention. Gave numerous speeches for the winning presidential candidate, James K. Polk. In November 1845 ran for Congress and won.

Personal

Full name: Jefferson Finis Davis. Born June 3, 1808, in Kentucky, son of a Revolutionary War officer. Grew up in Mississippi. In 1845 married Varina Howell; five children. Favorite pastime: reading Shakespeare and political treatises. Member of the Board of Regents, Smithsonian Institution. Received honorary LL.D. from Bowdoin College, 1858.

Assessment of Qualifications

Today, February 8, 1861, is a glorious day for the South: after four days of deliberation the convention of seceding states has announced the establishment of the Confederate States of America. Tomorrow it will be electing a provisional president to be inaugurated on the eighteenth.

Jefferson Davis is one of the South's most esteemed politicians, a rising star on the national scene. For over twenty-five years he has built up an impressive career as a U.S. congressman, war hero, senator, secretary of war, and once again senator. He has even been talked about as a potential president of the United States.

At the 1860 Democratic convention Davis got only one vote for the party nomination (eventually won by Senator Stephen Douglas). The leading vote-getters from the South were Vice President John Breckenridge of Kentucky and Senator Robert Hunter of Virginia, the youngest-ever speaker of the House and chairman of the Senate Finance Committee. Another prominent southerner is former Treasury secretary James Guthrie of Kentucky. Unfortunately none of these candidates is available for the Confederate presidency: neither Virginia nor Kentucky has seceded yet.

As a rump republic formed impetuously, the Confederacy consists of only seven states. The pool of talent for a president is very small. Other than Howell Cobb, the former Georgia governor, Treasury secretary, and speaker of the House (and now the president of the Confederate convention), Davis has little competition. For a nation about to embark on war, Davis is the only candidate who combines political experience with a military background.

What is the South fighting for? There are two groups: the moderates, represented by Davis, who argue that the war is about states' rights, and the hardliners, led by Georgia's Alexander Stephens, who argue that it is to protect and preserve slavery. Which is it? Fewer than 5 percent of southern whites own slaves.[3] When the euphoria of rebellion fades and tens of thousands of men get killed, how is Davis going to maintain morale in a war to preserve an institution that benefits only the wealthy few? The majority of southern whites are not going to fight to make others rich. To lead such an incongruous, bifurcated society requires a master juggler, a man capable of handling contradictory objectives simultaneously. This is one problem. A second problem is the contradiction between confederation and country. To win the war Davis needs to unite the states into a tightly integrated war machine. Yet these states, having rebelled against one central government, are not likely to yield their newfound freedoms to another one. These two problems are fundamental; there is no way around them.

President of the Confederacy has to be about the most difficult job one can imagine. The owner of that title must manage two tasks simultaneously: a start-up and a war. It's hard enough to lead a new country where most of the major players have never worked together before (many of them don't even know each other); how about a country at war when battles are being lost and everyone starts sniping at each other?

Davis has proven himself to be a superb government administrator and senator who commands the respect of his peers in the legislature. These are valuable skills for a president. But the job description for the Confederacy is unique: it is all about war because without victory, there's no Confederacy anymore. The Confederate States of America needs a leader with charisma who can articulate policy and wartime goals and keep everyone motivated to continue fighting for what may be a long and arduous struggle for independence (or conquest). He must work well with people, avoid making unnecessary enemies, and be pliant enough to adapt to incessant crises. Like George Washington, he must be decisive, resolute, and not given to bouts of darkness. He must be in extremely good health, able to handle the stress of war and never miss a day of work. He should be a risk-taker, ready to go for the knockout blow should the appropriate opportunity arise.

On all these counts there are legitimate concerns about this man. For starters, there is his health. It is alarming. He caught pneumonia and almost died when he was in the military and was stationed in the Northwest; three years later he caught pneumonia again. He and his wife came down with life-threatening malaria in 1835; his wife died. In 1847 his right foot was shattered by a bullet at the Battle of Buena Vista, putting him in the hospital for three months. He was on crutches for the next two years while his foot healed, and to this day he walks with a marked limp. During this time he had a second bout of malaria. In 1851 he contracted a painful eye disease that put him out of commission for two months because the pain was so bad; whatever this affliction is, it reappeared in early 1858 for four months and continues to burden him. He had major eye surgery in 1859, only partially successful, confining him to months in a dark room, unable to read. He can see out of his right eye, but his blind left eye is bloodshot, giving him an eerie appearance that many people find disconcerting. He is painfully thin. For an otherwise very handsome man, he looks worn-out and exhausted, almost as if he has one foot in the grave.

Much of this is due to overwork. He has enormous energy and drives himself at a pace that leaves most men in tatters. A perfectionist with a high opinion of himself, he is quick to find fault in others and does not like to delegate. He is a misfit, a rebel who follows his own drummer.

At West Point his performance was poor; three times he almost got thrown out due to insubordination. In the military he was court-martialed twice. At the second trial he stubbornly insisted on conducting his own defense. He attributes his losing the case to the unfairness of the military panel—not to the possibility he might have been wrong. All he will concede is a minor flaw: "I was right as to the principle from which it arose, but impolitic in the manner of asserting it." This seems to be one of his favorite expressions, especially when others disagree with him: "I was right."[4]

People like Davis make great warriors in battle, which he certainly proved to be in the Mexican War with his daring and bravery. Yet even then he had to have the last word: promoted to brigadier general, he threw the honor back in the government's face by saying the War Department had no right to involve itself in the affairs of a state militia. This is hair-splitting nonsense. His regiment, the Mississippi Rifles, was authorized not by the state but by the secretary of war; therefore he was serving under the command of the U.S. Army.

The man has "a chip on his shoulder." He bristles at insults—real or imagined—and is quick to overreact. During his military service in the Northwest Territory he challenged his commanding officer (and later father-in-law) Zachary Taylor to a duel. That was just for starters. Over the years, even as recently as two years ago as U.S. senator, he challenged five men to duels "in the name of honor." (In every case wiser friends interceded and told him "cool it.") Such impetuousness is not becoming of a leader; it suggests a rigid mind susceptible to self-delusion ("I was right"). Davis will go to extreme lengths to rationalize what makes no sense. How else to explain the following?

- He defends the slavery of blacks, even though he owes his life to his personal slave, who saved his life by taking care of him when he was stricken with malaria in 1848.
- He justifies being a slave master by claiming to be a benevolent man who never uses the whip, but he overlooks the fact that most southern slave masters are cruel tyrants.
- He says slaves have a better life in America than they would have as free men in Africa, but he fails to consider how much better their life might be as free men in America.
- He glosses over the fact that hundreds of so-called happy slaves are trying to run away to the North.

Even his Personal Statement stops short of being a complete thought; it sounds good as far as it goes but leaves a lot of unanswered questions. If a Union is so dear, what has Davis done to preserve it? If a rebellious state insists on using force, is not the Union equally justified? Are there not situations when the Union has no choice but to fight back?

For a man who spent ten years in seclusion reading books (1836–45), he has a distorted knowledge of history. Such is the peril of living alone for too long. He sees life through a narrow lens:

- He denies that the South had anything to do with the reprehensible African slave trade (abolished by the federal government in 1808), refusing to accept that the South created the market demand in the first place.

- He claims northern slave traders made more money out of slavery than did the southern plantation owners and that the only reason the North abolished slavery is because it was no longer profitable for the slave traders.
- In an 1858 speech at Boston's Faneuil Hall (built by a slave trader, no less) he reminded his Massachusetts listeners that they were the prime defenders of states' rights—as if the world in 1791 was the same as in 1858.*

* The story Davis told the audience concerned President George Washington's visit to Boston, where Governor John Hancock "refused to call upon the President, because he contended that any man who came within the limits of Massachusetts must yield rank and precedence to the Governor of the State."[5] Davis conveniently leaves out the fact that insulting President Washington was not a smart move.

How can a man who can't get his basic history facts straight be expected to make good decisions about the present? Is it not true that wrong assumptions lead to wrong conclusions? Closed-minded people tend to be obtuse in their certainty. Consider a scene in the Senate in 1850 when the senator from Wisconsin interrupted one of Davis's harangues to observe that "the Senator from Mississippi always speaks so very positively," to which Davis cavalierly responded, "Because I am very certain."[6]

"Against stupidity, the gods themselves contend in vain," said the great German philosopher and playwright Friedrich Schiller (1759–1805). Davis is a man who sees the world only from his own point of view.

Davis believes England and France will quickly support the Confederacy because the South is their only source of cotton—as if cotton were the primary concern driving their international balance-of-power calculations. But suppose he is wrong? That he could be naïve doesn't seem to enter into his thinking. For a man who has been proven rash so many times in the past, this continued bull-headedness is disturbing. It suggests a man who has not learned from his mistakes. He has advanced in years, but not in judgment.

In his personal statement Davis addresses his fitness to head the Confederacy. He says the job "is one of great responsibility and difficulty. [He has] no confidence in [his] ability to" handle it and will do the best he can. False modesty aside, this does not sound like the bold leader we need. Our Confederacy is a strong country, almost as strong as the North, but the North has a much larger population and massive industrial capacity. We know from George Washington's experience how to win against a stronger power: Don't lose it! . . . We must fight a defensive war, stay out of big battles, and go for the bold stroke (like crossing the Delaware or attacking at Yorktown). If our objective is to actually *defeat* the North, we must do so right away while our parity of strength lasts.

Davis has an enormous capacity for hard work; it has carried him far. His papers and communications to Congress are models of English composition. As secretary of war, he had responsibility for a full third of the entire federal budget. Unlike previous war secretaries, he made himself the leading man in the cabinet, even surpassing the secretary of state. He managed all aspects of the War Department in a thorough and professional manner, and made sure no money was misused or stolen. Most admirable of all, he never used his position to benefit the military preparedness of the South. Throughout his term he served national interests—not state interests—and appointed all fifty-five officers based on merit rather than on personal favoritism or sectional origin.

What's it like working for a man of such exacting standards? One of his fastest-rising officers in the military was George B. McClellan, who calls him "a man of extraordinary ability."[7] One of Davis's seven clerks in the War Department was William Lee, who says Davis was a very considerate and kind man to serve under and that nobody in the department had any complaints. However, Lee added a note of caution: "He was a regular bull-dog when he formed an opinion, for he would never let go." Even James Campbell, postmaster general in the Pierce cabinet and son-in-law of an Alabama slave owner, is nervous about Davis, whom he describes as "one of the most stubborn slavery men I ever met."[8]

As congressman and senator, Davis gave hundreds of speeches, all written out by hand and thoroughly rehearsed. He is a master orator: his farewell speech to the Senate when Mississippi seceded is one of the greatest Senate speeches ever given, leaving many men in tears. As a person he is very charming and has a ready ability to make friends, even with people on the other side of the political fence. (His closest friend in the Senate is the North's most prominent politician, William Seward.)He made a great impression on four presidents. John Quincy Adams predicted Davis the congressman would go far: "That young man is no ordinary man. He will make his mark yet."[9] Davis won over James Polk, was Zachary Taylor's most trusted confidant, and was Franklin Pierce's most important advisor. Both Taylor and Pierce continue to speak highly of him.

He is a superb administrator. But his perfectionism and narrowmindedness are likely to lead him astray as he faces one of the most difficult jobs ever facing the president of a country. While we recognize his remarkable achievements and many endorsements, we cannot recommend him with confidence. He is an overachiever: a stubborn workaholic with limited vision or common sense. He is closed-minded, rigid, and inflexible. He lacks personal charisma. He may be the right man to administer a country; he is the wrong man to lead a revolution.

Accomplishments	Intangibles	Judgment	Overall
excellent	poor	poor	poor

1861

Davis's intellectualism and lack of strategic thinking doomed whatever chance the Confederacy had to win.

The most important decision a president makes is whether or not to go to war and how to fight it. Davis understood that this would be a long, drawn-out war and that in the beginning the South had the advantage of having a more experienced president, better generals, and a better rationale for instilling patriotic fervor: defending the homeland. But he also had to know that his window of opportunity was closing: the North had five times as many ships and twice the density of railroad per square mile and produced fifteen times as much iron, seventeen times as many textile goods, twenty-four times as many locomotives, and thirty-two times as many firearms.[10]

To fight a superior enemy you need allies—in this case, England and France, both eager to maintain the lucrative cotton trade but not wanting to get involved in someone else's civil war. What faster way to impress them than to knock out the enemy's capital, a city conveniently located on the southern border?

The city of Washington was poorly defended, with only 1,500 troops. When Fort Sumter surrendered on April 12, the Confederate secretary of war bragged that the Confederate flag would "float over the dome of the old Capitol at Washington before the first of May."[11] Varina Davis sent invitations to her lady acquaintances in Washington inviting them to attend her reception at the White House in three weeks. A popular song, "Jeff Davis in the White House," caught the popular imagination: "What glorious news it will be, / Abe Lincoln in an inglorious flight, / In a baggage car we will see."[12]

Pessimism prevailed in the North. Edwin Stanton, soon to be the Union's secretary of war, expected Davis to be in possession of Washington within thirty days. Looming on the horizon was a large army under Gen. Pierre Beauregard in Charleston, a mere three days away by train. "If I were Beauregard I would take Washington," Lincoln said in despair.[13]

Yet Davis did nothing: he was fighting for independence, not conquest. In twelve days Gen. Winfield Scott was able to fortify the nation's capital with sufficient troops. By not attacking when the city was totally vulnerable, Davis had missed a once-in-a-lifetime opportunity. Benjamin Butler, one of the North's leading generals, wrote in his memoirs, "Why Washington was not captured within ten days after Fort Sumter was fired upon has always been a subject of careful consideration on my part, and a thing which I have been utterly unable to understand."[14]

A second opportunity soon presented itself for Davis to score a knockout blow, and once again he failed. On July 21, 1861, the rebels won a smashing victory in their first major engagement, the First

JEFF, DAVIS

IN THE WHITE HOUSE.

AIR—"Ye Parliaments of Old England."

Ye Northern men in Washington,
  Your administration, too—
Consider well what you are about,
  And what you are going to do.
Yankees gained the day with foreigners,
  Yet I am sure you'll rue the day,
When you meet the sons of Southern blood
  In battle's proud array.

You now confine our commerce,
  And say our ships shan't trade;
You first insulted Southerners,
  By stealing of their slaves.
And when they dare maintain their rights,
  The rights of all free men,
Old Lincoln with his Northern hordes,
  Thinks *he can coerce them*.

JEFF. DAVIS is a brave man,
  He will lead the Southern force;
I pity Lincoln's soldiers,
  For I fear they will fare the worse;
He will show the Union shriekers,
  The Union it is done—
The secession flag, ere many months,
  Will *wave o'er Washington*.

JEFF. DAVIS in the White House,
  What glorious news it will be;
Abe Lincoln in an inglorious flight,
  In a baggage car we will see:
With Seward as conductor,
  Gen. Scott as engineer,
Old Hicks, our traitor governor,
  Following, *panting in the rear*.

Take my advice, ye Northern men,
  Throw off old Lincoln's yoke;
Hurl down the tyrant from his seat,
  Who dares this war evoke.
Recognize the Southern Confederacy,
  Be brothers in heart and hand—
Peace, happiness and prosperity,
  Will shower its blessings on our land.

Battle of Manassas (known in the North as Bull Run). Gen. Irvin McDowell was sent fleeing back to Washington, leaving behind all his supplies and cannon. The North was in a panic; the poet Walt Whitman despaired, "The defeated troops commenced pouring into Washington . . . baffled, humiliated, panic-struck. Where are your banners and your bands of music and your ropes to bring back prisoners? . . . The president, recovering himself, begins that very night—sternly, rapidly sets about the task of reorganizing his forces, and placing himself in positions for future and surer work. If there were nothing else of Abraham Lincoln or history to stamp him with, it is enough to send him with his wreath to the memory of all future time."[15]

Gen. George McClellan agreed that the Confederacy could have won the war immediately after Manassas. Arriving in Washington to succeed McDowell as Union commander, he was horrified to find the city totally undefended: "I found no preparations whatsoever for defense. . . . There was really nothing to prevent a small cavalry force from riding into the city. . . . If the Secessionists attached any value to the possession of Washington, they committed their gravest error in not following up the victory at Bull Run." Observed Edwin Stanton, "The capture of Washington seems now to be inevitable; during the whole of Monday and Tuesday it might have been taken without any resistance. The rout, overthrow, and demoralization of the whole army is complete."[16]

Why didn't the Confederates pursue the enemy all day and all night? They were too disorganized, they were exhausted, they were bickering, and they had too many chiefs giving orders—one of them being the president of the Confederacy. Davis was there, on the scene. "We have whipped them!" Gen. Stonewall Jackson shouted to him. "They ran like sheep! Give me 5,000 fresh men, and I will be in Washington tomorrow morning!"[17] But Davis listened instead to his more cautious generals, who said the troops hadn't eaten for a day and needed a day or two to rest. Compare this to how Gen. George Washington would have acted: with his enemy on the run, no way would he have given his troops a day's rest. Davis made this ill-fated decision because he was too tired from overwork to think boldly. He fell back on his legalistic thinking: he wanted to be left alone; the South wanted to be left alone; the war was about independence—and nothing more.

Naturally the radicals in the South had a fit: "We should have gone to Washington!" exclaimed the Charleston *Daily Courier*,[18] to which the intellectual Davis responded that he could not justify invading "foreign" soil. This is specious thinking. How else did he expect to grab the North's attention? Only by capturing the nation's capital and forcing Lincoln's government to flee could he have brought the more powerful North to the negotiating table.

When Davis returned to Richmond he promptly got sick and took to his bed for two months. In the meantime the weaknesses of the South became apparent. Because of poor management of supplies and logistics, Gen. Joseph Johnston's army of forty-five thousand men stayed put while 25 percent of them got sick from drinking bad water and there was only enough food for five thousand men. Politicians started pointing fingers. Robert Toombs, the South's most outspoken politician, quit as secretary of state. A month earlier, before Manassas, he had written in despair to Alexander Stephens, "Davis works slowly, too slowly for the crisis."[19]

Both Davis and Lincoln had huge administrative problems trying to find the right generals and develop a winning strategy. Both leaders were unpopular and had draft riots in the streets and substantial desertions; both resorted to forced conscription and cessation of habeas corpus. Of the two men, it was Davis, the one with far more experience, who couldn't get his military act together. The structure of confederated rather than unified states was too much to overcome. Unlike Lincoln, Davis had to contend with state senators who insisted on having a say in how their state militias were to be used. There was constant bickering and backbiting over which generals to appoint, which troops should report to whom, which campaigns merited the most resources, and how the whole effort was to be financed. The more Davis meddled in states' rights, the more violent the arguments got, and little got resolved. With desertions mounting (a major disadvantage for the defender: home was a lot closer, making it very tempting to flee), the whole purpose of the war got turned on its head when

Lincoln's cabinet, meeting in the White House to hear from General Grant (on Lincoln's left).

Davis, getting desperate in 1864, implemented a stunning new policy: recruit blacks to fight in the Confederate Army. His confidence that slaves would want to kill the soldiers trying to free them revealed obtuse thinking bordering on mental illness.

Davis was adversarial to the end. In early 1865, when it became obvious that defeat was imminent, instead of surrendering graciously, as Gen. Robert E. Lee had done, Davis vowed to wage guerrilla warfare and fight in the woods. Finding only a handful of supporters, he tried to escape to Texas, got caught, and was imprisoned for two years. Released on bail (posted by wealthy northerners feeling compassion for the man), he returned to his plantation, only to find it looted and his "loyal" slaves gone.

He took lengthy trips to Europe and worked for several years as head of a life insurance company that eventually went under. In 1881 he published his memoir, *The Rise and Fall of the Confederate Government*. It was an apologia for the Lost Cause and reopened old wounds. Davis never changed his position on race

Here is the same White House painting, copied by a Confederate artist, with President Davis, the Confederate cabinet, and General Lee.

relations. He cheered the collapse of Reconstruction and the continued subservience of blacks to whites. For the rest of his life he maintained that the Civil War was about states' rights and the Constitution, not about slavery. He insisted that the South had fought for the noblest of principles: "the supremacy of law," "constitutional government," and "the natural rights of man."[20] In 1886, standing on the portico of the state capitol in Montgomery, Alabama, where he had been inaugurated president of the Confederacy a quarter-century earlier, Davis gave a speech bidding the audience to "fulfill all obligations and to [promote] the welfare of your country."[21] It was impossible for him to say *our* country." When he died in 1889 he had no place in America, like the man without a country in Edward Everett Hale's famous story.*

* A fictional short story about an American soldier arrested for treason in the War of 1812 and condemned to spend the rest of his life— fifty years—on a ship. He would never again enter a U.S. port or hear or see the words *United States*. The man covers his cabin walls with

American flags and goes insane. The story, which appeared in 1863, was intended to promote Union patriotism during the Civil War.

In closing the chapter on this brilliant but erratic man, it is worth remembering that the outcome of the Civil War, while in fact a rout, was not certain for most of the time. There was a period before the 1864 national election when it looked like Lincoln was going to lose and the Democratic Peace Party, led by General McClellan, would win and grant independence to the South. Had this happened, says the historian James McPherson, Lincoln "would have gone down in history as an also-ran . . . and Jefferson Davis might have gone down in history as the great leader of a war of independence, the architect of a new nation, the George Washington of the southern Confederacy."[22]

The following obituary, published in the *New York Daily Herald* after Davis's death in 1889, enumerates why one president won the war and the other lost:

> In the essential elements of statesmanship Davis will be judged as the rival and parallel of Lincoln. When the two men came face to face as leaders of two mighty forces, bitter was Northern sorrow that Providence had given the South so ripe and rare a leader and the North an uncouth advocate from the woods. But it was not long before the North was to realize with gratitude the wisdom of Providence in so ordaining it. Lincoln steadily grew to his work. Flexible, patient, keen, resolute, far-seeing, with pathetic common sense and a strange power over the hearts of men, Lincoln led and fashioned his hosts, never advancing to recede, outmatching Davis at every point by his diplomacy, his knowledge of politics, his power to wait as well as his power to strike crushing blows. It is painful to contrast this nimble, subtle genius, adapting himself to the mutations of every hour, with the cold mathematics of Davis, who managed politics upon the barren dogmas of Calhoun and conducted war like a tutor at West Point. The man who saw the skies above and the horizon about him was to overmaster the precise metaphysician who saw nothing but his tasks and lived in the traditions of an antecedent generation.[23]

6

Samuel J. Tilden, 1876

In our hundredth year ten million Americans, 20 percent of the population, are coming to Philadelphia to see the Centennial Exposition and celebrate the glories of our Republic. Alas, how far we have fallen! Unlike the early years of the Republic, led by political philosophers, intellectuals, patriots, and statesmen, politics today is dominated by spoilsmen, opportunists, freebooters, bribe takers, logrollers, machine politicos, and hirelings of the national plunderers.[1] If our Republic is to survive another hundred years, we must find a way to do better.

President Ulysses S. Grant leaves office the most popular American of the century despite a turbulent second term marked by scandals. The Republicans have held the presidency since 1860 and have nominated several candidates for this election. The powerful congressman and speaker of the House James G. Blaine was the clear front-runner but eventually lost out to a relatively unknown entity, Governor Rutherford B. Hayes of Ohio. The Democrats have nominated the governor of our biggest state, New York: Samuel Jones Tilden, a man who promises to drive the spoilsmen and freeloaders out of the temple of government. Over the past few months in almost every city and town massive torchlight parades have marched down the streets to the strains

of brass bands, proclaiming "Tilden and reform." His message is catching on, and with every passing day the odds are better than 50–50 he will be elected president.

SAMUEL J. TILDEN, 1876

SAMUEL J. TILDEN

Age: sixty-two
5-foot-9, 130 pounds
Fair health
Never married

Home address:
15 Gramercy Park
New York City

OBJECTIVE: Nineteenth president of the United States

POLITICAL AND CIVIC EXPERIENCE

Governor of New York, 1875–present

Elected head of the nation's largest state as a champion of reform. Fulfilled campaign promise: uncovered fraud, improved government administrative efficiency, and destroyed the Canal Ring, a consortium of businessmen and politicians who had accumulated fortunes by fraudulent bills for repairing the state's canals. Finalized cases against the Tweed Ring and secured the imprisonment of Tweed himself. Instituted vigorous new laws to punish government corruption. Promoted honesty in public works and economy in expenditure. Reduced New York State taxes from $15 million to $8 million. Commenced construction of magnificent capitol building in Albany.

Assemblyman, New York State Legislature, and Chairman, New York State Democratic Convention, 1871–1874

Led assault on the infamous Tweed Ring, a gang of political adventurers who controlled annual disbursements of $30 million, the patronage of over twelve thousand people, and the selection of judicial, police, and election officials in New York City. By developing detailed evidence tracing misappropriated municipal funds to private bank accounts, succeeded in smashing the Ring.

Chairman, New York State Democratic Committee, 1866–1874

Managed congressional campaigns and raised funds for candidates. Reelected in 1869 with 87 percent of the delegates' votes. Delegate, New York State Constitutional Convention.

Campaign Manager, U.S. Presidential Campaign of Democratic Candidate Horatio Seymour, 1868

Succeeded in garnering 47 percent of the votes against an enormously popular sitting president, Ulysses Grant.

Author, 1860

Published pamphlet, *The Union, Its Dangers, and How They Can Be Averted*, attacking Lincoln and the dangers of succession. Pamphlet reprinted widely throughout the nation.

Delegate, New York State Constitutional Convention, 1846

Active member of convention that produced a constitution for New York State; focused on commerce and drafted legislation for sinking funds to become the primary tool of state finance (as opposed to using traditional methods, such as loan guarantees or sale of state assets).

Assemblyman, New York State Legislature, 1845

Chairman of committee dealing with dispute between tenant farmers and landowners of huge tracts awarded by the Dutch before the American Revolution. Ensured orderly breakup of landed estates in favor of sale to tenants.

Editor, 1844

Created and served as coeditor of state party newspaper to unify the Democrats, win New York State, and ensure victory for presidential candidate James K. Polk.

Legal and Business Experience, 1841–1872

Developed highly successful law practice serving railroads, canals, coal mining companies, and other business entities; won difficult cases through dogged research and thorough preparation based on scientific fact-finding. Established reputation as expert advisor on railroad reorganization and finance; clients included over half the railroad companies between the Hudson and the Mississippi north of the Ohio River. Supplemented legal fees by investing in undervalued railroad stock and organizing mergers and acquisitions; enjoyed strong investment success. Board member of numerous railroad and mining companies. Phased out business activities in 1872 to devote all efforts to the Democratic Party and political reform. Now known throughout America as "the Great Reformer."

EDUCATION

Law school, New York University, 1838–41, Earned LL.D. and was admitted to the New York Bar.

College, New York University, 1835–37. Fulfilled course requirements but did not graduate. Spent time primarily involved in national Democratic politics as a pamphleteer; author of several widely acclaimed treatises on slavery and monetary reform.

Yale College, 1834. Dropped out after one term, for health reasons.

PERSONAL

Born February 9, 1814, in New Lebanon, New York, the fifth of eight children of a prominent political activist and close friend and confidante of President Martin Van Buren. Grew up fully conversant in politics and the traditions of the Democratic Party. As a teenager wrote an article defending President Andrew Jackson's bank veto that was reprinted by the Democratic Party and distributed throughout New York State. As an undergraduate and graduate student, helped write party literature for the Democrats. Delegate, Democratic Party National Convention, 1844, 1848, 1860, 1864, and 1868.

Awarded honorary degrees by New York University, 1867, and Yale University, 1865. Served as honorary member of numerous civic groups: the American Board of Foreign Missions, the New York Historical Society, the Metropolitan Museum of Art, the New York Bar Association, and the board of trustees of the New York Medical College.

Member of the New York Society Library and the Mercantile Library Association. Avid book collector: have amassed one of the largest private book collections in the United States. Favorite hobby: horseback riding. Member of various men's clubs: the Union, the Union League, the Century, the Yacht, the Manhattan, the American Jockey, and the St. Nicholas.

Assessment of Qualifications

In Samuel Jones Tilden, the reform governor of New York, we have a man who is a throwback to our Republic's early years, who believes politics should be guided "by the force of ideas" and not by "self-seekers" aiming to build up their personal fortunes.[2] This idealism is unusual for a man of his background:

- He is a self-made multimillionaire and one of the richest men in the country.
- He made his money speculating in railroads and hostile take-overs with no accusation of insider trading.
- He comes from a city known for corruption: New York, the "Golconda of fraudulent cupidity."[3]

Tilden has a razor-sharp legal mind and a masterful knowledge of government and political campaigns. He would bring to the presidency sophisticated professionalism concerning tariffs, taxes, and government bond offerings.

The Republican candidate, Rutherford B. Hayes, a former congressman and now governor of Ohio, is said to be everyone's choice for vice president[4]—hardly a rousing endorsement for a man seeking the presidency. And who did he choose as his running mate? William Wheeler, a political nonentity, a congressman unknown outside his home state of New York. How Wheeler got selected paints an unflattering picture of him and of Hayes. After Hayes clinched the presidential nomination, the Republicans decided his running mate should come from the number one state, even though the Democratic candidate was that state's governor—a most awkward situation. They couldn't find anybody substantial; finally someone said, "What about Wheeler?" and they all laughed, including Wheeler. When they eventually settled on Wheeler and told Hayes about it, he was baffled. "Who's Wheeler?" he asked.[5] Yet he went along with it.

Unlike the Republicans, the Democrat candidate acted much more professionally: he chose as his running mate Governor Thomas Hendricks of Indiana, a runner-up for the nomination and the leading Democrat in the U.S. Senate from 1863 to 1869. Hendricks is a highly regarded man, leagues ahead of Wheeler.

Hayes is out to win an election. Tilden, starting with his choice of vice president, is out to build an administration.

THE CANDIDATE

Tilden is one of the top corporation lawyers in the country. He is also a shrewd investor who has made a fortune restructuring bankrupt railroad companies. He is a wizard at numbers; in the 1874 congressional election he managed the county organizations so tightly that when the election returns came in, they were only 300 votes off his prediction.[6] Just like he calculates the swap of corporate bonds with disparate market values without putting pencil to paper, so he can calculate election returns off the top of his head. When he went after the Tweed Ring, his skill with numbers served him well in unraveling the complex money trail in Tweed's bookkeeping.

He has a passion for hard work. He insists on doing much of the work himself (his law firm has only three employees), and he works straight through the night, drinking cups of tea to keep himself awake. He gives the appearance of "a man pining in vain for sleep." Accused once of being too focused on work, he retorted, "A man who is not a monomaniac is not worth a damn!"[7]

He has never married. He dated a number of women when he was in his late thirties and early forties but never found one with his brains and interest in politics. Says one of his friends, "He never felt the need of a wife. . . . Women were, so far as he could see, unimportant to his success."[8] This is unfortunate. A president of the United States, no matter how brilliant, needs a confidential sounding board who knows him intimately, can temper his moods, and hopefully can prevent him from doing something foolish.*

* Our only bachelor president, James Buchanan, was a disaster as president. Andrew Jackson, a widower, freely admitted how much he missed the counsel of his beloved Rachel.

Tilden comes across as aloof and forbidding, especially in a first meeting. Friends and foes alike describe him as "shy," "nervous," "awkward," "cocksure," and "dogmatically assertive." He lacks the assets of a natural politician: good fellowship, sociability, wholeheartedness. He is not a man one relaxes with over a drink; with Tilden you sit down for formal afternoon tea. He speaks in a very low voice; hence his nickname, "Whispering Sammy."[9] He arouses little passion among his supporters; when the New York State Convention endorsed his nomination for president, there was no roaring applause or noisy demonstration.

POLITICAL EXPERIENCE

Tilden did not hold serious political office until he was fifty-nine. Some people may consider this a cause for concern. The eminent lawyer George Ticknor Curtis, cocounsel for Dred Scott in the famous 1857 antislavery case, thinks it is not: "I hear and see it said that he has never held office of any kind under the Federal Government. This is by no means a disqualification for the office of President of the United States." He continues, "It is possible for a man who has a natural and an acquired aptitude for public affairs, to know as much of the nature of our institutions, to understand as much of Federal jurisprudence and legislation, and to appreciate as well as questions that may have arisen or are likely to arise in the administration of the Federal Government, without ever having held an office under it, as he could if he had gone through the whole grade of its offices, from that of a postmaster to that of a senator or cabinet minister." Curtis goes on to say that Tilden has more political experience than most office holders and is "well qualified to be President."[10]

Tilden's experience as a political advisor and party boss is substantial and began at a very early age. He grew up in a household where politics was discussed at the dinner table; among the regular dinner guests was the senator and governor of New York who became president, Martin Van Buren. (For the rest of his life Van Buren remained a mentor and close friend of Tilden.) As a teenager Tilden did extensive volunteer work for the local Democratic Party.

During college and law school he wrote political pamphlets that were heralded throughout the nation. At age thirty-one, as a New York State assemblyman, he was directing the largest landowners of America on dividing up their 500-square-mile estates for their tenants. At age thirty-two, at the 1842 New York Constitutional Convention, he played a key role in restructuring New York State finances and succeeded in putting the state on a sound fiscal footing.

In 1848, after his mentor Van Buren lost the nomination to James K. Polk, Tilden left politics and plunged full time into private legal practice. On the side he continued to serve the Democrats as advisor, assemblyman, delegate, contributor, and fund-raiser. Van Buren once described him as "the most unambitious man he had ever known."[11] This is actually a backhanded compliment: Van Buren is really saying that he wishes Tilden would give up his law practice and run for a top public office.

Tilden is not a natural politician, used to backslapping and making lots of friends. He is not a man with a huge ego who seeks personal glory, who must be at the head of the line and loves power for power's sake. Rather he is a practitioner of public administration—and very good at it. He is a master organizer of political campaigns: as manager of Horatio Seymour's 1868 presidential campaign against Grant, he did an outstanding job, enabling the candidate to wage a surprisingly close race in a contest where few people gave the Democrats a prayer.

Tilden's razor-sharp mind and strong sense of civic duty came together in his assault on the Tweed Ring when he entered politics full time as a New York State assemblyman, and on the Canal Ring when he became governor. Against overwhelming odds he defined objectives, assembled evidence, and secured convictions that have made him famous. He promised as governor to get rid of corrupt state officeholders, reduce the size of government, and cut taxes. In just eighteen months he has done exactly that. He is proof that a single man, through sheer determination and hard work, can effect major change in our political system.

Tilden's good friend John Bigelow is impressed with Tilden's "profound and extensive knowledge of everything related to the

SAMUEL J. TILDEN, 1876

science of government."[12] We agree that Tilden is a master of the science of government. The question is: Is he also a master of the art of government?

PROSPECTS AS PRESIDENT

Tilden's vigor and drive stand in sharp contrast to his Republican opponent, Rutherford Hayes, who recently promised that if elected he will serve only one term.

Henry Adams raises an important point in last month's *North American Review*: "If there is one thing wholly opposed to the spirit of our institutions and the earlier and better usages of the country, it is the political trick of nominating unknown and untried men, on the ground that, being unknown and untried, they have no 'record' to defend. Every voter is thus left free to imagine what he pleases, and of course, *omne ignotum*, etc."[13] Nobody would say this about Tilden, governor of a state that accounts for 70 percent of national imports and 50 percent of all exports—a mini-country, if you will. Tilden has been a successful governor of New York, a logical stepping-stone to managing the United States.

But there are differences, and this is where one has reservations about the man. He is a lone wolf. He lacks the human warmth of an Abraham Lincoln. He is not a man of passion. He inspires no fervent loyalty from his followers. He is not a rousing speaker like William Henry Harrison. If anything, his subtlety of thought surpasses his capacity of language. He is superb at analyzing a complex situation and getting to the root of the problem (like many great lawyers), but he cannot communicate it to a large crowd.

A successful president must have his ear to the ground, able to discern vibrations emanating from the public. Tilden is tone-deaf. For example, he thought he had the winning issue in pushing for reform; it took a fellow politician, Horatio Seymour, to tell him reform wouldn't fly with the working men—they saw it as a loss of jobs. You need to go with a much punchier message, Seymour told Tilden: "Throw the rascals out!"[14] He is likewise insensitive to how demonstrations of his wealth may be interpreted. On winter rides in his horse-driven sleigh Tilden wears a luxurious sealskin coat, undoubtedly imported from the land of the Inuit in northern Canada. His enemies have quickly pounced on the image and started calling him "Sealskin Sammy."[15]

Tilden can spend all-nighters with his small staff of three identifying great arbitrage opportunities and speculating in railroads, but do we want a president who stays up all night? He can squash a corrupt Tweed Ring in New York City. Can he squash widespread corruption in America? He can do this only if he wins the presidential election by a landslide; if he wins by just a thin margin, he will not have this mandate. To continue as a moral reformer he will have to go on the campaign trail and get voters excited. If he couldn't do this at his own Democratic Party convention, how can he possibly do this for the nation?

Tilden is very much a lawyer: cautious, imperious, obsessive to the last detail just to prove that he is "right." Just this past August, for example, the Republican mouthpiece the *New York Times* came out with a story accusing him of tax fraud back in 1862—fourteen years ago! Instead of denouncing such tactics and laughing off the accusation, he spent an entire month preparing his detailed response as if he were filing a public offering document. The American people don't want a lawyer who marshals a fifty-page rebuttal filled with copious footnotes; they want a leader who gets mad when he's abused and calls it like it is. Tilden thinks people want reform, but that's not what his fellow Democrats want. They have been out of power since 1860—sixteen long years. They don't want reform; they want revenge.

The Republican Party, in the meantime, is in disarray. Just the other day William Evarts, attorney general under President Andrew Johnson, remarked to Senator Carl Schurz that the Republican Party today—controlling the presidency for sixteen years—reminds him of nothing so much as an army whose term of enlistment has expired. "The field is full of stragglers," he says.[16]

The two parties have virtually identical platforms; the choice therefore comes down to the man heading the ticket. No matter who wins, the South is likely to be left alone, free from interference by Washington. Who, then, is more qualified to deal with the other major issues of the day: civil service reform, the currency, and the tariff? On all three of them Tilden is the obvious choice. As governor he has displayed zeal and effectiveness in weeding out corruption. He has such a profound grasp of finance he could be his own Treasury secretary, and he brings proven expertise to managing the currency and the tariff.

He is not a natural leader. He is a man who leads by example rather than by inspiration. He is like a machine, austere and always correct, using his strong intellect to analyze all aspects of a problem, leaving nothing to chance. He is excruciatingly thorough at the expense of decisiveness. Voters who choose Tilden over Hayes are endorsing his ideals and taking a gamble that there will be no crisis calling for bold action. In this centennial year of our nation, we need a man who is idealistic and will stand up for government of the people and not of the politicians (many of whom are corrupt). A recommendation for Tilden is a bet—a prayer, if you will—that he will grow in the job and become more outgoing, more sociable, more political, more compromising, and less cocksure and holier than thou.

He has the brains and vision to be an excellent president, but he he's too cautious, gets caught up in details, and lacks the personality to build a strong team of advisors. Whatever happens, we know we can rely on his ethics and integrity. Henry Adams calls him "America's most distinguished reformer" and insists that the American people "cannot afford to risk the future of the Republic on supposed virtue or rumored ability."[17] There is nothing rumored about Tilden's ability; it's all in the record. Even James G. Blaine, once the favored candidate for this year's Republican nomination, has nothing but the highest respect for Tilden, whom he calls "the most striking figure in the Democratic Party since Andrew Jackson."[18]

This is an admirable candidate: he does not seek power or celebrity or glory; he seeks reform, a totally selfless objective. He will always strive to do the right thing. Imperfect though he may be, should we not judge a man by the goals he chooses?

Accomplishments	Intangibles	Judgment	Overall
outstanding	fair	excellent	fair

1876

The campaign of 1876 was the nastiest in American history. The Republicans, underdogs from day one, kept their candidate under wraps and focused their entire effort on attacking Tilden as a liar, a traitor, a briber, a conspirator, a thief, a counterfeiter, a defrauder, a perjurer, a robber, a swindler, a railroad wrecker, and more.[19]

But for Tilden, the real catastrophe was yet to come: he won the election but lost the presidency. That is, he won the votes of the people but lost the votes of the politicians. His strengths carried him only so far, and when it came time to be bold and step up to the challenge of an unexpected crisis, he responded too cautiously— just like before the election when he took five weeks to respond to accusations of tax fraud. Two months before the election Tilden's advisor and close friend John Bigelow had written in his diary, "The Governor . . . is scarcely fit or able to do anything. He can't write or control himself. He finds fault with everyone about him and makes the most childish complaints about others for his own omissions and commissions." Frustrated during the campaign that Tilden was taking forever to do what should have been done in a day or two, Bigelow wrote, "I begin to have my misgivings whether he will prove equal to the labors of the presidency."[20] He was to have even more misgivings after the votes came in.

Tilden's campaign started with serious handicaps. The Democratic National Party had not won a presidential election since 1860. The party had just $500,000 (of which 20 percent came from Tilden), whereas the Republicans had $15 million, plus plenty more from putting the squeeze on Grant administration office-holders to contribute 2 percent of their salaries to the party's campaign chest.

Tilden was caught in a Pandora's box: a wealthy man, he hesitated to give more than $100,000 to his campaign because he didn't want it to look like he was trying to buy the presidency. But wealthy Democrats, knowing he was rich, wanted him to foot the bill. As a result a lot of campaign work never got funded. Yet despite lack of money and a steady stream of vituperative attacks

With his intense, stern look, the cerebral Tilden intimidated many. Says one historian, "Tilden habitually looked as though he smelled something bad, and in the election of 1876, he smelled something very bad" (Butterfield, *The American Past*, 220).

by the Republicans, Tilden generated massive press coverage and kept his message focused on the need for reform. The message resonated with the public: as Election Day approached, the betting odds on Tilden were 5–2 and the Democrats jubilated at the prospect of their first presidential victory in sixteen years.

The turnout was 81.8 percent of all eligible voters—the greatest exhibition of participatory democracy the United States had ever seen (and never equaled since). Tilden had 51.5 percent of the popular vote, Hayes, 48.5 percent. Ten million voters chose Tilden by a majority of 260,000 and gave him 184 electoral votes to Hayes's 163. To win Tilden needed one more vote; still to be tallied were twenty-two votes from South Carolina, Florida, Louisiana, and Oregon. For Hayes to win, he needed them all. The major political leaders of both parties—Grant, Tilden, and Hayes—thought Tilden would be inaugurated on March 4, 1877, and "Tilden Elected President" was the common newspaper headline of the day.

But Tilden still needed that 185th vote. "Is Tilden's election a Snark or a Boojum?" cried the *New York Herald*.[21]* Was the uncertainty a misfortune, or was it a catastrophe?

* These two words were invented by Lewis Carroll in his 1874 poem, "The Hunting of the Snark," about an imaginary monster of childhood, a snark, who becomes particularly dangerous—a boojum.

The *New York Times* would make it a boojum. In a nefarious scheme hatched in the newspaper's offices, editor John Reid and his associates announced that the election was not a foregone conclusion and that a Republican victory could still be attained. Working closely with the Republican National Committee, Reid sent telegrams to Republican leaders instructing them how to claim the votes in the four states still being counted. Shortly thereafter, from each of the states came two sets of electoral ballots, one Democratic, one Republican. What to do?

Tilden's campaign manager urged Tilden to take to the stump and exhort voters to hold rallies and put political pressure on Congress not to play dirty. Tilden hesitated. Again his supporters begged him to make a public appeal to the voters, but to no avail. His campaign manager prepared a ringing address claiming the vote count was 203–166; the final paragraph called for a mass meeting to denounce the "outrage" and for supporters "to assemble at their usual places of meeting in every city, town and hamlet in the country on the 8th day of January."[22] Tilden struck out the paragraph, saying, "It would not be decent."[23] The *New York Tribune* commented that the Democratic Party was "in the position of an army waiting for orders from its general."[24] But no orders came. "The people," observed the *New York Herald*, "are today like a swarm of bees which has lost its queen."[25]

In South Carolina, Wade Hampton, the newly elected governor, wrote identical letters to Hayes and Tilden, demanding federal troops pull out of his state. Tilden refused; Hayes agreed. Hampton thereupon worked assiduously to deliver South Carolina's votes to Hayes.

In the meantime, unable to resolve the crisis, the House proposed the formation of a one-time Electoral Commission consisting of seven Republicans, seven Democrats, and an independent. At first Tilden rejected the idea, declaring, "I may lose the presidency, but I will not raffle for it."[26] But then he changed his mind.

Tilden's political advisors told him he was nuts: he had the popular vote; all they needed to do was go behind the returns and do a recount, if necessary. Tilden, however, persisted in his belief that rational behavior would rule the day. However, in agreeing to the formation of the Electoral Commission to resolve the dispute, Tilden lost his sure advantage, for the Constitution states that in case of deadlock the House shall elect the president and the Senate the vice president, and in 1876 the House was controlled by the Democrats. This would have given Tilden the presidency.

Instead of taking his case to the people, as Andrew Jackson would have, the intellectual Tilden preferred to rest his case on legal grounds. He spent most of his time buried in law books, preparing a 100-page legal brief on the history of electoral counts since 1789. His forty years in corporation law and finance had taught him to be cautious and thoroughly professional, dotting all the *i*'s and crossing all the *t*'s. Everything must be correct and beyond reproach. Except he forgot one thing: What if the client doesn't care?

While Tilden was busy with his law books, the Republicans were out hunting for votes. In Louisiana they managed to forge the names of two electors on the ballots. Same in Oregon: when one of the three Republican electors was disqualified, it was the Republicans who moved in first with a substitute.

Tilden disliked protracted, messy struggles. When "Tilden or blood!" became the battle cry of his supporters and they started printing up banners and stickers announcing a Tilden inauguration, he said no, it was going too far, people don't take to the streets in America as they do in France and Latin America. Asked how an emergency strategy session with Tilden went, one of his advisors retorted, "Oh, Tilden won't do anything; he's as cold as a damn clam."[27]

Eventually Tilden expressed reservations about the Electoral Commission and urged that the election be decided by the House, but by then it was too late. To further compound the fiasco, the local Democrats in Illinois—acting independently of the national Democrats—chose one of their members of the Electoral Commission to run for U.S. senator, thereby giving him an easy excuse to resign his seat and get out of a hot situation. (A man with presidential aspirations, he knew any decision he made would doom his prospects forever.) The man who eagerly replaced him was a Republican. Acting as kingmaker, this new member cast the deciding fifteenth vote in each of the four states in favor of Hayes, 8–7. All twenty-two electoral votes in dispute went to the Republican candidate, resulting in a final count of 185 to 184.

The *Cincinnati Enquirer* offered this epitaph: "It is done. And done fitly in the dark. . . . R. B. Hayes is 'Commissioned' as President, and the monster fraud of the century is consummated."[28] "Justice gibbeted and wrong enthroned!"[29] shouted the Democrats.

As for Tilden, his health deteriorated markedly and he declined to run again in 1880 or 1884. He died in 1886, convinced—like most Americans—that he had been elected nineteenth president of the United States. His running mate, Thomas Hendricks, went on to become vice president under Grover Cleveland in 1884.

The first thing Hayes did after assuming office was pull federal troops out of South Carolina and the other southern states, thereby disenfranchising black voters. The defeat of Samuel Tilden set back the black emancipation movement by at least twenty-five years. Shouted the agitator Wendell Phillips, "Half of what Grant gained at Appomattox, Hayes surrendered for us on the 5th of March."[30]

Had Tilden refused to submit to arbitration, the voting in the House would have been loud and messy, with plenty of shouting and threats, but he almost surely would have won.* Had there been a vehement Democrat protest, Blaine later admitted, the Republicans would have backed down.[31]

> * In an interesting preview of the 2000 election, someone suggested to Tilden that he reject the Electoral Commission findings as unconstitutional, organize a House filibuster denying Hayes the presidency, then claim the presidency by virtue of the quarter million popular vote plurality and take the case to the Supreme Court.

As president Tilden would have pushed the cause of reform, elevated the standard of political behavior in America, and spared the country some of the nonentity presidents we endured for the rest of the nineteenth century. His defeat is a reminder that in presidential politics, when nerves of steel are lacking, ethics and fair play do not always win.

7

William Randolph Hearst, 1904

This man is better known than almost any national politician, though few people know what he looks like; his daily newspapers mention only his name, "W. R. Hearst, editor and proprietor." He is William Randolph Hearst, owner of America's largest chain of daily newspapers, now seeking the Democratic Party presidential nomination.

The titular head of the party, William Jennings Bryan, the defeated candidate in 1896 and 1900, is no longer running. Hearst's major opponent is likely to be Alton B. Parker, the chief judge of the New York Court of Appeals in Albany. His Republican opponent will be the incumbent, President Theodore Roosevelt.

Hearst is barely forty-one years old. He has held elective office only one year, as a congressman from New York City. But he is no babe in the woods. As the publisher of eight major newspapers throughout the country, he is a public figure with extensive experience in political issues and controversies. He is also president of the National Association of Democratic Clubs. Should he win the nomination, he has two powerful tools to get his message across: his newspapers and his party's clubs. Plus he has his personal fortune, which is substantial. Time and time again he has bought a failing newspaper, injected capital, turned it around, and made it the leading newspaper in the city. He is a dynamic entre-

preneur, one of the most successful businessmen in the country. Blessed with tons of inherited money, he is beholden to no one. He is truly his own man. He claims to be a man of the people. Some fear he sees himself as a king. A superb self-promoter, he is one of the most colorful men to run for president of the United States.

WILLIAM RANDOLPH HEARST, 1904

WILLIAM RANDOLPH HEARST

Age: forty-one
6-foot-1, 200 pounds
Excellent health
Nickname: WR
Favorite hobbies: photography, flying kites, sailing, horseback riding, trout fishing, shooting quail, collecting antiques

OBJECTIVE: Twenty-seventh president of the United States

SUMMARY OF QUALIFICATIONS: One of the most successful business entrepreneurs in the country, with high personal visibility and name recognition and a massive public following. Proven ability to build a business from the ground up, operate in a highly competitive industry, and achieve strong profitability and dominant market share in a short period of time. Directed numerous groundbreaking investigations and newspaper stories exposing corruption, bribery, and other forms of political malfeasance. As publisher of the largest city newspaper in New York, Boston, Chicago, and San Francisco, thoroughly familiar with both regional and national political issues.

POLITICAL CAREER

U.S. Congressman, 1903–present

Elected congressman from New York City. Proposed stronger railroad rate regulations, construction of good roads, increased salaries for U.S. Supreme Court justices, an eight-hour day for government employees, a constitutional amendment providing for the popular election of U.S. senators, making railroad rebates a criminal offense, placing electric telegraphs under government control, making the U.S. government owner and operator of the Panama Railroad Company, and expanding the U.S. postal system to include packages as well as mail (parcel post).

Editor and Publisher, New York *American* (formerly New York *Journal*), 1895–present

Acquired money-losing newspaper and waged battle in the country's most competitive market, dominated by Joseph Pulitzer's New York *World* and James Gordon Bennett's New York *Herald*, followed by the New York *Sun*, the New York *Tribune*, the *New York Times*, and over forty other newspapers. Invested $7.5 million to finance additional staff, investigative reporting, circulation promotion, and acquisition of state-of-the-art printing presses and typesetting equipment. By setting ambitious goals and utilizing aggressive promotion, increased circulation from 30,000 to 100,000 in just one month. Hired superb staff of writers and reporters to ferret out scandal. Staff included the war reporter Stephen Crane, the artist Frederic Remington, and the satire columnists Ambrose Bierce and Mark Twain. Established paper as an important presence in New York. Through hard work, relentless enthusiasm, and personal leadership, increased circulation in four years to 500,000 to tie Pulitzer's *World* for first place.

Consistently beat the competition with news stories and exposés that served the public interest. Company motto: "While Others Talk, the *Journal* Acts." Stopped a $10 million Brooklyn gas franchise from being awarded to a group of insiders; exposed Spanish cruelties in Cuba that led to successful U.S. entry in the war; received the Cuban Grand Cross and was called "Cuba's best friend" by the Cuban leader Gen. Calisto Garcia;[1] led opposition to the Hay-Pauncefote Treaty and ensured that any canal built by the United States in Nicaragua or Panama will be properly fortified to protect American interests; hired Dorothea Dix and Susan B. Anthony to write stories about women's suffrage; ran numerous stories urging annexation of Hawaii, a larger navy, establishment of military bases in the West Indies, the need for an income tax, public ownership of public franchises, elimination of "criminal trusts," greater development of the public school system, and popular election of U.S. senators.

Started an evening edition, the New York *Evening Journal* (circulation 40,000), to compete with Pulitzer's *Evening World* (circulation 325,000). Achieved circulation equal to the *Evening World* in just seven weeks. In 1900 expanded into the Chicago market and started the Chicago *American*. Subsequently expanded into Los Angeles, Boston, and other large cities.

Appointed by the Democratic Party to be president of the National Association of Democratic Clubs. Led membership drive; increased membership to three million people.

Editor and Publisher, San Francisco *Examiner*, 1887–1895

Took over moribund newspaper (circulation 20,000); invested $500,000 of additional working capital to pay for new cylinder presses, a telegraph news service, and more editors and reporters. Plowed every dollar of cash flow back into the business. Within two years the newspaper was on sound financial footing and making a profit. More important, it became the most influential newspaper in California. Launched crusades and campaigns against public and corporate abuse. Most notable achievement: waging war on Collis Huntington for his illegal behavior (bribes, fake contracts, monopolistic pricing) to enhance the already outrageous profits of the Northern Pacific Railroad. Won the war; forced the railroad to give back much of its money.

In 1895 relinquished full-time duties to move to New York and acquire and develop a newspaper in the country's biggest and most important market. Still oversee paper as owner and chairman.

Trainee, New York *World*, 1886–1887

Worked as trainee at Joseph Pulitzer's newspaper, the leading newspaper in the country.

Harvard College, 1882–1885

Discovered true love in life, journalism, working on the Harvard *Lampoon*, the campus comedy and satire magazine, which was in serious debt. Took over as business manager and launched aggressive revenue-generating campaign; obtained 300 percent more ads and solicited substantial alumni contributions. Left magazine in strong financial condition. To learn about journalism at the professional level, worked part time for six months as a trainee at the Boston *Globe*, reporting directly to the editor in chief.

Member of the Porcellian Club (one of Harvard's Final Clubs) and the Hasty Pudding Theatricals. Participated in several plays. Member, Harvard Democratic Club: organized huge celebration in Harvard Yard to honor 1884 election of Grover Cleveland.

Expelled from college middle of senior year for disciplinary reasons. Joined the New York *World* to continue hands-on education in newspaper publishing; never returned to earn degree.

PERSONAL

Born April 29, 1863. Grew up in California. At age ten spent year in Europe traveling with parents; learned fluent French and German. Attended St. Paul's School in Concord, New Hampshire. Father a self-made multimillionaire in mining who served as U.S. senator from California from 1885 until his death in 1891.

Married Millicent Willson, 1903; one son, George Randolph, age thirteen months.

Favorite expression: "Wars are won by generals, not by armies."[2]

Assessment of Qualifications

If we ever wanted a firecracker in the White House, this would be our man. He loves firecrackers: he got expelled from Harvard for six months for throwing a huge firecracker party and almost burning down Harvard Yard,* and in his business and political activities he is a virtual firecracker himself, especially when he writes a sensational newspaper headline. He even managed to start an international war.

> * This was during his junior year, not to be confused with another prank during his senior year that led to his expulsion for good. He tested the good humor of his professors by giving several of them, as a Christmas present, a chamber pot with their name painted at the bottom.

He is irrepressible. He is rich. He throws money around like there's no limit. Whatever he wants, he gets; if he can't get it, he buys it. He is the son, the only child, of a man who made a fortune discovering the four richest mines in America: Nevada's Comstock Lode, Montana's Anaconda, South Dakota's Homestake, and Utah's Ontario Mine. When he toured Europe at age ten and saw Windsor Castle, he told his mother he would like to live there; when he visited the Louvre, he asked her if she would buy it. His father, who died when William was twenty-seven, left all his money to his wife, probably knowing the son would spend it all. But the mother (still living) was a soft touch, and the son is quite charming (as rich sons often are). The father, who nicknamed his son "Billy Buster," once observed, "When he wants cake, he wants cake; and he wants it now. And I notice that after a while he gets his cake."[3] Blessed with his mother's open checkbook, he buys castles and rare paintings like the rest of us buy a candy bar.

But he is no dilettante, not the typical rich boy. He has a will of iron, and he is ambitious, decisive, incredibly smart, and ruthless. Single-handedly he has built a huge empire in one of the toughest businesses of all: newspapers.

He is also a man of courage. Asked by the young, unknown William Jennings Bryan for support in the 1896 election against the favorite, Governor William McKinley, Hearst called a meeting with his news editor, his editorial manager, and his business manager to discuss the paper's position. All three employees favored going with the safe candidate and gave their reasons. Hearst made the decision to support Bryan. At a time when virtually all newspapers in the country were going for McKinley, this was a gutsy move, and it cost Hearst a lot of money when most of his advertisers pulled their ads. Still Hearst never wavered but stuck with Bryan to the very end. Hearst is afraid of nobody. We cite two more examples:

- Just several years out of college he declared war on the railroad baron Collis Huntington. Huntington was so powerful in California that the state was sometimes referred to as "Huntington's plantation."[4] No matter, Hearst would relentlessly follow the man like a shadow, exposing his bribes and nefarious dealings that had destroyed competitors and fleeced the public. Hearst also went after his late father's fellow California senator and Huntington's partner, Leland Stanford, forcing him to repay a $120 million government loan Stanford was trying to avoid.

- After making a success of his newspaper business in San Francisco, he moved to New York to take on the mighty Joseph Pulitzer.* Surely Hearst had lost his senses, leaving his comfortable San Francisco fiefdom to take on the powerful Pulitzer, number 1 in the most competitive market in the country, the home of forty-eight newspapers. Joseph Pulitzer laughed with contempt: "I'm afraid Hearst won't last long. He will find the going tougher than in his home town."[5] Several years later Pulitzer met with Hearst to shake hands; he had met his match.

* It seems that the two never met when Hearst worked for Pulitzer in his first job out of college. Too bad for Pulitzer. Little did he know he had a viper in his nest.

Hearst has a remarkable capacity for work. Every evening he

goes to the theater, followed by a stint at a nightclub, dressed in a dinner jacket and entertaining the chorus girls and popping open bottles of champagne (though he drinks very little), then around midnight he returns to the office to personally proofread and sign off on all the stories going into the morning paper. Finally, around two in the morning, he goes to bed, then rises at seven for another full day. He demands the same effort from his employees—and gets it. His organization is full of feverish excitement and electricity. None of his key people has quit on him; obviously he knows how to attract, motivate, and retain talented people.

His company's motto is "While Others Talk the *Journal* Acts." Hearst has created an organization in which people are challenged to accomplish exceptional feats. To help Bryan secure the 1900 presidential nomination at the Democratic National Convention in Chicago, he decided to start a Chicago newspaper. He called up his New York managing editor and told him to leave at once for Chicago: "The newspaper must appear in thirty days."[6] Thirty days to start a newspaper! Needless to say, the job got done. Despite Bryan's loss to McKinley in the presidential election, the Democratic Party chiefs were so astounded by Hearst's executive ability to get the newspaper out so quickly they made him president of the party grassroots organization, the National Association of Democratic Clubs.

For a rich man on such a plateau, he is remarkably generous. It appears he was always this way: in college he had a classmate whose family had suffered a financial misfortune, forcing the boy to drop out; Hearst promptly called his father and got him to pay the friend's tuition bills. Nowadays stories abound in the Hearst empire about the boss's warm generosity toward those in need. Hearst insists that these deeds go unpublicized, but there are enough known cases to conclude that the man's compassion is real. In addition to the usual stories of hospital bills and tuitions bills unexpectedly paid by an anonymous donor, there's the one about an employee who suffered a devastating brain impairment and had to live in an institution for the rest of her life, unable to take care of herself. Hearst got her an apartment. Hearing that she had fallen in love with another afflicted inmate while at the hospital, he got her a bigger apartment and arranged for the other person to move in, then got another apartment next door for relatives to live in and take care of the two—all bills paid for, for life. He may be obscenely rich, he may be a tough boss, but he is a man with heart.

Hearst is a superb problem-solver. Nothing fazes him. A huge storm in San Francisco Bay marooned five fishermen on a rock near Golden Gate, their boat long gone, death a howling wind. Hearst hired an ocean tugboat with a party of rescuers, including a champion English swimmer who leaped into the sea with a lifeline, swam to the rock, and brought the fishermen back to safety, one by one. The next day, while Hearst's newspaper featured pictures of the rescued men having coffee in the *Examiner's* office, feet propped up against the stove, competing newspapers described the men still huddled on the rock.

Newspapers are a special kind of business: they not only try to make money; they also try to influence public opinion and shape government policy. Being our only form of mass communication, newspapers enjoy enormous power. A profit-making newspaper baron has a responsibility to serve the public truthfully and responsibly and not resort to sensationalism to sell papers (like a bad kid yelling "Fire" in a movie theater). Unless he doesn't care and wants to appeal to the prurient and lowly, the newspaper baron should strive to increase the public's knowledge of current events— especially if he claims to be a man worthy of becoming president of the United States. "The newspapers of your country seem to be more powerful than the government," the Spanish prime minister once said to Hearst.[7] If Hearst has such power, which is what the Spaniard certainly implied, has he exercised it responsibly?

For years he and Pulitzer have waged a vicious war of yellow journalism with countless front-page headlines about headless corpses and bodies in the swamp. What fun to be a copyeditor at one of these tabloids! In Hearst's view, a newspaper needs some shocking news, lest it become "like reading a telephone book."[8]

"A newspaper without promotion," he opines in his usual colorful language, "is like winking at a girl in the dark."[9]

In his journalism Hearst has consistently stayed within the bounds of truth and performed a public service by seeking out stories that people should know about. He had no choice; just like Pulitzer, any fabrications or sloppy mistakes they made would be quickly discovered and pounced upon by gleeful competitors. Such competition is the best spur to being careful. In contrast to the staid *New York Times*, which never dared venture into investigative journalism, the sensational press was doing a lot more to expose corruption and injustice in high places and to help the needy.

The most controversial episode of his career began when he got a telegram from Frederic Remington, whom he had sent to Cuba to cover the revolution against Spain: "Everything is quiet. There is no trouble here. There will be no war. I wish to return." To which Hearst allegedly responded, "Please remain. You furnish the pictures and I'll furnish the war."

Yet no one has been able to get a copy of either telegram, so there are strong suspicions that they never existed in the first place. Perhaps the story is a plant by Pulitzer, or it may even have been invented by Remington himself. Remington certainly was no shrinking violet: as a varsity football player at Yale, he once went to a slaughterhouse and dipped his football uniform in cow's blood to give himself a more fierce appearance.

In the fifteen months before the Spanish-American War actually started, Hearst had a field day printing juicy stories about Cuba. But it wasn't he who invented them; they were handed to him on a silver platter by the Cuban revolutionaries looking to get the United States involved in overthrowing the Spanish. Sometimes Hearst went over the line, such as when he sent his men to rescue a young Cuban maiden from a Spanish prison, but nothing he did compares with President McKinley's sending the battleship *Maine* into the potential tinderbox of Havana Harbor. The *Maine* episode has to rank as one of the more reckless moves made by an American president. To this day we have no idea how the

Maine got blown up, but one thing we do know for sure: the last people to want to invite retaliation were the Spanish.

Unlike Assistant Secretary of the Navy Theodore Roosevelt, who, like a true jingoist, jubilated at the prospect of avenging the *Maine*, Hearst was actually quite moderate. At a time when everyone was pounding the war drums and over a million men were volunteering for an army needing only 290,000 soldiers, the *Journal*'s first-day headline was merely "Cruiser *Maine* Blown Up in Havana Harbor: Disaster a Mystery and Said to Be Appalling." The newspaper quoted the captain's entire telegraph to Washington—including the last line, "Public opinion should be suspended until further report"—and gave full credit to the Spanish soldiers and officers who assisted in the rescue efforts. On the second day the subhead was "Assistant Secretary Roosevelt Convinced the Explosion of the War Ship Was Not an Accident," and the article presented the increasingly popular theory that the ship was sunk because it accidentally bumped into a mine. Note that this theory came from Roosevelt, not Hearst. Subsequent articles described war preparations and explained how a mine could have been the cause, but never was any direct accusation made. In fact the *Journal*'s lead story on the second day explicitly stated, "Nobody thinks the authorities were party to the crime, if crime there was."*10

> * The Spanish authorities agreed with Hearst. Their investigation concluded that not even Cuban saboteurs were to blame, as the harbor was carefully guarded. The fault, said the Spanish investigators, probably lay with the American officers of the ship, who may have been sloppy in allowing coal to be stored too close to the boilers, causing an internal explosion—a common danger with these new, poorly designed ships.

. . .

After years of observing the spectacle and enjoying the taste of power, Hearst now wants to be a player in the arena. He sees a mess in government and thinks he can do better.

And he is a strong candidate for president. He is "smarter than any man who ever worked for him," his employees say.[11] He is courageous, a man of compassion, and a high achiever. Unlike men who are thrust into positions of political power or who seek it because they are consumed by ambition, Hearst is a leader with a burning desire for high achievement in business and will bend iron to get it. Politics is his avocation, not his passion. Plus, he has a special motivation: when you are born with lots of money, hopefully you feel the need to prove you deserve it. Even though you went to St. Paul's and Harvard, you must be self-educated. Even though you don't have to work, you must work harder than anybody else. You must rise above your wealthy social class and have a public conscience (like Theodore Roosevelt). Should there be times when you have everything to lose in pursuit of a principle, you must stick to your principles and take chances. Should the situation demand you be bold, you must be so.

For a man embarking on a career in elective politics, however, he does lack fundamental traits of a politician: he is painfully shy, he is a man of few words, he hates shaking hands, he gets no pleasure from giving speeches. But these skills can easily be learned. A greater concern is his lack of interest in the process of politics. He has the emotional maturity of an adolescent. As a member of Congress, he proposed many new bills and never followed up. He hardly ever appeared at roll calls: only four times out of two hundred, an abysmal performance. He made only a few friends. He evinced no interest in any complicated or important policy issue.

The candidate is only forty-one and, not counting his single year as a congressman, has spent his entire career in one activity. He is a megalomaniac, very sure of his own greatness. He is young and not fully tested in battle outside his obvious talent for rabble-rousing and appealing to the masses. He is a man used to having total command, like his idol Napoleon (whose huge portrait hangs over Hearst's desk). He excels in an environment wherein he can call the shots.

The presidency, however, requires compromise and willingness to work with others. Before recommending this brilliant man for the presidency, we would like to see him broaden his experience.

His achievements in business are outstanding. He is an incredibly hard worker. Yet what worthy goals has he achieved other than making a lot of money? Hearst is an opportunist, making millions of dollars by appealing to the lowest common denominator to boost his newspapers' circulation. Only in rare cases has he exposed corruption and chicanery and tried to enhance the public debate.

"To whom much is given, much is expected." For a man born to wealth and given an opportunity to be educated at our best schools, we expect much. Has he elevated himself to a higher level? Our answer is no. William Randolph Hearst possesses shrewd human instincts, but he is singularly lacking in judgment and discretion. He offers no particular insight on the critical issues of the day nor any compelling message why he should be elected president.

Accomplishments	Intangibles	Judgment	Overall
outstanding	fair	poor	poor

1904

Anybody who doesn't think politics is a nasty business can look to the Democratic Party in 1904. The titular head of the party was William Jennings Bryan, a man who owed everything to Hearst for sticking his neck out for him in 1896 and then spending millions in 1900 starting up a Chicago newspaper when the Democratic National Convention was in Chicago and Bryan desperately needed local support to clinch the nomination. With Bryan not running in 1904 and Hearst now running, was it not too much to ask that the favor be returned? Especially when Hearst sent Bryan on a luxurious nine-week trip through Europe to write some stories and make some quick easy money (which he desperately needed). But lo and behold, when Hearst looked around, Bryan was nowhere to be found. Worse, Bryan turned out to be a Judas. At the convention, as the voting went through several ballots, Hearst was starting to move up on the front-runner, Alton Parker. Then Bryan stunned everyone by endorsing a weak third candidate, stopping Hearst in his tracks. The dull Parker went on to win the nomination—and lose the election, as everyone expected. Apparently the last thing Bryan wanted was to have a fellow Democrat become president: he wanted the coast clear for himself so he could run again in 1908.

If Hearst had now learned not to trust his friends, he soon learned the other half of politics' golden rule: Don't trust your enemies. Reelected to Congress after losing the nomination, Hearst embarked on a ten-year quest for the presidency. It was a journey almost as astounding as his career in journalism, filled with bribery, corruption, opportunism, and double-dealing on all sides. For Hearst, Congress was just a stepping stone; he needed a high-profile political position, preferably in an executive capacity, so in 1905 he ran for mayor of New York. Because the incumbent was a Democrat Hearst ran as an Independent. Conducting a fiery denunciation of political parties, he garnered a substantial number of votes from the masses of people who read his one-cent newspaper: the lower middle class, the dispossessed, and the trade union workers. He also overcame his weakness as a public speaker and made himself a rousing orator. He won the popular vote, but the Democrats engaged in a massive campaign to turn away voters and stuff the ballots with fictitious votes by "floaters" and "repeaters." These extra votes turned a sure victory into an unexpected last-minute loss, exactly like what happened to Samuel Tilden in the presidential election of 1876.

In 1906 Hearst ran again, this time for governor of New York. Ever the opportunist, he mended his fences with the Democrats and rejoined the party. Even though he had castigated the Tammany boss as a crook who deserved to wear prison stripes, this time he gladly accepted the crook's support. Hearst's ambition had to be gratified at any price, inspiring one journalist to imagine a poem Hearst might write: "So I lashed him and I thrashed him in my hot reforming zeal / Then I clasped him to my bosom in a most artistic deal."[12] No way was Hearst going to be cheated a second time. Everyone knew that if he were elected governor, he would be the Democratic candidate for president in 1908.

If the Republican Party was going to knock off Hearst, it had to do so now. Operatives recruited the esteemed lawyer Charles Evans Hughes to run for governor of New York. Even the president got involved. Theodore Roosevelt plotted every step of the Hughes campaign to destroy Hearst: "We must win by a savage and aggressive fight against Hearstism and an exposure of its hypocrisy, its insincerity, its corruption, its demagogy." The president viewed his fellow member of the elite Harvard Porcellian Club as a charlatan and a radical. "He has an enormous popularity among ignorant and unthinking people," thundered Roosevelt. "He preaches the gospel of envy, hate and unrest. His actions so far go to show that he is entirely willing to sanction any mob violence if he thinks that for the moment votes are to be gained by so doing. . . . He cares nothing for the nation. . . . He is the most potent single influence for evil we have in our life."[13]

Five days before the 1906 election the president sent Secretary of State Elihu Root to New York to give a speech. It got very nasty, probably the lowest point ever in presidential politics. Said Root, "I say to you, with the President's authority, that he regards Mr. Hearst to be wholly unfit to be governor, as an insincere, self-seeking demagogue."[14] That was for starters. Root then went on to drop a bombshell: Hearst, by his sensationalist comments in his newspapers, had implicitly created the climate of hate that fostered the crime of the decade, the assassination of President McKinley.

Hearst never recovered. "Root the Rat!" screamed his supporters, but every newspaper in the country grabbed the story. Despite Hearst's putting up $500,000 and wildly outspending Hughes, Hughes won the governorship and went on to become a presidential candidate ten years later. Many Americans cheered, including many Democrats who never forgave Hearst for abandoning the party to run for mayor. Even now, though he had accepted the Democratic nomination, he had run a campaign distant from his party and its leaders—not a winning strategy. Hearst found himself a man with few allies. He had "greatly changed in the last few years," observed one of the Democratic Party bosses. "Now, apparently, he is controlled by the idea that he is greater than the Democratic Party. . . . He is [a] slave to passion and egotism. His creed is that everybody who is for him is an angel, while everybody who is against him is a demon."[15]

The downward path continued. In 1908, when Bryan won the Democratic Party nomination for a third time, Hearst insisted on putting a third-party ticket in the field, thus splitting the Democrats and making a Republican victory certain. (The winner was Taft.) Asked why his candidacy had done so poorly, Hearst responded, "We have no prominent men associated with us. I don't want any prominent men. If I have prominent men connected with me, I will have to consult with them—and I don't consult with anybody."[16]

Bullheaded as ever, in 1909 he ran again for mayor of New York. This time he lost by twenty times the four thousand votes he had lost in 1905—and this time there were no irregularities. In the 1916 Wilson-Hughes presidential contest he was nowhere to be found. In 1918 he ran for governor of New York and got trounced by Al Smith. In 1922, when Hearst tried to get nominated for U.S. senator from New York, Governor Al Smith, calling him "a pestilence that walks in the dark," made sure he got nowhere.[17] Hearst's once-promising political career was finished.

"Learning that political office lay beyond his power to attain," says one historian, "despite all his wealth and brains, meant a profound shock." Be that as it may, he still retained the power of a press tycoon, capable of starting another war. Which he almost did. In 1935 he announced with great fanfare that he had uncovered incriminating documents showing that Mexico was planning with Japan to wage war against the United States. After several weeks of frantic phone calls and telegrams burning the wires of three nations on both sides of the Pacific Ocean, it was determined that the documents were fake. Hearst refused to admit guilt or accept blame. So what if the Mexican documents were blatant forgeries? "The essential facts contained in the documents were not fabricated, and the facts—the political facts, the international facts—are the things which are of vital importance to the American people."[18]

Not true. A responsible leader must always seek the truth, not the "facts" he likes. By now Hearst has descended into the self-delusion and paranoia so brilliantly captured in the movie *Citizen Kane*. Ever the spoiled child, the lord and master of his universe, "Billy Buster" could no longer distinguish between a lie and a truth. Anything that corroborated his own views must be true because he wanted it so. Anything that conflicted, well, that could be disregarded.

We can be grateful he never became president.

8

···

William Gibbs McAdoo, 1920

The leading candidate for this year's Democratic Party nomination is the crown prince of American politics, the president's son-in-law and treasury secretary, William Gibbs McAdoo.

This assumes, of course, that the president himself doesn't run. Washington is rife with rumors that Woodrow Wilson, incapacitated for over a year now, is almost back to normal and plans to run for a third term. That would be a major problem for the Democrats. Increasingly over the past few years Wilson has turned his administration into a one-man show and staked his prestige on a long, ongoing, bitter fight with the Senate over the League of Nations. Since his stroke in October 1919, the government has ground to a halt. The United States, says one journalist, is like "a ship at sea with its engines stopped."[1] Americans are reverting to isolationism and conservatism and turning their backs on the progressive movement of Roosevelt and Wilson.

Rumors that Wilson is still seriously incapacitated from his stroke make people nervous about his ability to do his job, especially when he sends mixed signals about running for a third term. Party strategists believe that if there is a deadlock at the convention, there may be a clamor for the president to throw his hat in the ring. Naturally this prospect has put all the candidates into a state of great anxiety and hindered their active campaigning. As

a result, with the convention about to start soon, there is no commanding front-runner. The most prominent candidate is McAdoo, but he has just announced he will not seek the nomination. For a man known to be very decisive and ambitious, many of his supporters wonder if his declaration is sincere.

The sudden death of Theodore Roosevelt, who had been expected to win a third term this year, has given the Democrats hope they may still retain the presidency. The Republicans are without vigorous leadership. In what appears to be a sign of the times, they have nominated a ticket of Warren Harding and Calvin Coolidge, two small-time politicians who promise "a return to normalcy." With each passing day wartime idealism is fading: labor unrest, inflation, and collapsing farm prices dominate the news. A new, modern age seems to be upon us. There are now eight million automobiles on the road and thirteen million telephones in use. Railroads are carrying twice the number of passengers compared to 1900, and newspapers are booming. The average factory work week has dropped to just fifty-one hours, and it is expected that women will get the right to vote before the presidential election in November. Should McAdoo win the nomination, his consistent support of women's rights could garner a substantial majority of the female vote.

WILLIAM GIBBS MCADOO

Age: fifty-six
6-foot-1, 180 pounds
Excellent health
Hobbies: tennis, playing cards, dancing
Nickname: Mac

Office address:
120 Broadway
New York City

Home address:
863 Park Avenue
New York City

OBJECTIVE: Twenty-ninth president of the United States

Secretary of the Treasury, 1913–1919

Appointed the forty-sixth secretary of the Treasury by incoming president Woodrow Wilson. Confronted major currency crisis at the outbreak of the Great War, July 1914, when many foreign investors, strapped for cash, started selling shares on the New York Stock Exchange and demanding to convert their money into gold, thereby threatening a run on U.S. gold reserves, a collapse in the value of the dollar, and an economic depression in the United States. Averted currency collapse by shutting down the New York Stock Exchange for four months in order to ensure a gradual and orderly liquidation of foreign assets without increasing U.S. national debt. Avoided a recurrence of the 1907 Panic and managed to keep the banks open by invoking provisions of the 1908 Aldrich Vreeland Act, allowing issuance of special bonds. Instituted strong measures to maintain strength of the U.S. dollar against the British pound. Against strong opposition kept the dollar on the gold standard. Thanks to these efforts, the U.S. dollar is now a fully transferable, fully recognized international currency (along with the British pound).

Created the Federal Reserve System, the nation's first national bank since 1832. Negotiated with senators and bankers on the number and location of reserve banks, established headquarters in New York City, and served as the first chairman of the Federal Reserve.

Assisted Wall Street bankers in creating a fund of short-term, gold-backed dollar notes that saved New York City from going bankrupt.

In addition to serving as head of the Treasury and the Federal Reserve, served as director general of the U.S. Railroad Administration, an entity formed to run America's transportation system during the war. Gave 40 percent pay raise to 1.4 million workers. Instituted equal pay for women and blacks. Ensured smooth delivery of war armaments and supplies to the eastern seaports. Also served as chairman of the Federal Farm Board (to promote farm exports) and the War Finance Corporation (raised $16.94 billion in Liberty Loans). Resigned, effective January 1919, to pursue private law practice.

Volunteer, Wilson for President Campaign, 1911–1912

Met Wilson in 1910 and commenced volunteer work to support his campaign. Raised funds. In 1911 became vice chairman of his campaign: directed nationwide efforts to derail the front-runner, Champ Clark, and enlist the vital support of William Jennings Bryan. Successfully secured Wilson the Democratic Party nomination. Encouraged by Wilson to run for governor of New York; rejected offer in order to continue managing his presidential campaign, on the firm promise that the president-elect will not feel obligated to offer a government position as a reward.

President and CEO, Hudson & Manhattan Railroad Company, 1901–1912

Put together financing plan to revive the Hudson River tunnel project and get business up and running. Raised $6 million to acquire the project. Promoted to president and CEO by investors. Completed first tunnel and undertook second tunnel. Selected architects and engineers and personally supervised all construction with no delays or cost overruns. Acquired substantial land in downtown Manhattan and developed network of subways to link Manhattan to New Jersey. Above tunnel terminal built world's largest office building complex (1.18 million square feet). Acquired rights from the Pennsylvania Railroad and built third tunnel. Total business value in 1905: $60 million, a tenfold increase in five years. Secured $72 million in debt financing. By 1908 company had created the largest tunnel network in the world. Upon completion of new line into Jersey City, service inaugurated by President Theodore Roosevelt pressing a button in the White House. By 1910 company had fifty million passengers a year and fewer than fifty complaints. Perfect safety record. Company motto: "Let the public be pleased." Instituted equal pay for female employees.

Partner, McAdoo & McAdoo, 1894–1901

Formed partnership with former New Jersey congressman and undersecretary of the navy William McAdoo (no relation). Served clients in New York and in Kentucky. Reorganized the Wilkes-Barre & Hazelton Railroad. During this assignment learned about half-completed Hudson River tunnel project; resolved to take advantage of this business opportunity and left law firm.

Partner, Pemberton & McAdoo, 1892–1893

Set up law and securities firm in New York City to sell railroad securities.

Self-employed, 1886–1892

As sole-practitioner lawyer, first year earnings were $280. Through aggressive salesmanship and high energy, acquired new clients and related business opportunities. Took over a local manufacturer of agricultural implements, built new factory, and served as president. Speculated in real estate; made $25,000. Saw opportunities in electricity and resolved to replace horse-pulled streetcars with electric cars. Secured bank financing in Philadelphia and purchased the Knoxville Street Railway Company for $200,000. Served as president. Business went into receivership in 1892; at great personal sacrifice, paid back all company debts. Moved to New York in search of bigger business opportunities.

EDUCATION

Attended University of Tennessee in Knoxville 1880–83 on special tuition waiver (father a history professor). To help pay expenses worked part time in the local circuit court. Promoted to a deputy clerkship in Chattanooga. Dropped out of college to get practical experience in the law. Attended Democratic National Convention in 1884; served as an alternate delegate. Admitted to the bar in 1885, age twenty-one.

PERSONAL

Born in Georgia on October 31, 1863. Grew up in Chattanooga and Knoxville, Tennessee. Married Sarah H. Fleming in November 1885; six children, one deceased: Harriet (age thirty-three), Francis (thirty-two), Nona (twenty-eight), William III (twenty-five), Robert (nineteen), and Sally (sixteen); wife died in 1912. In May 1914 married Eleanor ("Nellie") Wilson, the youngest daughter of President Wilson; two daughters: Ellen (five) and Mary (two months). Member of the New York Social Register and numerous private clubs.

Assessment of Qualifications

McAdoo is one of the most dynamic men in many years to run for president of the United States:

- A brilliant secretary of the Treasury, widely acknowledged to be the greatest since Alexander Hamilton.[2]
- A superb campaign manager who succeeded in helping Wilson overcome the front-runner and win the 1912 party nomination.
- A visionary entrepreneur who pulled off a public works project even more impressive than the Panama Canal, says the *New York Times*, where he performed every role: originator, promoter, financier, political manager, and construction manager.

To top it off, he is an outgoing, charming man who loves to go to nightclubs and dance all night and win the hearts of the ladies. He has won the hand of none other than the president's favorite daughter, a young woman half his age.

Perhaps most interesting of all, he has succeeded in creating a new form of capitalism: a profit-making public utility that serves the interests of the people. "Let the public be pleased!" is his slogan. This has never been done so successfully in the regulated quasi-public sector of the economy (public utilities, mass transit). In government too he created a new agency, the Federal Reserve, to deliver, as he puts it, "a blow in the solar plexus of the money monopoly" and provide badly needed stability to the national currency.[3]

McAdoo is an innovator of the rarest type: a public entrepreneur. If there ever was a man capable of coming up with an original approach to solving an intractable public sector problem—be it in transportation, currency, railroads, or agriculture—this is a man who has done it repeatedly and obviously can do it again. He knows how to bring competition to government monopolies and make them more accountable and efficient. "Unregulated competition is better than regulated monopoly," he says, "but regulated competition is better than either."[4] He is a visionary—but a practical one, not a dreamer. He has a phenomenal memory for detail. He not only knows how to start up a new venture; he possesses the political astuteness to make whatever compromises are necessary to see the venture through and arrive at a sound, permanent footing.

The New York–New Jersey region owes a great debt to this man. So too do the bankers of the United States for his single-handedly creating the Federal Reserve System. So too do the free nations of Europe: while President Wilson hemmed and hawed for months about whether or not to go to war, the cabinet member who was the most forceful advocate for intervention was McAdoo. Finally, the greatest debt is owed by the president himself. Wilson will never say so, but at the 1912 Democratic National Convention, trailing Champ Clark by a wide margin in the delegate count, he had already drafted a telegram conceding the nomination. McAdoo, his campaign manager, refused to give up and went out on the convention floor and negotiated a last-minute alliance with William Jennings Bryan that revived Wilson's candidacy. Had it not been for McAdoo, Wilson never would have become president.[5]

REFERENCES

"Nobody can do things better than Mac," Wilson says, "but if Mac ever reflects, I never caught him in the act." George Creel, head of the Office of Public Information, the propaganda organization created by Wilson before World War I, describes the lengthy debates in the cabinet meetings that would absorb the president and various officers. Not McAdoo. "He shot ahead with the speed and directness of a bullet," says Creel.[6] Walter Lippmann, the eminent political columnist frequently given to cavalier statements, calls McAdoo "a statesman grafted upon a promoter."[7] Who else, after successfully stopping the gold drain in July 1914, would brag that he succeeded because he "did not hesitate to bludgeon the crisis with a sledgehammer"?[8] Bellicose words, yes, but the point is: he succeeded.

Every venture, truth be told, needs a promoter. What's important is that the promoter do more than make an introduction; he must follow up and make sure the deal gets done properly. McAdoo has done this in his Hudson River tunnels project where he raised the money and served as a superb CEO for ten years. He did this again, after Wilson's nomination victory, in executing all the myriad details in the national campaign for president. He did this too as Treasury secretary, gathering the necessary political support and executing the details of how the Federal Reserve System should function. The man does not stop.

Anyway, the word *promoter* is a bit of a cheap shot. Is not a politician campaigning for elective office a promoter?

Other criticisms are of a more personal nature. Secretary of War Newton Baker says, "McAdoo has the greatest lust for power I ever saw." George Creel is even more pointed: "Mac has never been largely concerned in anybody but himself."[9] Others view McAdoo as arrogant and pushy.

Such traits are weaknesses in a regular citizen, but not in a president. People don't become president because they're sweet and accommodating; they become president because they're hard-driving, competitive people. One-on-one they have to be charming and likeable, which McAdoo certainly is. As for arrogance and conceit, the man is remarkably modest. He freely admits he got a big break in life when he happened to be talking with another lawyer and learned there was an abandoned, half-completed tunnel under the Hudson River. The tunnel was a potential gold mine, but equally a potential folly: it had failed twice, and it was widely believed that the technology to complete it did not exist. McAdoo had the vision and drive to grab the project and run with it. "I was never anything more than an outsider in the community of interest that is known as Big Business," he says. "I appeared in Wall Street with a constructive idea, and managed to get it turned into reality. Anybody else might have done the same thing, but it just happened that nobody else did." Ask him about the Hudson tunnels and he sounds like a poet: "Under the Hudson River, in slime and darkness, lay the ruins of a partly constructed tunnel that was intended to connect New York and New Jersey. It was the grave of a daring idea, the last resting-place of an ambition and an energy that had been crushed by insuperable obstacles."[10]

Many people think McAdoo made millions from the tunnels project. He did not. To get the deal financed he took no equity, just a salary of $50,000—a nice salary, but not for a widower with six children. All he really cared about was getting the deal completed; lining his own pockets was secondary. His subsequent seven years earning $25,000 as Treasury secretary, at the peak of his career with a wife and two more children, was a major financial sacrifice. No, he is not a rich man.

"Swift to move," says Lippmann about McAdoo, "he picks his course quickly, moves fast upon it and with great audacity. . . . Instinctively he prefers the bold and the decisive to the prudent and tepid course."[11]

RELATIONS WITH THE PRESIDENT

When you marry the boss's daughter, beware. The president was thrilled when his daughter Nellie got engaged: "The dear girl is the apple of my eye: no man is good enough for her. But McAdoo comes as near being so as any man could."[12] But when a controlling older man runs into a brilliant younger man who is not afraid to voice his opinions, relationships can quickly change. McAdoo, the dynamic, take-charge executive, established himself as the most vocal and obstreperous member of Wilson's cabinet. Such a role was not appreciated by other cabinet members or by the president. According to Col. Edward House, Wilson's key advisor, McAdoo annoyed Wilson in cabinet meetings with his "emphatic manner and language."[13] If presidents have ambiguous feelings about a vice president sitting around with little to do but wait for the president to die, imagine what it must have been like for Wilson facing a successor for the 1920 nomination—a son-in-law, no less.

"Off with his head!" says the mythical king to the messenger bearing bad tidings. In 1915 the president was conducting a love affair with Edith Galt, causing great concern among his advisors that such news—if it ever got out—would kill his chances for reelection in 1916. Even more worrisome were rumors that a packet of love letters had surfaced about Wilson's earlier relationship with a certain Mary Peck. At the urging of Colonel House (nobody else was willing to do it), McAdoo took it upon himself to have lunch with the president and bluff him with the fictitious story that he and House had received anonymous correspondence from Los Angeles alleging that Mrs. Peck was talking about her $7,500 and 227 love letters from Wilson. As McAdoo hoped, the news put the president in a panic. But instead of motivating the president to stop seeing his new lover, it had just the opposite effect: he promptly married her.

Pillow talk knows no secrets. McAdoo now not only had a father-in-law who resented bad news; he also had a stepmother-in-law who was an implacable enemy. (Even Colonel House found himself shunned.)

No president likes admitting his dependency. As Wilson was just getting ready to leave for Europe for six months to propose his League of Nations, McAdoo announced his resignation, thereby depriving the president of a key cabinet member when he most needed him. Wilson, who demanded control and loyalty to an extreme degree, was not mollified, no matter how justified McAdoo may have been in leaving to take care of his family (Wilson's daughter and grandchildren). When McAdoo—who had done so much for Wilson—wanted Wilson's endorsement for his 1920 candidacy, Wilson blew up in a rage.

WILSON'S EVALUATION OF MCADOO

In the midst of all this family brouhaha it may be worth listening to Stockton Axson, the brother of Wilson's deceased first wife, who had a conversation with the president last August about the likely 1920 candidates. Wilson told him he didn't want to run for a third term, and as possible successors he mentioned Newton Baker, David Houston, and William McAdoo. Wilson added that he did not think Baker and Houston were abler than McAdoo, but they were "both *reflective* men—and I am not sure Mac is a reflective man."[14]

This is certainly true. McAdoo is not a reflective man who thinks in terms of broad philosophical concepts like Wilson does; McAdoo is an entrepreneur who solves problems. What makes him special is his proven ability to solve *huge* problems. Reflection, while help-ful, is not a criterion for president. President don't have the time; hopefully they did their reflecting before they became president.

Wilson always complained that what he disliked most about the presidency was that he had so many tedious chores—signing papers, attending ceremonial functions, and so on—that he had no time to sit back and think like the college professor he used to be. In commenting that McAdoo is not a reflective man, Wilson is saying more about himself than about McAdoo. For voters the important fact about McAdoo is his manic energy and fifteen-hour days. Look at the workload this man had as a member of Wilson's cabinet: Treasury secretary, chairman of the Federal Reserve Board, chairman of the Federal Farm Loan Board, chairman of the War Finance Corporation, chief sales manager of Liberty Loans, finan-cial negotiator with the Allied Powers, administrator of the huge soldiers' and sailors' insurance plan, director general of 250,000 miles of railroads. That's eight jobs at the same time!

Asked how he did it all, he offers up the usual pabulum about good management: selecting good people, giving them full respon-sibility, monitoring them closely, and creating a positive atmo-sphere of what the French call "esprit de corps." Nothing startling or new here. Then he throws out a nugget: the ability to get at the core of a problem. "Remember what I told you about the Hol-land Tunnels," he says. "The secret of doing a big job is to reduce it to its simplest elements. . . . There is a key to every problem. I always endeavor to find the key, and then I shape everything else around it."*[15]

> * This confirms what he said in 1911 when he gave a speech about subways: "The subway problem is not so intricate and complex as is generally supposed. It is, in fact, quite simple."[16] This is a very per-ceptive insight: if you view a problem as potentially simple, you may well find it to be so.

He goes on to make another interesting point: "Neither inter-est, nor loyalty, nor energy takes the place of brains. Nothing can supersede ordinary common sense; it is a fundamental quality. I have always tried to avoid fools. . . . A fool can cause more mix-ups in two hours than a dozen men can disentangle in a month."[17] In other words, a president's job is to avoid being a fool. Whatever you do, find the key and don't make a major mistake. There's a name for this. It's called good judgment, caution, prudence, a quality Washington and Lincoln had in spades.

IS MCADOO RUNNING?

With no word coming from the sick president—the new Mrs. Wilson is keeping everyone in suspense—McAdoo stayed out of the primaries. Growing frustrated as the convention drew near, he put the word out that though he wasn't running he was still very interested: "It would be my duty to accept the nomination if it came to me unsolicited."[18] To make sure everyone got the message, on June 18 he announced that he was pulling out (though he had never announced he was jumping in). Quipped the *Chicago Tribune*, "Mr. McAdoo wishes us all distinctly to understand that if the San Francisco convention does not offer him the nomination, he will not accept it."[19] To make things even more confusing, he just announced that due to "increasing demand" he will accept the nomination if it is forced on him.[20] According to a June 12 *Literary Digest* poll of five thousand people, even though he isn't actually running McAdoo is the front-runner; President Wilson is second. Navy Secretary Josephus Daniels says, "McAdoo seems our strongest man," and the newspaper columnist Walter Lippmann calls him "brilliant in genius . . . by all odds the keenest politician in America today."[21]

A DARING PROBLEM-SOLVER

The man is daring and imaginative. In the Hudson Tunnels project he took on risks that no railroad company was willing to undertake. Above one of his terminals he built an office complex consisting of twenty-seven acres of office space—the biggest in the world. This man does not think small. Though he is not an engineer and had no experience in construction management or real estate development, he made himself an expert and supervised the engineering

WILLIAM GIBBS MCADOO, 1920

and construction companies flawlessly. He showed the same der-ring-do as Treasury secretary. When a flood hit the Ohio Valley and the city of Dayton was under twenty feet of water, Treasury officials told McAdoo there weren't any funds to pay for the res-cue boats. "To hell with appropriations!" shouted McAdoo. Told what he wanted to do was illegal, he responded, "Send the boats immediately and I will serve the jail sentence."[22] The man is an absolute ball-buster. He has more *cojones* than just about any man in America. He is the ideal described by Alexander Hamilton in the *Federalist 70*: "Energy in the executive is a leading character in the definition of good government."

In his management of the 1914 external payments crisis threat-ening the loss of all the U.S. gold reserves, McAdoo devised a solution to the outflow: promote farm exports to food-starved Europe to generate incoming payments. Not a single banker on Wall Street had come up with this creative idea. To make sure it would happen, he took control of the Farm Relief Board and the railroads. By balancing cash IOUs with farm exports, he said, he could stop the hemorrhage. Needless to say, it worked.

McAdoo had a very delicate political problem trying to convince our allies that we were not going off the gold standard. In the cab-inet with McAdoo, in the powerful position of secretary of state, was none other than the famous William Jennings Bryan, who had run for president in 1896 on the ringing slogan "You shall not press down upon the brow of labor this crown of thorns, you shall not crucify mankind on a cross of gold!" What irony—here's McAdoo pushing gold! Yet McAdoo managed to keep Bryan quiet and convince America's creditors that he was the boss and Ameri-ca's commitment to gold was solid. Obviously this man possesses a politician's gift for salesmanship and persuasion.

CONCLUSION

When the president surprised McAdoo by offering him the Trea-sury position, McAdoo demurred, saying he had no qualifications. Wilson responded, "I don't want a banker or financier. The Trea-sury is not a bank. Its activities are varied and extensive. What

I need is a man of all-around ability who has had wide business experience."[23] Wilson was absolutely right. And he picked the right man for the job.

"All-around ability" is also one of the criteria for president. Equally important is that the candidate has mastered a crisis. In his Holland Tunnels project and in setting up the Federal Reserve System, McAdoo has twice proven such mastery.

He rates extremely high on accomplishment, integrity, and judgment. In ideological clarity, however, he falls short: on issues on which he has an opinion, he is so forceful he comes across like a sledgehammer, to use one of his favorite images. He lacks subtlety and reflection. Conversely, whenever he comes to a fork in the road and is confused about what to do—such as whether or not to seek the Democratic Party nomination—he appears evasive.

However, he relishes making difficult decisions. "Nothing else gives me so much joy as the solution of a difficult problem," he admits.[24] He also brings a talent rarely seen in a presidential candidate: the ability to manage a large organization. As Treasury secretary, reports the *Nation*, he had "staggering responsibilities" and generated "an extraordinary record of accomplishment."[25] In doing this job well, McAdoo established himself as the second most powerful man in the United States.

Now running for the presidency, he is a natural choice for the number 1 position.

Accomplishments	Intangibles	Judgment	Overall
outstanding	fair	outstanding	outstanding

1920

What happened to McAdoo is so bizarre it almost belongs in a novel.

The most dangerous person ever to occupy the White House was a first lady. Exercising presidential prerogatives while her stroke-ridden husband lay practically comatose, she issued proclamations pretending all was well and that Wilson would soon emerge and run for a third term. She was the ultimate power-grabber. But she had a problem: she had a stepson-in-law, married to her husband's favorite daughter from his first marriage, who had committed an unpardonable sin: trying to persuade Wilson not to marry her. Edith Wilson ordered that McAdoo never be allowed in the same room alone with the sickly president. She told her friends they must never mention his name in her presence. In the weeks leading up to the convention, McAdoo tried five times to see the president; every time he was rebuffed. He was a pariah.[26] No matter that this man was the front-runner for the 1920 party nomination; she wanted her revenge. She must destroy him.

In addition his own wife didn't want him to run. He could not fight both his wife and his stepmother-in-law.

McAdoo, the crown prince waiting to be anointed by his father-in-law as the next president, was stuck: he couldn't announce his candidacy without Wilson's blessing, lest he look like a rebel. All he could do was declare himself "an undeclared candidate."

. . .

The 1920 election proved Woodrow Wilson was senile. He never imagined that if he didn't support McAdoo the Democrat nominee would end up being Governor James Cox of Ohio, a man viewed by many as a weasel; even Wilson called Cox "a fake."[27] Despite his illness, Wilson still harbored dreams of running again. When the party nomination ended in a deadlock, he allowed his name to be entered as a candidate, only to be utterly rejected, one more stab to the heart after the League of Nations fiasco. An invalid to the end, Wilson died three years later.

. . .

The problem for McAdoo—for all the Democrats in fact—was the Democratic Party rule that the presidential nominee must win two-thirds of the delegate votes, a supermajority. (The Republican Party required only a simple majority.) McAdoo had a majority on the first eleven ballots, but he couldn't clinch the nomination. He fell behind Cox, pulled ahead on the twenty-ninth ballot, then faded for good on the forty-fourth. Cox went on to lose to the Republican nominee, Warren Harding, who illustrated his profound thinking with the slogan "Let's be done with wiggle and wobble."[28] McAdoo was aghast: What kind of nonsense was this? Harding's speeches, he said, left "the impression of an army of pompous phrases moving over a landscape in search of an idea."[29] So began America's sorry descent into the 1920–32 Era of Complacency, when idealism lost out to stock market speculation, making money, Prohibition, flappers, and boodles.

Thinking ahead to the 1924 election, McAdoo—brash as ever—gave the 1920 delegates something to mull over. He gave each of them a large bronze medallion, on one side a likeness of himself and on the other his two major titles: "Secretary of the Treasury" and "Director General of the Railroads."

In 1922 McAdoo left New York City, where he had spent twenty years, and moved to California and immediately secured hefty legal retainers from oil companies and movie companies. Here he violated a major rule for presidential candidates: stay out of unnecessary controversy. Against the advice of his former colleagues Josephus Daniels and Joe Tumulty (Wilson's private secretary, a position now called chief of staff) he entered into a business relationship with Edward Doheny for $50,000 up front and a $900,000 potential bonus if he negotiated a successful deal with the government of Mexico. Doheny was a well-known figure and a vice chairman of the Democratic Party in California, but he was also considered a slippery character, possibly a crook. In 1923 he was exposed in the Teapot Dome scandal and admitted to paying a bribe to the secretary of the interior for drilling rights to oil in Wyoming. Although McAdoo was not implicated in any way, the association was a deadly blow for a man claiming to be a champion of the people against the vested interests. Everyone predicted that McAdoo's political career was finished.

McAdoo would have none of it. This time he would run aggressively. In its January 7, 1924, cover story featuring McAdoo, *Time* magazine editorialized, "None of the candidates wiped his feet on the doormat of New Year's Eve with more gusto than William

G. McAdoo. The old jingle made on him four years ago still rings with startling poignancy."

> The Who, predominantly Who
> Is William Gibbs, the McAdoo . . .
> He's always up and McAdooing;
> From Sun to Star and Star to Sun
> His work is never McAdone.

Surprising everyone, McAdoo won 60 percent of the primary vote, making him the clear front-runner. He arrived at the convention, held in New York, the city where he had made his name, took a ride on one of his subway trains (affectionately called "McAdoos"), and pronounced the city of Wall Street financiers to be "reactionary, sinister, unscrupulous, mercenary and sordid."[30] No one could say this man wasn't blunt.

Here McAdoo ran into the quintessential problem confronting a strong-willed candidate who's been around for many years: he had enemies. "We love him for the enemies he has made!" his supporters chimed.[31] Such cockiness is all right if you need only a majority and your friends outnumber your enemies—but not when you need a supermajority and have to assemble a coalition. Opponents can be cajoled, but not enemies.

In what turned out to be the most hotly contested nomination battle of all time, the voting went on for fifty-eight ballots. McAdoo was in the lead, but not a commanding lead: he was stuck in a deadlock with Governor Al Smith of New York. The voting went on and on for so long that the humorist Will Rogers commented about the delegates, "This thing has got to come to an end. New York invited you people here as guests, not to live."[32] Each passing day reduced the value of the nomination. Finally, in the sweltering summer heat, on the 100th ballot both contenders released their delegates, and on the 103rd ballot the nomination went to the bland New York lawyer John W. Davis, former solicitor-general under Wilson.

Had the Democratic Party employed the simple majority rule,

McAdoo would have won the nomination and possibly become president.*

* It wasn't until 1936 that the Democratic Party finally changed the rules to a simple majority.

McAdoo declined to run in 1928, knowing his advanced age (sixty-six) and twice-loser status would work against him. But he wasn't finished yet. At the 1932 convention, now running for senator like a phoenix rising from the ashes, McAdoo arrived as the chief delegate of the state of California. Franklin Roosevelt was the front-runner, but he had to nail down the victory so it wouldn't drag on for countless ballots. Roosevelt's opponent was Al Smith, the man who had thwarted McAdoo in 1924. On the fourth ballot, with Roosevelt's backers extremely nervous—it was now or never—McAdoo stepped up to the podium and thundered, "California casts forty-four votes for Franklin D. Roosevelt!"

Roosevelt was astounded. "Good old McAdoo!" he roared as the balloting quickly culminated in a victory.[33] Helping to deliver FDR as America's next president was McAdoo's finest hour in American politics.

He returned to Washington the following year as a senator from California and spearheaded New Deal legislation setting up the Federal Deposit Insurance Corporation. He divorced Nellie and married a twenty-six-year-old. To everyone's surprise he lost reelection in 1938 to a political hack who promised to write a check to every voter over fifty. FDR and every respectable economist denounced the "ham 'n eggs" movement against McAdoo as political quackery, but to no avail: California voters wanted their entitlements and would vote for whoever promised the most goodies. (The movement died out a year later.)

FDR, concerned about having enough ships in case of war, arranged for McAdoo to be appointed chairman of a large passenger shipping company that had gone into receivership. Showing his old zeal as a business entrepreneur, McAdoo turned the company around in three years and made the American President Lines the country's most prominent ocean liner company.

(Renamed APL, the company is now the world's fourth-largest container transporter.)

McAdoo died in 1941 and nowadays is nearly unknown. No full-scale biography has been written about him. In 1931 he penned a first-rate autobiography, but the book covers his life only up to 1919; he said he would have to write another to finish telling his fascinating story. He never got around to it, which is a shame; the book is filled with marvelous insights, such as these three:

It is impossible to defeat an ignorant man by argument.

I do not like ideas that are suspended in the air.

Big Business has a passion for unearned money.[34]

Certainly the economy after the Crash would have been better managed if McAdoo had been in charge. In 1933 very few people had any idea of how to combat the Depression: the 1924 Democratic candidate John W. Davis admitted, "I have nothing to offer, either of fact or theory," and the noted banker Bernard Baruch suggested only, "Delay in balancing the budget is trifling with disaster."[35] McAdoo could only throw up his hands in exasperation: "Our entire banking system does credit to a collection of imbeciles."[36]

McAdoo's story illustrates the importance of timing. A progressive to the core, he bridged the gap between the Progressive Era and the New Deal. It is our nation's loss that he ran for the presidency without family support and when it was impossible for a bold and rebellious Democrat to win the endorsement of a supermajority of delegates, no matter how impressive his résumé. He was a great man at the wrong time.

9

···

Herbert Hoover, 1928

Back in 1920 a leading Democrat politician, Louis Wehle, asked his college classmate Governor Franklin D. Roosevelt what he thought of Herbert Hoover, "the Great Humanitarian" food administrator in World War I. "He certainly is a wonder," said Roosevelt, "and I wish we could make him President of the United States. There would not be a better one."[1]

How about running on a ticket with him? Wehle suggested. Sounds good to me, replied the governor. Better check it out with Col. Edward House. Wehle went to House, President Wilson's advisor, who jumped at the idea: Hoover-Roosevelt, a dream ticket in 1920![2] But when House approached Hoover, Hoover was less than thrilled. He wasn't sure what party he would run on, his wife was leery of national politics, and he didn't like the idea of a slate put together by a group of politicians. The proposal died then and there.*

* Which was just as well: considerable doubt existed about whether Hoover, having spent most of the previous twenty-three years abroad, satisfied the constitutional fourteen-year residency requirement. (Hoover claimed he was a resident of California, but he could not demonstrate that he had paid local property taxes as proof of U.S. residency: his home was built on land rented from Stanford University, a nonprofit.)

Hoover eventually decided to become a Republican and seek the nomination, so long as he could make it look like he was being drafted. His friends entered his name in several primaries. He came in third in Minnesota, fourth in the Michigan, and fourth in Montana and failed to win his home state of California, so he dropped out.

Appointed secretary of commerce by President-elect Warren Harding, Hoover displayed dynamic leadership over eight years and earned the sobriquet "Secretary of Commerce and Under-

Secretary of Everything Else"—quite a compliment, considering this was one of the great cabinets of all time, with Charles Evans Hughes at State and Andrew Mellon at Treasury.

Still, having spent so much time abroad performing humanitarian work for of the Wilson administration and never elected to any public office, Hoover was distrusted by the Republican Party bosses and lagged behind five other candidates seeking this year's nomination. Then Mother Nature intervened. The Mississippi River Flood, the greatest natural calamity ever to hit America, devastated eight states and made six hundred thousand people homeless. Overnight Hoover's name and photograph appeared on the front pages of newspapers as he raced around the southern states giving orders for the feeding and housing of victims. Once again he became the Great Humanitarian.

At the Republican National Convention he was touted as a miracle man almost too good to be true: an "engineer, practical scientist, minister of mercy to the hungry and the poor, administrator, executive, statesman, beneficent American, kindly neighbor and wholesome human being."[3] He won the nomination easily and is now a clear favorite to win the presidency.

Hoover has no forceful position on any political issues, except to promise he will lead us on the path of continued prosperity. He eschews controversy. He is running solely on his résumé of past achievements. Is this enough? Says *Time* magazine in a recent cover story, "The central fact militating against candidate Hoover is that many people cannot understand what he stands for. A technologist, he does not discuss ultimate purposes. In a society of temperate, industrious, unspeculative beavers, such a beaver-man would make an excellent King-beaver. But humans are different. People want Hoover to tell them where, with his extraordinary abilities, he would lead them."[4]

HERBERT HOOVER

Age: fifty-four
5-foot-11½, 200 pounds
Nickname: Bert

Temporary home address:
2300 S Street
Washington DC

Permanent home address:
623 Mirada Drive
Palo Alto, California

OBJECTIVE: Thirty-first president of the United States

PERSONAL STATEMENT: "We in America today are nearer to the final triumph over poverty than ever before in the history of any land. The poorhouse is vanishing from among us. . . . We shall soon with the help of God be in sight of the day when poverty will be banished from this nation."[5]

GOVERNMENT EXPERIENCE

U.S. Secretary of Commerce, 1921–1928

Widely recognized as the most influential member of the Wilson cabinet. Earned sobriquet "The Secretary of Commerce . . . and Under-Secretary of Everything Else." Added thirty-five overseas offices to help U.S. businesses sell their products abroad. Settled trade disputes. Instituted standardized measurements and design to minimize product variations and improve manufacturing and shipping efficiency. Worked with banks to develop long-term, low-cost mortgages. Held conferences to regulate radio licenses and create an effective national network of radio stations. Held conferences to set up codes and safety regulations for the aviation industry and mandate the use of radio beams and landing lights at all airports. Hosted the two-part National Conference on Street and Highway Safety to develop safety standards and traffic rules for automobiles. Persuaded the steel industry to reduce the working day from twelve hours to eight. Commissioned nation's first study of national petroleum reserves. Saved Alaska's salmon from extinction. As chairman of the Colorado River Commission, negotiated water-sharing compact of seven states.

Provided vigorous leadership and response to the 1927 Mississippi River flood, which inundated nearly twenty-six thousand square miles in seven states (the size of South Carolina). Director of Mississippi Flood Relief: managed all aspects of humanitarian relief, emergency rescue, and provision of food, clothing, and housing. Personally visited ninety-one communities to inspect damage and boost local morale.

HUMANITARIAN EXPERIENCE

Director-General, American Relief Administration (New York, Paris), 1918–1920

Organized shipments of 27 million tons of food (worth $5.5 billion) to people in Central Europe, Germany, and Russia at end of World War I. Helped feed more than 300 million starving people in more than twenty countries. Work involved financing and distributing food, reviving coal production, reopening ports and canals, and rebuilding telegraphic and postal communications. Coordinated with Congress, the Treasury, and the U.S. Armed Forces. Served on twenty committees, chairman of six of them, including the Allied Food Council, the U.S. Grain Corporation, the Sugar Equalization Board, and the Inter-Allied Food Council. Member of the War Trade Council. In the United States raised $30 million for the European Children's Fund. Founder and president, American Child Health Association. Known worldwide as "the Great Humanitarian." Nominated for the Nobel Peace Prize, 1921.

Administrator, U.S. Food Administration, 1917–1918

Set up successful voluntary program whereby Americans refrained from consuming certain food items on assigned days in order that conserved food could be sent to soldiers overseas. Supervised 8,000 employees and 750,000 volunteers. Secured food conservation pledges from thirteen million American homes. Launched extensive publicity program. Slogan: "Food will win the war!"

Chairman, Commission for Relief in Belgium (London), 1915–1917

Led major relief effort to provide food for Belgium after country was invaded and occupied by German troops. Created major enterprise with its own flag, ships, factories, and railroads to feed 10 million people in Belgium and northern France. Negotiated with the British government to ensure safe passage of ships through its naval blockade of the continent. Conducted over forty negotiations with German authorities to successfully ensure observance of international law permitting distribution of food to citizens. Shipped 2.5 million tons of food; 99.57 percent of funds went directly for purchase of food, and only 0.43 percent for expenses and overhead. Awarded the French Legion of Honor and named Citizen and Friend of Belgium, a one-time special award.

Member, Committee of American Residents in London for Assistance to American Travelers (London), 1914–1915

Helped organize the return of 120,000 Americans stranded in Europe at the outbreak of the Great War (known in America as World War I). Raised funds and provided boat tickets and cash, much of it from my own pocket.

PRIVATE SECTOR EXPERIENCE

Founder and managing general partner, Burma Mines Ltd., Zinc Corporation Ltd., and others (London), 1908–1914

Established numerous limited partnerships to provide financing and management services for mining companies. Opened offices in London, Paris, New York, and St. Petersburg. Took equity stake in client mining projects outside the British Empire (in conformance with noncompete agreement with Bewick Moreing). Acquired controlling interest in mining operations in over a dozen countries, with a payroll of 175,000 employees. Provided technology assistance to extract value from depleted mines and make them profitable. Companies in portfolio include one of largest mining companies in Australia and the number one producer of zinc in the world.

Partner, Bewick Moreing, Ltd. (London), 1897–1908

Pretending to be the minimum age of thirty-five, hired at age twenty-two by leading British mining company with operations in over twenty countries. Sent to Australia to identify and evaluate potential mines for investment. Discovered huge mine known as the Sons of Gwalia and introduced cyanide metallurgy technology that yielded a return of 65 times the original investment.

Promoted to junior partner in 1900 and transferred to China. Traveled extensively through China, Mongolia, and Tibet, evaluating potential mines. Helped organize relief of Tientsin during the Boxer Rebellion. Acquired the assets of the partner Chinese mining company and achieved a very profitable return for Bewick Moreing's investment syndicate. Acquired fluency in Mandarin.

In 1901 promoted to partner and transferred to London. Traveled extensively throughout the world and acquired mining rights, almost all highly profitable. Focused on New Zealand, Tasmania, Burma, India, Egypt, Italy, Canada, and United States. While traveling through China and visiting ancient gold mines, hired native scholars to read ancient manuscripts; learned of the existence of a great silver lode in Burma known as the Bawdwin Mine. In 1905 visited the mine and acquired rights. Raised financing for construction of railroad tracks, roads, bridges, a two-mile tunnel, smelter, mills, hydroelectric plants, houses, towns, schools, hospitals, and other infrastructure to support what is now the largest silver mine in the world.

EDUCATION

Stanford University, 1891–1895

Enrolled in newly founded university, tuition-free for its first class of students. Earned BS in geology. During summers worked for U.S. Geological Survey.

Personal

Born August 10, 1874, in Iowa. Orphaned at age nine; at age ten, transferred to care of an uncle in Oregon. Worked in uncle's business office and attended night school before attending college. Married Lou Henry (also a geology student at Stanford), 1891; two sons, ages twenty-five and twenty-one, both graduates of Stanford.

In 1909 published *Principles of Mining*, a compilation of lectures at Stanford and Columbia Universities. In 1912 coauthored with wife a translation of the 1556 Latin mining classic *De Re Metallica* (*On the Nature of Metals*). Both books still in print. Awarded first gold medal given by the Mining and Metallurgical Society, 1912, for "distinguished contributions to the literature of mining." Elected president of the American Institute of Mining and Metallurgical Engineers.

Named "One of Ten Greatest Living Americans" in *New York Times* survey, 1920. Author, *American Individualism*, 1922. Founder, Hoover Institution on War, Revolution and Peace, Stanford University. Trustee, Stanford University, 1912–present. Received honorary degrees from a dozen universities, including Brown, Georgetown, Swarthmore, Columbia, and Harvard.

Assessment of Qualifications

Not since George Washington has there been a presidential candidate as exalted as Herbert Hoover. His performance as director of Mississippi Flood Relief brings back memories of his magnificent performance in World War I: "The story of the Commission for Belgium Relief . . . is an account not only of philanthropic enterprise, but also of business venture and management without parallel in history. No Argonautic legend or Arthurian romance can match this story of the succor of a whole people by an organization conceived and directed by one man."[6] Called "the Little Republic of Relief" by the *New York Times*, Hoover's operation issued its own passports, flew its own flag, operated its own fleet of ocean vessels and canal boats, requisitioned food supplies, operated mills and factories, and rationed and distributed food at its sole pleasure. It was like a country unto itself.

It is said that the best executive experience for being president is being governor, but there may be an even better one: being chief of an international relief organization. The responsibilities are awesome, the pressure to perform is tremendous, one has multiple governments to report to, and one must be decisive. In this, Hoover certainly excelled.

Another high-ranking position providing preparation for the presidency is cabinet officer. Here too Hoover proved his mettle. As secretary of commerce for a full eight years, he demonstrated that his vaunted administrative ability was no fluke. His reputation has become so renowned that letters addressed to "The Miracle Man, Washington DC" got delivered to him.[7]

In addition to his proven skill managing large, complex organizations, Hoover brings a wealth of international experience, having spent the vast bulk of twenty-three years, from 1897 to 1920, living in England, Australia, and China. A British leader, writing to President Wilson recommending Hoover for a war-time office, even referred to Hoover as "a former citizen of your country."[8] Finally and not least, he is a modern-day Horatio Alger, a self-made multimillionaire in business. In his midthirties he was allegedly the richest man in the world among men his age.[9]

Everything he touched seemed to turn to gold. Never once in his career had he known failure. No wonder so many of his supporters are giddy at the prospect of his becoming president. "Oh, what a great president he will make!"

Now the negatives: He is arrogant and thinks he knows best. An engineer, he believes in scientific exactitude. He is used to running the show. A Quaker, he is convinced of his moral purity, to the point of being extremely stern and tough. Asked what his ambition as a boy was, he responded, "To be able to earn my living without the help of anybody, anywhere." Asked his favorite motto, he answered, "Work is life."[10] He is an utter workaholic, dismissing appeals to leisure: "Who wants a short day, who wants to work only eight hours?"[11]

People call him the Great Humanitarian, but many people who know him say he is cold-blooded and never sheds a tear for the unfortunate he has helped. He lacks compassion and empathy. In his work for Belgian relief Hoover assiduously avoided coming into personal contact with famine victims, even little children; it was too heart-wrenching, he said, and he had a job to do. Touring Mississippi after the flood he traveled in a private railroad car and never bothered to step out and talk with the survivors.

Josephus Daniels, secretary of the navy in 1917, recalls the time he invited Hoover to lunch and how much he was looking forward to hearing all about the Belgian relief effort. "I was never more disappointed," Daniels says. "He told of the big work in Belgium as coldly as if he were giving statistics of production. . . . I felt I had been talking to a capable administrator who either had no heart, or whose heart had been atrophied by his experiences around so much suffering. . . . His reserve and cold manner had chilled my enthusiasm."[12] Here is how another politician describes a visit to Hoover's office:

> He is abnormally shy, abnormally sensitive, filled with impassioned pride in his personal integrity, and ever apprehensive that he may be made to appear ridiculous. . . . He rises awkwardly as a visitor is shown to his desk, and extends his hand only halfway, in a hesi-

tant fashion. His clasp is less than crushing. Then he sits down and waits for questions. His answers are given in a rapid, terse manner and when he is finished he simply stops. Other men would look up, smile, or round off a phrase. Hoover is like a machine that has run down. Another question starts him off again. He stares at his shoes, and because he looks down so much of the time, the casual guest obtains only a hazy impression of his appearance.[13]

He has an engineer's passion for efficiency. He dropped his middle name, Clark, because he had to sign his name hundreds of times and not having to write a "C" would free him to do more important duties. He believes an engineer can create a more handsome waterfall than any found in nature, and he thinks God did a poor job designing the horse. He splits his sleep in two to give himself two opportunities to get the most intense rest: the period after falling asleep and shortly before waking up. He goes to bed at ten, gets up at two, and reads until five, then goes back to sleep and gets up at seven.[14] That's six hours of sleep, but he claims it's more like eight. (Efficient though it may be, such tampering with his metabolism may account for his frequent surly mood.)

The only physical exercise he gets is to play medicine ball; he has figured out that it burns three times more calories than tennis and six times more than golf. Other than reading, he has only one hobby: trout fishing. By his own admission Hoover has very few friends, maybe half a dozen. He likes to give big dinner parties at his home, but he says very little during the dinner conversation other than his favorite sound, "Uh." He has a forbidding personality and a frigid demeanor. There is hardly any mirth or ribald camaraderie. After a while casual conversation starts to sound like a business meeting. One friend who has known Hoover for thirty years claims he has never heard the man laugh once.

Ever so serious, he promotes himself incessantly. In five hundred working days as food administrator he issued no fewer than 1,840 press releases—"like flakes of snow in a heavy storm," the *Nation*'s editor Oswald Villard called them.[15] As commerce secretary Hoover had 11,000 copies of the Commerce Department

annual report printed and sent to government officials, companies, trade associations, chambers of commerce, and the press,
much of it paid for out of his own pocket.[16]

He is very bright. According to the financier Bernard Baruch,
"To Hoover's brain facts are as water to a sponge."[17] He can read
a memo and recite the numbers from memory. He is extremely
well-read and has broadened his knowledge far beyond the geology
he studied in college. By the age of forty he had spent over seven
hundred days—equivalent to two years—on a ship. He claims
that from 1904 to 1907, during "two hours nightly and all spare
time on long voyages," he read "several thousand" books by Balzac,
Dumas, Voltaire, Zola, Hugo, Rousseau, Montaigne, Mirabeau,
Confucius, Mencius, Plato, Shakespeare, Schiller, and Goethe.[18]

Spending so many years abroad has given him opportunity to
learn foreign cultures firsthand. When he worked on his own in
1908–12 he participated in archaeological digs in Egypt and northern Italy and learned about the Egyptian and Roman empires.
With the help of his wife, who knows Latin better than he does,
he labored for over a year producing a translation of a classical
Latin text on ancient mining, *De Re Metallica*—an intimidating
document!

For a man with such a rich education, it is surprising that he
is so handicapped verbally. He is a horrendous public speaker: he
reads from the manuscript, mumbles, and can't be heard by anyone past the third or fourth row. His writing too is atrocious. In
1922 he wrote *American Individualism*, a short book setting forth
his philosophy of patriotism, society, and government in America. There is one paragraph that Hoover considered so important
he italicized it:

> *While we build our society upon the attainment of the individual, we*
> *shall safeguard to every individual an equality of opportunity to take*
> *that position in the community to which his intelligence, character, abil-*
> *ity, and ambition entitle him; that we keep the social solution free from*

GEORGII AGRICOLAE

DE RE METALLICA LIBRI XII, QVI,

bus Officia, Inftrumenta, Machinæ, ac omnia deniç ad Metalli-
cam fpectantia, non modo luculentiffimè defcribuntur, fed & per
effigies, fuis locis infertas, adiunctis Latinis, Germanicisç appel-
lationibus ita ob oculos ponuntur, ut clarius tradi non poffint.

EIVSDEM

DE ANIMANTIBVS SVBTERRANEIS Liber, ab Autore re-
cognitus:cum Indicibus diuerfis, quicquid in opere tractatum eft,
pulchrè demonftrantibus.

BASILEAE M, D, LVI,

Cum Priuilegio Imperatoris in annos v.
& Galliarum Regis ad Sexennium.

An unusual hobby: for several nights a week for over a year Hoover and his
wife struggled to translate this obscure sixteenth-century treatise, including
giving names to objects not known today.

the frozen state of classes; that we shall stimulate effort of each individual to achievement; that through an enlarging sense of responsibility and understanding we shall assist him to this attainment while he in turn must stand up to the emery wheel of competition.[19]

What gibberish! To be sure, a president of the United States is not expected to be a literary giant, but he should be able to able to communicate his message in a clear, forceful manner. Hoover's pedantic writing suggests a lack of imagination and originality. People won't have a clue what he is talking about. Try this for illogic: two short sentences from his book: "We cannot ever afford to rest at ease in the comfortable assumption that right ideas always prevail by some virtue of their own. In the long run they do."[20] No wonder not a single phrase from this book is being used in his campaign literature. This must be a presidential candidate first. He may be very smart, but he has no communications skills whatsoever.

More fundamental is the curious disconnect between the self-made multimillionaire and the orphan boy he once was. He has lost touch with the average voter. When Senator Thomas Gore of Oklahoma asked about the price of beans per bushel, Hoover innocently replied, "I have always bought them by the ton."[21]

BUSINESS PERFORMANCE

Mining is a boom-and-bust business. Fortunes have been made, but even more fortunes have been lost. How did Hoover manage to be so phenomenally successful?

Unlike most miners, Hoover did not look for virgin mines; rather he looked for distressed, overworked mines that other people had given up on. Calling himself "a doctor of sick mines,"[22] he would buy cheap and exploit the remaining lodes to the fullest. He based his financial projections on output and cost of production, not on the ups and downs of investment bubbles. Result: while many mine owners lost their shirt chasing market manias, Hoover, by being disciplined and focusing on intrinsic value, kept his losses to a minimum and stayed in the game long enough to reap the upside.

Hoover in his midthirties, allegedly the richest man in the world for his age.

Out in the field, looking for mines to buy

The mining business attracts its share of get-rich-quick scam artists. His employer Bewick Moreing prided itself on being one of the high-end players known for its honesty and integrity. But in 1902 one of the firm's partners embezzled half a million dollars and fled to Canada. Hoover, acting alone, insisted that the firm—though it had no legal obligation to do so—assume full liability to preserve its reputation. It took three years for the partners to pay back the money, all from their own pocket. This bold action suggests Hoover is a man of principle and integrity.

Everyone thinks Hoover is a brilliant engineer, a miner on a burro with pickax in hand, discovering precious metals in exotic parts of the world. In actual fact he pretty much stopped doing mining and engineering three years after finishing college. He is a man who knows how to juggle the numbers and extract maximum value out of a business deal. The finance world calls the function he performs "promoter," meaning the person who raises money to invest in developing a business venture. (In Hoover's case, the vehicle was a limited partnership, and the venture was a mining property.) Some of his deals have worked out; most have not. In every case Hoover made money by charging management fees borne by the partnership (whether or not the partnership made money, he still got paid), plus taking a percentage override of any profits. He is superb at structuring complex partnerships involving interlocking ownership of mines that are so complicated only he can understand who owns what, thereby giving him a ready opportunity to buy for his own account when he has inside information of a mining success. While there is no evidence of financial chicanery on his part, one wonders why he made his mining deals so complicated. Either he wants to hide something or, more likely, he wants to be in total control and doesn't want investors asking lots of questions.

As a managing partner at Bewick Moreing, Hoover was paid a salary of $100,000 (plus 25 percent of the profits). His salary, by his own admission, was $5,000 as a mining expert and $95,000 as a financial expert in reconstructions and reorganizations. Financiers reconstruct a company by imposing a huge capital write-off, which reduces the original capital almost to the vanishing point, and then they enhance the value of their own holdings by issuing fresh preference shares (carrying majority voting power) on the grounds that new capital is required to avoid bankruptcy. Hoover did this in his two big deals, Burma Mines, Ltd. and Zinc Corporation, Ltd. The incorporation papers of these ventures contain two clauses that clearly favor the general partner over the investors: the discovery clause (which prevents shareholders from inspecting the corporation books) and the waiver clause (which permits directors to invest reserve funds at their discretion without consulting the shareholders). It is also worth noting that these two companies—as well as most of Hoover's other deals—are registered in Australia, not in Britain where the waiver clause is not allowed.

Hoover did twelve major deals. How successful were they? A review of the original offering memoranda and results reveals that most of these deals were flops, one was so-so, and only two made money. These two, Burma and Zinc, made a pile of money.[23]

Deal	Result
Anglo-Continental Mines, Ltd.	Absorbed into Yuanmi Gold Mines, Ltd. at an 80% loss (£300,000)
Babilonia Gold Mines, Ltd.	£200,000 raised; company now suspended
Bellevue Proprietary, Ltd.	Total loss (£195,000)
Burma Corporation, Ltd.	Highly profitable holding company, with interests in Burma Mines, Ltd. and Burma Trust, Ltd.; shares skyrocketed to 26 times original value
Great Fitzroy Gold & Copper Mines, Ltd.	Total loss (£466,000)
Lake View Exploration, Ltd.	Merged into Oroya Exploration, Ltd., a holding company of mining interests, capitalized at £1,617,000 and eventually liquidated at £600,000

Lancefield Gold Mining, Ltd.	Total loss (£250,000)
Oroville Dredging Co., Ltd.	£563,000 invested in several mines; modestly profitable
Oroya Leonesa, Ltd.	Failed (£225,000)
Oroya Links, Ltd.	£312,000 investment; lost 88%
Yuanmi Gold Mines, Ltd.	Total loss (£350,000)
Zinc Corporation, Ltd.	Substantial moneymaker

In London, Hoover was well-known for putting very little of his own money into a deal, selling a lot of his promotion stock early in the flotation, and keeping only shares in those deals he knew were likely to pay dividends. There is nothing illegal in this, but such sharp practices did not make him many friends in London.

WAR PROFITEER

Hoover claims he gave up his business career when he took on the job of Belgian relief during the war. Not true. He still kept his fingers in the pie, profiting handsomely from the war-time explosion in prices of precious metals. According to the British registration records for 1915 and 1916, Hoover was still listed as chairman or director of Granville Mining Company, Inter-Californian Trust, Inter-Mexican Syndicate, Kystim Corporation, Russo-Asiatic Corporation, Tanalyle, and Zinc. He didn't resign from Burma until 1918, Zinc until 1920, and Oroville Dredging until 1924. Call him the Great Humanitarian, but he still qualifies as a war profiteer.

Also during the war, as part of his business operations he bought chemicals from Germany—not because they were unavailable anywhere else but because he could buy from Germany cheaper.[24] Such practices are illegal in the United States, but because his companies were registered in Australia he could not be prosecuted.

One of his government deals is particularly unsettling: the Austria loan. As head of the American Relief Administration he had a problem getting food for Austria because U.S. law prohibited lending to former enemy states. Hoover got around this restriction by arranging for the United States to lend $45 million to our allies Britain, France, and Italy, who would then turn around and lend the money to Austria. Austria would repay the three countries, and they in turn would repay the United States. A stipulation in the deal was that the Austrians buy their food only from American farmers. When Austria was unable to repay and defaulted, Congress insisted the three allies repay, though they had received no benefit whatsoever.[25] Hoover stood by quietly and did nothing, causing considerable ill will among our wartime allies. He had used them, and when he no longer needed them, he stiffed them.

COMMERCE SECRETARY

Traditionally the Commerce Department was considered a backwater in the government hierarchy, an agency whose major responsibility was "turning on the lighthouses at night and putting the fish to bed."[26] Under the leadership of a dynamo like Hoover, this quickly changed, and the Commerce Department found itself on the front pages for its activities in tariffs and flood relief.

His tenure as secretary was not without its share of controversy. Hoover favored the interests of big business over small business. His allocation of radio licenses, for instance, put many small operators out of business and helped create a powerful franchise for General Electric. In his treatment of the salmon fisheries industry, Hoover placed property rights above human welfare. He claims that he saved Alaska's salmon from extinction; this is a material misstatement. From 1914 to 1918 the number of cases of salmon harvested each year was 26.1 million. After the war demand during 1919–23 dropped to 21.2 million. In 1924–28, after the Commerce Department started to regulate the fisheries, the number of cases was 26 million; there was absolutely no disruption in the supply and certainly no "extinction" as Hoover claims.

What did change under Hoover was who got the money. Hoover persuaded President Harding, under the guise of "conservation," to bar independent fishermen—the native Indians of Alaska— thus conferring a virtual monopoly on a half-dozen big packers. Thirty-three percent of Alaskan Indians depend on salmon fishing for their livelihood. There was such uproar about this injustice that in 1924 Congress enacted a special law guaranteeing equal rights to all citizens participating in Alaska fishing, but Hoover administered the law in such a way that many native fishermen were still driven out of business anyway. Furthermore the corporations operating the canneries proceeded to bring in hordes of cheap immigrant labor from Washington State and California to usurp the work performed by the native Indians of Alaska— akin to union-busting. (In Canada it is against the law to import nonresident fishermen without paying a prohibitive penalty tax.)

WHAT OTHERS SAY ABOUT HIM

Andrew Mellon, the esteemed secretary of the Treasury during the eight years Hoover was commerce secretary, says Hoover is too rigid and inflexible to be a good president: "Hoover is an engineer. He wants to run a straight line, just one line, and then say to everyone, 'this is the only line there is, and you must come up to it, or else keep out.'"[27] Adds Col. Edward House, President Wilson's foremost advisor, Hoover is "the kind of man that has to have complete control in order to do well. . . . He does not know how to work with Congress or politicians."[28] To the banker Bernard Baruch this is no surprise; he says Hoover suffers from "delusions of grandeur—he really believes all the wonderful things written about himself."[29]

Hoover has worked directly for three presidents. What do they think? Back in 1920 Warren Harding, who admired Hoover as the smartest man he'd ever met, warned that he should not be president because he was too "dictatorial and autocratic."[30] A year earlier Hoover complained to reporters that he wasn't getting enough food for overseas shipment because the railroads weren't running properly. Secretary of the Treasury William McAdoo, responsible for the railroads (and doing an excellent job at it), read about Hoover's allegations in the newspapers and blew up. He called Hoover into his office and demanded to know why Hoover hadn't come to him first—to which Hoover had no answer; all he could do was look down at the floor like a chastened schoolboy.[31]

President Wilson confirms McAdoo's opinion and says Hoover "cannot be trusted": "I have a feeling that he would rather see a good cause fail than succeed if he were not the head of it. . . . One of the most selfish people I have ever known."[32]

The president who knows Hoover best is Calvin Coolidge, who says Hoover has been giving him "unsolicited advice for eight years, all of it bad."[33] To be fair to Hoover and his eight years of excellent service as commerce secretary—not to mention the many times Coolidge invited him to the White House for a private dinner and cigars—this may be the comment of a curmudgeon leaving the White House and resenting his potential successor. Presidents, like kings, don't give up the throne easily.

CONCLUSION

The wisdom and judgment required to perform the highest office in the land do not come from analyzing data; such qualities come from seeing reality in its entirety—above and beyond what can be measured in numbers. Rational problems, such as calculating how much food is needed and how to get it from point A to point B, are easy for Hoover. Nonrational problems, like figuring out how to inspire people, are another matter entirely.

In his campaign literature quoting from his Republican Party acceptance speech of August 11 a phrase has been left out of the last sentence. This sentence reads in full (deleted words italicized): "We have not yet reached the goal, but given a chance to go forward with the policies of the last eight years, we shall soon with the help of God be in sight of the day when poverty will be banished from this nation."[34] "The last eight years" is a vital omission in almost all of Hoover's speeches. He claims the United States is enjoying unprecedented economic progress under Harding's and Coolidge's "New Era." Yet he himself admits that the materialism and prosperity of the New Era has been based largely on easy credit, conspicuous consumption, and market speculation—meaning the economy could collapse tomorrow.

Right now we enjoy peace and economic prosperity. We have no political, military, or economic crises looming on the horizon. The times call for a proven administrator who can provide high energy to keeping our ship of state afloat. Such a man is

Herbert Hoover. His fitness for the presidency would appear to be obvious.

But suppose our economy is running out of gas, as Hoover privately admits? Should an unexpected crisis occur, one questions whether Hoover, the ultimate engineer and dynamo dealing with well-defined problems, has the imagination to cope with the unknown. He made his money on only two out of twelve major deals. Two successes out of twelve may work in finance, but not for the presidency. A president must be able to handle any crisis that comes up; he does not have the luxury of picking and choosing. On any given day a half-dozen problems can land on his desk: he must be able to handle all of them, some of them totally out of left field.

Furthermore the presidency is more than an executive job; it is a symbolic position. Hoover is a straight arrow, with no talent for flattery or exhortation. He has no social skills. He never indulges in witticisms or tells a story or a joke. Imagine him having to deal with powerful congressmen who have their own power bases and demand accommodation! Can he manage the necessary give-and-take, unpleasant though it may be? He dislikes being a public figure; he calls giving speeches "agony."[35] "You can't make a Teddy Roosevelt out of me," he says—almost as if he didn't want to even try.[36]

A completely different view of the presidency is offered by Hoover's former admirer, Franklin Roosevelt. In his speech nominating Governor Alfred Smith at the Democratic Convention, Roosevelt said that to be a great president requires "the quality of soul which makes a man loved by little children . . . that quality of soul which makes him a strong help to those in sorrow or trouble, that quality which makes him not merely admired but loved by all the people—the quality of sympathetic understanding of the human heart, of real interest in one's fellow man."[37] Clearly Roosevelt is not describing Herbert Hoover, the efficiency expert.

Throughout his career Hoover has had jobs where he was in complete control. In seeking the presidency he hopes to try his hand at a quite different job. When attacking a social problem he is superb at logistics but is frequently tone-deaf to its complex human and social ramifications. Says the *Nation*, "Competent observers say that Mr. Hoover's Administration will either be, on the purely executive side, one of the most memorable in our history, or that he will be one of the greatest failures in the presidency."[38] Is this a risk we want to take? Hoover's achievements are glittering: he brings an incredible résumé to the presidential office; he is a superb manager and chief executive, with proven ability to solve problems, identify opportunities, and implement solutions. Voters will find it difficult to say no to a candidate with such a stellar record of accomplishment.

But as a leader—especially a moral leader—he is sorely lacking. *Inspiration, faith, emotion,* and *hope* are not words in his vocabulary. He exudes no warmth or compassion; he attracts no cadre of followers. He has never demonstrated a talent for compromise, it's always been his way or no way. He is stubborn, rarely questions himself, and seldom seeks diverse opinions. His aggressive business dealings smell of hucksterism and self-dealing. He is an extreme introvert and fails to comprehend that there are other issues involved in making money besides the bottom line. The only reason his financial success hasn't made him look like a money-grubber is the veneer of having done charity work. Were it not for the patina provided by food relief, he might be perceived as just another Babbitt, a man of small-town midwestern values who happened to hit the jackpot.

Accomplishments	Intangibles	Judgment	Overall
outstanding	poor	fair	fair

1928

Promising "a chicken in every pot and two cars in every garage," Herbert Hoover won by a landslide. Upon taking office he pursued his foremost priority and met with Federal Reserve officials to authorize measures to curb speculation and clamp down on easy money. As president he followed up on his 1925 letter to the Senate Banking and Currency Committee, wherein he had warned that the Federal Reserve's loose-money policies would bring "inevitable collapse."[39] There would be no economic collapse on his watch as president. Unemployment at the time was just 3 percent.

Eight months into his presidency Hoover ran into a tsunami known as the Crash. For a while it looked like the worse was over. Andrew Mellon said there was nothing to worry about; John Maynard Keynes predicted there would be no more crashes; Bernard Baruch announced that the financial storm had passed. When President Hoover received a delegation requesting a public works program to help speed the recovery, he told them, "Gentlemen, you have come sixty days too late. The depression is over."[40]

Yet every time the stock market rebounded, it promptly sank back to a new low. This happened five times. There were actually two depressions during Hoover's term. The first was the result of overspeculation during the previous years. The second—hitting just as Hoover's efforts were beginning to show results—occurred in 1931, when the fiscal and financial structure of Europe started to collapse and Britain and eighteen other countries went off the gold standard. What had started out as a U.S. depression had now become an international depression. Unemployment soared, banks closed, and Hoover started making incredible statements like "Many people have left their jobs for the more profitable one of selling apples."[41]

No president ever worked as hard as Hoover: sixteen-hour days, seven days a week. He called conferences of business leaders and got them to keep paying good wages. He called conferences of state and local politicians and got them to refrain from waging strikes. He tried to get the governors to back a plan for a $3 billion reserve fund, only to be rejected. (The governors called the plan "socialistic.")[42] He initiated what under FDR became the Glass-Steagall Act to clean up Wall Street; he also signed the Hawley-Smoot bill to protect American businessmen against European competition. He spent more money on public works than all his predecessors combined. He lowered taxes, then he raised them;

he got an increase in the Fed discount rate; he balanced the budget, then he ran a deficit. There was hardly anything he didn't do. When the 1932 presidential campaign came around, FDR accused Hoover of presiding over "the greatest spending administration in peacetime in all of history," and FDR's running mate, John Nance Garner, declared that Hoover was "leading the country down the path to socialism."[43]

What the Democrats conveniently ignored, of course, was the magnitude of the obstacles Hoover faced. The worse the economy got, the harder Hoover worked, to the point that he sometimes got only three hours of sleep a night. He was sure he could beat the Depression—but then, who ever thought it would last thirteen long years, until 1942, when massive war spending started to kick in?

The American people never saw the real Herbert Hoover because he wouldn't let them. There's a marvelous story about the man that was never publicly told: One day three children appeared at the front gate of the White House and rang the doorbell. Apparently their father had been jailed for stealing a car while in search of work. The children had hitchhiked all the way from Detroit in childlike faith that the president could return their father to them. White House aides checked out the story and confirmed it was true.

"Three children resourceful enough to get to Washington to see me are going to see me," said Hoover. The thirteen-year-old girl and her two younger brothers were ushered into the president's office. After hearing their tale of woe, Hoover said he would help. "I know there must be good in a man whose children are so well behaved and who show such loyalty and devotion to him," he said. "I will use my good office. You may go home happy." He gave each of them a little gift. "Now run along and go straight home. Dad will be there waiting for you."

After the children left, Hoover, visibly distraught, ordered his aide to get the father out of jail immediately. After this was done with a quick phone call, the aide begged the president to release the full human-interest story to the press, just as Lincoln had done after hearing a woman's pleas to pardon her son about to be executed for being a deserter. But Hoover would have none of it; only the barest announcement would be made. "Let's not argue about it," he said. "That will be enough. Now we will have to get back to work."[44]

This thoroughly decent man was unable to communicate his humanity. At a time when Americans needed reassurance and human warmth, all they got from Hoover were technical analyses, long-range plans, and exhortations for more volunteerism. Even the press—which had for so many years touted his achievements—turned against him. When Hoover gave his regular press conferences he simply handed out prepared statements. He almost never answered questions, even written questions submitted in advance. When he most needed the press to calm Americans' worries about economic collapse, he had lost this critical ally.

In the White House he was a terror. Even the servants were frightened of him; walking down the hall, he would never look at them or say "Good Morning" or "Hello." He was like a machine, working nonstop, always rushing off to another meeting.

The low point of his presidency came in 1932, when forty-three thousand army veterans from around the country came to Washington seeking an advance payment on their military pensions. A deal was reached, and 90 percent of the Bonus Marchers went home. But instead of sending out coffee and sandwiches to those remaining, Hoover gave them Gen. Douglas MacArthur. Ordered to prevent any further marches that might erupt into violence, MacArthur disobeyed Hoover's orders and commanded his troops to beat up the marchers. The result was a public relations disaster. Instead of blaming MacArthur for insubordination, Hoover assumed all responsibility, hoping the mess would blow away. It didn't, and the president became even more despised. He was his own worst enemy.

"No president must ever admit he has been wrong," he told his good friend Julius Barnes.[45] Hoover refused to sack MacArthur, refused to admit Prohibition was a mistake and should be repealed, refused to provide direct relief to citizens, and refused to meet with the Bonus Marchers (just as he never wanted to meet the starving Belgian children or the Mississippi homeless). Comparing Hoover to the eight other presidents he had worked for, beginning with Benjamin Harrison, the head of the household staff in the White House observed, "Hoover seemed to wish to discuss matters with people whom he knew in advance would agree with him, whereas often I have heard other presidents say, 'I do not wish to talk with So-and-So, for he thinks just as I do.'"[46] For this multimillionaire who had started life as an orphan, anyone seeking a dole must be a subversive. Isolated in the White House, he became even more stubborn and puritanical in his convictions. When congressmen came to see him, he doodled, looked up at the ceiling, looked out the window—and would not change his mind. "One, with God, is a majority," the Quakers say.[47]

Finally, in 1932, he admitted that voluntarism had failed; he would now create the Reconstruction Finance Corporation, modeled after the War Finance Corporation. This was a major, almost radical undertaking, the first program ever mounted by the federal government to intervene directly in the economy during peacetime. Still Hoover insisted that the RFC was only a temporary agency and would loan only to large businesses and banks, not to individuals. As in Alaska when he was commerce secretary, individuals and small businesses would be left to fend on their own.

When the newspaperman Byron Price visited his friend in the White House, he got an earful from a man under siege. Hoover complained he had done everything he could but his efforts had been undermined by European nations, Republican Party leaders, and Congress's "stupidity and stubbornness." "Is it my fault that cheap politicians [and] selfish men over the whole world have refused to see the folly of their policies until it was too late?" he thundered. Marveled Price, "I've never heard anybody do a better job of laying out some of his political enemies than Mr. Hoover did, in language that he must have learned in a mining camp."[48]

As the lights dimmed on the waning days of his administration, Hoover—who had benefited from exaggerated publicity and a compliant press—complained to one of the Republican senators, "I have been absurdly over-sold. No man can live up to it."[49] (No mention, of course, of who had been doing most of the overselling.) Come Election Day 1932, unemployment had skyrocketed to 25 percent and apple-sellers were everywhere. A vote for Hoover, said Roosevelt, was like voting for the Four Horsemen of the Apocalypse, "Destruction, Delay, Deceit, and Despair."[50] Hoover returned the animus, declaring that a vote for Roosevelt would mean "the grass will grow in the streets of a hundred cities, a thousand towns; the weeds will overrun the fields of a million farms."[51]

Hoover went down to crushing defeat. Several days after the election a resolution to impeach him was introduced in the House to get him out of office immediately. It was voted down, 361 to 8. In the long five months before Roosevelt took over, Hoover reached out to his successor to discuss how to ameliorate the banking crisis, but Roosevelt stayed far away. The very name *Hoover* was a plague: shantytowns filled with the homeless were called *Hoovervilles*; horses pulled *Hoovercarts* because their owners couldn't afford gas; the newspapers under which homeless people slept in parks were *Hoover blankets*; empty pockets turned inside out were *Hoover flags*.

Roosevelt had a particular reason for animus bordering on hatred for Hoover. At a White House governors' reception earlier that year, with all the governors standing around waiting for the president to arrive, Hoover had deliberately delayed his entrance almost an hour so Roosevelt would get tired standing in his leg braces and have to ask for a chair, thus exposing his physical weakness. Eleanor Roosevelt never forgave Hoover for that stunt.

It got even worse. On the day before the inauguration Roosevelt and his son paid a courtesy visit to the White House. Hoover surprised Roosevelt by bringing in Treasury Secretary Ogden Mills to discuss the banking crisis. Roosevelt said no, this was a social call, he would discuss policy only with his advisors present. At the end of a very frosty half-hour of afternoon tea, Roosevelt, not wanting to inconvenience the president, told Hoover not to wait, it would take time for him to adjust his leg braces, stand up, and leave. Hoover rose, eyes glaring, and told the president-elect, "Mr. Roosevelt, after you have been president for a while, you will learn that the President of the United States waits for no one!" Then he stormed out. Roosevelt's son was so angry he wanted to punch the president in the face.[52]

Roosevelt got his revenge. The next day, upon leaving the White House and arriving at Union Station to board the train to New York, Hoover learned that FDR had ordered the Secret Service to stop giving him protection. (The Washington and New York police departments immediately jumped in and volunteered their services.) Soon after FDR took office Washington's Hoover Airport, named for the man who had set up the civil aeronautics system, was renamed National Airport (now Ronald W. Reagan Airport). Then Hoover's name was stripped from the magnificent dam under construction near Las Vegas and renamed Boulder Dam, and Hoover was excluded from the guest list for the opening ceremony. (In 1947 President Harry Truman put an end to the personal vendetta and restored Hoover's name to the dam.)

Many years later the New Deal administrator Rexford Tugwell admitted that "practically the whole New Deal was extrapolated from programs that Hoover started."[53] Today Hoover is increasingly given credit for having originated much of the New Deal. By the time he died in 1964 he had acquired an astonishing eighty-seven honorary degrees and five nominations for the Nobel Peace Prize. The most progressive of presidents, he was trapped between individualism and collectivism, and for the rest of his life he opposed the welfare state America was becoming. Nothing could shake his fear that once Americans willingly went on the dole, they would be giving up much of their liberty and freedom.

Probably the greatest difference between Hoover and Roosevelt was how they handled the overwhelming issue of fear. One man treated it as a fact; the other used it as inspiration. Said Herbert Hoover in 1931, "Ninety percent of our problems are caused by fear."[54] Said Franklin Roosevelt in 1933, "The only thing we have to fear is fear itself." In those two sentences lies the difference between the brilliant president who fell short and the less than brilliant president who inspired hope and confidence. Sometimes personality and emotion is everything.

10

Wendell Willkie, 1940

Never has a man come out of nowhere as fast as Wendell Willkie. He has never held public office or served in the military. He is a lawyer and corporate CEO—of a monopoly, no less (a public utility, about the most unpopular business there is in America). He is a former Democrat who suddenly switched to the Republican Party and got told by a former Republican senator he didn't have a prayer in the Party: "It's all right if the town whore joins the church, but they don't let her lead the choir the first night."[1]

Yet here he is now, leading the choir, a man who never ran in any of the Republican primaries, who back in May had only 3 percent support among Republicans, far behind New York's district attorney Thomas E. Dewey with 67 percent, followed by Senator Arthur Vandenberg and Senator Robert Taft. All three men represent the isolationist wing of the party, whereas Willkie emphasizes the Nazi menace and the need to help Britain.

As the situation in Europe worsened, public support for Willkie grew. "Willkie for President" clubs sprung up all over the country, generating four and a half million petitions for Willkie and a million letters and telegrams to the delegates at the Republican National Convention. Professional politicians could only shake their heads in disbelief as gallery spectators chanted "We want Willkie!" and Willkie came from behind to capture the nomina-

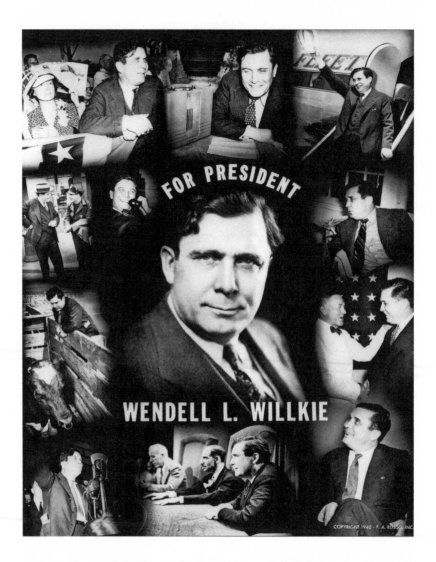

FOR PRESIDENT

WENDELL L. WILLKIE

COPYRIGHT 1940 - F. A. RUSSO, INC.

tion on the sixth ballot. "The Miracle at Philadelphia," people call it. One Republican national committeeman summed up the situation this way:

> So I am supposed to go back to the clubhouse and tell the boys that we all have to pull together now to get the nomination for Wendell Willkie. They'll ask me "Willkie, who's Willkie?" And I'll tell them he's the president of the Commonwealth & Southern. The next question will be, "Where does that railroad go to?" And I will explain that

it isn't a railroad, it's a public utility holding company. Then they will look at me sadly and say, "Ken, we always have thought you were a little erratic, but now we know you are just plain crazy." And that would be without my even getting to mention that he's a Democrat.[2]

As a man new to his political party, Willkie has his work cut out for him. His Democratic opponent is President Franklin Roosevelt, running for a third term. In the last presidential election Roosevelt beat his Republican opponent, Alfred Landon, by eleven million votes. Willkie is figuring he can get eight million votes more than Landon did, but that's still three million short. So how does he expect to win? By persuading a lot of Democratic voters to stay home.

Should Roosevelt get the same number of votes as before, then Willkie has to do a lot better than eight million votes. That's a tall order. Willkie has already pulled off one miracle. Can he pull off another? To do so he is mounting what he calls "a crusade." The Democrats, mocking his background in the electric utility industry, call it "the charge of the electric light brigade."[3]

WENDELL WILLKIE

Age: forty-eight
6-foot-2, 230 pounds

Home address:	Office address:
1010 Fifth Avenue	20 Pine Street
New York City	New York City

OBJECTIVE: Thirty-third president of the United States

SUMMARY OF QUALIFICATIONS: Dynamic and visionary corporate executive with proven leadership skills and charisma. Compelling personality, able to inspire others.

PERSONAL STATEMENT: Having never held public office, I will provide a fresh perspective that is lacking in most politicians and government officials who think "government knows best."

Qualifications

LEADER OF LARGE, COMPLEX ENTERPRISE

CEO of one of the largest and most successful companies in America.

EXPERIENCE IN A HIGHLY REGULATED INDUSTRY

Perfect compliance record managing a public utility subject to myriad local and state regulations and the 1935 Public Utility Holding Company Act.

RESTORED PUBLIC CONFIDENCE

In industry with a reputation for high prices and poor service, provided exemplary service at low prices, resulting in increased volume and customer satisfaction.

Skilled Negotiator and Communicator

Negotiated government-forced sale of company to a government monopoly (the TVA) at a price that achieved maximum value for the shareholders. Won nationally televised public debate with Assistant Attorney General (now Attorney General) Robert Jackson.

National Perspective

Extensive travel throughout the United States to supervise far-flung business operations, especially in the South and Midwest.

Will Bring Prosperity to All Americans

Developed an ingenious rate structure that enabled Americans to enjoy cheap electrical power and an improved standard of living, especially in rural areas.

Public Affairs, 1924–present

Delegate to the Democratic National Party Convention, 1924 and 1932.

Author of widely acclaimed articles on public affairs and government administration: "Campaign against the Companies," *Current History*, May 1935; "Horse Power and Horse Sense," *Review of Reviews*, August 1936; "Political Power: The Tennessee Valley Authority," *Atlantic Monthly*, August 1937; "New Deal Power Plan Challenged," *New York Times Magazine*, October 31, 1937; "Brace Up, America!," *Atlantic Monthly*, June 1939; "Idle Money, Idle Men," *Saturday Evening Post*, June 17, 1939; "Evening Star of the Great Day of the Whigs," *Herald Tribune Book Review*, August 27, 1939; "The Faith That Is America," *Reader's Digest*, December 1939; "With Malice toward None," *Saturday Evening Post*, December 30, 1939; "The Court Is Now His," *Saturday Evening Post*, March 9, 1940; "We, the People: A Petition," *Fortune*, April 1940. This last article generated over two thousand speaking invitations.

Also participated in numerous radio and television interviews, including "How Can Government and Business Work Together?," a debate with Robert Jackson, NBC *Town Hall Meeting of the Air*, January 6, 1940, on the merits of the free enterprise system. Won debate and attracted attention as a potential presidential candidate.

Commonwealth & Southern, 1929–present

> 1934–present: Chairman and chief executive officer
>
> 1933–1934: President and chief operating officer
>
> 1929–1933: Legal counsel

Took over nation's largest electric utility holding company,[4] with far-flung operations (165 companies) and in total disarray after the stock market crash. (C&S stock plummeted from 23¾ to 1⅝, dividends from 70 cents to 1). Turned around money-losing operation and restored it to substantial profitability. Within six years doubled sales of electricity, established company on a sound financial footing, and lowered household electricity rates to a level 27 percent lower than the national average.

Led battle in the courts and the media against the Tennessee Valley Authority (TVA), a newly created government entity designed to compete with private industry. Testified before numerous congressional committees. Supervised legal team making vigorous argument before the U.S. Supreme Court. Upon ruling by the Court that it lacked jurisdiction, negotiated successful sale to the TVA at a fair price reflecting the value of one of the most successful businesses in America.

Unlike holding companies of the past, Commonwealth & Southern made customer service its number one priority. Under my direction, company invested over $1 billion of its earnings back into the business to provide electricity to homes in rural areas. Financed extensive property improvements and construction of new power-generating plants with capacity of five million kilowatts—a 150 percent increase over 1930 capacity.

Mather, Nesbitt & Willkie, 1921–1929

Partner in small law firm in Indiana serving electric utilities. Specialized in litigation. Elected president of the Akron, Ohio, Bar Association, 1926.

Firestone Tire & Rubber Company, 1919–1921

In-house legal counsel.

EDUCATION

Indiana University, 1938, received honorary LL.D. degree.

Indiana Law School, 1914–1916, JD degree, graduated first in class.

Indiana University, 1909–1913, AB degree in history; class orator.

Attended Officer Training School. Received commission as first lieutenant, discharged as captain.

PERSONAL

Born February 18, 1892. Grew up in Ellwood, Indiana, the fourth of six children. Both parents were lawyers. Attended local high school; was class president. During summers while in college rode freight trains out west and worked in an iron mill, a cement plant, the oil fields of Texas, and the farmlands of California. Taught history in high school in Kansas for one year. Switched affiliation to the Republican Party, 1939. Married; one son: age twenty, a student at Princeton. Listed in the New York Social Register. Member of the Century, University, Recess, Lawyers, and Blind Brook clubs.

Assessment of Qualifications

It's been three months now since Willkie pulled off his astounding win of the Republican nomination, and many people—Republicans as well as Democrats—still can't believe it. Was it a fluke, or is this man for real?

The man who arrived at the Republican National Convention was not the midwestern hick his opponents like to portray. ("The barefoot boy from Wall Street," FDR's advisor Harold Ickes called him.)[5] To the contrary, he is a shrewd lawyer who rose to the top of the business world as CEO of the biggest utility in the country, fought tooth and nail against the TVA and the New Deal, negotiated a hefty purchase price from the government for one of his companies, and established a national reputation as a spokesman for free enterprise.

To win the nomination Willkie had two things going for him that traditional politicians don't have. First, he had a national network of two thousand Willkie Clubs that sprung up like mushrooms on a summer night, staffed by volunteers. Second, there was Willkie himself: a dynamo, a force of nature. He arrived in Philadelphia several days in advance to put the squeeze on any early delegates he could find, whereas his three competitors didn't arrive until the evening before the convention. By the end of the first day, holding court in his modest two-room suite, Willkie had personally met six hundred of the one thousand delegates.

Imagine a delegate going to meet Taft in his 102-room complex, or Dewey in his seventy-eight rooms, or Vandenberg in his forty-eight.[6] When you went looking for Senator Taft's room, assuming you could find the right floor, you had to fight your way through a crowd of handlers and curiosity-seekers; with Willkie you went to The Man right away. Your conversation may have been brief, but you will remember his good cheer and certainly his handshake. He is a bear of a man, with a grip that can pop open a can. Willkie has enough personal money to rent two hundred rooms if he wanted to, but he was careful to communicate the image of a regular man of the people. No one can say this man is not cunning and shrewd.

Willkie is colorful and exciting—the first such Republican since Theodore Roosevelt. And like many successful presidential nominees, he has had his share of astounding good luck. All his opponents were isolationist conservatives, whereas he stood out as an internationalist and a liberal. He could talk about the New Deal with the credibility that comes from having been on the firing line for eight years, whereas his opponents could talk only in theory. He could take an aggressive attitude toward the Nazis storming through Europe and occupying Paris, whereas Taft and Vandenberg were locked into their long-standing isolationism of earlier years. He had substantial experience, whereas Dewey was young— only thirty-seven.* Finally and most fortuitous of all, his opponents let their egos get in the way. Between them Taft and Dewey had 650 ballots—more than a majority. Had they joined forces the contest would have been over on the first ballot. But neither man was willing to play second fiddle and be the vice president, so the deal floundered. In fact Dewey offered the vice presidency to Taft, Taft offered it to Dewey, Dewey offered it to Vandenberg, and Vandenberg offered it to Dewey. There were no takers.

* The acerbic Harold Ickes had a biting witticism about Dewey: "He threw his diaper into the ring."[7]

This left the field wide open for the darkest of dark horses.

The Republicans may have been half-asleep, but Franklin Roosevelt wasn't. He knew Willkie: they had first met at the 1924 Democrat convention, where Roosevelt was keynote speaker and Willkie was a delegate. Roosevelt's aides say Willkie is the candidate he fears the most. The president has even gone on record saying that if hostilities in Europe were to end tomorrow and there be no threat of war, Willkie would win this election hands-down.

A PUBLIC BUSINESSMAN

Other than William McAdoo or Herbert Hoover, who were known for their years in public service, hardly any businessman has run for president. It would seem that the two professions call for entirely different skills. At the convention, in an obvious dig at

Willkie, Senator Taft's campaign manager distributed a declaration exclaiming, "[The] next president should be a Republican . . . deeply experienced in the science of government. He should know by experience how to cooperate with the legislative branch."8 But there is nothing unique or impressive about being a Republican per se—or a Democrat. Government is not a "science," which implies precision and certainty; it is an art. As for experience, what matters is not so much what the experience was in but what the candidate accomplished and learned from it. A legislative background, while helpful, is no assurance of success in dealing with the legislature—and certainly is no help in dealing with all the other sectors a president must face, such as the Supreme Court, Congress, the public, and our allies and enemies abroad.

The Taft statement of qualifications is obviously describing Taft. But it could also describe Willkie. He has been battling the TVA for years, arguing and negotiating power cost, prices, fixed costs, capitalization rates, excess generation—the kind of hard facts a scientist must work with. Facing a 600-pound gorilla that could put him out of business any day, he has cooperated with the TVA and managed to close a deal that made millions for his company even though he had the weaker hand. This is a much more impressive accomplishment than horse-trading with fellow congressmen over some esoteric legislation where you have nothing personal at stake. He is a master of the "science" and precision of numbers, and he is also a master of the "art" of negotiating.

When Willkie took over Commonwealth & Southern, the company was in deep trouble: it was a bloated, overextended colossus reminiscent of the infamous holding companies of the 1920s whose profits got siphoned off by the parent at the expense of the operating divisions. The founder and former chairman of C&S had recognized Willkie's talent and promoted him over fifty senior executives to be president at age forty-one, even though Willkie was only a legal counsel with no business experience. Willkie took to the road and spent over a hundred days a year visiting the subsidiaries and talking with the local managers. And he did more: to learn more about the local market and improve community relations, he visited the local newspaper editor, the library, the Chamber of Commerce, and the superintendent of schools in every town. The man has real sensitivity to people.

Observing the dictum of Justice Louis Brandeis, who bemoaned the devastating effect on corporations of directors who understood finance but knew nothing about business, Willkie removed the bankers from his board and replaced them with operations executives. Together they took a gamble and introduced an incentive rate system whereby the householder receives a bonus of free electricity once he uses a certain amount; for example, use ten dollars' worth of electricity, get another three dollars' worth for free. The federal government wanted the utility companies to lower their rates, which would have forced them to either go bankrupt or be sold to the government. Willkie, following the business model of Henry Ford, would protect himself against bankruptcy by generating so much volume he could still make money. Result? He produced electricity 27 percent cheaper than the national average. Brilliant.

Also, instead of complaining about the New Deal, like most other public utilities did, he would fight. When the TVA gave him a "take it or leave it" offer, he refused. He made himself a public figure and attracted national media attention by writing articles and speaking out in public. He was careful not to attack the idea of government regulation per se but rather specific, poorly drafted regulation and imperious bureaucracy insensitive to local concerns. He testified before Congress and gained national prominence as the spokesman for the public utility industry, an industry Roosevelt had promised to make the poster child for his New Deal reforms. Roosevelt wanted to wipe out all holding companies; Willkie had already cleaned up the financial abuses in his own company, making such criticism moot. Roosevelt pledged to give America more electric power at cheaper rates; Willkie had already done it—an example of "good" private enterprise. Under his leadership C&S sales more than tripled in five years. Earnings per share rose from one cent in 1935 to thirteen cents in 1936; 1940 earnings are projected to be eighteen cents.

Despite this impressive record the government still wanted to own C&S's subsidiary company in Tennessee, so under duress Willkie—after tough negotiating and getting a high price—sold it in early 1939. In his press release announcing the sale of Tennessee Power to the TVA, he issued a blunt warning to the government that sounded like a shot across the bow: "This transaction has demonstrated that no business, however well run, can endure against the competition of the Federal Government with its vast financial resources. But the loss of these properties will not be in vain if it serves to arouse the American people against government invasion of their business."[9]

Clearly this is not a man to go off quietly in the night. He may have lost one of his companies, but he had gained national stature. He was now in a position to enter politics at the highest level. On July 31, 1939, he appeared on the cover of *Time* as "the only businessman in the U.S. as a presidential possibility." Should Willkie defeat Roosevelt in the upcoming election, Roosevelt will rue the day he attacked the public utilities so cavalierly and turned one of its executives into a barnstorming political leader.

Make no mistake about it, Willkie is crystal-clear about who the enemy is. In a speech to a joint meeting of the Economics Club and the Harvard Business School Club of New York he said, "Any public-government service, no matter what zeal or humility its leaders may desire otherwise, tends to become arrogant, truculent and arbitrary in its attitude towards those it serves. The 'I issued the order—it must be obeyed' attitude is the inevitable accompaniment of bureaucracy and the vesting of independent power in the hands of public officials."[10] Thus Willkie tapped into the great public concern about big government and the excesses of the New Deal, which has done little to bring us out of the Depression over eight long years—and no relief in sight.

PERSONAL

Willkie has been married for twenty-four years. The cliché "Behind every great man there's a great woman" is certainly true of Willkie, with an unusual caveat: the woman is not his wife but his mistress.

Irita Van Doren is a divorcée and the influential book review editor of the *New York Herald Tribune*. They have been together since 1937 and spend weekends at her country home in Connecticut. Willkie makes no secret of their relationship; when he threw a party announcing his candidacy, he did it at Mrs. Van Doren's apartment. They spend most of their evenings with her media friends, who can be helpful to Willkie's political career. Their relationship appears to have broadened Willkie's horizons and sharpened his keen intellect. Having outgrown his Indiana wife and appalled by what he calls the "pedestrian thinking" of most politicians, he finds the intellectual friends of Mrs. Van Doren stimulating and challenging.[11]

Willkie's home address, according to the *New York Social Register*, is 1010 Fifth Avenue, across from the Metropolitan Museum of Art. But he is hardly ever there. When reporters want to get hold of him for a juicy quote, they know to call Mrs. Van Doren's apartment at 123 West 11th Street. Where this leaves Willkie's wife, Edith, is uncertain. Obviously they have an arrangement; a presidential candidate must be happily married, at least in public—that's part of the job description—and Edith is always at his side at political functions, playing the role of loyal spouse. The closest she's come to acknowledging her strange marital situation is to say, "Politics makes strange bedfellows."[12] One wonders if the pun was intended.

A tangled love life is not a virtue in a presidential candidate. Should the campaign get rough, the Democrats may be tempted to make an issue of it—or use it to blackmail Willkie to stop him from using any damaging information he has on them. And should he win the presidency, it will be interesting to see which woman moves into the White House; as president he certainly can't have both. (Most of his friends say it will be Mrs. Van Doren.)

Financial Disclosure and Charitable Activities

Willkie's net worth is around $500,000, all properly accounted for. His annual salary is $75,000. He was offered a pay raise but turned it down, saying he shouldn't be paid more than the president of the United States. (Actually he should be making more: unlike the president, he has to pay for his own housing.) He lives frugally, spending only $20,000 a year. The rest of the money he invests, mostly in the purchase of five large Indiana farms covering 1,500 acres; that's where he goes for vacation. He also donates a lot of money to charity. One of his gifts is quite remarkable: he has put fifty boys and girls through college, all on his own nickel.[13]

One day a young marketing executive in one of his companies came to him with a 1,200-page draft of a Civil War novel written by the man's wife, titled *Tomorrow Is Another Day*. Would Mr. Willkie, known to be a voracious reader and a fan of southern history, be kind enough to take a look at it? Willkie read it, then passed it along to Mrs. Van Doren, who loved it and arranged for it to be published by Macmillan. Today that book, retitled *Gone with the Wind*, has made the author rich. Willkie gave the husband a fat pay raise: It's not good for the wife to be making all the money, he joked with a hearty laugh.

Personality and Intellect

If personality and intellect were the sole criteria for choosing a president, we could do no better than Wendell Willkie. The man has a marvelous sense of humor. He proposed to the young Edith Wilk by asking, "How do you feel about adding a couple of letters to your name?"[14] At a meeting of utility executives where President Roosevelt announced his plan for the TVA to take over much of their business, Willkie reminded him that Commonwealth & Southern had been his power provider when he was recovering from polio at a health spa in Warm Springs, Georgia. "We give you good service, don't we?" he quipped. And when Willkie sold his Tennessee company to the TVA and received a big check from David Lilienthal at the public ceremony, Willkie teased him, "This is a lot of money for a couple of Indiana farmers to be kicking around."[15] Shortly thereafter Gen. Hugh Johnson suggested he run for president. Willkie responded, "If the government continues to take over my business, I may be looking for some new kind of job. General Johnson's is the best offer I've had so far."[16] Noting that he and FDR both became president of their enterprises in early 1933 and for the exact same salary, he cracked, "Roosevelt and I took office at the same time, only my company is running at a profit while his company is running at a loss."[17]

How can you not love a man like this? Many people do. He is such a natural, genuine person, reminiscent of William Henry Harrison. He is gregarious, outgoing, warm-hearted, and extremely likeable. Forget what Alice Roosevelt Longworth said about him;* this is a man who relates easily to people: factory worker, delivery boy, congressman, or fellow CEO. He likes to play the role of simple Indiana country bumpkin, but it's all an act: he is extremely well-read and can converse intelligently on a variety of topics in history and literature, not just business. What makes him unique is that he can also write intelligently and has written many articles for national magazines and newspapers such as the *Saturday Evening Post*, the *Atlantic*, *Reader's Digest*, and the *New York Herald Tribune*. He has made himself a darling of the media, who are entranced by his openness and winning personality and his mastery of the issues. Unlike most politicians or corporate executives, this is a man who thinks and can be counted upon to utter an original thought.

* Alice Roosevelt Longworth, the doyenne of Washington society and a woman known for her biting wit, was having a conversation with the journalist Joe Alsop. When Alsop commented that the movement for Willkie came from the grassroots, Mrs. Longworth gave a loud snort and said, "Yes, from the grass roots of 10,000 country clubs."[18]

He has enormous energy and drive. In a *New Yorker* interview he describes himself as the "best gadget salesman in the country," referring to the electrical appliances his company sells to boost usage of electricity.[19] He has the optimism of a super-salesman who believes he can sell anything and bend the world to his will.

He is an extraordinary presidential candidate for a party floundering for lack of leadership. Back several months ago, before the Philadelphia convention, the journalist Raymond Clapper made a prescient observation: "Republicans can nominate somebody who looks good in ephemeral straw votes, or some plodding politician. Or they can take a bold and audacious course, look at the job to be done, and select, regardless of tradition, the man best qualified to do it."

And who might that man be?

"They can leap over the 'keep off the grass' signs and nominate Wendell Willkie."[20]

The critical issue of the day is the war in Europe and whether the United States should become involved. The German flag is already fluttering over the Eiffel Tower, yet many leading Republicans seem to want to look the other way. Says Senator Arthur Vandenberg, "Protected by a great ocean on either side, the United States fear no other nation if we mind our own business."[21] Even more adamant is Herbert Hoover. American rearmament would arouse fear of America and "make us suspect of the whole world."[22] Were America to enter the war, he says, "we shall have sacrificed liberty for generations."[23]

In supporting the president on Lend-Lease, Willkie has drawn the ire and wrath of the isolationists in the Republican Party. Still he remained firm, demonstrating courage and adherence to his principles. Criticized by Democrats and Republicans alike for his perfidy in switching parties and then setting out a new course at odds with many Republicans, he responds, "I did not leave my party, my party left me."[24]

CONCLUSION

Willkie gave $150 to the Roosevelt campaign in 1932. He now says he would like his money back.

Being an internationalist liberal like Roosevelt, he has very few opportunities to stake out a different position. How can he attack Roosevelt if he essentially agrees with what he is doing? The socialist politician Norman Thomas points out that Willkie is in an impossible situation: "He agreed with Mr. Roosevelt's entire program of social reform and said it was leading to disaster."[25] Certainly on foreign affairs their views are very similar.

A president after two terms will have a lot of enemies. FDR, with his extensive New Deal programs that have yet to prove successful, is no exception. Governor Harold Stassen, Willkie's floor manager at the convention, says Willkie is the candidate "best fitted for the job" because he "can mobilize and unify the country to make it strong."[26] For sure, Willkie's lack of baggage and prior commitments will help him pursue whatever policies he chooses.

Willkie will bring more honest accounting to government. As head of a utility, he is thoroughly familiar with the shenanigans the TVA and other government programs perform to hide their true costs. Our country is running a dangerously large deficit that threatens to explode if we go to war. We need a president who possesses a sophisticated knowledge of finance and knows how to run a huge enterprise (a war machine).

He promises to bring to Washington a zeal to curb government arrogance. Many of the bureaucrats in charge of New Deal programs act as if they are running their own fiefdoms. Having borne the brunt of the TVA's ruthless ambition, Willkie knows how one-sided it can be. "Power is just as destructive on Pennsylvania Avenue as it was in Wall Street," he says. "Power goes to men's heads."[27]

He is a superb salesman; countless people who have had dealings with him say it is impossible to say no to him. His personal charisma and persuasiveness will serve him well in dealing with foreign leaders and in twisting the arms of congressmen to get legislation passed. As an administrator capable of running a large organization Willkie has few peers. He turned around a floundering company and made it one of the most successful corporations in the country. In his many public speeches and written articles he has demonstrated a passionate concern for public affairs. In his private charitable activities he has shown himself to be a man with heart.

We have three reservations about Willkie: he has no experience in foreign affairs at a time when the world is falling apart; he has no experience managing a government entity, in either an executive or a legislative capacity; he has never weathered the storms of running for elective office. (Only three men—Zachary Taylor,

Ulysses Grant, and Herbert Hoover—have won the presidency without having previously run for public office.)

The relationship between a leader and his public is symbiotic, as expressed in this marvelous quotation from the French: "There go my followers. I must follow them, for I am their leader."[28] Two months before he was nominated Willkie observed, "I seem to be in front of a trend."[29] Unlike either Dewey or Taft, who try to figure out what voters want and then try to give it to them, Willkie believes that "a public man must express his conviction and then try to persuade the people to follow him."[30] But he mustn't be too far in front. As FDR said after a lackluster reaction to one of his speeches calling for a quarantine of aggressor nations, "It is a terrible thing to look over your shoulder when you're trying to lead and find no one there."[31]

Although Willkie has achieved much, he will need to overcome his apparent dislike of politicians and become more disciplined in his frenetic activities lest he burn out. There is reason to be confident he can do so, for he had the discipline to become a lawyer, then a CEO, then a political party nominee for president. He possesses a high degree of executive ability, intellectual curiosity, and personal warmth, and he has the judgment and vision to be a first-rate president.

Accomplishments	Intangibles	Judgment	Overall
excellent	outstanding	outstanding	excellent

1940

Late in the campaign a treasure trove arrived at Republican Party headquarters: a collection of letters written in the 1930s by Roosevelt's running mate Henry Wallace to a Russian mystic who claimed to have found "the inner light." Among the "Dear Guru" letters were juicy tidbits like "I have been thinking of you holding the casket—the sacred most precious casket. And I have thought of the New Country going forth to meet the seven stars under the sign of the three stars. And I have thought of the admonition, 'Await the Stone.'" That was just for starters. "Long have I been aware of the occasional fragrance from that other world which is the real world. . . . Yes, the Chalice is filling."[32]

An astrologer and mystic for FDR's vice president? The letters could have destroyed the Democrats; instead they gave FDR's advisor Harry Hopkins an idea: using a candidate's private affairs as an election issue. He phoned Willkie and let it be known that the Democrats would be more than delighted to talk about his relationship with Irita Van Doren. Willkie got the message; he refrained from saying anything personal about FDR's running mate, as did Hopkins about Willkie's paramour. The 1940 election would be decided solely on the issues. Tabloid newspaper sales would remain low, and American voters would miss an opportunity to boost their spirits with salacious gossip.

. . .

Looking back, it is hard to imagine the isolationism that once gripped America's political leaders. In 1940 John Foster Dulles, Dewey's chief foreign policy advisor and later secretary of state under Eisenhower, called Hitler "a passing phenomenon."[33] Asked if Hitler would threaten the existence of France and England, Hoover dismissed the question: "It was too impossible an event to warrant comment."[34] On another occasion Hoover said that because Hitler was going to rule the world, America should have a president who had not alienated him and could do business with him. Fortunately the man who won the Republican nomination was neither Dewey nor Hoover but a man with quite different ideas.

The campaign season in those days was brief, running from Labor Day in early September to the election in early November. Just like he promised, Willkie ran his campaign as a crusade: he traveled thirty thousand miles in fifty-one days, almost all by train, and gave 550 speeches to 2.5 million people. Never very well-organized, he neglected to pace himself, and after several weeks of giving so many speeches, his booming bear-like voice became a froggie croak. His handlers tried hard to get him to slow down and take better care of himself and to focus his message and not talk about so many issues at once.

Rarely has a candidate stirred the voters like Wendell Willkie, a man out of nowhere.

Willkie had three-quarters of the nation's newspapers behind him as he attacked Roosevelt's lack of military preparedness and poor economic performance (unemployment was at 15 percent). However, because he strongly supported Roosevelt on lend-lease and the draft and did not blindly embrace the Republican platform, he got only lukewarm support from Party loyalists. In fact the journalist Marquis Childs observed that many Republican congressmen had "an antipathy toward Willkie almost greater than their hatred of Roosevelt."[35]

Roosevelt trounced Willkie by five million popular votes and won 449–82 in the Electoral College. Still Willkie got more popular votes than any Republican candidate had ever gotten, even more than Dewey would get in 1944 or 1948. Running against one of the greatest presidential campaigners of all time, Willkie's winning ten states "was equivalent to a man staying ten rounds with Joe Louis," said the journalist John Gunther.[36] Roosevelt won the election only because he had a lock on the South and the urban poor; everywhere else Willkie was the leader. Willkie was handicapped because he was too good a man to attack the New Deal and Roosevelt's foreign policy, both of which he essentially agreed with. The only message he could deliver was that he could manage better—hardly the stuff that wins elections. With the nation facing the prospect of war, such a claim was too big a risk for the voters to take.

A week after the election Willkie gave his "Loyal Opposition" speech calling for an end to acrimony and for the nation to support the president in dangerous times. The isolationist Republicans would have none of it. Never terribly enthusiastic about Willkie, they now wanted little to do with him, especially after he agreed to serve as Roosevelt's emissary on a three-week trip to Great Britain in 1941. Roared the *Chicago Tribune*, "He was a Republican by name for less than a year and that period was much too long. The party will take leave of its late standard bearer with the hope that it will never again see him or he it."[37] Several Republican congressmen stood up in House and called him a "Roosevelt stooge" and "the Dr. Jekyll and Mr. Hyde of American politics." For supporting the president and meeting with Winston Churchill, they said, he had become "America's Number One Warmonger."[38]

A year later he was Roosevelt's personal envoy to the Middle East, the Soviet Union, and China. He became alarmed at the dreams of glory uttered by Churchill and de Gaulle, who wanted to keep their colonial empires; in his talks with leaders of emerging nations, all looking for moral leadership from the world's strongest democracy, he saw a quite different future—and danger for America. "When the aspiration of India for freedom was put aside to some future date," he wrote, "it was not Great Britain that suffered in public esteem in the Far East. It was the United States."[39] Upon his return in October 1942 he gave a radio talk to an audience of thirty-six million people, a number exceeded only by Roosevelt's announcement of the Japanese attack on Pearl Harbor. "There are no more distant points in the world any longer," he said. "The myriad millions of human beings of the Far East are as close to us as Los Angeles is to New York. . . . What concerns them must concern us, almost as much as the problems of the people of California concern the people of New York."[40]

Roosevelt agreed entirely, but it was not a message the Republicans wanted to hear. Then Willkie drove a stake into their isolationist heart: he wrote a book about his trip in which he declared that the United States had better start planning for the future after the Allies won the war. Edited by Irita Van Doren, *One World* became "the most widely-read and discussed non-fiction book of the 20th century," selling three million copies in over twenty languages.[41] The isolationists went ballistic; the military obviously didn't like it; even Roosevelt was put in a bit of an awkward position. But the American people loved it.

Willkie decided to run again for president, but the Republican chiefs wanted no more of this crusading Judas in their midst. For a man of such vision and talent, there was no worthy job in America except president. He couldn't run as a Democrat because Roosevelt was a Democrat, and as a Republican he couldn't expect an open door at the top, like he enjoyed in 1940; he had no enemies back then, but he had lots of them in 1944. This time he would have to undertake a long slog through the Republican local primaries—all unfriendly territory.

Going against his political advisors, Willkie listened to his financial managers, who argued that to raise the huge amounts of money required for a national campaign he must score a high-risk knockout victory in an extreme isolationist state like Wisconsin. Willkie, his judgment clouded by anger at the way he was being treated by the party bosses, went for the gamble. For two weeks he tromped through the state giving forty speeches, including driving two hundred miles in a snowstorm to give three of them. He was confident he would win the majority of Wisconsin's twenty-four delegates; his local coordinator believed he could win them all. None of his opponents campaigned, but Willkie gave it everything he had.

The result was a stunner. Wisconsin voters didn't want a new world and international responsibilities; they wanted their boys back home. Of the twenty-four delegates, Willkie failed to win a single one. Hoping for a 24–0 showing, it was 0–24, one of the greatest reversals in all politics. Willkie abruptly withdrew from the campaign. He would try again in 1948, he vowed.

Then fate intervened. In September 1944, after writing seven newspaper articles about key issues facing a postwar America, Willkie developed chest pains and checked into a New York hospital for observation. Over the next few weeks he had fourteen heart attacks. In between them he was as busy as ever, reading newspapers, entertaining a continuous stream of visitors (including his wife and his lover, careful to arrive at different hours), negotiating to buy a Chicago newspaper, and starting work with a close friend, the executive secretary of the NAACP, to write a book about the struggle for racial equality. In early October, just as he was getting ready to leave the hospital, he fell over dead, age fifty-two.

. . .

In his five years as the second most influential man in America, Wendell Willkie had sharpened the public debate and written a blockbuster book. "In a life unbelievably full of satisfaction," he said, the success of *One World* had brought him "the richest satisfaction of all." Some heard echoes of Henry Clay, who said, "I'd rather be right than president."[42] One of his last visitors in the hospital was the journalist Roscoe Drummond to whom Willkie afterward wrote, "If I could write my own epitaph, and if I had to choose between saying 'Here lies an unimportant president' or

'Here lies one who contributed to saving freedom at a moment of great peril,' I would prefer the latter."[43]

After Willkie's death Walter Lippmann observed, "Second only to the Battle of Britain, the sudden rise and nomination of Willkie was the decisive event, perhaps, providential, which made it possible to rally the free world when it was almost conquered. Under any other leadership but his, the Republican party would have turned its back upon Great Britain, causing all who still resisted Hitler to feel that they were abandoned."[44] When FDR's top advisor Harry Hopkins, hearing about Willkie's death, made a caustic comment, Roosevelt whirled around in anger: "Don't ever say anything like that around here again! Don't even *think* it. You of all people ought to know that we might not have had Lend Lease or Selective Service or a lot of other things if it hadn't been for Wendell Willkie. He was a godsend to this country when we needed him most."[45]

Roosevelt, more than any other man in America, appreciated Willkie. Back in 1941, after winning the lend-lease battle, he had startled the guests at a big political dinner by standing up and announcing, "Wendell Willkie—in word and in action—is showing what patriotic Americans mean by rising above partisanship and rallying to the common cause."[46] The president even instructed his son James to have a little fun with the party regulars and inform them that he and Willkie just might run together in 1944—sending the party leaders into temporary panic.

Probably the finest compliment Willkie received came from the man who had beaten him for the presidency. "I'm glad I won," FDR said, "but I'm sorry Wendell lost."[47]

In losing Wendell Willkie, America lost one of the most dynamic and creative men ever to run for president. Of the several hundred candidates who never got the nomination or who won the nomination but lost the election, only a few have gone on to achieve greater stature. This is a very small club: the elite also-rans, the true greats. They include DeWitt Clinton, George Marshall, and Wendell Willkie. In his decision to address the most divisive question of the day, Willkie showed the kind of vision that marks a great leader.

In 1937, three years before he became world-famous, *Fortune* magazine predicted this smart, savvy, homespun "simplifier of national issues" out of Indiana could be another Abraham Lincoln.[48] Willkie was the most forceful candidate since Lincoln to champion the rights of African Americans; he also was the first to run on a platform advocating equal rights for women. In economic and international affairs he identified the critical issues facing the nation and proposed the proper response:

1. We needed the New Deal and greater regulation of business, but excessive bureaucracy was a serious brake on economic recovery and personal liberties.
2. Hitler was a threat that must be obliterated; there could be no compromise.
3. Wars don't end when the fighting stops; to win the peace America must exercise the boundless goodwill it enjoys while it lasts (which won't be long).

Based on what we know now, Roosevelt had it half-right on the first, right on the second, and never got to do the third.

Willkie had it right on all three. In losing him America lost a remarkable man who would have made an excellent president anytime from 1940 to 1952. Very few candidates are fit over such a broad time period. Such breadth is a mark of true greatness.

11

· ·

George C. Marshall, 1944

In the middle of a war, with victory starting to look imminent, we are hardly going to change leaders. Franklin Roosevelt, now completing a third term, intends to run again and finish the job he set out to do. It doesn't take a genius to see that we have a problem: the president's health. His pallor, his trembling hands: it is impossible to believe the man can live another four years, especially under the strains of the presidency. Unless he can be persuaded to step down, he must take special care in choosing his vice president. The current vice president, Henry Wallace, has outlived his usefulness: FDR no longer needs the farm vote. Now that the war is going reasonably well, the president is sure to win and has no need to balance the ticket. He can select his running mate solely on the basis of qualifications.

Among the politicians, advisors, generals, and other leaders available to him, one man stands out: Gen. George Marshall, the army chief of staff and *Time*'s Man of the Year in 1943. "The closest thing to 'the indispensable man,'" the magazine called him. "He has armed the Republic. He has kept faith with the people. In a general's uniform, he stood for the civilian substance of this democratic society. Civis Americanus, he had gained the world's undivided respect."[1]

Senator Edwin Johnson of Colorado recently proposed General

Marshall as the Democratic candidate in 1944. Several columnists took this up; one wrote, "On the basis of personal merits, can you think of a more desirable successor to President Roosevelt?" Marshall immediately put out a disclaimer: "General Marshall would no more think of lending himself to such a proposition than he would resign his post in the midst of a battle."[2]

Unless, of course, he was ordered to do so by the president. Were that to happen, according to *Time*, Marshall would become "a trustee for the nation."

GEORGE C. MARSHALL

Age: sixty-three

6 feet tall, 180 pounds

Excellent health

Married; two stepchildren living,
one killed in action, 1944

Home address:

Dodona Manor

Leesburg, Virginia

OBJECTIVE: Whatever position the president asks me to accept.

MILITARY CAREER

Chief of Staff, U.S. Army, 1939–Present

Led U.S. effort in World War II as architect of America's military strategy and director of personnel and logistics. Named *Time*'s Man of the Year, 1943.

Strategy: supported the president in his Europe-first policy, despite the objections of the navy, Gen. Douglas MacArthur, and many politicians and media who argued for making Japan our primary target; juggled needs of national defense to provide sufficient arms and supplies to ensure survival of Britain; kept together coalition of difficult allies (Russia, Britain, France); demonstrated diplomatic skills at numerous international conferences; regarded by President Roosevelt as "the best man at the conference table";[3] joined president at all major international conferences with leaders of Allies: at sea (Atlantic Charter), Quebec, Casablanca, Teheran, and Cairo; developed winning strategy for the war; rejected British strategy of blockade, bombing, and insurrection as being too complicated and lengthy; convinced president the war would be decided in a major land battle, not in the air, and to increase budget requests for non-airplane expenditures: increased number of planes from 1,064 to 69,000, troops from 174,000 to 8.5 million, and officers from 13,000 to 764,000.[4]

Personnel: transformed the world's seventeenth-largest army into number one in just five years; reorganized army by dividing

234

it into three commands (Ground Forces, Air Forces, and Supply) reporting to Operations Division; eliminated antiquated fiefdoms such as infantry, cavalry, field artillery, and coast artillery; reduced number of subordinates reporting directly to the chief of staff from sixty officers to six and gave these six new officers increased power; played key role in winning the support of congressmen in successful extension of the draft in 1941 (passed by one vote, 203 to 202); broke with tradition and eliminated the "hump" in the officer corps ranking by seniority, thereby allowing younger men to bypass older men no longer fit for fighting; successfully pushed for unified command in the field over coalition of different nationalities of soldiers; selected Dwight Eisenhower over hundreds of more senior officers to be the U.S. general in North Africa and eventual commanding general of the Allied Invasion of Normandy.

Logistics: master-minded and directed the greatest logistical operation in history: ordering and delivering equipment, spare parts, supplies, food, and accommodations for over eight million men and women in Europe, the Middle East, Asia, and the Pacific; successfully pushed for allocation of war production to be handled by the military, not by civilians; cooperated with and earned commendation from Senator Harry Truman's congressional investigation of national defense spending.

Deputy Chief of Staff, U.S. Army 1938–1939

Pushed for a balanced army in opposition to proposal to build fifteen thousand planes; lined up support in Congress and testified before congressional committees; promoted by the president to chief of staff over thirty-three more senior generals.

Various ranks, U.S. Army, 1902–1938

Brigadier general, 1936–38: commander of brigade stationed in state of Washington; responsible for thirty-five Civilian Conservation Corps camps. Chief of Staff, National Guard, Chicago, 1933–36: chief training officer, appointed by Army Chief of Staff Douglas MacArthur. Colonel, 1933: stationed in South Carolina; set up fifteen Civilian Conservation Corps camps.

Lieutenant colonel, 1924–32: assistant commandant at Fort Benning and Fort Screven; instituted major reforms to modernize training and replace rigid operational thinking; stressed new infantry tactics and mobility; instituted "the Benning Revolution" of "move, shoot and communicate" (and show concern for your men); lecturer, Army War College, 1927; stationed in China, 1924–27. Major (promoted 1920), 1918–24: aide to Gen. John J. Pershing, army chief of staff; stationed in France and Washington, DC; in France directed movement of six hundred thousand men and nine hundred thousand tons of supplies and munitions in the successful Meuse-Argonne offensive, 1918; awarded Legion of Honor from the French government, 1919; earned nickname "Wizard" for quality staff work. Commissioned second lieutenant in army, 1902.

EDUCATION

U.S. Infantry and Cavalry School, 1906–1908

Entered as the youngest and lowest-ranking officer. Ranked first in class in first year; no class rank given in second year, but selected as one in five students invited to stay on as instructor (declined, to go straight into the army).

Virginia Military Institute, 1897–1901

Graduated fifteenth in class of thirty-four survivors of original class of 121; no demerits; majored in civil engineering; appointed by faculty to be first captain (highest-ranking cadet). Tackle on varsity football team; All-Southern selection.

PERSONAL

Grew up in western Pennsylvania. Married Lily Coles in 1902; she died in 1927. Offered position as superintendent of the Virginia Military Institute in 1927; turned it down. Married Katherine Tupper Brown in 1930. Hobbies: horseback riding, hunting, tennis, bird shooting, and gardening.

GEORGE C. MARSHALL, 1944

Assessment of Qualifications

Naming Marshall its 1943 Man of the Year, *Time* magazine avers he is someone the American people "trust more than they have trusted any military man since George Washington." In fact as a candidate Marshall bears an uncanny resemblance to our founding president that goes far beyond their shared first name. Both have reached the very top of the U.S. Army and have superb political skills, getting along with congressmen and with other countries in a coalition war. Although Marshall is a "staff" executive and has never commanded troops in battle, whereas Washington was a "line" executive, both have over forty years of leadership experience, are master strategists, have demonstrated superb executive ability in assigning responsibilities and choosing good subordinates, and enjoy enormous respect from their peers. *Time* concludes that Marshall is "the one and only U.S. citizen who (as a Republican Congressman once suggested), could get at any time a unanimous vote of confidence from Congress."[5] Does that not remind you of Washington, unanimously chosen four times (as head general, convention president, and twice president)? It has taken 150 years, but we have another Washington.

Like Washington, Marshall supports civilian control of the military. Also like Washington, he disdains messy politics and the idea of running for office. If he is to be president it will be because he was chosen. Roosevelt is now in his third term and in failing health, highly unlikely to live long. This means that the delegates at this year's Democrat National Convention are nominating *two* presidents, not one. Rumor has it that FDR is unhappy with his current vice president, Henry Wallace, and is looking to replace him. Who will it be? Certainly a logical choice is his most trusted advisor, General Marshall, the architect and likely commander of the pivotal battle of the war, our invasion of France (expected to take place before the convention in mid-July).

Says nationally syndicated columnist Westbrook Pegler, "Gen. George Marshall may be unavailable because of his commitments and his sense of loyalty and duty, but just on the basis of personal merit can you think of a more desirable successor to President

Roosevelt?"[6] Adds Senator Edwin Johnson from Colorado, "The Democratic Party owes it to the people to draft Gen. Marshall for President. He is not a candidate and he will emphatically say no, but no patriotic American from George Washington down can refuse such a call."[7]

Marshall says he is not interested in running for high office, but if his boss asks him, he will never say no. Should he get the call to become vice president (and thus likely president someday), we best be prepared. Hence this appraisal.

. . .

General Marshall is a military statesman, a master of bureaucracy, a man behind the scenes. He is not a field commander or war hero. He is no Douglas MacArthur, seeking military glory for himself. He is the ultimate team player.

Typical of Marshall, he does not state in his résumé that he is ranked first as "the individual who has made the greatest contribution to the nation's leadership in the past two years," according to a *Newsweek* poll of newsmen and historians. (FDR ranked second.)[8] Ask him about his accomplishments and you will find a man extremely modest and taciturn. He does not push his own agenda or reach for power. To the contrary, he has had power thrust upon him.

Our favorite reference check on him is a performance appraisal dated 1916, when he was thirty-five. In response to the standard form question, "Would you like to have this officer under your command?," Marshall's superior officer wrote, "This officer is well qualified to command a division, with the rank of major general, in time of war, and I would like very much to serve under *his* command."[9]

In World War I he was Gen. John Pershing's fastest-rising officer, eventually becoming Pershing's right-hand man, responsible for the operations and logistics of over one million American soldiers. Pershing recommended that General MacArthur promote Colonel Marshall to brigadier general, but MacArthur refused. Years later MacArthur found himself under Marshall's command in matters of coordination (albeit both men were then four-star generals).

Ever since he was an instructor at Fort Benning, Marshall has disdained officers who go by the book and lack independent thought. In pushing for the draft and building up a huge citizen army, he discarded the monotonous drilling and blind obedience he saw in the French Army when he was fighting in the trenches of World War I. In his words, military discipline must grow out of "respect rather than fear; on the effect of good example given by officers; on the intelligent comprehension by all ranks of why an order has to be and why it must be carried out; on a sense of duty, on *esprit de corps.*" "It is morale that wins the victory," he says.[10] Certainly this stance is not new. What is new is where the responsibility lies: in the commander. Commanders who complained to Marshall about the morale of their troops quickly got sacked.

Three years ago, when he promoted Dwight Eisenhower over 366 more senior officers, Marshall told him precisely what he expected: "Eisenhower, the department is filled with able men who analyze their problems but feel compelled always to bring them to me for final solution. I must have assistants who will solve their own problems and tell me later what they have done."[11] Eisenhower recalls Marshall insisting, "When you disagree with my point of view, say so, without an apologetic approach; when you want something you aren't getting, tell me and I will try to get it for you."[12] Such is Marshall talking to a subordinate. How about Marshall to his boss? Here is what he said to Assistant Secretary of State Dean Acheson: "I shall expect of you the most complete frankness, particularly about myself. I have no feelings except those I reserve for Mrs. Marshall."[13]

Marshall has never been afraid to take the initiative and speak up, even at the risk of offending his superiors. In 1917, stationed in France during his first combat assignment, he was the only officer willing to bluntly tell General Pershing that inadequate supplies were affecting troop morale and performance. Similarly in May 1940, in a meeting with the president, Marshall was the only man in a room of ten to speak up and disagree, asking "Mr. President, may I have three minutes?"[14] If you're going to contradict your boss in public, you better be on firm footing and know your facts. Marshall did. In what turned out to be a lot longer than three minutes, he laid out a devastating critique of America's lack of preparedness and carried the day.

An army is not a democracy; it operates on a merit system. Throughout his career Marshall has strived to improve that system. He changed the rules so that graduates of Ivy League schools don't automatically become officers; they have to take several weeks of accelerated basic training to bring them up to the level of their fellow soldiers who have undergone the entire program. In addition, concerned about the blockage of advancement opportunities because of too many officers at the top waiting to retire, Marshall instituted a two-track system: a merit system as well as a system based on seniority. This caused howls of protest by senior officers bypassed for promotion but resulted in improved morale and a more professional army.

PLANNING AND LOGISTICS

Nothing gets a soldier more riled up and discouraged than to arrive at a post with no blankets, no food, and a gun that doesn't work. Hard to believe, but the basic infantry rifle in 1940 was a Springfield rifle made in 1903. Basic planning was woefully out of date: when Adm. Ernest King took over as commander of the Atlantic fleet in 1941, he found in the locked safe of his ship's cabin a strategic plan—for a war with Mexico.

Isolated instances of a fossilized military living in a time warp? Hardly. Taking over as the new chief of staff, Marshall found that little had changed in the army bureaucracy since his days in Texas thirty years earlier, when he needed fourteen signatures to get food for his men.

Marshall single-handedly undertook a massive reorganization of the U.S. Army. He divided the army into three commands and streamlined reporting relationships so that logistics would always get high priority. This required a level of strategic thinking rarely seen in the military. What good would extra planes be, for example, without trained pilots, crews, and ground support? And how about the planes themselves? When Roosevelt glibly talked about "clouds of airplanes," it was Marshall who had to remind the president that it normally took five years to design a new bomber, plus another year to build it.[15] (An airplane has 165,000 parts, plus 150,000 rivets.)[16] When Gen. Hap Arnold wanted more bombs to support his raids on Germany, the problem wasn't lack of money; it was lack of time: manufacturing a bomb could take months. Same for machine guns and semi-automatic rifles: first you have to set up a whole network of parts suppliers.

Marshall is an extraordinary decision maker: he doesn't fight problems; he decides them. Under his vigorous leadership the U.S. Army became a high-powered procurement and production machine. While there were mistakes and cost overruns (many of them identified by Truman's Senate Committee to Investigate the National Defense Program), there was not a whiff of scandal about Marshall. If anything, there was just the opposite. "I got to know General Marshall really well," says Truman, "and I got to know that you could depend on every word he said, and that he just never would lie to you, and that he always knew what he was talking about."[17]

The complexity of managing America's wartime production machine was staggering. For example, it was discovered that eight Liberty ships could carry the same number of 2.5-ton trucks disassembled as it took one hundred ships to carry assembled trucks. By setting up local facilities to do the simple assembly, the army could deliver twelve times as many trucks.[18]

Of all the general's many deeds, perhaps the most significant occurred on August 7, 1940: he shocked Congress with a supplemental request for $4 billion for supplies and housing before Congress had even voted for the draft! This is a man who thinks ahead. When he took over as army chief of staff, he found the War Department had developed six different plans for fighting a two-ocean war. Marshall revised and combined them into one plan, with Germany as the priority target.

He has a demonstrated track record in working well with Congress. He testified eighteen times in his successful 1941 effort to get Congress to approve extending the draft. (The measure passed by only one vote.) Had it not been for Marshall, this bill would not have passed and America would have found itself in severe straits when Pearl Harbor occurred. When he goes to Congress to plead for more money for his military programs, he deliberately wears a business suit, not a military uniform, making it clear that he is a servant of civilian authority. Marshall always conducts himself with dignity and rectitude. No matter how silly or exasperating a congressman's questions might be, Marshall responds respectfully and invariably wins over his adversaries.

A COALITION GENERAL

Napoleon once said that enemies are bad, but allies are even worse. World War II is unique in being the first war largely fought by a coalition, requiring many divisions to fight under the leadership of other countries' generals. Coordinating so many men in different parts of the world put enormous strains on supply and logistics, but even more important it required deft dealing with egotistical generals. Marshall had to manage not only his own generals; he had to keep Churchill and Stalin happy, each of whom could rightfully claim his country was carrying a greater burden of fighting than the United States was. Furthermore he had his own commander in chief—not the easiest man to deal with.

Not a single one of these leaders has a critical word to say about Marshall. Roosevelt thinks his support invaluable. Churchill praises Marshall effusively. So too does Stalin. Anybody who can handle these giants can surely handle any senator or adversary a president might face. Marshall's skills at coalition management should readily translate into the give-and-take of political management. Rarely does one find a potential presidential candidate skilled at both coalition management and executive management.

On the criteria of administration and diplomacy, Marshall's performance is outstanding: he correctly perceived the need for dramatic remobilization. But on questions requiring vision and imagination as chief planner for the army, Marshall—like everyone in Washington—failed to foresee the attack on Pearl Harbor.

Early in the summer of 1941 he was asked by the president if there was any threat to Hawaii. Marshall told him that Oahu, a mountainous island with fortifications and garrisons, was "the strongest fortress in the world" and that "a major attack against Oahu is considered impractical."[19]

On December 4, 1943, in Cairo, FDR and Marshall had a lunch to discuss his future role in the administration. At the urging of General Pershing, the members of the Joint Chiefs, and many members of Congress, the president decided that Marshall—in charge of armies on four continents—was too essential to be spared to go to Europe and take field command of a single theater. It would be, in effect, a demotion. Much though he wanted Marshall to be "the Pershing of World War II" and get the battlefield glory he deserved, FDR vacillated. He asked Marshall what position he wanted. Obviously Marshall wanted the Normandy command, but he didn't feel it was his duty to say so. Disappointed when Marshall told him such a decision was up to the president and not up to him as a subordinate, FDR reluctantly chose Eisenhower instead, telling Marshall, "I could not sleep at night with you out of the country."[20]

The president's decision is understandable: America must win the war, doing whatever it takes. We only hope the war will end before Roosevelt has to decide about a successor. Then Marshall will be free of his wartime responsibilities and be available for a civilian position. Like FDR, all Americans will sleep better should this man eventually become our next president. Very few men who are ideal in war are ideal in peace; this is one of them.

Accomplishments	Intangibles	Judgment	Overall
outstanding	excellent	excellent	excellent

1944

The call for Marshall to be FDR's running mate never came. With the stunning Allied victory in June in Normandy (the invasion—

Marshall and FDR at the Casablanca Conference, early 1943. The mole on the side of FDR's face is the melanoma that would cut his life short.

masterminded by Marshall and carried out by Eisenhower—succeeded in just one day), Roosevelt knew he was well on the way to achieving victory in Europe. It was only a matter of time before the Third Reich collapsed—but not in time for the Democratic National Convention.

Even though he was in frail health, FDR insisted on running for a fourth term. He gave no serious thought to selecting a successor should he die in office—a possibility he had to know was extremely likely. He kept Marshall in his position of chief of staff and left it to the convention to choose between a man he didn't want (Wallace) and a man he barely knew (Truman). After winning in November, he never bothered to bring Truman into his inner circle as he had with Marshall. No man ever became president more ill-prepared than Harry Truman, which is why Eleanor Roosevelt's first words to him were so poignant: "Is there anything we can do for you? You're the one in trouble now."[21]

The war continued. FDR's dismal performance at Yalta, where he excoriated Churchill and let himself be manipulated by the wily Stalin, showed he had no business serving a fourth term. He had lost so much weight he seemed to be dying. One glance at him and the ruthless Stalin privately rejoiced, while Churchill winced, knowing full well what was coming. For Marshall it must have been excruciating.

In December 1944, along with MacArthur, Eisenhower, Arnold, and Admirals Leahy, King, and Nimitz, Marshall was awarded a fifth star, putting these men on a virtual par with Ulysses Grant and John Pershing as the highest-ranking officers in American history after George Washington.[22]

After the war Marshall went on to an even more illustrious career as special envoy to China, secretary of state,* and secretary of defense. He was *Time*'s Man of the Year again, in 1947, making him the only nonpresident to win it twice. He conceived and executed America's most imaginative foreign aid program, which he called the European Recovery Plan and everyone else called the Marshall Plan. The man he personally picked to command the Normandy invasion and reap all the glory eventually became president in 1952. Compared to all the people in our history who ran for president and didn't win, few men came as close as this man who never ran but was seriously considered. All it would have taken was the vote of his greatest admirer. Had FDR picked him as running mate, he would have become president in 1945. Had FDR insisted he command the Normandy invasion, he—not Eisenhower—would have been the war hero and elected president by popular acclaim in 1952. That's two times he could have become president.

* For six months this position under Truman made him second in line to the presidency, there being no vice president at the time, until the Presidential Succession Act of 1947 was enacted to make the Speaker of the House the next in line.

Dean Acheson got to know Marshall well toward the end of the war and afterward, when he served as Marshall's number 2 man in the State Department and succeeded him as secretary of state. In his book about the leaders he had known, Acheson writes, "The moment General Marshall entered a room, everyone in it felt its presence. It was a striking and communicated force. His figure conveyed intensity, which his voice, low, staccato, and incisive, reinforced. It compelled respect. It spread a sense of authority and of calm. There was no military glamour about him and nothing of the martinet."[23]

The accolades accorded Marshall after World War II were glittering. "The greatest Roman of them all," said Churchill. Stalin, the man who trusted nobody, declared, "I would trust General Marshall with my life."[24] Henry L. Stimson, secretary of war during World War II and a man who had served seven presidents, from Taft to FDR, told Marshall, "I have seen a great many soldiers in my lifetime and you, sir, are the finest soldier I have ever known."[25] Giving him an honorary degree at its 1947 commencement, where he announced the Marshall Plan, Harvard University compared him to George Washington. President Truman, who gave him three of the most critical jobs in his administration, called him "the greatest living American" and "one for the ages."[26]

In choosing to hang on to the presidency in 1944 without making serious plans for succession, FDR may have committed one of the most irresponsible acts ever made by a president. That we ended up with Harry Truman was due only to good luck.

12

Henry A. Wallace, 1948

This summer has seen the hottest politics in Philadelphia since the Constitutional Convention of 1787. Both parties held their convention here, in the sweltering 103 degree heat. The Republicans came first and nominated two hugely popular governors, Thomas E. Dewey of New York for president and Earl Warren of California for vice president—a dream ticket. Then came the Democrats, renominating President Harry Truman. In what was expected to be a dull convention, Truman brought the delegates to their feet with the greatest acceptance speech ever given, vowing to fight to the finish and win.

Following this pandemonium came a third party, also holding its convention in the heat of the City of Brotherly Love: the Progressive Party, headed by Henry Wallace, vice president of the United States until FDR suddenly replaced him with Truman. Had Wallace stayed on as vice president for just another eighty-two days until FDR died, he would now be the thirty-third president of the United States.

Wallace's defection from the Democratic Party has put party strategists in a panic. Opines the *New York Times*, "He is ready to run for President on a third ticket, and he is not deterred by the thought that this action may chiefly injure the party which twice honored him with Cabinet Office and once elected him to the

Vice Presidency."[1] Wallace has other ideas. In his radio broadcast announcing his candidacy, he laid it on the line: "We have assembled a Gideon's army, small in number, powerful in conviction, ready for action. . . . We face the future unfettered by any principle but the general welfare. . . . By God's grace, the people's peace will usher in the century of the common man."[2]

At the convention, packed with three thousand delegates, he

unveiled a platform advocating arms reduction, economic aid to Russia, termination of the Marshall Plan, abandonment of overseas military bases, greater control of Big Business, and elimination of discrimination against blacks and women. His subsequent public appearances have become rallies not unlike religious festivals, and to his young followers he is a modern Isaiah. America has never seen anything like it before.

The political establishment views him with derision—and fear. Says the Democratic national committeeman from Indiana, "He is a much confused man and always had his thingamajigs mixed up with his whatchamacallits."[3] Adds one of the senators from Illinois, "He won't get enough votes to wad a shotgun."[4]

He is such an idealistic oddball pursuing his own drummer that Washington insiders can't figure him out. He neither smokes nor drinks. He is not a social type who enjoys parties and small talk. He is enormously wealthy yet lives very modestly, even plainly. He is the Lone Ranger of American politics. And he has a sixteen-year record of accomplishment in the federal government that no Democrat or Republican candidate can match. In 1932–35, while Wallace was dazzling Washington with his administrative brilliance as secretary of agriculture, Harry Truman was a local county judge in Missouri and Thomas E. Dewey, fresh out of law school, was beginning his career as a federal prosecutor in New York.

HENRY A. WALLACE

Age: fifty-nine

Married; three children,
ages thirty-three, thirty,
and twenty-eight

Favorite hobbies: gardening,
reading, playing tennis

Fluent in Spanish (self-taught)

Home address:

South Salem

New York

(fifty miles north of New York City)

OBJECTIVE: Thirty-fourth president of the United States

PUBLIC SECTOR EXPERIENCE

Founder, Progressive Party, 1947

Editor, *New Republic*, 1946–1947

Hold honorary title at liberal political magazine.

U.S. Secretary of Commerce, 1945–1946

Offered any cabinet position other than State by FDR, chose Commerce. Overcame opposition by conservatives and ensured passage of the 1946 Employment Act. Author, *60 Million Jobs*. Created the Office of Science and Technology to assist small businesses. Strengthened the Department of Commerce's foreign trade offices and promoted postwar economic development. Last surviving member of FDR's cabinet; fired by President Truman for giving speeches advocating a conciliatory approach to the Soviet Union.

Democratic Party Nominee for Vice President of the United States, 1944

Lost party nomination to Senator Harry Truman.

Vice President of the United States, 1940–1944

Transformed meaningless office into supervisory role over postwar planning, national defense, and the economy; cited by *New York Times* columnist James Reston as "not only Vice President, but 'Assistant President.'"[5] Chairman of the Board of Economic Warfare, responsible for overseeing war production. Member of the Top Policy Group, a five-man committee advising the president on the atom bomb. Gave numerous speeches, the most notable being "The Price of Free World Victory," translated into twenty languages and distributed throughout the world. Compendium of speeches published as a book, *The Century of the Common Man*. Conducted highly acclaimed tour of Latin America, drawing massive crowds.

U.S. Secretary of Agriculture, 1932–1940

Created the most successful department of the New Deal, known as "the Idea Factory": increased number of employees from 40,000 to 146,000 (easily the largest department in the federal government); created a government national granary to store crops in good years for distribution in lean years, thus ensuring a stable market and dependable supply; instituted extensive programs to encourage farmers to curtail production so as to support farm prices; foresaw Supreme Court objections to the Agricultural Adjustment Act farm relief program and instituted the Soil Conservation and Domestic Allotment Act of 1936; created the Farm Security Administration to combat rural poverty; successfully raised farm prices and income 70 percent; prolific public speaker on foreign policy; helped FDR combat the national mood of isolationism.

Predicted by many newspapers to become FDR's successor president at the end of his second term in 1940. When FDR decided to run for a third term, selected by him to be his running mate; played lead role in campaign and gave numerous speeches in all forty-eight states to help the FDR-Wallace ticket win by a landslide.

Founder, *Pioneer Hi-Bred, Inc.*, 1926

Created highly successful company providing hybrid corn seeds. Company now playing major role spearheading the "Green Revolution" and agricultural productivity throughout the world, thus ensuring sufficient food for millions of hungry people. Currently chairman and major shareholder.

Various Positions, *Wallaces' Farmer*, 1910–1932

Joined family-owned weekly newspaper serving the farm market; promoted from staff writer to assistant editor; replaced father as editor when father became U.S. secretary of agriculture (1920–24); continued as editor after father's death in 1924. Wrote *Agricultural Prices*, the nation's first econometric study of farm prices and markets, and *Corn and Corn Growing*, a textbook widely used in colleges and still in print to this day. After appointment to the cabinet in 1932, stayed on masthead as honorary "editor on leave" until 1945.

EDUCATION

Earned BS at Iowa State College of Agricultural and Mechanical Arts, 1910.

PERSONAL

Born October 7, 1888. Grew up in Des Moines, Iowa. Honorary Editor of the *New Republic*, a leading liberal magazine, 1946–48.

Assessment of Qualifications

Rarely has there been a man whose career rose like a rocket, only to suddenly run out of fuel and fall back to earth. Such a man is Henry Wallace, who established a stellar career in government and rose to be vice president of the United States, and now he is out in the wilderness, rejected by his party and friends, seeking solace in a quixotic third party.

For the first twenty-two years of his professional life he worked as head of a family-owned trade newspaper in Iowa before being chosen in 1932 to be FDR's secretary of agriculture, a position once occupied by his father under Harding and Coolidge. In a town where "accomplished bureaucrats have gone so far in perfecting the art of governing by *not* doing things," Wallace hit Washington like a midwestern storm.[6] Working almost eighteen hours a day he inaugurated numerous programs that helped bring the farming industry out of the Depression. The number of employees in his agency quadrupled, to become the largest in the federal government. A prolific writer and public speaker, he became so widely known after eight years that many newspapers were talking about him as a potential presidential candidate. He became FDR's running mate in 1940. Dropped from the ticket in 1944, he returned to the cabinet as FDR's secretary of commerce. After a year and a half he was fired by President Truman for giving foreign policy speeches at odds with administration policy. Over the past year he has been busy doing what he likes to do best: give speeches.

Wallace is a visionary, a dreamer, a man of ideas. He cites as his favorite poem a verse used by the three-time presidential candidate William Jennings Bryan in 1909:

> I am tired of planning and toiling
> In the crowded hives of men,
> Heart-weary of building and spoiling
> And spoiling and building again.
> And I long for the dear old river.
> Where I dreamed my youth away,
> For the dreamer lives forever,
> But the toiler dies in a day.[7]

Wallace was a toiler once, and a very good one. But that was many years ago. Many people, as they grow into their fifties, tend to become wiser with experience and less dogmatic. Wallace, on the other hand, in the six years from age fifty-two when he became vice president to age fifty-eight when he left the Commerce Department, has become increasingly doctrinaire and opinionated. His middle-of-the-road liberalism has turned to the left—to the far left, in the view of many.

A VISIONARY

From the time he was a teenager Wallace has been precocious. Visiting Iowa corn shows where judges graded corn by its appearance, Wallace questioned the prevailing belief that appearance meant quality. "Looks mean nothing to a hog," he pointed out.[8] Conducting his own scientific tests, he showed that there was no connection between appearance and yield.

He bought a farm, experimented with different grains of seeds, and started a company to develop and market high-yield hybrid corn. Capitalized with $7,000 (mostly from his wife's inheritance), the company started slowly, barely making a profit of $30 in the first year. With corn going for ten cents a bushel, selling hybrid seed for $5.50 a bushel was impossible, so Wallace agreed to take as his payment half of the back end, gambling that the yield would be substantial. It was a good bet, and Wallace started to become a wealthy man.

The hybrid seed movement started by Wallace led to a revolution in the growing of corn in the United States. In 1931 less than 1 percent of all corn in the Corn Belt came from hybrid seeds; by 1941 the figure had skyrocketed to 78 percent. The revenues of Wallace's company, Pioneer Hi-Bred, grew from $20,000 in 1933 to approximately $4 million today, making him a millionaire. (His annual dividends exceed $150,000.) At current rates of growth he will become fabulously rich.

Most interesting of all, this company has no patents. The key to sustainable business success, says Wallace, is not the negative restrictions of patent protection but the positive edge provided by continuous scientific research. Pioneer Hi-Bred, he says with pride, spends more on corn research every year than does the entire U.S. Department of Agriculture and all the state farm bureaus combined. Clearly this is not your normal nuts-and-bolts businessman.

Appointed secretary of agriculture after a catastrophic 66 percent drop in farm income during 1929–32, Wallace showed a manic energy and "can do" determination rarely seen in government. Within a week of taking office he spoke on national radio, convened an emergency conference of national farm leaders, and secured sweeping executive authority subsequently enacted into law. A prolific writer and speech maker, he took his message to the people: in 1934 he traveled over forty thousand miles by car and train and made public appearances in all forty-eight states. To ensure local participation in the Agricultural Department's efforts to reduce production and raise farm prices, he directed the formation of four thousand local committees. When the Supreme Court struck down many New Deal farm programs as an infringement on states' rights, Wallace was able to salvage the aid to farms; thinking ahead, he had already put in place alternative programs the Court could not strike down.

He was the most successful cabinet officer in the New Deal, probably FDR's best cabinet appointment. During his tenure as secretary farm income rose from $39 billion in 1933 to $66 billion in 1939. Shortly before taking on the position of vice president, he took an unofficial trip as ambassador extraordinary to Mexico. He was so appalled by the poor farming methods in Mexico that when he came back, he persuaded the Rockefeller Foundation to set up an agricultural experiment station in that country to teach proper food production. The program has been so successful that Mexico has now become self-sufficient in food. One almost wishes Wallace had never left the Agriculture Department.

VICE PRESIDENT

Almost everyone—especially the men who have held the position—say the job of vice president of the United States is a one-way path to oblivion and obscurity. Wilson's vice president, Thomas Marshall, wisecracked, "Once there were two brothers. One ran away to sea; the other was elected vice president of the United States. And nothing was heard of either of them again."

Even Theodore Roosevelt couldn't accomplish anything in the brief time he had the job. So it is no surprise that for a man as talented as Wallace the job was a dead end. He engaged in numerous activities and committees, only to find himself so frustrated by the position's lack of power and executive authority that he rebelled: as president of the Senate—the one function the job entailed—he performed with obvious lack of enthusiasm. Many times during Senate debates, bored with the tediousness of it all, he would sit slumped in his chair with his eyes closed, his thoughts elsewhere. Obviously not a good way to make friends.

A vice president who can't please the senators might try to please his boss. But not Wallace. At the end of 1943, trying to prepare the American public for the catastrophic casualties that would occur in the strong push to beat Germany and invade Japan, FDR admitted in a press conference that "Dr. New Deal" had been replaced by "Dr. Win-the-War."[9] *Time* magazine announced the "death" of the New Deal in its obituary column:

> **Death Revealed.** The New Deal, 10, after a long illness; of malnutrition and desuetude. Child of the 1932 election campaign, the New Deal had four healthy years, began to suffer from spots before the eyes in 1937, and never recovered from the shock of war. Last week, its father, Franklin Roosevelt, pronounced it dead.[10]

Wallace immediately jumped in and gave speeches asserting that the New Deal was not dead. Espousing the ideals of Woodrow Wilson, he argued that the U.S. military should be relatively small, and peace enforced by international collective security. His "common man" speech put him squarely at loggerheads with the "America first" vision for the postwar world embraced by most Americans, and it cost him the president's support. Another lost supporter was the Bronx boss Ed Flynn, now chairman of the Democratic Party. Flynn, who had supported Wallace for vice president in 1940, four years later remarked that Wallace "seemed to have become the candidate of the radicals of the country."[11]

Seeing how his views were drifting away from FDR's policies, Wallace's friends warned him he was in trouble and that if he hoped to retain the vice presidential nomination in 1944, he better create an organization to solicit convention delegates. Wallace refused. "Presidential politics of this kind simply did not appeal to me," he said. His assurance he would be renominated was misplaced. After losing the nomination to Harry Truman, Wallace had a meeting with FDR. The president related how he had once successfully handled a similar situation: back in 1932, to maintain his chances for the presidency, he had made a deal with John Nance Garner, giving Garner the vice presidency. Wallace responded, "Mr. President, I could have made a deal, too, but I did not care to do it."[12]

SECRETARY OF COMMERCE

As secretary of commerce Wallace once again failed to make the most of his situation. (Look how thin his résumé description is of this job.) Instead of focusing on administration, where he is so brilliant, Wallace spent most of his time giving speeches on foreign policy. Not surprisingly this got him in trouble with the State Department. It also got him into trouble with President Truman for not toeing the party line concerning Russia and Communism. Truman got rid of him in a full-blown public dismissal.

Wallace had forgotten who his client was. He thought he was still working for FDR, carrying the liberal message and executing FDR's vision for a postwar world. But FDR was dead, and visions of a strong UN and a community of nations looked increasingly problematic in the face of an aggressive Soviet Union. Wallace failed to see the handwriting on the wall, and he had no power base. The only way he could keep his job was to buckle down and do the work—and not go running off giving internationalist speeches.

The Commerce Department is an unusual agency in the federal government in that it has no direct supervisory or regulatory authority; it is a service organization. Yet it has far-reaching impact and offers ample opportunity for a strong leader to exercise enormous power and influence (like Herbert Hoover did). As the New Deal's most successful cabinet head—of Agriculture, a much larger department—Wallace should have been the perfect man for the job at Commerce. But his heart wasn't in it. The man had changed: details now bored him. The times had changed too. And he didn't see it.

COMMENTS ON RÉSUMÉ

Wallace's résumé contains a fair amount of fluff. He leaves out the fact that in 1929 he went along with an ill-advised expansion of his family's business, the *Wallaces' Farmer* publication. A year later the company went bankrupt and Wallace ended up working for a new owner.

He claims that as vice president he transformed a meaningless office into a supervisory role and quotes James Reston's comment that he acted like an "assistant president." Now everyone knows FDR had no assistant presidents; he treated people like pawns on a chessboard. No way Wallace could have played such a powerful role. (If FDR had any really close advisors, they would be Harry Hopkins and Jim Farley.) Had Wallace been as successful as he claims, FDR would have kept him on the ticket. Likewise Wallace claims that for his next position he was offered the choice of almost any cabinet post. This is disingenuous. FDR offered him any position *but* State, the one job Wallace really wanted. The offer was not a promotion; it was more like a demotion.

One needs to look skeptically at claims of New Deal successes and place accomplishments in context. For example, while it is true that under Wallace's leadership farm income increased 70 percent, that rate was calculated on an artificially low base. The 1939 figure of $66 billion is more than the 1933 figure but *less* than the 1930 figure. In other words, despite all the money spent over eight years and the addition of a hundred thousand government employees, Wallace failed to restore farm income to its pre-Depression levels.

Wallace claims he is a reformer seeking to protect the common man, but a close look at his farm programs shows quite the opposite: Wallace was protecting the interests of the "400-acre farmers," such as his own family enterprise. These programs were structured to raise farm prices by reducing output. To achieve this the government paid *landowners*, encouraging them to force tenants and sharecroppers off the land—and out of a job.

When the inequity of his farm programs was pointed out in a congressional committee meeting, Wallace responded evasively, "It is inevitable in a period of emergency that such disturbances occur."[13] "Disturbances" is a callous way of putting it, especially when people are being put out of work. If the government is going to pump a lot of money into the farm economy, should it not have some say on how the money is to be distributed?

In his "Dr. Win-the-War" comment FDR was perfectly willing to admit that the best hope for ending the Depression was the war mobilization, not the New Deal programs. One wishes Wallace could be equally forthright. He claims that he created a national granary program to ensure a stable market and dependable supply. Once again this is only part of the story. What really happened was that the capitalist farmers outsmarted the government planners by taking advantage of good prices and maximizing their production, resulting in far more product than the government could possibly store and sell. And as is usually the case, free-market commodity traders made tons of money. Wallace's program was a disaster. Like many New Deal programs, the only thing that saved it was the war's artificially huge demand for more output.

FDR recognized that Wallace speaks out of both sides of his mouth. He once commented, "You never know what Henry will do. He's in favor of one thing today and something entirely different tomorrow."[14] Coming from a man not known for consistency himself, this is quite an accusation.

Wallace claims he has written many books and given countless speeches. But quantity should not be confused with quality. (He cranks out ten thousand words a day.)He has mastered the glib, not the profound. "New frontiers beckon with meaningful adventure," he once said, leaving everyone wondering what he was talking about. Says the literary critic Dwight Macdonald, "Wallace's words don't spring, they don't leap, and they don't even stumble; they just ooze." This man who has written more books and given more speeches than anyone in the New Deal says, "Strangely enough, I don't even like to write." Hence such profundities as "The job of reconciling Jeffersonian democracy to the impact of machine civilization is one which is going to take the most imaginative resources in all of us" and "I believe that in a democracy every individual ought to define the general welfare in his own way."[15]

CONCLUSION: PRINCE VERSUS SAINT

Henry Wallace is a man of enormous talent and energy and zero self-discipline. He is a man, as Disraeli said of Gladstone, "inebriated with his own verbosity."[16] Like many intellectuals, he loves to play with words as if the mere utterance of them reflected serious thought. A scientist at heart, he relates to theories more than to people. He is a mystic and an idealist. "To understand Henry Wallace," says Frances Perkins, another FDR cabinet officer, "you had to understand his religion."[17] Rexford Tugwell, undersecretary of agriculture during Wallace's term in the Agriculture Department, comments, "Henry's worst trait is his habit of rationalizing, as direct messages from God, the dirty deals and compromises that all politicians must engage in."[18]

Many people wonder how being a farmer could qualify a man for being president of the United States. To Wallace the link is quite obvious: he describes his New Deal farm programs as a "Declaration of Independence, a recognition of our essential unity and our absolute reliance one upon another."[19] He extends this to politics and religion on a global scale, making himself a bona fide internationalist. He preaches cooperation and unity among nations, not "America first." He eschews organized religion in favor of the Theosophy Society and its doctrine of pantheism, which holds that God is an infinite and universal presence. Problem is, reassuring and sublime though it may be, such a view is perilously close to pacifism. In a speech last year in Oslo, Wallace asserted, "It would be unfortunate for world peace if anything happens inside Russia to upset its system of government at the present time."[20] Two months later, pressed for details, he urged President Truman and Secretary of State George Marshall to meet with Stalin "for the avowed and announced purpose of drawing up an agreement which will cover all points at issue between the United States and the Soviet Union."[21] Noble sentiments, yes. But realistic? Countries, as Machiavelli wrote, are ruled by princes, not saints.

Harry Truman, the street politician, is your typical prince. Same for Thomas E. Dewey, a prosecutor. Wallace, on the other hand, is the opposite: a saint who believes in the goodness in everyone. Consider how each would answer the question, Is England as great a threat to world peace as Russia? Wallace would answer yes. He says of Churchill, "He would have England and the United States really run the world. . . . As far as the world is concerned, we owe him a great debt of gratitude. As far as peace is concerned, he's one of the architects of World War III."[22] If you agree with this description, vote for Wallace. If you disagree, vote for Truman or Dewey.

Accomplishments	Intangibles	Judgment	Overall
outstanding	poor	poor	poor

1948

For Henry Wallace there was no light at the end of the tunnel, just pitch black. He who once enjoyed such a stellar government career followed it with four years in the wilderness and an utter debacle in the 1948 election. Not only did he fail to make a dent against either the Democratic nominee or the Republican nominee, but he didn't even come in third. At the last moment a group of southern Democrats espousing segregation broke away and formed their own third party, headed by Senator Strom Thurmond. Truman got 303 electoral votes, Dewey 189, Thurmond 39, and Wallace 0.

Wallace never got his campaign going. He pleaded for world peace, claiming America was "on the road to ruthless imperialism" and damning the Marshall Plan as an act designed "to revive Germany for the purpose of waging a struggle against Russia." Such promises fell flat during the Berlin airlift and an attempted Communist overthrow of the Greek government. Wallace could never shake off suspicions that he was a front for the U.S. Communist Party. His idealism and loose words let his opponents paint him into a corner as a wooly-eyed radical.

Do scientists make good presidents? Ever the scientist, Wallace found it very difficult to disbelieve anything until it was proven wrong. This is a luxury available in science, but not in the real world of politics and government affairs.

Liberals abandoned him en masse, fearing he was a radical. Viewed from the perspective of today, however, many of his ideas seem quite mainstream. Desegregation of public schools, equal rights for women, creation of a cabinet-level Department of Education, immigration reform, collective bargaining for federal employees, a minimum wage for farm employees, home rule for Washington DC, the vote for eighteen-year-olds, and national health insurance are now law.

His public career obviously finished, Wallace retired to a large farm he had bought in South Salem, New York. Only he was hardly retired; he searched for the perfect chicken capable of breeding the perfect egg (though many people may find the egg a perfect shape already). Reporters paying him a visit to learn his latest political views were astonished to find him surrounded by five thousand chickens and fifteen thousand chicks. They were even more surprised when, asked what the secret to successful plant breeding was, he answered, "Sympathy for the plant."[23]

In his newfound profession raising chickens, Wallace once again found the success he had in corn breeding and his early days in government service. His chicken operation, a subsidiary of Pioneer Hi-Bred, grew so big that at one point it accounted for three-quarters of all egg-laying chickens sold commercially throughout the world. He who couldn't run a newspaper or stimulate the economy became a very, very wealthy man.

In *Gulliver's Travels* by Jonathan Swift there appears the following paragraph: "And he gave it for his opinion, that whoever could make two ears of corn, or two blades of grass, to grow upon a spot of ground where only one grew before, would deserve better of mankind, and do more essential service to his country, than the whole race of politicians put together." Wallace changed the world more than most presidents do. By 1981 an acre of farmland could produce almost ten times more corn than in 1931, half of which was due to hybrid seeds. He claimed the hybrid revolution was "as dramatic and important as the history of the automobile," and for once he was not exaggerating.[24] Pioneer Hi-Bred became so successful that it was purchased by DuPont in the late 1990s for $9.4 billion; approximately 25 percent of this money went to Wallace's three children.

"He was a mystic who made an awful lot of money," commented the *Des Moines Register*.[25] "An agricultural expert . . . a man whose judgment could never be trusted when he strayed more than six feet from a manure pile," said columnist Joe Alsop.[26] A less withering comment comes from Roald Dahl, a British secret service agent during World War II, before he started writing children's books: "He was a lovely man, but too innocent and idealistic for this world."[27]

13

....

Barry Goldwater, 1964

The Democrats arrived at their national party convention in Atlantic City, New Jersey, only to find—to their horror—a huge billboard on top of their convention hall touting the Republican candidate Barry Goldwater: "In your heart you know he's right."

Barry Goldwater, one of the true conservatives in the U.S. Senate, is running on a platform of limited government, preservation of individual liberties, and a strong stance against Communism. As chairman of the Republican Senate Campaign Committee, he has traveled nonstop all over America and given hundreds of speeches. With no party organization or personal fortune to back him up, he has single-handedly built a huge following by dint of his ideas.

His opponents, Republican and Democrat, have launched a campaign of extremism and fear, calling him a racist, a fascist, a trigger-happy warmonger, and a man who can't win. Worn out by all these accusations, in his party nomination acceptance speech he threw down the gauntlet: "I would remind you that extremism in the defense of liberty is no vice. And let me remind you also that moderation in the pursuit of justice is no virtue!"[1]

With that thundering line, the battle for Armageddon was joined, and we are now in the nastiest political campaign since 1876. It is a fight to the death, with visions of street riots and

Goldwater slipped into town during the Democratic National Convention to pose for this photo. The Republicans had a good laugh.

nuclear holocaust in the background. "The stench of fascism is in the air," warns the governor of California, Edmund Brown. "Goldwater Republicanism," says Senator J. William Fulbright, chairman of the Senate Foreign Relations Committee, "is the closest thing in American politics to . . . Russian Stalinism."[2]

Who is this man his supporters say is an ardent patriot? Is he as dangerous as his opponents say?

BARRY GOLDWATER

Age: fifty-five

6 feet tall, 185 pounds

Married Margaret "Peggy" Johnson, 1934: four children: Joanne, Barry Jr., Michael, Peggy

Health excellent

OBJECTIVE: Thirty-sixth president of the United States

PERSONAL STATEMENT: "I offer you a choice, not an echo. . . . We can deny self-indulgence. We can restrain our pressure groups from seeking special privilege favors at the expense of the general public taxpayer. We can meet our obligations and not postpone the debt payment and place that burden on the next generation. . . . My aim is not to pass laws, but to repeal them. It is not to inaugurate new programs, but to cancel old ones that do violence to the Constitution, or that have failed in their purpose, or that impose on the people an unwarranted financial burden."[3]

U.S. Senate, 1952–1964

Won 1952 election against a long-standing incumbent in a state where Democrats outnumbered Republicans 2 to 1, becoming the first Republican senator from Arizona since 1920. Won reelection in 1958 against an all-out effort by the Democrats and the AFL-CIO. Gained respect as a free-thinking conservative. Promoted states' rights, limited government, preservation of individual liberties, labor union reform, anti-Communism, and a strong military. Opposed unbalanced budgets and deficit financing.

Member, Senate Rackets Committee: conducted high-profile, bipartisan investigation of abuses by AFL-CIO's Walter Reuther and the Teamsters' Jimmy Hoffa; cast the sole vote against the Kennedy-Ervin labor rackets bill for being too weak. Supported increases in Social Security benefits (1956, 1958, 1964). Urged freedom of choice in retirement plans (including Social Security). Supported the 1957 and 1960 civil rights acts; with great reluctance, voted against the 1964 Civil Rights Act because of Titles II and VII, which restrict personal choice. Voted against public housing, foreign aid, Medicare, and increases in minimum wage. Opposed nuclear test ban treaty. Opposed limited involvement in Vietnam, urging instead that we either go for victory or get out immediately.

As twice-elected chairman of the Republican Senate Campaign Committee, traveled the country extensively and gave over a thousand speeches for Republican candidates. Resigned in 1964 to run for the U.S. presidency.

Civic Affairs, 1946–1952

Upon returning home from war, decided to pursue civic interests full time rather than rejoin family business. Got involved in the right-to-work movement: returning veterans couldn't find jobs because unions made sure new jobs went to people based on seniority. Created the Arizona Air National Guard. Appointed to the Colorado River Commission; defended Arizona's fair share of water under the seven-state compact of 1922. As chairman of advisory board, led successful effort to replace the city council, upgrade the Phoenix city charter, combat vice and crime, and end segregation in public schools. In 1950, when Democrats won every other state office by 2-to-1 margins, served as campaign manager of Republican upset in the state gubernatorial race.

President of the Phoenix Chamber of Commerce, chairman of the Community Chest drive. Board member of the YMCA, the Boys' Club, the Civic Center Association, a local museum, and two hospitals. Member of club of business professionals performing Native American dances in full regalia to publicize and boost the community and local culture. Member, Planned Parenthood.

Military Service, 1940–1945

Joined the U.S. Air Force as a reservist in 1940 and became a pilot. Flew over a thousand missions in World War II in China, India, Africa, and South America. Stayed a reservist after the war. Flew 165 different kinds of aircraft. Retired with rank of major general.

Business Experience, 1929–1953

Joined the family business, Goldwater's Department Store in Phoenix, on a full-time basis in 1929 and assumed positions of increasing responsibility. With brother, took over management of store in 1936. Concentrated on fashion and merchandising and attracted national attention: cited by *Women's Wear Daily* as a "creative merchandising dynamo." Became president in 1937. Established liberal employee benefits program: high wages; full health care insurance and life insurance; pension plan; sick leave; profit-sharing plan; in-house psychologist; a lake cabin for vacations; a farm for growing vegetables, along with a recreation hall, picnic area, and swimming pool; and a company plane and instructor to teach employees how to fly. Employees rejected two unionization attempts. Became chairman (an honorary position) 1953. Business sold in 1962.

EDUCATION

Graduated from Staunton Military Academy in 1928, awarded Legion of Honor as "best all-around cadet" in school. Turned down appointment to West Point to attend University of Arizona (father in failing health required my being near home); president of freshman class. Dropped out upon father's death to help manage the family business.

PERSONAL

Born January 2, 1909. Religion: Episcopalian. Father a Jewish American; mother an Episcopalian and a direct descendant of the theologian Roger Williams of Rhode Island.

Hobbies: amateur radio, assembling electronics kits, outdoor hiking, and white-water rafting. Avid collector and owner of America's largest collection of kachina dolls (made by the Hopis). Accomplished amateur photographer: published two-volume book of photographs, *Arizona Portraits*, in 1940 and 1946; elected member of the Royal Photographic Society of London. Keen interest in science and technology.

Author of three books, including the 1960 best-seller, *The Conscience of a Conservative*; seventeen printings, 3.5 million copies sold to date.[4] Write weekly column for the *Los Angeles Times*, carried in 150 newspapers throughout the country.

Assessment of Qualifications

Controversy aside for the moment, in Barry Goldwater we have one of the most attractive and personable players on the national political scene, a man *Time* magazine says is "the hottest political figure this side of Jack Kennedy."[5] Goldwater stresses our glorious national heritage and preaches a brand of rugged individualism that made our country great. He also represents the future: the West, the fastest-growing sector of the country.

He is enormously well-liked by his fellow senators, including liberals and Democrats. He was a close friend of our late president John Kennedy; they were planning to stage their 1964 presidential debates traveling across the country together. Bobby Kennedy, now running for senator, who worked closely with Goldwater on the 1953–54 Senate Rackets Committee, says, "I was personally very fond of Senator Goldwater. He worked extremely hard, was tough, had a sense of humor. He played politics to the hilt and sometimes slightly beyond. He could cut you to ribbons, slit your throat, but always in such a pleasant manner that you would have to like him."[6]

Is Senator Goldwater qualified to be president? His résumé of accomplishments is not particularly strong. He freely admits he is a man of only average intelligence: "I really haven't got a first-class brain."*[7] His greatest pleasure is flying fighter jets and demonstrating his control over the machine. He is the ultimate outsider, an angry rebel who frequently shoots from the hip. Lacking in introspection, he makes rash statements that he has not thought through.

* His IQ is 103.[8]

Goldwater went to a state school for just one year and spent most of his time chasing girls and driving around in his flashy 1925 Chrysler. He dropped out not because his father was dying, as he claims in his résumé, but because he was bored with academics.

He took over the family business with his brother and worked hard to keep it going during the Depression. His brother managed the finances, while he was the promoter who drummed up new business by developing stunts such as a brand of men's underwear printed with large pictures of red ants, called "Antsy Pants." It didn't sell for very long.

During World War II Goldwater volunteered his services as a pilot and flew dangerous missions over the Atlantic and the Himalayas. When he returned home, he decided to plunge into the more exciting world of civic affairs rather than rejoin the family business. He could do this because he never had to work to make a living: his wife had a large inheritance. In no way is Goldwater the entrepreneurial self-made man he makes himself out to be. He is the beneficiary of a privately held business from his father and the wealth of his wife, giving him the freedom to be "the lone ranger." The cartoonist Herblock skewed him mercilessly for saying that many people are poor because they are lazy and don't want to work. The tagline read: "If you had any initiative, you'd go out and inherit a department store."

In his new avocation Goldwater excelled, proving to be one of the most diligent and relentless men in the Senate. When necessary he worked well past midnight, living on five hours' sleep. As chairman of the Republican Senate Campaign Committee, he was constantly on the road and never said no to a local Republican candidate's plea to fly in and give a speech to help raise money. Other than President Eisenhower, no man has done more for the Republican Party than this dedicated man.

In the 1930s, under the New Deal, for every dollar Arizona paid in federal taxes the state received twenty-one dollars in assistance;[9] in the 1960s dams built by the federal government fueled the booming growth of Arizona, transforming the state from a backwater into an agricultural and tourism paradise. Yet Goldwater, who disdains federal benefits, still says, "The Government never did a thing for us," and jokes, "I was born in a log cabin equipped with a golf course, a pool table and a swimming pool."[10]

His twelve-year record in the Senate is mostly one of opposition, frequently as part of a very small minority, a protest vote in defense of a principle. He is proof that one man can make a difference. As a member of the Senate Rackets Committee, he cast the sole vote

"IF YOU HAD ANY INITIATIVE, YOU'D GO OUT AND INHERIT A DEPARTMENT STORE"

against the Kennedy-Ervin bill, calling it "like a flea bite to a bull elephant."[11] The unions, he said, "stand now across the nation like a colossus and no power outside of Government can compare with them in magnitude." Criticized by Senator John Kennedy for dissenting, Goldwater called it "one of the proudest votes I ever made."[12]

Watching this vote was President Eisenhower, who had a serious interest in the issue and was curious about the one man who voted no. The very next day the president summoned Goldwater to the White House to elaborate on his dissent. Several months later the Eisenhower administration followed up with a bill of its own, a much tougher bill, the Landrum-Griffin Act, and after lobbying hard finally managed to get it passed. Much of the credit for today's labor union reform belongs to Goldwater, who by virtue of his courageous dissent accomplished more than all the rest of the Rackets Committee put together. He eventually earned the admiration of both Kennedys, especially John, with his interest in profiles in courage.

Goldwater the campaigner offers many one-liners about the oppressive size and power of the federal government. He is like a breath of fresh air against the standard orthodoxy, and he identifies a very serious problem: the growth of central government and the potential erosion of personal liberties. He is an unusual politician: he promises the voters there's no such thing as something for nothing and urges them to rely on personal initiative and self-reliance rather than on government's largesse. That he has attracted such a large following astonishes many politicians.

Who are his followers? Writes Vermont Royster for the *Wall Street Journal*, "Far from being the crackpots of the stereotype images, the supporters of Senator Goldwater are mostly lawyers, doctors, small businessmen, farmers and white collar workers, with a sprinkling of those from the more skilled labor groups. . . . The secret of Senator Goldwater, if that's the word for it, is simply that he speaks for this somewhat amorphous middle class."[13]

Barry Goldwater is a crusader and a man of ideas. In *The Conscience of a Conservative* he has written the most widely read political primer since Thomas Paine's *Common Sense*. He has made himself a leader of the Republican Party through his hard work and by getting to know every politician and potential delegate and amassing a huge bank of ious. As a presidential candidate he never had the benefit of an advance organization or personal war chest; he won the critical California primary against Governor Nelson Rockefeller of New York even though he was outspent 10 to 1, and he came into the Republican National Convention with a huge lead in the number of delegates. The eastern liberals in the party wouldn't give him their support; at the last minute they banded together around a candidate who hadn't done any campaigning, Governor William Scranton of Pennsylvania. In their desperation to stop the Goldwater movement they resorted to horrendous invectives, calling Goldwater a fascist, a demagogue, a man who could never win. The tactic didn't work. When Goldwater stood up to give his acceptance speech, he was facing legions of excited supporters who had pulled off a revolution in the party. Also in the convention hall were many disgruntled party regulars, angry that they had been beaten by upstarts and looking for the slightest provocation to become even angrier. In this high-charged atmosphere Goldwater flashed his lightning bolt: "Extremism in the defense of liberty is no vice. Moderation in the pursuit of justice is no virtue!"

It's an excellent line, and it comes from Cicero: "I must remind you, lords, Senators, that extreme patriotism in the defense of freedom is no crime. And let me respectfully remind you that pusillanimity in the pursuit of justice is no virtue!" The problem was the setting: mentioning extremism in a national acceptance speech. It was like a teenager screaming "Fire!" in a crowded movie theater. In a nanosecond whatever fears people had about Goldwater as a polarizing figure coalesced. The former vice president Richard Nixon, watching the speech on television, pronounced, "It's over. He's lost it."[14] Afterward Goldwater tried to explain away his use of the E-word by citing the American Revolution and D-Day as "extremist" actions "in defense of liberty."

Responding to Nixon's request for clarification, Goldwater wrote, "If I were to paraphrase the two sentences . . . I would do it by saying that whole-hearted devotion to liberty is unassailable, and that half-hearted devotion to justice is indefensible."[15] Hardly the most rousing oratory, but at least it doesn't repeat the E-word. Not that the change did much good. In a top-secret emergency meeting with the top political figures of the Republican Party (Eisenhower, Nixon, Rockefeller, Scranton, and George Romney) Goldwater attempted to heal the rift. Despite the fact that the future of the party was at stake, only Eisenhower and Nixon stuck with Goldwater, and one of the people in the room leaked the full transcript of the meeting to the Democrats.

In politics, never trust your "friends."

. . .

To be sure, all politicians make gaffes, and it's easy to find inconsistencies and misstatements in the words of someone who has given as many speeches as Goldwater has. According to a tally by *Life* magazine, Goldwater has "probably written or spoken on the record 10 million words—the equivalent of 100 average-size novels."[16]

He opposed the 1964 Civil Rights Act on strict constitutional grounds,* which he now admits was a mistake. (He supported two earlier civil rights bills, 1957 and 1960.) As a private employer he was ahead of his time in his treatment of African Americans: he was one of the first merchants to offer equal opportunity employment; he integrated the Arizona Air National Guard—the first state air guard to be integrated; and his first Senate assistant was an African American woman—a choice so unusual for that era that the FBI opened a file on this newly elected senator because of his perceived left-wing leanings and support by a large percentage of blacks in the Phoenix area.

* Also opposing were other Senate luminaries: Albert Gore Sr., Sam Ervin, and J. William Fulbright.

In his department store business, which was doing well but not extravagantly, he lavished substantial employee benefits directly affecting his personal wealth. He not only set up a generous pension plan for his employees; he also bought a twenty-five-acre farm near Phoenix where they could go for free vacations. To be sure, he was defending his company against attack by the unions, but the benefits he provided made him one of the most liked employers in all of Arizona. If *Fortune 500* corporations were as far-sighted and generous as Goldwater's department store in Phoenix, American capitalism would enjoy a better reputation.

He is not your narrow-minded businessman solely concerned

about profit. In his political manifesto, *The Conscience of a Conservative*, he is a progressive, urging conservatives to "make war on all monopolies . . . whether corporate or union" and to "fight against the concentration of power wherever they find it."[17]

Like any good public speaker, Goldwater is a master at the pithy phrase. But he is also provocative, perhaps unnecessarily so, saying, "Let's lob one into the men's room of the Kremlin." Or suggesting the best way to deal with the offensive "Eastern money interests" is to "saw off the Eastern seaboard and let it float out to sea." Selling the TVA "for one dollar" gets people's attention but does not address the fundamental problem with privatization: how to guarantee that a profit-driven corporation will provide the public with reliable, cheap electricity twenty-four hours a day with no blackouts (an issue that Wendell Willkie, for example, handled with great tact). Another idea that's gotten a lot of attention—and unwarranted panic—is Goldwater's proposal to give the NATO commander control over the use of atomic weapons. In actual fact both the NATO and the NORAD commanders *already* have the authority to press the Red Button in carefully defined circumstances, such as incapacitation in the chain of command. There's nothing new here, except that the public was unaware of the facts. So why did Goldwater bring it up unless his aim was to provoke a reaction?

Hostile media immediately jumped at the opportunity to portray him giving nuclear weapons to trigger-happy generals. A more balanced appraisal comes from Hanson Baldwin, the *New York Times* military editor, who described Goldwater's proposal as "neither very revolutionary nor very new. It has been made to appear far more sensational than it is by Mr. Goldwater's own occasional imprecision, the distortion of his remarks, and by the political reactions they have evoked."[18]

He is rightfully angry at the way he has been treated by the media, which often misquote, ignore, or underestimate him. On Social Security, for example, Goldwater has consistently argued that the system needs to be strengthened. But in the New Hampshire primary he made a comment about making the system voluntary, and the next day the headline in the Concord *Monitor* was "Goldwater Sets Goals: End Social Security." He never said this, of course. The respected journalist Theodore White, author of the best-selling *The Making of the President, 1960*, pointed out that Goldwater gave an excellent speech on civil rights violence, "but if it was reported anywhere in more than a paragraph, I do not know of it."[19] A typical example of the media's underestimation of the senator was the sneer by the national columnist Stewart Alsop: "No serious Republican politician, even of the most Neanderthal type, any longer takes Goldwater seriously."[20] Four months later Goldwater won the Republican Party nomination.

Goldwater is a true original: he has the courage to see obvious problems and speak up, whereas most politicians shy away from anything controversial. But such courage, while commendable, is no excuse for being sloppy and unprofessional. He must learn to think through the repercussions of his slogans and stop handing a knife to his enemies. When talking about hot-button issues like Social Security, nuclear weapons, TVA, and civil rights, he should have detailed position papers to back him up. But with no serious party support, Goldwater has acted alone.

As president he will have all the professional staff support he needs to make sure he doesn't have these kinds of problems. A man of honor and integrity, he might well make an excellent president. One on one he is extremely persuasive and sincere. He has a strong conscience, and he questions orthodox thinking. He is ahead of the crowd. He is a terrific public speaker. But to attain the presidency you have to be a good candidate, and here his performance is poor. He should have known that he must clarify his position on certain critical issues. Most important of all, he must capture the mood of the country. In his one triumphant moment at the Republican Party Convention, when he had a chance to put everyone at ease, he blew it. He showed poor judgment.

A presidential campaign must run like a well-oiled machine. It's true that Goldwater is battling a vicious Democratic campaign and a hostile mass media, but he has also failed to identify his key message (other than protest) or develop a strategy to counteract the climate of fear propagated by the Democrats. He has only himself to blame. An honest man who will bring a high standard of ethics to the presidency, Senator Goldwater lacks the flexibility and toughness it takes to survive in an environment of wolves. By his own admission he has never been much of a leader and has shown little interest in coalition building, an essential part of the president's job. He is more of a pusher, an outsider in charge of an ideological movement.

Barry Goldwater is one of the most decent men in Washington today, esteemed by his fellow senators. He scores high in intangibles. But he is too honest to a fault, so he scores poor in judgment. He lacks the guile, canniness, and discretion required of a successful president.

Accomplishments	Intangibles	Judgment	Overall
fair	outstanding	poor	fair

1964

> From time to time a great event, ardently desired, does not take place because some future time will fulfill it in greater perfection.
> —Jacob Burkhardt

Robert Dole, Walter Mondale, Michael Dukakis, Alf Landon, Alton Parker—also-rans long forgotten. Barry Goldwater, on the other hand, was not. "Goldwater was a man ahead of his time," says former president George H. W. Bush.[21]

The first Republican since Coolidge to question the tenets of progressive "me too" Republicanism, Goldwater was so demonized in the mainstream media that he never had a chance. Daniel Schorr of CBS Evening News claimed Goldwater was linking up with neo-Nazi elements in Germany, and the New York Times stooped to accept a full-page ad announcing that 1,189 psychiatrists had diagnosed Goldwater as not "psychologically fit" to be president.*[22] The Democratic candidate, Lyndon Johnson, accused Goldwater of "sowing prejudice and bigotry and hatred and division" in America.[23] The Democrats ran a TV commercial featuring a little girl in a field of daisies, while a somber voice-over intoned a countdown—"Ten . . . nine . . . eight"—followed by an explosion and the girl swallowed up in a mushroom cloud. The Federal Communications Commission was so outraged it ordered the ad taken off the air, but of course the damage was done. The three networks had repeated the ad incessantly as "news."

* The ad was based on a magazine article that touted its findings as scientific, whereas the sample was flawed and none of the so-called psychiatrists signed their name. The American Psychiatrists Association denounced the advertisement as slander. Goldwater later took the magazine to court for deliberate misrepresentation and defamation of character—and won.

"I was depicted as a grotesque public monster. Hell, if half the things they said about me were true, I'd never have voted for myself," said Goldwater.[24] A lot of people agreed. As the election drew near, the betting odds were that Goldwater would get only 33 percent of the popular vote. He did only slightly better: 38 percent. His political obituary appeared immediately and definitively. Intoned the dean of the Washington columnists, James Reston, "Barry Goldwater not only lost the Presidential election yesterday but the conservative cause as well. He has wrecked his party for a long time to come."[25] Intellectuals exulted in the Goldwater defeat; the historian Richard Hofstadter declared it "broke the back" of American conservatives, and the New Republic announced that the Republican Party "has no future unless it returns to the moderate platforms and candidates."[26] Walter Lippmann invoked his usual high-blown style: "There is no more unfounded claim than that Barry Goldwater is a conservative. Sen. Goldwater is in fact a radical opponent of conservatism who, under the banner of personal freedom, would compound the moral disorder which is the paramount problem of the modern age."[27] What exactly he meant by "moral disorder" or what "the paramount problem" was, he did not say.

Other pundits predicted the death of the Republican Party, overlooking the fact that the Republicans lost no more congressional seats or governorships in 1964 than they had in the 1958 midterm election. Rumors of the death of the conservative movement were greatly exaggerated. Ronald Reagan, who later admitted he went into politics only because of Goldwater, soon became governor of California and later president; Newt Gingrich became speaker of the House; and William Rehnquist became chief justice and Antonin Scalia became associate justice of the U.S. Supreme Court.

In the meantime Goldwater went back to Arizona, then returned to the Senate in 1969 and went on to serve three more terms before retiring in 1986. He displayed a fierce independence that surprised many conservatives and even delighted a few liberals. When it became clear that Nixon had lied about the Watergate cover-up, an outraged Goldwater led a small group of Republicans to the Oval Office and demanded that the president resign. "Nixon is the biggest liar I ever met," he fumed.[28] When Reagan challenged President Gerald Ford for the 1976 party nomination, Goldwater backed Ford, saying that the man had proved his competence; ability— not ideology—should trump one's preference for a candidate.* At the end of Reagan's second term, when he got into serious trouble over Iran-Contra, the Republican who denounced him the loudest was Goldwater. Feisty as ever, he criticized Reagan for not following through on his promise to rein in the budget. What had Reagan done to cut back on spending, stop welfare, reduce the bureaucracy? "Had I been in Reagan's place, this country would never have gone $3 trillion in debt," he asserted.[29]

* This doomed any close relationship between the two conservatives. When Reagan eventually became president, he and the first lady never invited Goldwater to any White House social functions.

An advocate of a strong defense, Goldwater shared Eisenhower's concern about the military-industrial complex. Seventy-six years old, past his prime, but still a fighter and ready to take on the world's largest and most complex bureaucracy, he was angry that "Duty, Honor, Country" had become "Turf, Power, Service."[30] To his dismay he found that his strongest opponents were his Republican colleagues. But no matter: he teamed up with two Democrats, Senator Paul Simon and Representative William Nichols, and called the generals to task. The military brass marched into the committee room, defiant and confident they had a friend—only to find they had a well-informed foe determined to make major changes. Goldwater's committee demanded that the military services work together as a team and be subject to performance accountability. The effort took four years and 241 days—longer than America's involvement in World War II—but in the end Goldwater won. The 1986 Goldwater-Nichols National Defense Authorization Act passed 95–0 in the Senate and 406–4 in the House. It was his finest achievement. He received the Presidential Medal of Freedom for accomplishing what no president or senator had been able to do. Only Goldwater could have done it, marveled Joe Biden, the Democratic senator and later vice president.

Goldwater's reforms quickly bore fruit. Shortly after America's astounding victory in Kuwait in 1991, Gen. Colin Powell said a key reason for the success of the well-coordinated invasion was the reforms instigated by Senator Goldwater.[31]

When Goldwater died in 1998, hundreds of eulogies came from Republicans such as John McCain and Colin Powell but also Democrats such as Senator Edward Kennedy and Senator Hillary Clinton, a "Goldwater Girl" in her high school days. It seems the animosity of the liberal Republicans and media reporters in the 1964 campaign was not shared by the Democrats and moderate Republicans who knew Goldwater personally.

. . .

Do honorable men make good presidents? Yes. Do honorable men make good candidates? Not necessarily, especially if they are running against a man bent on winning at all costs. For Lyndon Johnson, who pulled off every possible dirty stunt to win, extremism in pursuit of victory was no vice.

Apparently Goldwater paid a visit to Johnson during the campaign and got his agreement that neither side would play the "race card." However, that didn't stop LBJ from sending Hubert Humphrey to play the "nuclear bomb card." Humphrey, decent man though he was, was only too happy to play attack dog.

When politicians in their zeal to win stoop to such gutter politics, the victim is not the loser but the American voter. In 1964 the better candidate (and lesser human being) won the presidency. Yet the campaign itself was abominable. Anybody who thinks American democracy and the election of presidents has improved since the hoary days of Reconstruction should take another look. And hope it doesn't happen again.

The final word on Barry Goldwater belongs to the renowned columnist George Will, who characterized the senator as "a man who lost forty-four states but won the future."[32] The twenty-seven million people who voted for Goldwater grew to fifty-four million twenty years later and voted for Ronald Reagan.

14

Robert F. Kennedy, 1968

On March 16, only four days after Senator Eugene McCarthy pulled off his stunning 41 percent upset against President Johnson's 49 percent in the New Hampshire Democratic primary, Robert Kennedy joined the race: "I am today announcing my candidacy for the presidency of the United States to close the gap that now exists between black and white, between rich and poor, between young and old. . . . I do not lightly dismiss the dangers and difficulties of challenging our incumbent president. But these are not ordinary times and this is not an ordinary election. At stake is not simply the leadership of our party and even our country. It is our right to moral leadership of the planet."[1] Coming after a year of denying he was a candidate, this sudden change of heart struck many as opportunism. "He is like a man who comes down from the hills after the battle and shoots the wounded," says one well-known columnist. His reversal reminded everyone of Jules Feiffer's famous cartoon about the two Bobbys: the man of noble sentiments and the man with an unbridled appetite for power.

Two weeks later, on March 31, Johnson shocked everyone by announcing he would not run for reelection. The contest for the Democratic Party nomination is becoming a three-way fight between McCarthy, Kennedy, and Vice President Hubert Humphrey. In the meantime the assassination of Martin Luther King

Jr., race riots in the streets, and growing student unrest on college campuses have added a toxic mix to this year's campaign, already dominated by the Vietnam War.

In Robert Kennedy we have one of the most controversial and divisive candidates ever to run for president. He inspires both intense adoration and widespread loathing. Many people who work with him speak highly of him as a man of principle and morality. Others see him as a ruthless bully riding on the coattails of his martyred brother.

ROBERT F. KENNEDY

Age: forty-two
5-foot-10, 165 pounds

Permanent address:	Current address:
Hickory Hill	860 UN Plaza, 14th floor
McLean, Virginia	New York City

OBJECTIVE: Thirty-seventh president of the United States

PERSONAL STATEMENT: "The cruelties and obstacles of this swiftly changing planet will not yield to obsolete dogmas and outgrown slogans. It cannot be moved by those who cling to a present that is already dying, who prefer the illusion of security to the excitement and danger that come with even the most peaceful purposes. It is a revolutionary world we live in; and this generation, at home and around the world, has thrust upon it a greater burden of responsibility than any generation that has ever lived."

SUMMARY OF QUALIFICATIONS: As a cabinet member and chief advisor to President John F. Kennedy, have gained extensive experience and familiarity with the job of president of the United States. Possess proven leadership and administrative abilities and total commitment to worthy causes.[2]

LEADERSHIP EXPERIENCE

U.S. Senator, 1965–Present

Opposed military escalation and bombing of Vietnam; advocated cease-fire, establishment of a coalition government, and withdrawal of U.S. troops. Led Senate lobbying effort to increase appropriations for job creation programs for the poor. Founded innovative community renewal corporation for Bedford-Stuyvesant, the nation's second-largest ghetto; secured support of national business leaders to provide funding and jobs.

U.S. Attorney General, 1961–1964

Launched intensive civil rights effort: eliminated racial discrimination in interstate transport; helped James Meredith enroll peacefully at the University of Mississippi; negotiated the release of Martin Luther King Jr. from prison; played key role in initiating and drafting the Civil Rights Act. Promoted equality of justice for the poor and initiated the Bail Reform Act and the Criminal Justice Act. Chairman, President's Committee on Juvenile Delinquency: conducted demonstration projects in sixteen cities to give local communities greater role in managing welfare programs. Pursued union corruption: increased convictions 1,400 percent and secured the imprisonment of Jimmy Hoffa. Wrote *The Pursuit of Justice*, published in 1964.

Served as President John F. Kennedy's most trusted advisor on all matters of state. Played key role in developing U.S. response to the Cuban missile crisis of October 1962. Conducted secret diplomacy with Russian ambassador Anatoly Dobrynin that resulted in the withdrawal of Russian nuclear missiles from Cuba. In follow-up negotiations with the Cuban government secured release of Cuban prisoners. Wrote widely acclaimed book, *Thirteen Days*, published in 1967.

Campaign Manager, 1960 Democratic Presidential Campaign

Directed successful effort to win the presidential election for John F. Kennedy. Secured the Democratic Party nomination on the first ballot after scoring wins in early primaries against Hubert Humphrey, Lyndon Johnson, Stuart Symington, and Adlai Stevenson. Won national election against Richard Nixon.

Chief Counsel, Labor Rackets Committee, U.S. Senate, 1957–1960

Initiated and led exhaustive investigation of Jimmy Hoffa and the Teamsters Union; secured the downfall of union president Dave Beck. Generated widespread publicity and increased public awareness of the evils of trade union corruption. Wrote *The Enemy Within*, a national best-seller, published in 1960.

Chief Counsel, Permanent Subcommittee on Investigations, U.S. Senate, 1954–1956

Pursued waste and graft in government. With newspaperman Charles Bartlett, investigated wrongdoing by the secretary of the air force and forced his resignation; Pulitzer Prize awarded to Bartlett.

Minority Counsel, U.S. Senate, 1954

Appointed to newly created position by senators of the minority Democratic Party. Played key role in the nationally televised Army-McCarthy hearings. Prepared minority report rebuking Senator Joseph McCarthy and his attorney Roy Cohn, which ultimately led to censure of McCarthy by the full U.S. Senate. Selected by the Junior Chamber of Commerce as one of the Ten Outstanding Young Men of America, 1954.

Assistant Counsel, U.S. Senate, 1953

Investigated illegal shipping of strategic materials to Communist China. Earned public commendation by journalist Arthur Krock for "congressional investigation at the highest level." Due to policy differences with Senator Joseph McCarthy and chief counsel Roy Cohn, resigned after six months and worked for my father, Joseph P. Kennedy, a member of the second Hoover Commission.

Assistant Campaign Manager, John F. Kennedy Senatorial Campaign, 1952

Responsible for campaign organization in effort to elect John F. Kennedy to the U.S. Senate. Due to lackluster support from the Democratic Party in Massachusetts, had to set up new organization to generate exposure for a candidate facing a powerful Republican incumbent, Henry Cabot Lodge. Campaign scored upset victory in a year that witnessed a Republican national landslide.

Staff Member, U.S. Department of Justice, 1951–1952

EDUCATION

University of Virginia, 1951. Earned LL.D. President of the Student Legal Forum. Graduated 56th out of class of 124. Admitted to the Massachusetts Bar.

Harvard College, 1948. Earned AB. Varsity Football. Varsity Club, Pi Eta Club, Hasty Pudding Institute of 1770.

Military Service, 1943–1946

U.S. Naval reservist. Completed Officers Corps Training Program.

PERSONAL

Born November 20, 1925, the seventh of nine children. Married Ethel Skakel, 1950: ten children: Kathleen, Joseph III, Robert Jr., David, Courtney, Michael, Kerry, Christopher, Matthew, and Douglas. Favorite athletic activities: touch football, skiing, white-water rafting, mountain climbing. Avid reader of history, biography, poetry, and classical Greek plays.

Assessment of Qualifications

Many men, especially vice presidents, have tried to claim the mantle of "assistant president." Other than perhaps Alexander Hamilton when he was Washington's Treasury secretary, only one man in almost two hundred years has come close: this man, the brother and confidante of a president. Robert Kennedy has dedicated his career to supporting and protecting his older brother, and he has done it superbly.

He is not blessed with extraordinary talent. He is no orator; he does not make friends easily; he is not particularly charismatic. He is not even physically imposing: of average height, he actually looks shorter because of his hunched back. Kennedy is an ordinary man who has managed to make himself extraordinary. With his piercing eyes and obvious intensity, he looks like a dynamo poised to explode.

. . .

A helpful—though not absolutely necessary—trait of a president is that he have a sense of humor; it helps him maintain his balance and perspective. Almost all of our recent presidents had it: FDR, Truman, Eisenhower, especially JFK.

This man has absolutely none. He is awkward, extremely intense, and emotional. He behaves like a battering ram, threatening, "You will do this, or else!" He is always in motion. His Senate office is like a political campaign headquarters: phones ringing incessantly, visitors coming in every half hour, staff assistants and speechwriters scurrying about, long checklists of tasks to do. The man is always on the move, rushing to his next appointment. Does he ever stop to think and reflect? In just three years as a senator he has assumed leadership of the state Democratic machine, Vietnam policy, the antiwar movement, political reform in Latin America and South Africa, community development in inner-city slums, and job creation for the poor. He is the standard-bearer of the John F. Kennedy legacy, with its numerous ceremonial functions and public appearances. When he goes home, he has a wife and ten children to look after, with an eleventh child due soon.

How does he find the time to do all this? His late brother offered an answer: "Bobby's the best organizer I've ever seen." Asked why he had such high regard for his younger brother, the president replied, "He has this terrific executive energy. We've got more guys around here with ideas. The problem is to get them done."[3]

In his zeal to get things done Bobby Kennedy has run roughshod over a lot of people, many of whom hate his guts. The renowned lawyer Melvin Belli calls him "arrogant, rude, even ignorant of the law . . . the little Lord Fauntleroy of government."[4] "A dangerous ruthless man," adds Gore Vidal, "a Torquemada-like personality with none of his brother's gift for seeing things other than black and white. . . . He has none of his brother's ease—or charity."[5] Says the columnist Jim Bishop, "When he concludes a short chat with a political leader, the man feels that if he doesn't do as Robert tells him, God will strike him dead. . . . I would not like to see him appointed to high office."[6]

Alice Roosevelt Longworth, who knows just about everybody in Washington, including every president this century, says Bobby Kennedy could have been "a revolutionary priest, a member of Sinn Fein,"[7] the Irish revolutionary group. Kennedy seems to agree with this characterization. When the journalist Jack Newfield asked the candidate, "If you weren't born a Kennedy, what would you have been?" he responded, "Either a juvenile delinquent or a revolutionary."[8]

At age forty-two, a month before his twentieth college reunion, this juvenile delinquent–revolutionary is a leading candidate for the nation's highest office. Were he to win, he would be the youngest president ever. He attracts crowds of followers like no other man in America. Brother of a martyred president, his name is known in virtually every household. When he travels abroad, he is addressed as "the future president." He is adored by many who know him well. Yet he is also feared by many as a demagogue, a man who cannot be trusted with power.

"I was the seventh of nine children," he says. "When you come from that far down, you have to struggle to survive."[9] He had additional pressures to cope with: he had a domineering father and two very popular older brothers, and he never lived in one town long enough to form lasting friendships. His parents moved from place to place, and he went to no fewer than ten schools. He followed his two older brothers to Harvard and achieved a feat neither of them did: making the varsity football team. The team captain at the time, Kenneth O'Donnell, who later became President Kennedy's appointments secretary, recalls, "It was just after the war and all the men were back from the service. We had eight ends who were bigger, faster, and who had been high-school stars. [Bobby] wasn't fast, he wasn't shifty. But he was a quick, tough guy who worked five times as hard as anybody."[10] To this day Kennedy views his varsity letter as one of his proudest achievements, a test of his manhood, his way of outclassing his two big brothers. "Except for war," he says, "there is nothing in American life—nothing— which trains a boy better for life than football."[11]

His scrapper personality is further evident in his choice of friends. He disdained his fellow preppies and dropped out of the Spee Club, one of the prestigious undergraduate social clubs at Harvard. Instead he spent all his time with jocks and servicemen, most of whom were on scholarship. These down-to-earth people were the ones he felt most comfortable with. He is the son most like his father, who was also a Harvard varsity athlete, shy and socially uncomfortable, fiercely competitive, and with a chip on his shoulder about privileged people. Joseph P. Kennedy, who made over $400 million and became one of one of the half-dozen richest men in America, said of his son, "Bobby's like me. He's a hater."[12]

He has a trust fund that more than pays for a country estate in Virginia, an apartment at the UN Plaza in New York, servants and babysitters, and private schools for his ten children. Every salaried job he has had has been in the federal government. He's worked in the private sector only once, and that was a long time ago: as a ten-year-old boy selling magazines to his neighbors from the backseat of his parents' chauffeur-driven Rolls-Royce.

A CAREER FUELED BY NEPOTISM

Rarely has a career owed so much to nepotism. After a brief stint with the Justice Department in the Brooklyn borough of New York City, all of his subsequent jobs were created for him by his father:

- Assistant to his father in managing John Kennedy's first Senate campaign.
- Assistant to his father's good friend Senator Joseph McCarthy.
- Assistant to his father on the Hoover Commission.
- 1960 presidential campaign manager.
- U.S. attorney general.

As minority counsel in the nationally televised Army-McCarthy hearings in 1954, he was cited as one of Ten Outstanding Young Men of America. Only three years out of law school with a mediocre school record, Kennedy obviously got this award because of all the media exposure (again thanks to his father).

As chief counsel to the Senate Rackets Committee, he was the first to make the public aware of underworld crime syndicates and the need for a new crime-fighting strategy. He attacked his job with passion, announcing, "My first love is Jimmy Hoffa."[13] When he finally met Hoffa he promptly challenged him to a push-up contest, *mano e mano*. Hoffa laughed at such playground behavior and walked away.

It is true that Kennedy "embarked on a number of purely punitive expeditions" characterized by "relentless, vindictive battering" of witnesses, as the Yale law professor Alexander Bickel has asserted. Yet his effort to send Hoffa to jail was an attempt to imprison a dangerous mobster. Unlike the FBI and other law enforcement agencies that preferred to focus on small-time criminals and alleged Communists, Kennedy had the courage to go after the big fish.

His major talents are not legal, but managerial. For his work on the Rackets Committee he built a large staff of investigators and accountants, who he claimed were "the best . . . of any Congressional committee," and instilled in them some of his own passionate enthusiasm.[14] In his next job, as his brother's presidential campaign manager, his performance was masterful. He traveled relentlessly from state to state stirring local Democrats into activity. He was able to make decisions on the spot and to generate active enthusiasm among volunteers. "I don't have to think about organization," marveled the candidate John Kennedy. "I just show up."[15]

After winning the presidency JFK had no plans to appoint a thirty-five-year-old with no legal or courtroom experience to be attorney general. But their father insisted, and the president-elect obeyed. Asked by *Newsweek* how he planned to announce the appointment, JFK must have looked like a man facing the seven knives: "Well, I think I'll open the front door of the Georgetown house some morning about 2 a.m., look up and down the street and if there's no one there, I'll whisper, 'It's Bobby.'"[16]

Bobby did not disappoint. Single-handedly he transformed a sleepy bureaucracy into an agent of change. Under his direction the department vigorously went after organized crime and launched initiatives in the emerging area of civil rights. As his brother's closest advisor, he also involved himself in international affairs having nothing to do with the Justice Department. During the Cuban missile crisis he squelched the idea of air strikes, pushed for a peaceful blockade, and conducted secret negotiations with Russia with tact and circumspection. Throughout the crisis, said Defense Secretary Robert McNamara, he "remained calm and cool, firm but restrained, never nettled and never rattled."[17] According to President Kennedy, Adlai Stevenson, and British prime minister Harold Macmillan, Bobby's leadership and good judgment were major factors in averting a nuclear war. His coolness under fire, his friends say, is his major qualification to be president.

This later coolness under fire, however, does not absolve him from his hot-headed impetuosity in the beginning of his term as attorney general. He showed horrendous judgment in trying to get Castro assassinated—a clear violation of American policy and international law. He ordered illegal wiretaps to try to nail Hoffa; had this been widely known at the time, the nation's highest law enforcement officer could have been impeached.

Justice and politics is a dangerous mix. Hiring lots of ambitious young lawyers to staff the Justice Department runs the danger that they will get so carried away in their zeal they will run roughshod over basic constitutional rights. For instance, Nicholas Katzenbach, Kennedy's deputy (and successor attorney general), says the law doesn't have to be neutral, that it can be used "creatively to achieve social and political objectives."[18] This is a radical idea quite different from the traditional Anglo-Saxon principle that the law must be impartial and nonpartisan, devoted only to pursuing justice (however defined). The prospect of using the nation's law enforcement and judicial apparatus to enforce one's political views frightens many people out of their wits.

Kennedy's coolness under fire in the Cuban missile crisis overlooks a more important point: how did John and Robert Kennedy manage to get us into this mess in the first place? It is a long-forgotten fact that a full year before the October 1962 crisis, President Osvaldo Dorticos Torrado of Cuba had told the UN General Assembly that Cuba was prepared to give up missiles if the United States gave assurances "by word and by deed that it would not commit acts of aggression against our country." Also not widely known is that President Kennedy had ordered the removal of "unreliable, inaccurate, obsolete" missiles from Turkey as early as late summer 1961 (orders which, to everyone's surprise, had never been followed). "What if Khrushchev hadn't backed down?" asks the columnist I. F. Stone.[19] That Khrushchev did back down mustn't obscure the fact that the Cuban missile crisis was due to U.S. bumbling as well as Russian aggression. More important than resolving a crisis is making sure it doesn't happen in the first place (especially when it comes to nuclear warheads). This is not a touch football game calling for a "Hail Mary" pass or a macho game in which you exult in making the other guy blink.

Any praise for Bobby's masterful handling of the Cuban missile crisis must be tempered by the fact that he was a major cause of the crisis in the first place.

ON HIS OWN

After his brother's death, Kennedy decided to run for senator from New York, even though he lived in Virginia and Massachusetts and had barely stepped foot in New York since the age of ten. Despite being an obvious carpetbagger, he won, thanks to his celebrity.

One can hardly imagine a job less suited to such a man of action: he who had negotiated with the Kremlin now found himself unable to get a seat on the Senate Foreign Relations Committee. But the Senate did provide him a platform from which to seek more power. Over the past three years he has been spending most of his time on the road, giving speeches and attracting huge crowds attracted by his name and memories of his late brother.

Almost everyone points to his sudden decision to run for president as a sign that he is an opportunist. His supporters disagree; they see it as a gutsy decision on his part. Kennedy's plan always was to run in 1972, after LBJ finished his two terms and was out of the way. One simply does not seek the party nomination against an incumbent president.*

> * This happened only once before, in 1884, when James G. Blaine won the party nomination over President Chester Arthur, then lost the general election.

Eugene McCarthy's supporters say their man is the courageous one because he was the first to challenge LBJ. They overlook the fact that McCarthy took no risk; his was a quixotic campaign, a prayer based on a whim: he had no money, no strong base of supporters, no strong qualifications to be president, not even a desire to be president. For him, running for president was a lark. For Kennedy, it meant he could lose everything, including his future in 1972. Even with so much to lose he chose to gamble.

Asked to name the best quality a man can have, Kennedy threw out Churchill's line about courage—"the first of human qualities because it is the quality which guarantees all others"—then added "judgment" and "sensitivity." The worst quality? "Being ruthless, impatient." Asked what his favorite aphorism was, he referred to Emerson's *Essays*: "Always do what you are afraid to do."[20] In taking on an incumbent president Kennedy must have been afraid. It showed courage—or possibly recklessness. Whether it showed good judgment will depend on how well he does in the next few primaries, especially in California.

CREDIBILITY

Kennedy makes a number of statements in his résumé, which were repeated throughout the campaign, that show a serious disregard for truth:

- "Opposed military escalation and bombing of Vietnam" is disingenuous, if not outright false. For years, beginning in the JFK administration, he was one of the country's fiercest war hawks. He voted in favor of the 1965 Tonkin Gulf resolution and approved more money for the war. He started opposing the Vietnam War only in 1967, when he was looking for a cause on which to focus his presidential aspirations.

- "Founded imaginative community renewal corporation for Bedford-Stuyvesant" is only partially true: he failed to provide the follow-up leadership required to keep the project going. Today the project is virtually moribund.

- "Launched intensive civil rights effort" is not true: he did little more than visit burned-out ghettoes to ensure that he would get 90 percent of the black vote. This smacks of opportunism and hypocrisy. At a time when the civil rights movement was in desperate need of federal government support to enforce national laws over state obstructionism, Kennedy's Justice Department was nowhere to be seen, fearful of upsetting southern senators who controlled key congressional committees needed to support JFK's legislative programs.

- "Negotiated the release of Martin Luther King Jr. from prison": this occurred only after he spent several years as attorney general doing little to protect the Freedom Riders and local African Americans in Mississippi from being abused and attacked. (After JFK's assassination he declined to invite King to the White House for the funeral ceremonies. King was left out on the street, watching like millions of other mourners.)

PROBLEM SOLVING

Give him the assignment of beating a single opponent in an election, and he will do an excellent job. Give him a specific task, like negotiating with Khrushchev over the Cuban missile crisis, and he is focused. But ask him to explain his policy or overall strategy, and he is ineffective. Speaking out against the Vietnam War is not policy unless backed up with specifics; otherwise it's just hot air. Voters want to know how he will act. He urges the formation of a coalition government and withdrawal of our troops—fair enough—but he provides no specifics for how this is to be done. He evades the key question: How can we trust the Chinese Communists and Viet Cong to keep their side of the bargain after we've pulled out?

Big ideas bore him. Speaking to a student group after President Kennedy's inauguration, he was unable to recollect his brother's major theme: "You people are exemplifying what my brother meant when he said in his Inauguration address: 'Ask what you can do for—uh—uh—do not ask what you can do—ask not what you can do for your country but—uh—.' Well, anyhow, you remember the words. That's why my brother is president."[21]

His performance in a national debate was equally appalling. In May 1967 he engaged in a CBS "Town Meeting of the World" with Governor Ronald Reagan of California. Called "the first eyeball-to-eyeball test of the two men who may very well meet on the road to the White House,"[22] the debate had Kennedy speaking from a studio in New York and Reagan from a studio in California, taking questions from a group of eighteen students in London about America's role in Vietnam and the world. The show was watched by fifteen million people. Their verdict was virtually unanimous:

"Reagan destroyed him."[23] Reagan came across as knowledgeable and forceful, whereas Kennedy was lame and uninformed. Observed *Newsweek* magazine, "Political rookie Reagan . . . left old campaigner Kennedy blinking when the session ended."[24] So bad was Kennedy's performance he told his aides to never again put him on the same stage with "that son-of-a-bitch." He was even overheard yelling at them, "Who the f— got me into this?"[25]

In his zeal to solve specific problems Kennedy forgets that some problems occur in the context of an abstraction, and there is no greater abstraction in America than the Constitution. It is essential that a president understand it. Consider Kennedy's experience as chief counsel to the Senate Rackets Committee investigating labor corruption, for which he pursued Hoffa and Dave Beck but squelched any investigation of Walter Reuther of the United Auto Workers. The minority report from senators headed by Barry Goldwater (a close friend of Kennedy's) concluded:

> We are deeply disappointed that the Chief Counsel, who had been delegated broad authority, was not only reluctant, but actually refused in more than one instance to probe into areas which would have fixed the responsibility for the clear pattern of crime and violence which has characterized and has generally been associated with UAW strikes.
>
> When investigating unions other than those affiliated with the leadership of Walter Reuther, the Chief Counsel worked effectively and cooperatively with all members of the Committee—Democrats and Republicans alike. But whenever an investigation touched upon the domain of Walter Reuther, an altogether different procedure was followed. . . . A double standard prevailed.[26]

Despite this stinging rebuke, Kennedy never learned his lesson. When he became attorney general, he continued his campaign to get Hoffa.

It is a cliché and a truism that the most important civil rights in America are those of our enemies. When a public official, acting in the name of every citizen, engages in selective prosecution, he is violating the Constitution.

ROBERT F. KENNEDY, 1968

He projects the image of a loyal family man, devoted to his wife and many children. The truth is more complex: like his older brother, albeit to a lesser degree, he has had his share of marital affairs, sometimes showing no regard for discretion. It's risky enough to have a fling with an unstable celebrity like Marilyn Monroe, but even more so to be openly brazen and have a hot four-day tryst with Candace Bergen in Paris when she was supposed to be on a movie set. According to Jack Valenti, not only did everyone know about this affair, but Kennedy had the nerve to seat Bergen next to him at an official dinner with President de Gaulle. Even worse was his behavior with his Washington mistress, where he opened himself to potential blackmail. According to newspaper columnist Drew Pearson, Bobby would park his official Justice Department car in front of the woman's Georgetown home and vanish inside for an hour or two. He and the woman never bothered to pull down the blinds, little knowing that on the other side of the house lived Harold Gibbons, vice president of Jimmy Hoffa's Teamsters union. (Fortunately for Kennedy, Gibbons told a friend who tipped off RFK, and he discontinued his noonday visits.)[27]

Bobby seems to have a sense of entitlement, that he's above it all, can do whatever he pleases. Back in 1962 the Kennedy brothers wanted Marilyn Monroe to appear at a Madison Square Garden rally in honor of JFK'S forty-fifth birthday. Problem was, she was working on a movie that was far behind schedule. Bobby called Milton Gould, a member of the board of directors of 20th Century Fox, and demanded he release her. Gould refused, upon which Kennedy screamed at Gould, called him "a Jew bastard," and hung up. (As it turned out, Marilyn defied the studio and came to New York for the event anyway.)[28]

Now calling someone a "Jew bastard" isn't the end of the world, but to do so over an unimportant matter having to do solely with vanity and self-gratification is disturbing. Kennedy needs to control his temper and not blow up like a spoiled brat.

His supporters, all chomping at the bit for the resurrection of a Kennedy presidency so they can get back their old jobs, claim he has matured into "a good Bobby." Be that as it may, Kennedy has made so many enemies that his ability to get his programs through Congress will be difficult. He will be hamstrung as president.

With the party bosses now pledged to Humphrey and the anti-war activists pledged to Eugene McCarthy, Kennedy has chosen to create his own coalition of the young and poor. It is a coalition based on emotion and nostalgia for the good old days of Camelot. His campaign rallies are like rock concerts.

"I do best among people who have problems," he asserts.[29] Fair enough, but promising lots of new benefits to the poor—on top of those mandated by LBJ's Great Society—is fiscally irresponsible. It is pandering to the masses just to get votes. Most people in America do *not* have problems: they have a job; they may even own a house; they pay taxes; they pay their bills. What does Kennedy have to say to these people?

Kennedy has shown no talent in attracting the middle class and unifying the country at a time when America is a veritable tinderbox. He seems to revel in extremism, in being an outsider, the seventh child, overshadowed by two bigger brothers. The most common word used to describe him is *ruthless*, a description he makes no effort to dispel; on the contrary, he treats it like a badge of honor. He seems to enjoy being the runt of the litter, turning every fire into an explosion.

He claims to be the conscience of America, yet he is one of the most undemocratic men to run for president. Where would he be had he not been born with a silver spoon in his mouth and a president for a brother? Many people remember with trepidation his claiming New York as his home so he could run for senator. They abhor his current kowtowing to the Left to get votes and are not at all convinced that "the good Bobby" has surpassed "the bad Bobby." Anyway, being the conscience of America is not the same as being president.

He is a superb executive who needs a lot more seasoning and

humility. He may become an excellent president someday, but not in 1968.

Accomplishments	Intangibles	Judgment	Overall
excellent	fair	poor	poor

1968

Robert Kennedy was assassinated in June 1968, hours after he had narrowly beaten Eugene McCarthy in the California primary. Admirers—and they were fervent—touted the victory and asked, "What might have been?" as if he would have become president. He became even more of a martyr than his brother; some booksellers reported they were selling more books about Bobby than about JFK.

In actual fact Kennedy was assassinated when he was falling short, not when he was rising. He had started the race by entering the Indiana primary and winning, but the results were merely "an inconclusive victory," according to the *New York Times*.[30] He was a long way from capturing the nomination. "Students were suspicious, party chiefs were unresponsive," says the historian Ronald Steel, "the whole South was hostile, and the vast middle class could not be gauged."[31] To build momentum and mount a credible campaign against McCarthy, Kennedy admitted he needed at least 50 percent of the California vote, and he hoped to get a lot more. But he got only 47 percent (McCarthy got 41 percent). Kennedy's win was not a victory; it was a setback. The next battleground on the long road to the party nomination was the state of New York, where there were relatively few African Americans and Hispanics ready to give Kennedy a 90 percent share of their vote. McCarthy would have trounced Kennedy there and ended his campaign, thereby forcing a showdown with the Democratic Party's establishment favorite, Vice President Hubert Humphrey (the eventual nominee). "Couldn't they see," said Democratic Party chairman Lawrence O'Brien about Kennedy's supporters, "he didn't have a chance?"[32]

O'Brien knew what he was talking about. Kennedy's problem was twofold: (1) there were not enough primaries left for him to win a large number of delegates, and (2) at the convention, where the contest would be decided, Humphrey could count on three-fourths of the delegates. In 1972 the rules were changed to make primaries the major determinant of who would be the nominee (which is how Jimmy Carter got the 1976 nomination). In 1968 this was not the case.

Kennedy followers imbued with nostalgia confuse the excitement of a campaign with what the voters were actually saying. A pre-election poll indicated that 40 percent of those declaring for McCarthy actually favored *escalation* of the war. "Many Democratic voters were registering a protest against the president for not *winning* the war, not because he was losing it," explains the historian Lewis Gould.[33] Kennedy's strident views on Vietnam and race were out of synch with the views of most voters.

Humphrey lost the presidential election to Nixon by less than a percentage point. Had the Democrats put up a united Humphrey-McCarthy ticket (or Humphrey-Kennedy), they probably would have beaten Nixon.

Bobby Kennedy had a morbid fear of assassination, for obvious reasons. Yet he, the father of eleven children, refused close Secret Service protection, plunged into crowds to shake hands, and refused to ride in bubble-top limousines—just as JFK, against the pleas of the Secret Service, had refused to do in Dallas. It's almost as if he had a subconscious wish to become a martyr like his brother.*

* His brother Ted urged him not to run. His strongest supporter in running was his wife, Ethel.

How one wishes he had been more circumspect! Or had shown better judgment. He put his own selfish emotional needs ahead of the nation's, and certainly ahead of his family's.

He had always insisted that he never intended to run for president in 1968, that he would wait until 1972. But when Johnson threw in the towel, he became a young man in a hurry, too impatient to wait. The opportunist in him took over, and he entered a race he probably knew he couldn't win.

15

Ronald Reagan, 1980

The presidency is an office under siege. Lloyd Cutler, President Carter's legal counsel, says the job has become too much for one man and maybe it's now time for a parliamentary system in the United States.[1]

Harry Truman isn't the only president to call the White House the "great White Jail."[2] Ever since Theodore Roosevelt virtually every president has left office a shadow of his former self. Wilson had several strokes; Harding and FDR died in office; Taft, Hoover, and Coolidge were totally exhausted; and Truman left with a humiliating approval rating barely above 20 percent. Our last four presidents have fared no better: Kennedy was assassinated; Johnson fell into a state of frustration and despair; Nixon was impeached; and Ford lost the re-election, the first time for an incumbent since Grover Cleveland in 1888.

Now President Carter is saying we are suffering a national malaise, exacerbated by the oil embargo, rising oil prices, Soviet adventurism in Afghanistan, and the Iranian imprisonment of fifty-two American hostages. Economically our country is in a state of stagflation. Four years ago the inflation rate was 4.9 percent; now it's in the double digits and rising.

The Republican nominee is a former governor of California who ran for president in 1968 and 1976, both times failing to win the

nomination. A political conservative, he says he aims to cut taxes, strengthen the military, and restore American optimism and confidence. In a March 17 speech to the Chicago Council on Foreign Relations, he attacked the Carter administration for harping on our allies for their human rights violations while ignoring our real enemy: the Soviet Union: "May I suggest an alternate path this nation can take, a change in foreign policy from the vacillation, appeasement and aimlessness of present policy? That alternate path must offer three broad requirements. First, it must be based on firm convictions, inspired by a clear vision of, and belief in, America's future. Second, it calls for a strong economy based on the free market system which gives us an unchallenged leadership in creative technology. Third, and very simply, we must have the unquestioned [military] ability to preserve world peace and our national security."[3] He promises to end the malaise and restore America to its true greatness. In his nomination acceptance speech of June 20, he quotes Thomas Paine, "We have it in our power to begin the world over again," and he excoriates Democrats who "say that the United States has had its days in the sun, that our nation has passed its zenith. My fellow Americans, I utterly reject that view."[4]

A Hollywood movie star in his early career, he once auditioned for the part of U.S. president in a movie, *The Best Man*. The studio turned him down, saying he didn't look presidential enough. Now, sixteen years later, he is trying again, this time for real.

RONALD REAGAN

Age: sixty-nine
6-foot-1½, 200 pounds
Married twice; divorced once
Excellent health
Nicknames: Dutch, Ronnie

Temporary home during campaign:	Permanent residence:	Weekend ranch:
Wexford Middleburg, VA	668 St. Cloud Los Angeles, CA	WS Refugio Road, Rancho del Cielo Solvang, CA

OBJECTIVE: Fortieth president of the United States

SUMMARY OF QUALIFICATIONS: Successful two-term governor of America's largest state; outstanding public speaker; proven negotiator with outstanding record of achievement; fully developed political views advocating smaller government, military security, and preservation of personal liberty.

LEADERSHIP EXPERIENCE

Pundit, 1976–Present

Write weekly newspaper column appearing in 174 newspapers. Have delivered over a thousand five-minute radio broadcasts on various political topics.

Candidate for President of the United States, 1976

Ran against incumbent president Gerald Ford for the Republican nomination. Lost by narrow margin: 70 votes short of the 1,140 needed for nomination.

Governor of California, 1967–1975

Two-term governor of America's largest state and the seventh largest economic political entity in the world. In first election, upset incumbent and won by one million votes (3.7 to 2.7 million).

Faced a horrendous budget deficit upon taking office. Raised taxes and eventually brought the state's finances under control. After generating a budget surplus, issued rebates to taxpayers and reduced taxes.

Undertook welfare reform to eliminate welfare fraud while at the same time providing increased aid to the truly needy. Passed the California Welfare Reform Act of 1971. Initiated reform of state prisons to improve living conditions.

Established strong environmental protection record: halted construction of new freeway and new dam; strengthened state regulation of industry and utilities; set aside 145,000 acres and expanded the Redwood National Park.

Undertook to instill order and fiscal discipline at the University of California. Fired the university president and called in the National Guard and the Highway Patrol to quell student riots and keep the university functioning. After restoring order, increased the education budget.

Elected chairman of the Republican Governors Conference. Featured in *Life* magazine, 1970, as "the hottest candidate in either party."

Candidate for President of the United States, 1968

Lost the Republican Party nomination to Richard Nixon.

Cochairman of California Republicans for Goldwater, 1964

Gave widely acclaimed, nationally televised speech, "A Time for Choosing."

Host, *Death Valley Days*, 1964

Hosted weekly television drama sponsored by the Borax Corporation.

Host, *The GE Theater*, 1954–1962

Hosted highly successful weekly television show sponsored by General Electric. Spent three months a year touring the country to meet company executives and 250,000 employees at 135 plants. Gave several thousand speeches on civic topics; over the years speeches became more political, warning of the dangers of big government to the independence of the worker. Acquired reputation as a prominent conservative spokesman.

Film and Entertainment Career, 1937–1964

Acted in fifty-three movies, beginning with *Love Is on the Air* (1937) and ending with *The Killers* (1964). Worked alongside many of the great Hollywood actors of the era. Starred as George Gipp ("Win one for the Gipper") in *Knute Rockne—All American*. Starred with Errol Flynn in *Santa Fe Trail*, with Lionel Barrymore and Wallace Beery in *The Bad Men*, and with Ann Sheridan in *King's Row* (where I awake from surgery, horrified that my legs have been amputated, and scream, "Where's the rest of me?," the title of my 1965 autobiography).

Became increasingly involved with the Screen Actors Guild and the growing concern with infiltration by Communists. As SAG president in 1959–60 led six-month strike against the movie studios: won revenue-sharing and pension plan for the actors. Led effort to clean the union of Communist spies and sympathizers. Testified before the House of Representatives Un-American Activities Committee, 1947; served as informant for the FBI. Reelected president of the Screen Actors Guild, an AFL-CIO affiliate every year between 1947 and 1952. In 1949–50 also served as chairman of the Motion Picture Industry Council, an organization dedicated to improving the public image of the movie industry.

Member, U.S. Army Air Corps, 1942–1945

Due to poor eyesight, performed military service in a civilian capacity. Member of the First Motion Picture Unit, a group of 1,300 people responsible for producing training films and documentaries. Acted in *This Is the Army* (an Irving Berlin musical) and *Hollywood in Uniform* (with Clark Gable, Alan Ladd, and Tyrone Power).

Commissioned as a second lieutenant; honorably discharged as a captain. Demonstrated ability to spot talent: encouraged a seventeen-year-old brunette named Norma Jean Dougherty to color her hair blonde and go into movies. She changed her name to Marilyn Monroe.[5]

Sports Announcer, WHO Radio Station, 1933–1937

Announced over six hundred Chicago Cubs and Chicago White Sox baseball games for radio station in Des Moines, Iowa. On visit to spring training camp in California, secured interview with Warner Brothers and obtained job as an actor.

EDUCATION

Eureka College, 1928–32, small (250 students) liberal arts private college in Illinois. Awarded 50 percent scholarship; paid the balance with earnings from summer and part-time jobs. Majored in economics. Three-sport varsity athlete: football, swimming, and track. Also served as varsity swimming coach. Member of the Drama Society: earned Honorable Mention in national competition. President of senior class.

PERSONAL

Born February 6, 1911. Grew up in Dixon, Illinois. Worked seven summers as a lifeguard and saved the lives of seventy-seven people. Married Jane Wyman, 1940, divorced 1949; one daughter, Maureen, age thirty-nine, and one son, Michael, age thirty-five. Married Nancy Davis, 1952; one daughter, Patti, age twenty-seven, and one son, Ron, age twenty-two. Favorite hobbies: reading, horseback riding, fine wines, watching movies, and working on the 688 acres of my mountaintop home, Rancho del Cielo.

Assessment of Qualifications

The first thing people want to know about Ronald Reagan, age sixty-nine, is the state of his health. The last time we elected an old man for president, he died after a month in office. Could it happen again? Highly unlikely. William Henry Harrison died because the medical treatments at the time were primitive. For a man about to turn seventy, Reagan is remarkably fit. His blood pressure is normal; he has never been hospitalized for anything serious; he exercises regularly; and he doesn't smoke or drink, except for an occasional glass of expensive wine.* A former life-guard and movie actor, he is proud of his physique and keeps himself in top condition, mostly by horseback riding and chopping wood at his ranch. He makes no apologies for his age. He compares himself to Verdi, who composed *Otello* at age seventy-four; to Falstaff at eighty; to Stradivarius, who made his best violin after he had reached sixty and was still making them up to age ninety-two. We see no reason why Reagan won't live to eighty-four, the average life expectancy for men his age.

> * During cocktails at a dinner party he is seen with a martini glass in his hand. What people don't know is that the glass is always filled with water (and the obligatory olive). Always an actor!

The second question people ask is: How can a movie star think he's qualified to be president of the United States? Asked a similar question in 1966, when he ran for governor, Reagan responds, "I don't know, I've never played the role."[6] This humor leaves his opponents flummoxed. What they forget is that Reagan was no B-grade actor, as his political opponents claim; in his prime he was one of the highest-paid actors in Hollywood and played alongside some of the biggest names on the screen. On his thirty-ninth birthday five hundred actors, known as the Friars, honored him as one of the top actors of the 1940s.

Not only was he a major box-office draw, but he got elected six times as president of a huge organization—the fourteen-thousand-member Screen Actors Guild—and led a successful strike against the movie studios, one of the toughest monopolies in the country.

Though he got into politics quite late in life—age fifty-five—he has well-developed political views due to many years of serious reading and writing. His convictions are so strong he has even put his life on the line. He learned firsthand about Communist efforts to infiltrate Hollywood and use the movies as a tool for spreading propaganda. ("Of all the arts," said Lenin, "cinema is the most important.") Reagan spoke up in opposition and received threats that acid would be thrown in his face, but still he became an FBI informant and testified before Congress. It was a patriotic effort so dangerous he had to carry a loaded Smith & Wesson .32 (a major reason his first wife left him). He refused to be cowed. Asked why the Communists had failed to take over Hollywood, the pro-Communist actor Sterling Hayden testified before Congress, "We ran into a one-man battalion named Ronald Reagan."[7]

Reagan has a wonderful sense of humor and loves to tell jokes. Many people make the mistake of confusing this humor with the light-headedness of a Hollywood celebrity. A visit to his home reveals a far more serious man than most people give him credit for. In his library are many books by James Madison, Thomas Jefferson, Friedrich Hayek, and Ludwig von Mises—all dog-eared and underlined with comments in the margin. He writes his own speeches. Every week he writes a newspaper column. His output is prodigious: over a lifetime he has churned out more political copy than any president since Jefferson (and that includes intellectual luminaries like Theodore Roosevelt and Woodrow Wilson). His writings may lack the intellectual sophistication of Wilson, but they are well-written and to the point. He knows how to write simply and clearly—a rare talent.

He is probably the best public speaker in America, so good that it is said he "could get a standing ovation in a graveyard."[8] A look at how he prepares his speeches reveals an ingenious and creative mind. He is extremely nearsighted and refuses to wear glasses in public, meaning he cannot see his notes on the podium when he is giving a speech. So he developed a unique method. He writes out his entire speech, word for word—no ad-libbing. Then he takes key words, shortens them by eliminating particular vow-

OF " MILs. " CM. " THS. CITY ECH ←
YR. THR --- ALWls " STOP " BE MD.
HR. --- BASE " REFLECTING POOL &
" STATUE " BE SN. --- BCKWOODsMN
" BCM. " LAWYR, " CONG.MN & " PRES.

IT " SD. --- BY STNDNG " I SD. " THS.
STATUE THR CN. --- SN. --- PROFILE --- MN.
--- STRNGTH & WISDOM ⌐& BY STNDNG
--- OTHR SD: " PROFILE --- MN. --- COMPASSN

THS. 2 VIEWs " LINCOLN SYMBOLIZE
OUR OWN MEMRY " HM. TODAY⌐— LINCOLN
" NAT. LDR. WHO " TM. " CRISIS CALLD
" COUNTRY MN " GRTNSS ⌐& LINCOLN
" MN. WHOSE GRACE, COMPASSN &
EARNEST COMMITMNT --- REMEMBRD "
COUNTLESS BIOGs. FOLK TALES & POETRY

els and consonants, and writes them in block letters on a 4" by 6" index card, big enough so he can read them. Thirty cards are enough to make a twenty-minute speech. He has a phenomenal photographic memory. As he gives the speech he glances down at a card and reads the block of abbreviations below a line. It is an ingenious form of shorthand, enough to challenge anybody.*9

* "Of the millions who come to this city each year, there is always a stop to be made here at the house of the Reflecting Pool and a statue to be seen, of a backwoodsman who became a lawyer, a congressman, and a president. It is said that by standing to one side of this statue there can be seen the profile of a man of strength and wisdom and by standing on the other side the profile of a man of compassion. These two views of Lincoln symbolize our own memory of him today: Lincoln, the national leader who in a time of crisis called his countrymen to greatness; and Lincoln, the man whose grace, compassion, and earnest commitment is remembered in countless biographies, folktales, and poetry."[10]

With the advent of teleprompters, he rarely uses index cards, but he still uses his unique system of shorthand. His development of this technique shows a man who takes his job seriously and makes an extraordinary effort to do it well. Certainly it shows imagination.

In May 1967 Reagan engaged in a debate with Robert Kennedy on an international TV show sponsored by CBS and viewed by fifteen million people. "The Ronnie-Bobby Show," *Newsweek* called it, "the first eyeball-to-eyeball test of the two men who may very well meet on the road to the White House."[11] After the show was over, virtually everyone agreed Reagan had clobbered Kennedy. "It was the political rookie Reagan who left old campaigner Kennedy blinking when the session ended," *Newsweek* declared.*

* Kennedy was so furious at being humiliated by "that son-of-a-bitch" Reagan that he allegedly ordered CBS to never release the tape for repeat viewing. When Reagan wanted to use the tape for the Oregon primary, CBS refused. The blackout of Reagan continued. To this day not a single biography of Bobby Kennedy discusses this highly publicized debate. Even Arthur Schlesinger's thousand-page *Robert Kennedy and His Times*, published in 1978, makes no mention of it.

Kennedy had done no preparation for the show. In contrast Reagan had studied lengthy memos on Vietnam and conducted a full question-and-answer rehearsal the day before the debate. He came armed with statistics that left the audience astounded.

Friends of Kennedy would complain that Reagan had the advantage of being a former movie actor, but they had to admit he had worked a lot harder and had done his homework.

As governor, Reagan usually managed to get home by six o'clock, leading many people to think he is lazy. This is incorrect: he is extremely self-disciplined and has tremendous powers of concentration. And he does a lot of work at home. According to his wife Nancy, Reagan never watches TV; he reads. After he gets up in the morning and takes a shower, he immediately goes to his desk in the bedroom and starts writing. Reagan's two security guards confirm this propensity for work. One of them is Dennis LeBlanc, a member of the security detail when Reagan was governor who stayed with Reagan after he left public office in 1975, traveling with him as he went around the country giving speeches. On the plane, with the lights out and everyone sleeping or watching the movie, Reagan had his light on, reading and writing. "The minute the meal service was done, he'd whip out the legal pad and start writing," says LeBlanc. "He wrote to fit the exact time he needed to record. I was always amazed at how hard he worked. I'd be exhausted from traveling with him; I could start reading something and quickly fall asleep, and when I woke up he'd still be working, just writing away."[12] A second confirmation comes from David Fischer, Reagan's executive assistant in 1978 and 1979. During the many drives from Los Angeles to Reagan's ranch in the mountains, a two-and-half-hour trip, Reagan would be in the backseat, writing.

Over the past three years Reagan has delivered over a thousand five-minute radio shows, titled "This Is Ronald Reagan Speaking." Broadcast over 286 stations and published as a weekly newspaper column in 226 newspapers, these have reached an audience of twenty million Americans. Where does this love of political issues come from? How is it that a man who excelled in the cinema and television world has a passion to bury himself in books, memos, and position papers?

Reagan grew up in a small town in Illinois, the younger of two sons of a poor but happy family. "Our family didn't exactly come from the wrong side of the tracks, but we were certainly always within sound of the train whistles," he writes in his 1965 autobiography.[13] Dinner often was oatmeal mixed with hamburger meat, cooked on a single-burner hot plate in a two-room apartment. His father was a shoe salesman and an alcoholic who never had a steady job until he landed a position with FDR's Works Progress Administration. Like many children of alcoholic fathers, Reagan learned to suppress bad news and uncomfortable facts in order to get along. His great savior was his religious mother, who taught him that whatever happens "is God's plan."

To help his family put food on the dinner table, he worked seven summers as a lifeguard, twelve hours a day, seven days a week. He says this experience saving people taught him a lot about human nature: "They felt insulted. I got to recognize that people hate to be saved. Almost every one of them later sought me out and angrily denounced me for dragging them to the shore. 'I would have been fine if you'd let me alone,' was their theme."[14] He set a record in his hometown for the number of lives he saved: seventy-seven. Only one person ever thanked him: a man who was blind. This experience exerted a major influence on him when he became governor of California and set out to control the skyrocketing cost of welfare programs; he was compassionate for those truly drowning and tough on everyone else.

Reagan worked his way through college as a janitor, construction worker, and dishwasher. He was a big man on campus: a three-sport athlete and president of his class. But his pivotal moment in college came in a different arena: when he stood up to give a political speech and got treated to a rousing ovation at the end. "They came to their feet with a roar. . . . It was heady wine," he writes. He had one goal after leaving college: "I decided to find the rest of me. I loved three things: drama, politics and sports, and I'm not always sure they came in that order."[15]

His years as a Hollywood actor and union leader and his eight-year stint for General Electric shaped his political philosophy. After one of his speeches, workers would tell him all the problems they were having with government bureaucrats who were constantly telling them how to run their business. "It was almost like a postgraduate course in political science for me," he recalls. "I was seeing how government really operated and affected people in America, not how it was taught in school. . . . No barnstorming politician ever met the people on quite such a common footing."[16] He was on the road three months a year, giving as many as fourteen speeches a day. He calculates that he was on his feet in front of a mike for about 250,000 minutes. At twenty-five minutes a speech, that's 10,000 speeches. No wonder he's such a good public speaker.

He got involved in the 1964 Goldwater campaign and offered to give a speech as Election Day approached. Problem was, the Republican finance chest was running low and the cost of a national telecast was $60,000. Fortunately for Reagan, help came from two of his friends: John Wayne, the actor, and the former chairman of General Electric, Ralph Cordiner, now chairman of the Republican Finance Committee. Utilizing his experience on the "mashed potato" circuit for GE, Reagan delivered his speech, "A Time to Choose," and a political star was born. David Broder, the famous Washington columnist, called it the greatest speech since the "Cross of Gold" speech by William Jennings Bryan in 1896. It raised $8 million for the party.

Ronald Reagan had found his calling.

RECORD AS GOVERNOR

What chance did a neophyte—a former actor, no less—have against Governor Pat Brown, a powerful politician who had won the governorship in 1958 by defeating the state's senior U.S. senator and won reelection by defeating Richard Nixon in 1962? The neophyte furthermore was a Republican in a state where Republicans were outnumbered by Democrats 2 to 1.

As one might expect of a man who once had to carry a gun for two years, Reagan does not scare easily. By campaigning relentlessly, giving magnificent speeches, and positioning himself as an outsider mocking his opponent's experience, Reagan pulled off a stunning upset, trouncing Brown by a million votes. Upon taking office, when he found the state treasury nearly bankrupt, out the window went his campaign bromides about cutting taxes. Instead he raised taxes and increased government spending. In so doing he confounded not only his conservative Republican friends but also the Democrats who couldn't believe he was getting away with it: having just raised taxes, he was coasting on a 70 percent public approval rating. "How in the devil a governor can push through a billion-dollar tax increase and win popularity doing it is beyond me," a frustrated Democratic legislator told *Time* magazine.[17]

He proved to be such a dynamic governor that *Life* magazine called him "the hottest candidate in either party."[18] Reelected by another huge margin, he set about reforming the state's bloated welfare system. Facing fierce opposition from Democratic legislators, he went over their heads and made dozens of banquet speeches appealing directly to the people. Bob Moretti, the speaker of the assembly, was so inundated with angry letters he begged the governor to stop the juggernaut. The two men sat down and over several months crafted a deal everyone could live with. Reagan got stricter standards, forcing many people off the rolls, and permitted increased benefits for the truly needy. California, once denigrated as "the welfare capital of the nation," became the national standard for welfare reform.

One test of a man's fitness for political office is how he treats his enemies. Reagan, a conservative in a liberal state, certainly had a lot of them. Yet he thrived. Wilson Riles, upon being elected state superintendent of public instruction over one of Reagan's conservatives, was understandably nervous about how he would be treated by the powerful governor. He was pleasantly surprised to discover that Reagan had an open door and was always willing to talk. Said Riles, "He did not try to manipulate [education] in a partisan way, he did his homework, and he was well-organized."[19]

Whereas Governor Brown had forty department heads reporting directly to him, Reagan consolidated them into four "cabinet"
agencies. Each semiweekly cabinet meeting was conducted like a
board of directors meeting, but with only one person voting: the
governor. Many issues got resolved quickly; others, such as help
for the truly needy and fighting to add 140,000 acres to the Redwood Forest Park, took as many as thirty or forty meetings. Like
Churchill and Eisenhower, Reagan insisted on every issue being
reduced to a one-page memo, though, when necessary, he would
ask for the customary fat briefing book. He was such a forceful
executive that he used his line-item veto authority 943 times—
and never once was he overridden by the legislature.

He restored the state budget to a healthy surplus and returned
over $5 billion in taxes to taxpayers. Now a national figure, he was
elected chairman of the Republican Governors Conference and
was offered several top jobs by the Ford administration: ambassador to the Court of St. James, transportation secretary, commerce
secretary. He turned them all down; he didn't want an advisory
job. Every job he has held—lifeguard, radio announcer, movie
star, union leader, television personality, and governor—has been
a line position, putting him in direct control.

Being a governor is a logical stepping-stone to the presidency:
almost half our presidents (seventeen of thirty-nine) have been
former governors. Reagan believes his record as governor qualifies him for the presidency: "For too long a time we have turned
to the legislative branch of our government for our candidates
for president and have ignored the fact that those with the most
executive experience are governors."[20]

RUNNING FOR PRESIDENT

Upon leaving public office, Reagan found himself the most sought-
after speaker in the country. As governor in 1974, his income was
$49,100; in 1975 speaking fees pushed it over $800,000.

Reagan had always planned to run for president in 1976, after
Nixon completed his second term. But with Nixon's impeach-
ment and a new man as the Republican president, the presidency

RONALD REAGAN, 1980

looked like a lost cause. But Reagan knew something about politics most politicians and political pundits apparently did not: Gerald Ford's strength was wide but shallow. A political poll may measure popularity and name awareness, but it doesn't measure depth the way a focus group does. To win elective office, argued Reagan, you need to have a powerful message. Stick to your core message, keep hammering away, and your base will grow.

He surprised everyone by coming within a whisker of beating Ford for the 1976 presidential nomination. At the Republican National Convention he gave a powerful peroration that left many feeling they had elected the wrong man. Another run for the presidency, in 1980? Highly improbable, given his age. In a meeting with his staff as he prepared to leave the convention, Reagan told them to be ready, the battle had just begun. "We lost, but the cause goes on! . . . Nancy and I, we aren't going to go back and sit in a rocking chair and say, 'Well, that's all for us.'"[21]

Reagan clearly has the drive—and the stomach—required to run for president. Nothing fazes him. When he was governor and student radicals and protestors were rioting, he didn't hide in his office like many professors and administrators; he went out on the street to talk to them, face to face. "I wouldn't miss this for anything," he said.[22]

He possesses two qualities that make for a transformative leader: intense willpower and personal humility. It's a rare combination. On his desk in the governor's office is a sign: "There is no limit to what you can accomplish if you don't care who gets the credit." In describing his record as governor, he uses the pronoun *we*, not *I*. He explains, "I use the plural 'we' because, as governor, I had the help of some very fine people."[23] (Such modesty stands in sharp contrast to President Carter, who repeats *I* fifty to a hundred times in a speech.) Reagan is a man comfortable in his own skin.

The former Democratic senator and presidential candidate Eugene McCarthy, the man whose 41 percent of the New Hampshire primary vote drove LBJ out of office in 1964, has stunned everyone by endorsing Reagan for president. McCarthy calls him "the only man since Harry Truman who won't confuse the job with the man."[24] A similar point is made by John Sears, even though Reagan fired him as campaign manager: "Reagan knows himself better than most presidents and has kept his identity separate from politics. Reagan knows who he is and therefore he possesses the first prerequisite for being a good president."[25]

On the negative side, he is prone to make numerous gaffes and inaccurate off-the-cuff remarks. He says trees contribute 93 percent of the atmosphere's nitrous oxide, that Alaska has more oil reserves than Saudi Arabia, and that the federal government spends three dollars in overhead for every dollar of welfare benefits (the actual amount is twelve cents). Such gaffes have cost him the support of all three past Republican candidates, Goldwater, Nixon, and Ford, who regard him as a lightweight. Probably the strongest of these critics is Goldwater, who in 1976 accused Reagan of "gross factual errors" and warned he might "take rash action" and "needlessly lead this country into open military conflict."[26] Yet there is no question who better crystallizes the issue at hand: the giveaway of the Panama Canal. Said Reagan, "We bought it, we paid for it, it's ours, and we're going to keep it."

Gerald Ford writes in his memoirs that Reagan has a "penchant for offering simplistic solutions to hideously complex problems."[27] Be that as it may, Reagan is better able to get at the root of a problem and express it in language everyone can understand.

CONCLUSION

The political pollster Louis Harris, advisor to JFK in the 1960 election, once offered this comment about elections: "If you're running for political office, and you succeed in getting three messages to your electorate, you stand a chance. If you succeed in getting just two messages to your electorate, you take the lead. . . . And if all you do is communicate just one message, you become president of the United States."[28] Jimmy Carter had such a message four years ago when he promised a Watergate-weary public, "I'll give you government as good as the people." Reagan has crafted an equally compelling message for today, after four years of Carter: "Are you better now than you were four years ago?"

Reagan is a formidable candidate. He has won two state elections by a huge margin and almost upset an incumbent president in a party nomination. He has successfully managed America's largest state by reorganizing the executive office, treating his adversaries with respect, and being decisive. He's a bit like Wendell Willkie: a tough negotiator with a winning smile and pleasing personality. He is an exceptionally congenial and charming man, with a terrific sense of humor. Nothing rattles or depresses him. He promises to be a different type of president from what we normally see:

- He is a man of conviction.
- He is not interested in chalking up lots of small victories to make himself look like a successful president; he is more likely to gamble and go for the big win.
- A master of public speaking and persuasion, he will go over the heads of legislators and appeal directly to the people if he doesn't get what he wants.

What does he hope to accomplish? Asked by his son Michael what disappointed him most about losing the 1976 party nomination to Ford, Reagan responded, "I wanted to sit down with Brezhnev. I wanted to listen to him for fifteen or twenty minutes. Then I was going to get up from my chair very slowly while he was talking, and I was going to walk around to the other side of the table. And I was going to lean over and whisper in his ear, '*Nyet*.'"[29]

However, if he has any idea about how to attain this opportunity, he has yet to reveal it (probably to avoid controversy during a campaign). How will he cut taxes, increase military spending, and still balance the budget? Even his own running mate—when running against him for the nomination—called this "voodoo economics."

He dislikes messy contradictions, which is to be expected of the son of an alcoholic. "There are no easy answers," he says in his Goldwater speech, "but there are simple ones." For most of his life he has excelled in familiar surroundings: being in command of the microphone, hammering away at the same points. Says the columnist George Will, "It is hard for Reagan to avoid sounding like an echo of an echo."[30] This constant hammering away is a virtue when running for president, but not when being president. In the presidential chair he will face new and unusual problems, many of them bizarre and complex. To cope with them, persistence and perseverance may not be enough.

As governor of California he compiled one of the most impressive records of any modern-day governor. He is not to be underestimated; he has the potential to be an excellent president. We would be surprised, however, to see him become a great one.

Accomplishments	Intangibles	Judgment	Overall
outstanding	outstanding	excellent	excellent

1980

Reagan won by a landslide, winning forty-four of fifty states. He immediately laid down his marching orders in his Inaugural Address: "We are a nation that has a government—not the other way around." At his gala inauguration ball he set the tone for a rejuvenated America: gone were the cardigan sweaters and turned-down thermostats of the Carter era; this would be like FDR's campaign slogan of 1932, "Happy Days Are Here Again." The contrast between the sunny and optimistic Reagan and the gloomy Carter reminded people of the contrast between FDR and Hoover. The release of the hostages, through no effort of his own, was a sign that good luck was on his side.

His mission in becoming president may have been to say *nyet* to the Soviets, but that would not be among his first three priorities. They were "the economy, the economy, the economy."[31]

He moved with business-like alacrity. In his first hundred days, he held sixty-nine meetings with 467 members of the House and the Senate, prompting many of them to say they had seen more of Reagan in four months than they had of Carter in four years.[32] He worked relentlessly on matters he cared about. In trying to get his tax cut passed, he held numerous meetings and worked the phones from dusk until the late evening, scrounging for votes. For a man known to be hands-off and an excessive delegator, he surprised many aides with his energy. He read everything that was given to him, and throughout his presidency he kept up a hectic daily pace, holding an average of ten meetings a day and seeing eighty people. He worked as hard as Samuel Tilden or Herbert Hoover, but he kept George Marshall's hours.

Seriously wounded in an assassination attempt, he amazed everyone with his calm and equanimity. How could voters not respond to a man who tells his wife, "Honey, I forgot to duck"? Or to the doctors as he is being wheeled into the operating room, "I hope you are all Republicans"? After the life-saving operation the chief surgeon said he had never seen such a strong man. He had lost 50 percent of his blood.

After leaving the hospital, he sent a handwritten letter to the Soviet premier, urging that they get together to talk. There was no acceptance.

He was bull-headed in pursuit of his principles, and once he made up his mind there was no going back. Offended by the audacity of the air traffic controllers to demand a 100 percent pay raise and then to strike in violation of their "no strike" pledge, he threatened to fire them, even though their union had been one of the few to support his election. His advisors told him he was taking a huge risk: with the nation's airports understaffed and manned by substitute controllers, a crash would have been a political disaster. He fired them anyway.

He was relentless in his drive to curb inflation. By the end of 1982 inflation had "dropped like a rock,"[33] from 21 to 3.8 percent, and the United States was on its way to a nonstop economic expansion for the rest of his eight years. Blocked by the Democrats from implementing deep cuts in government spending, he ran up a deficit every year he was in office. By the time he left the federal deficit had increased to over $1.5 trillion. Roughly half, $800 billion, was increased defense spending. His rationale: he was waging a war; the United States always runs a deficit during wartime; and only after the war was won could military expenditures be decreased and the budget balanced (which is exactly what happened in the 1990s under Bill Clinton).

He implemented two widely publicized tax cuts in 1981 and 1986 that reduced the top tax rate, eliminated six million low-income earners from the tax rolls, and indexed the tax rate to inflation to eliminate "bracket creep." Despite his antitax rhetoric, he also passed two huge tax increases in 1982 and 1984 to try to stem the deficit problem. The result was that overall federal taxes remained the same: 19.4 percent in 1980 and 19.3 percent in 1989. Still tax revenues were not enough. By the time he left office the nation had a $155 billion deficit, nearly twice the deficit he had inherited from Carter. He called himself a conservative and railed against big government, but in truth he was a big spender.

Try though he might, he could not halt the automatic growth of federal spending due to cost-of-living increases. Many of what Democrats decried as tax cuts were not absolute cuts but reductions in the rate of growth. Carter had tried to address this issue by proposing a new procedure called zero-base budgeting and gotten nowhere. Reagan tried by using a line-item veto, with limited success. As the deficits mounted, the only way to pay for government programs was with increased borrowing—a fundamental violation of prudent fiscal management espoused by the Founding Fathers. Said Thomas Jefferson, "I wish it were possible to obtain a single amendment to our Constitution . . . an additional article, taking away the power of borrowing."[34]

Daring to take on "the third rail" of American politics, he proposed cuts in Social Security—and got rebuffed by the Senate, 96–0. Undeterred he appointed a commission to make alternative recommendations. In 1983 he got legislation passed that increased taxes, gradually increased the retirement age by two years, and taxed a portion of benefits for higher-income individuals. These reforms kept the system in surplus until 2008.[35] In saving Social Security for twenty-five years, Reagan showed the kind of leadership largely forgotten today; from the time he left office to the present, not a single president or candidate has made any attempt to address this entitlements crisis, which only gets worse with each passing year.*

* Countless studies have confirmed the magnitude of this problem. In 2011 the International Monetary Fund estimated that in order to pay for entitlements, a double whammy was necessary: all taxes must rise by 35 percent and all benefits be cut by 35 percent "immediately and for the indefinite future." [36]

To the dismay of many conservatives Reagan refrained from pushing favorite causes like permitting school prayer and outlawing abortion. He had his mind fixed on another issue, easy to remember. All he had to do was put his hand in his pocket and be reminded: "As president, I carried no wallet, no money, no driver's license, no keys in my pockets—only secret codes that were capable of bringing about the annihilation of much of the world as we know it."[37]

Back in 1977 he had told a visitor that he had been thinking about the cold war and he had a solution: "We win and they lose."[38] Now he upped the ante, terrifying many people, especially in Europe, with his blunt talk about the Soviet Union—"the evil empire," he called it. To the British Parliament he announced, "The march of freedom and democracy . . . will leave Marxism-Leninism on the ash heap of history."[39] Such fighting words, reminiscent of Truman's "Carry out your agreements and you won't be talked to like that!" reinforced Reagan's image as a gun-slinging cowboy.

Not that the Soviets made it any easier. In 1983 they shot down a Korean Airlines 747 with 269 passengers aboard, including sixty-one Americans, one of them a member of Congress. Reagan, though outraged, refused to respond in a provocative manner. If anything, the incident reinforced his fear of an accidental nuclear war and the need to overcome the bankrupt thinking called MAD, mutually assured destruction. If a fighter pilot could make such a horrendous mistake, how about the commander of a missile launch crew?*

* Unbeknownst to the United States at this time, such a disaster almost did occur. Three weeks after the Korean airliner incident, Lt.-Col. Stanislav Petrov received five separate electronic notifications of a U.S. ICBM missile headed for Russia. He had only ten minutes

to notify his superiors to launch a retaliatory attack. Fortunately he questioned why there were only five missiles and suspected the electronic information might be a false alarm. It turned out that the Soviet satellites had detected sunlight reflections off Montana clouds. First heralded as a hero, Petrov was later reprimanded and forced into early retirement for failing to inform his superiors in a timely manner. This incident was covered up and did not become public until the late 1990s. It was the closest the world came to nuclear war.[40]

Equally simplistic, thought Reagan, was the U.S. military plan for presidential security in case of nuclear attack: just fly away in a helicopter. Given that the maximum amount of time between detecting a missile and being hit by it is a mere six minutes, the odds of getting out of the White House safely were problematic. More important than the president's survival was the survival of the office itself. The president must not leave the White House. "I want to sit here in the office," he said, "getting into the helicopter is George's job" (referring to Vice President George H. W. Bush).[41] Reagan initiated and approved "Enduring National Leadership," a top-secret plan in the event of a nuclear attack, whereby several teams would vanish to secure locations, each with a successor "president" equipped with "the world's biggest laptop" so he could continue to govern if the real president was killed.[42] The program was a high-tech way to deal with a threat not envisioned by the Founding Fathers. Reagan pulled his most imaginative move yet, however, in announcing the Strategic Defense Initiative, whereby the United States would build a missile shield to defend itself against Soviet attack. It caught everyone by surprise, including many of his own military advisors. It was also, observes the historian David Hoffman, "extra-legal and extra-constitutional, and established a process of presidential succession that is nowhere in the Constitution."[43]

The Russians were stunned. Then Reagan pulled another surprise: he would share the technology with the Russians so they would feel safe knowing they had parity.

In 1984 he won the biggest reelection landslide in history, taking forty-nine states. In the meantime the Soviet general secretary Konstantin Chernenko had died, and the contest for his successor boiled down to a hard-liner, Grigori Romanov, and a young reformer, Mikhail Gorbachev. Unnerved by Reagan's rhetoric and realizing the Soviet Union was falling behind the United States, the party chiefs selected Gorbachev to make the reforms needed to enable the Soviet Union to compete.

On his second day in power Gorbachev announced he would negotiate on arms control. Reagan sent him several handwritten letters, and an extensive correspondence ensued. To get ready for his first summit meeting, Reagan—like a movie actor getting ready for a prime role—mastered an intensive Soviet Union 101 tutorial and conducted a mock summit with a former U.S. ambassador playing the role of Gorbachev. Whatever curveballs would be thrown at him, Reagan would be well-prepared. But there was more: years later, when asked why his personal negotiations had been so successful, Reagan referred to his Hollywood days as a labor union leader: "After the studios, Gorbachev was a snap."[44]

With the economy booming, Reagan was on a roll. In July 1986 *Time* magazine ran a cover story entitled "Why Is This Man So Popular?" There were two basic reasons, concluded *Time*: he was consistent, and he was authentic. He outlined a clear set of goals, and people trusted him even if they disagreed with what he was doing.[45] In August there appeared a *Fortune* cover story, "What Managers Can Learn from Ronald Reagan." In the *Fortune* interview Reagan espoused his theory of good management, akin to that of George Washington and George Marshall: "I encourage all the input I can get. And this has led to some of those press stories, since the walls of the [White House] building leak profusely, saying that we're torn with dissension or something. No, I want to know. And when I've heard all that I need to make a decision, I don't take a vote. I make the decision. Then I expect every one of them, whether their views have carried the day or not, to go forward together in carrying out the policy."[46]

Two months later came Iran-Contra, the botched attempt to reach out to moderates in Iran that ended up becoming an effort to trade guns for hostages and divert money to help the Contras in Nicaragua. It was such a cockamamie scheme many people wondered if Reagan had lost his senses. The answer was simple: nobody was minding the store. Reagan's famed management-by-delegation had broken down, not because of oversight or laziness but because of a fluke in organization. Back in 1973, in a letter about Nixon and Watergate, Reagan had written, "If my staff wanted to keep something of this kind from me, it would be very easy for them to do so."[47] To prevent this from happening, President Reagan had appointed a strong man to be chief of staff, first James Baker, then Donald Regan. Anyone wanting to see the president had to go through Regan, who usually sat in on all meetings. But there was one notable exception: John Poindexter, head of the National Security Council, who had his own office in the basement of the White House. After getting Reagan's approval on a policy to seek communications with moderates in Iran, with release of hostages as proof of sincerity, Poindexter and CIA director William Casey embarked on a quite different effort, a straight arms-for-hostages swap. Helping them was a Rambo named Oliver North, a midlevel military officer who spun fantasy tales about "private meetings with the president" and "taking walks with the president in the woods of Camp David"—complete fabrications. Before long North was heading a top-secret program, unknown and unapproved by the president, to divert arms sale monies to the Contras in Nicaragua.

How to deny something that was never said or never happened? Reagan said he couldn't remember giving such particular instructions, and his chief of staff couldn't help him because he was hardly ever in the meetings with Poindexter, who had direct access to the president. It was a managerial mess of the first order—not a crime, but a mess. Reagan was subjected to a political lynching over Iran-Contra, and after it was over, in early 1987, most people gave him up for dead politically. With less than two years left on his term and his credibility badly damaged, his prospects looked bleak.

But the seeds of his greatest political success had been sown and now came to fruition. In 1987 Reagan and Gorbachev signed their historic agreement, the Intermediate-Range Nuclear Forces Treaty, eliminating midrange conventional and nuclear-armed missiles. It was the crowning achievement for a president who dared to fight for an issue other politicians veered away from. Americans forgave Reagan for botching the Iran-Contra affair and now hailed him as a hero. Thomas Jefferson probably would have understood. In 1810 he wrote, "A strict observation of the written laws is doubtless one of the highest duties of a good citizen, but it is not the *highest*. The laws of necessity, of self-preservation, of saving the country when in danger, are of higher obligation."[48]

Presidents are rated on what they achieve: passing legislation, creating new programs, winning wars. In Reagan's case a new dimension should be added: preventing harm. If in the years ahead Armageddon fails to happen, a great debt will be owed to the man who helped prevent it. To be sure, "What if?" conjectures are impossible to prove, but to whatever extent he saved the world from potential nuclear war one could argue that Reagan achieved the greatest single feat of any post–World War II president.

Ten months after leaving office the Berlin War came down. Reagan had won his war. Or had he? Liberal detractors claimed the wall would have come down anyway and that equal credit should be given to Pope John Paul II, to Lech Walesa, and to the Solidarity movement. But most people who knew the situation firsthand, including the Polish people, Walesa, and the Democratic senators Edward Kennedy and John Kerry, gave almost all the credit to Reagan. At a state dinner in England for Gorbachev in 2001, when a British academic mocked Reagan as "rather an intellectual lightweight," Gorbachev, astounded and offended, retorted, "You are wrong. President Reagan was a man of real insight, sound political judgment, and courage."[49]

Certainly he was a man who baffled politicians and academics. Polls of academics rank him in the middle tier of presidents, whereas many polls of voters rank him as one of the greatest, alongside Washington, Lincoln, and FDR. A 2012 Harris poll of the public found Reagan ranked the best president in modern times, even ahead of FDR.[50] During his eight years as president, according to a Gallup poll, he was the most admired man in America.[51] In his two presidential elections he had captured 94 percent of the electoral vote, the highest percentage since George Washington's 100 percent. When he left office his approval rating was higher than any president's in forty years: 68 percent.

How to explain his success? In his Farewell Address he said, "I won a nickname, 'the Great Communicator.' But I never thought it was my style or the words I used that made a difference. It was the content. I wasn't a great communicator, but I communicated great things."[52]

One of which was his "11th Commandment": "Thou shall not speak ill of any fellow Republican."[53] It applied also to the Democrats. Contrary to what the media portrayed as a warm relationship between Reagan and House Speaker Tip O'Neill, a Democrat, the truth was that the two men detested each other. The first time they met at the White House, O'Neill lectured the man from California, "A governor plays in the minor leagues. You're in the big leagues now." O'Neill would go on to publicly denounce Reagan as "callous," a "tightwad," and an "Ebenezer Scrooge" with "no concern for the working class of America."[54] Throughout such insults Reagan controlled his temper and acted graciously.

He wasn't a particularly sophisticated man. Robert Gates, then CIA deputy director and later secretary of defense, called his perception of the Soviet Union "primitive."[55] But Reagan possessed remarkable clarity that allowed him to see the future in ways that eluded more sophisticated thinkers. Few people believed him when he said he would bring down the Soviet Empire. When he walked out on Gorbachev at the Reykjavik summit, he got hammered by critics for refusing to give up his Strategic Defense Initiative, now mocked as "Star Wars," and walk away with no agreement. But Reagan knew a bad agreement would have been worse.

Observes Dr. Eugene Jennings, author of several books on leadership, "The ability to adapt and adjust tactics while sticking to principles is extremely important. One of the biggest problems with CEOs is that they are flexible on principles and inflexible on plans."[56] No one could say that about Reagan; he was inflexible on principles and flexible on plans. There is more to leadership that knowing when to bend a little; one also needs a vision. In recognizing the frailty of the Soviet economy, Reagan had come up with a brilliant insight from which all actions flow. "Reagan," said Gorbachev, "was a visionary, making great decisions."[57]

Conclusion

Appraising the Candidates

An examination of overall appraisal ratings reveals that two of the three highest-rated candidates never became president. Among the four candidates with an "excellent" rating, three never got the chance to demonstrate what they could do as president; this includes Harrison, who served only one month. Two of the four with a "fair" rating became president. Among those with a "poor" rating, only Jefferson Davis won his election, which proved to be as disastrous as might have been expected, so he never became president of the United States.

With two or three exceptions, each of our fifteen candidates was a person of substantial accomplishments. But to pick a candidate because of his accomplishments can be shortsighted (see Hearst and Wallace). Conversely to pick a candidate who is likeable and "one of the boys" is narcissistic and misguided. Harrison, who rejected his aristocratic Virginia upbringing to seek his fortune out west among the settlers, was one of the most gregarious and well-liked men, our first celebrity candidate. Yet he also possessed insight, judgment, and nerves of steel: there was nothing average or common about him. Certainly there was nothing common about Marshall, who single-handedly assembled the most powerful fighting force of all time. No way was he a one-shot wonder or lucky unknown plucked out of nowhere, nor were

		Accomplishments	Intangibles	Judgment	Overall
Qualified					
1789	Washington	I	I	I	I
1812	Clinton	I	2	I	I
1920	McAdoo	I	2	I	I
1840	Harrison	2	I	I	2
1940	Willkie	2	I	I	2
1944	Marshall	I	2	2	2
1980	Reagan	I	I	2	2
Less Qualified					
1860	Lincoln	3	I	2	3
1876	Tilden	I	3	2	3
1932	Hoover	I	4	3	3
1964	Goldwater	3	I	4	3
Unqualified					
1861	Davis	2	4	4	4
1904	Hearst	I	3	4	4
1948	Wallace	I	4	4	4
1968	Kennedy	2	3	4	4

I = Outstanding 2 = Excellent 3 = Fair 4 = Poor

men who lost, like Clinton. To the contrary both men went on to accomplish even greater feats after the election.

Several of our candidates were exceptionally well prepared. As a military governor Harrison had exercised the responsibilities and prerogatives of a ruler with unlimited power and demonstrated the wisdom not to overreach. Hoover and Marshall had provided superb multinational leadership under wartime conditions. Reagan had been a highly successful governor of California.

Hoover, McAdoo, Marshall, and Kennedy were superb administrators, but managerial skill, although a valuable trait, is not as important as leadership skill. What made Washington particularly unusual was that he was both a leader and a manager.

Many candidates would win a personality contest; some would

not. Washington, Harrison, Lincoln, McAdoo, Willkie, Goldwater, and Reagan would be delightful dinner companions, always telling jokes and stories. Were you to find yourself stuck in a hunting lodge somewhere, you could do no better than have these people as companions. You might not get excited at the prospect of having dinner with "Whispering Sammy" Tilden or Herbert Hoover, who would light up a cigar and say little while you talked. Equally reticent were Marshall and Clinton. Having dinner alone with DeWitt must have been daunting, as he could talk so intelligently about so many things. On the other extreme was Wallace, whose talking speed frequently outraced his thinking speed.

A candidate who cannot score a single top rating is probably not worthy of serious consideration. The same goes for a candidate who scores a "poor" in any criteria. A president cannot have glaring weaknesses; a "fair" is acceptable, but not a "poor." Hoover had a terrific résumé but gave his enemies good reason not to vote for him because his intangibles, in particular his frigid public demeanor, were so abysmal, not to mention his somewhat questionable dealings in his early career as a business promoter. Tilden was a beacon of honesty and probity and also had a sterling résumé, but he too had a cold personality and seemed to regard it as a virtue. A candidate's glaring weaknesses will almost always catch up with him, especially if he serves a second term. Davis's weaknesses caught up with him pretty quickly. It also did for candidates Hearst, Kennedy, and Wallace in their later years.

It is no accident that almost all our candidates who scored highest in accomplishments were exceptionally bright: Clinton, Tilden, Hearst, McAdoo, Hoover, and Wallace. Probably the most brilliant of these was Wallace, a renowned scientist. But he had no common sense; he espoused ideas without thinking them through and offended virtually everyone in his political party. Same for Hearst, so cocksure he became his own worst enemy.

Our other three candidates rating high in accomplishments—Washington, Marshall, and Reagan—were noteworthy for their ferocious self-discipline and hard work, proving that exceptionally high IQ is not necessary.

One of the men who ran against Willkie was even smarter than Willkie. Son of a president and first in his class at Yale and Harvard Law School, Senator Robert Taft couldn't see the obvious. In urging American accommodation to Hitler in 1940 he stated, "I don't understand why if peace is once restored we could not trade as well with Germany as with England."[1] What planet was he living on?

All our candidates were exceptionally hard workers. Few colleagues could keep up with Davis, Tilden, Hearst, Hoover, Willkie, or Goldwater—five hours' sleep was the norm for them. But hard work is not to be confused with working eighteen hours a day— that's a grind. Often our most powerful insights happen not when we're glued to our desk coping with memos or spending hours in committee meetings but when we're taking a shower and relaxing, or walking down the street, or reading a novel, or going out on a rented sailboat for the day (which is how FDR came up with the lend-lease idea).

The banker J. Pierpont Morgan once joked that he could do a year's work in nine months but not in twelve.[2] What matters is concentration, the ability to absorb massive amounts of information and locate the key issue without getting bogged down in details. For being able to get work done in the shortest period of time, the prize would go to McAdoo, Marshall, and Kennedy.

Marshall said no one had a fresh thought after three in the afternoon. He knew his limits and pushed unimportant duties for the end of the day. He also made sure to keep himself in top physical shape and not end up like Harrison or Willkie, who died prematurely.

Nobody put in the hours in the White House like Hoover. FDR thought Hoover would make a great president, yet Hoover didn't do as well as FDR. Why not? Until late 1942 Roosevelt looked very healthy. People wondered how in the world he managed to hold up so well facing the problems of economic depression and world war for eleven long years. His secret? He stopped working at seven, went upstairs to his book-lined library, poured himself a stiff drink or two, and spent an hour chatting with friends and family. He had a cardinal rule about "happy hour": no talk about politics. Reagan also took a break at the end of the day; he exercised in the specially built White House gym before going out for a state dinner, fresh and invigorated. He paced himself. He focused on a few big priorities and generally got them right. We are not paying presidents by the hour; what matters are results. Says the historian Richard Reeves, "We pay our presidents for . . . one or two big decisions . . . when something happens at the point of crisis and judgment."[3]

So much for accomplishments and judgment. Particularly interesting are intangibles; this is where personality and character come in. Washington, Lincoln, and Reagan lacked the brilliance of, say, Clinton or Wallace, but by sheer force of personality and human traits they achieved exemplary success. What about persuasiveness, clarity, honesty, and integrity? While we don't expect a president to be a saint, he must set a high standard for honesty and probity. This was Kennedy's problem: his zealousness and lust for power scared off a lot of people.

Rectitude and honesty can take a candidate far: look at Washington or Harrison or candidates whose "reputation had been built not only on brilliant work but on steadfast subordination of self to national needs."[4] This was one historian's description of Marshall. It also describes two candidates who might have become president had they put ambition ahead of principles in their campaign: Tilden and Willkie. In refusing to bend and pursue votes at any cost, these two also-rans set the highest possible standard of integrity to be hoped for in a presidential candidate.

Finally there are the issues of timing and context. Napoleon was once asked what he looked for in selecting generals. "Lucky ones," he responded. Some candidates ran into a situation where it was impossible to develop a coherent policy and satisfy the progressive and conservative wings of their party, especially when it came to war. Clinton and Willkie faced this problem, and both lost—not because they waged a poor campaign but because it was impossible to win. A fair question to ask future candidates, therefore, is "Is this a difficult election in which to make your case, or is it an easy one?" In 1980 Reagan had it easy; Tilden, on the other hand, was in a losing situation no matter what he did.

Anyone who thinks elections don't matter should reflect on what a disaster it would have been if Wallace had become president, either by staying on the FDR ticket in 1944 or by winning on his own in 1948. Consider an even more intriguing election: 1812. Had Clinton beaten James Madison, the Civil War almost surely would not have occurred and we would not have needed a Lincoln as president.

The stories of the fifteen candidates in this book raise the following issues pertaining to how we appraise candidates today.

Experience

Harvey Mansfield, a professor of government at Harvard, offers this shrewd insight on age and political wisdom:

> If you're not a famous mathematician by the time you're twenty-five, I suppose you won't be one. But philosophy, especially political philosophy, depends on or uses experience. You have to learn what human beings are like. That's one point. And then another point is that with something like mathematics or different branches of science, you're on a frontier. Everything that's being done now is the best that's ever been done. But with political philosophy, that's by no means the case. What's being done now is not as good as what used to be done in the great books or in the classics. It takes a long time to develop a mature understanding of these books, reading them over and over, and teaching them helps as well. So you'll get better. And you would be at your best, I would say, in your fifties or sixties, even.[5]

Why is experience more valuable than youthful energy? Because experience is what psychologists call pattern recognition, "the ability to see the relevance of other non-identical situations."[6] Pattern recognition is a key component of sound decision making.

History is full of examples of leaders who benefited from time spent out of power or in exile, giving them a chance to reassess themselves. The historian Arnold Toynbee wrote about the "withdrawal and return" of the hero; Charles de Gaulle, in exile for many years, described it as "crossing the desert." In his memoirs Nixon observed, "De Gaulle in his 'wilderness' years, Adenauer in prison and in the monastery, Churchill out of power . . . all had time to reflect, and all used it well."[7] So too did Washington; after resigning as general until he got back into politics at the Constitutional Convention he spent four years on his plantation, giving him plenty of time to think and reflect. Davis didn't get much benefit from his ten years of reading because he lived in total solitude, whereas Washington surrounded himself with dinner guests with whom he could share and test his ideas.

Hopefully the wise older candidate will, like Harrison, have the optimism and forward-thinking mind-set of a young man. Equally energetic was McAdoo, who wrote in his memoirs at the age of sixty-seven:

> Youth does not think of the present, but only of the future. It does not live on memories, but on expectations. Many times I have seen men of mature talent and experience fumble and hesitate, and turn back just as they were about to scale the high walls of achievement, and the thought has occurred to me that their lackadaisical stumbling was only a mental reverberation of past failures and discouragements. If they could have swept the past out of their minds and looked at their problems with the eyes of unbeaten youth, they would have gone ahead. There is a wise Chinese proverb which says: "Do not follow on the heels of a sorrow; it may turn back."[8]

One candidate who did not gain wisdom from his many years of experience was Hoover. In the 1940 campaign he hoped to stage a comeback—a quixotic effort. Did he really think the Republicans would gravitate to a man who had resoundingly lost the 1932 election 59 to 472? Asked about Nazi barbarism in 1939, all he could say was "Chivalry is certainly dying in our world." Hoover even chastised those Americans who reacted strongly to the German conquest of France and much of Europe. In an effort to be witty—certainly never a talent of his—he remarked, "Every whale that spouts is not a submarine."[9] Hoover's dilemma was that he had seen so much brutality in World War I (albeit as an observer, not as a soldier) that he wanted nothing to do with war ever again.

Insider vs. Outsider

Many presidential campaigns invoke the merits of Insider vs. Outsider, such as the one waged by Ronald Reagan against President Carter: "Are you better off now than you were four years ago?" At least Reagan had the experience and credentials to offer an alternative to Washington DC; Goldwater did not. Nor did Henry Wallace, who ran a quixotic third-party campaign. DeWitt Clinton and Lincoln, though they had limited Washington experience, ran as outsiders. So, too, did Harrison and Tilden, with their extensive national experience. They are the moderate outsiders.

Then there are the extreme outsiders like Hearst and Willkie. Whenever such a candidate appears out of the clear blue, voters are taking a considerable risk. It can safely be said that in almost 230 years of presidential elections, only one such outsider has won the presidency: Carter. And only one Also-Ran has merited serious consideration: Willkie.

Promoting Bipartisanship

The continual cry for bipartisanship in today's gridlocked Washington obscures a fundamental truth: politics is the art of compromising as little as possible. Candidates with vision stick to their goals and don't compromise until they absolutely have to, and then only just barely.

But the road is long, and choice of language becomes important. Goldwater and Kennedy were impressive human beings one-on-one but failed to attract majority support because they were intemperate and denigrated the opposition. They had a talent for getting angry, making extreme statements and creating enemies. Richard Nixon used to say, "When the action gets hot, keep the rhetoric cool." Certainly no candidate faced a hotter fire than Tilden, yet throughout the recount crisis he kept his cool and remained civil. Harrison managed to finally become president because of his ability to keep many friends, many of them from decades earlier. Compare this to Hoover, who, when surrounded by a million troubles, found himself with hardly any friends. He simply didn't know how to make them.

Probably no candidate worked harder at making friends than Washington. He lacked the easy conversational skills of a Lincoln or Reagan, but he made himself into a man respected and liked by all. For him this personality trait was essential for being a president. "I would fain hope," he wrote Alexander Hamilton in 1792, "that liberal allowance will be made for the political opinions of each other; and . . . that there might be mutual forbearances and temporizing yieldings on all sides. Without these I do not see the Reins of government are to be managed."[10]

Why Does the Candidate Want This Job?

Other than Harrison, who loved the excitement of campaigning and politics, very few candidates enjoyed politics as a vocation. Even Lincoln was wary of what he called "the wriggle and struggle for office," "a way to live without work."[11]

The need to actively campaign and raise enormous amounts of money discourages many people from running for high office. "We always want the best man to win an election," said the cowboy humorist Will Rogers. "Unfortunately he never runs." To win the presidency one must have a love for the process involved in running for office and leading a coalition of political factions. Clinton had an appetite for it; Marshall definitely did not.

It takes a person of thick skin and ruthlessness to get in the political game and stay in it. Even McAdoo, one of the most hard-driving and toughest men to run for president, had this to say about his last job as senator from California: "Why does any decent man want to stay in politics when there are so many skunks unremittingly acting to make things unpleasant? If I can be permitted to serve here (the Senate) without reference to office-seekers, skunks, cranks, and everyone else who has some personal ax to grind, so that I could devote my energies and what little brain I have to the great problems which are crying for solution, I might enjoy the job."[12]

No modern-day president got insults like Reagan did, the most memorable of which—and endlessly repeated—was Clark Clifford's description of him. Yet Clifford hardly knew the man. What happened was this: Clifford, a former defense secretary and subsequently a Washington power broker (later indicted for banking fraud), had requested a meeting with the president, no reason given. Reagan and Clifford met in the Oval Office for five minutes, discussing nothing more than vague pleasantries. It was one of those thousand perfunctory meetings that take place in the Oval Office, so brief the two men didn't even bother to sit down. That night, at a dinner party of big-wig Democrats, Clifford bragged that he had just come from a lengthy meeting with the president and found the man "an amiable dunce."[13] Such is Washington DC, where many people thrive on scurrilous gossip and inflated self-importance.

If the job is so unpleasant, why would anybody want it? Henry Stimson, secretary of war for three presidents and who had such a high opinion of Marshall, made this observation: "I have been accustomed throughout my life to classify all public servants into one or the other of two general categories: one, the men who were thinking what they could do for their jobs, the other, the men who were thinking what the job could do for them."[14]

The Importance of Integrity

Because of their prominent position, candidates frequently have access to inside information and a chance to make a lot of money. Washington, Clinton, and Harrison could have made a fortune flipping land deals under their control in the West; same for Tilden and McAdoo in their railroad financings. How easy it would have been! And nobody would have known. Yet they kept their hands clean.

What temptations have come the candidate's way, and how did he respond? What was his reaction when approached by people seeking a quid pro quo? Has he ever had to make a decision that might cost him a shot at the presidency? In 1876 Tilden refused to make a deal with the Republicans and lost the election. Same for Wallace when he was vice president: refusing to adhere to FDR's policies, he lost his place on the ticket. George Marshall had the opportunity of a lifetime: to lead the Normandy invasion and become world-renowned; instead he chose to stay in the background job of chief of staff, where he was needed most. Lincoln feared his Emancipation Proclamation would cost him reelection, but he issued it anyway, just like Willkie in supporting Lend-Lease, though it cost him any chance of becoming the Republican nominee in 1944.[15] That's what separates a statesman from a politician: "A politician thinks of the next election; a statesman thinks of the next generation."[16]

"Father, I cannot tell a lie," said young George Washington about the cherry tree. We all know the Parson Weems story is a myth, a part of our national folklore, yet we love it because we know it's just a story, no harm done, and it suggests a standard we should hold our presidents to. Beware the candidate who makes noncredible promises like Wilson's "he kept us out of war" or Nixon's "peace is at hand." Warned William Howard Taft about false promises, "The president cannot make clouds to rain, he cannot make the corn to grow, he cannot make business to be good."[17] Or balance the budget, or guarantee a health care plan promising you can keep your current doctor.

A Deep Capacity for Moral Outrage

Washington, Lincoln, and Reagan had it. So did Kennedy, though his moral outrage was so extreme he turned off a lot of people. Tilden, a moral zealot who had built a career fighting corruption, demonstrated remarkable balance in refusing to contest "the stolen presidency," no matter how outraged he must have been. A lesser man would have drawn America into an abyss. A humanitarian, Hoover had deep moral principles, but he couldn't communicate them to the public. Compare this lack of passion with the behavior of one president in a moment of crisis. The year: 1834. A group of bankers from Philadelphia (the Wall Street of the time) went to the nation's capital to call on the president. "Gentlemen," said Andrew Jackson, "what can I do for you?" For an hour the men made their pitch: that he restore the government deposits in the Bank of the United States. Many years later an employee at the U.S. Treasury stumbled on the minutes of this meeting and wrote the following account of what happened:

> When they had finished, he made no comment and they thought they had won him to their cause. Then he spoke, "Have you anything more to say, gentlemen?" They admitted they had not. Then he arose from his seat and gave them this answer: "Gentlemen! I too have been a close observer of the doings of the Bank of the United States. I have had men watching you for a long time, and am convinced that you have used the funds of the bank to speculate in the breadstuffs of the country. When you won, you divided the profits amongst you, and when you lost, you charged it to the bank. You tell me that if I take the deposits from the bank and annul its charter I shall ruin ten thousand families. That may be true, gentlemen, but that is your sin! Should I let you go on, you will ruin fifty thousand families, and that would be my sin! You are a den of vipers and thieves. I have determined to rout you out, and by the Eternal [bringing his fist down on the table] I will rout you out!" The minutes then recorded that the committee were frightened out of their boots at the vehemence of the president and were glad to get away with their lives.[18]

Breadth of Intelligence

More important than being a child prodigy like Wallace is having breadth of intelligence. Justice Oliver Wendell Holmes, no lightweight in the brains department, gave a wonderful definition of intelligence: "There are one-story intellects, two-story intellects, and three-story intellects. All fact collectors, who have no aim beyond their facts, are one-story men. Two-story men compare, reason, generalize, using the labors of fact collectors as well as their own. Three-story men idealize, imagine, predict; their best illumination comes from above, through the skylight."[19] Three-story men are the ones who have vision. Back in 1812 everyone mocked the canal project as "Clinton's folly," but Clinton was right to follow his vision. The presidency is not a job for bean counters or control-obsessed types who follow every rule by the book, like Davis, Tilden, and Hoover did. At the 1787 Constitutional Convention one of the delegates, fearful of creating a strong presidency, argued that the army be limited to three thousand men. Good idea, responded Washington, just so long as the Convention passed a resolution that no foreign power be allowed to invade the United States at any time with more than three thousand men. Lincoln, urged by a mother to give clemency to her deserter son, was put in a bind because he didn't want to override his secretary of war, Edwin Stanton. He solved the problem by ordering that the boy could be executed only by an order from the president, which of course was never issued.

While he didn't have the kind of imagination Washington and Lincoln had, Marshall had his own way of seeing all points of view: encouraging people to speak up and disagree with him. At one staff meeting he told his top officers, "Gentlemen, I am disappointed in you. You haven't yet disagreed with a single decision I've made."[20]

Knowing how to execute takes more than decisiveness; it takes judgment and reaching out. A president, said Lyndon Johnson, needs "operational intelligence."[21] He wasn't referring to brainpower; he was referring to getting up at six in the morning to call congressmen at home and ask for their help in getting an important bill passed. Johnson was hands-on. When it came to signing the 1968 Fair Housing Act, he didn't give the first pen he used to sign the law to one of the black civil rights leaders; he gave it to the Republican senator who had helped gather the necessary votes.

Operational intelligence means being smart and going the extra mile to get done what needs to be done. It's the executive ability to turn ideas into reality, an ability Marshall as a general and McAdoo as a businessman and treasury secretary had in spades. Such leaders assume responsibility and don't blame others when things go bad. They are decisive and get involved, and they don't leave the messy hard work to others. In business parlance it's called "the will to manage." Most people wrongly assume this means determination. It actually means having the intelligence to know what to do and the discipline to do it.

Reagan referred to this intelligence when he said, "The President must deal with things as they are, not as he would like them to be."[22] Which is why, when he took office, he postponed his dream of saying *nyet* to the Soviet premier and focused on "the economy, the economy, the economy." Like Johnson, who knew that without the help of the Republican senators there would be no bill to sign, Reagan knew he wouldn't be in a strong bargaining position to threaten to bankrupt the Soviets unless he got the U.S. economy turned around. To do this he had to get his tax cuts passed. Using his actor's memorizing skills, he impressed skeptical legislators by making himself so familiar with the intricacies of the tax code that the only congressman who could keep up with him was the chairman of the House Ways and Means Committee.[23]

A Crisis Manager More than an Administrator

"To fill the Presidential chair with success," wrote the nineteenth-century historian Henry Adams,

> a man must have a great deal more than those good purposes, fair talents, and high character which serve to make him locally respectable. He must have judgment, firmness, insight, and above all, experience in a much more ordinary degree.
>
> And that he has these is only shown by trial.[24]

Just as the candidate's résumé should be judged primarily by instances where he has overcome extremely difficult challenges, especially unforeseen ones, so this in all likelihood becomes the major criterion for his success in the Oval Office.

There is no greater, more vivid illustration of disparity in presidential performance than the cases of Jefferson Davis versus Abraham Lincoln and Herbert Hoover versus Franklin Roosevelt. Davis and Lincoln were direct competitors in war; Hoover and FDR were mutual admirers until the Depression came and FDR turned on Hoover for being too extremist and "socialistic"— only to become even more so himself when his turn came to face the same problems.

Davis and Hoover were superb administrators, renowned during their day as among the very finest administrators ever to serve as cabinet officers. They certainly had more impressive overall résumés than their two opponents and probably would have made better presidents than Lincoln and FDR in normal times. Times of crisis, however, called for a different kind of leader. Davis and Hoover may have been superb as managers of complexity, but they were not great managers of change, able to take on new roles, new relationships, and new approaches. They reacted in fits and starts, lacking overall consistency or firm policy. Nor could they relate to people easily; neither had a sense of humor about himself. When things went wrong, they lost their temper and became a prisoner of their job. "People with fiery temperaments," says Daniel Goleman, author of *Emotional Intelligence*, "are frequently thought of as 'classic' leaders—their outbursts are considered hallmarks of charisma and power. But when such people make it to the top, their impulsiveness often works against them. . . . Extreme displays of negative emotion have never emerged as a driver of good leadership."[25]

More modest men like Lincoln and FDR demonstrated optimism in the face of failure and had faith that they would eventually prevail. Marshall lacked the charisma normally associated with great leaders, but he inspired confidence. He thought in terms of *we* instead of *I*, identified what needed to be done, developed action plans and ran productive meetings, and took care to communicate his decisions promptly and clearly. Repeatedly tested in a high-pressure job, he simply didn't have the word *crisis* in his vocabulary. No matter what challenges World War II threw at him, he always managed to handle stress with grace and aplomb, as did Washington during the Revolution and McAdoo as secretary of the treasury.

Addressing Our Greatest Foreign Threat

In our early days having been a secretary of state was pretty much a requirement for a presidential résumé. Jefferson, Madison, Monroe, John Quincy Adams, and Van Buren brought this experience to the presidency. Nowadays this method of advancement seems to have gone into "innocuous desuetude."[26] With the world so much smaller, one would think international experience would be mandatory, yet more important than a candidate's world experience is his worldview.

Relying on the State Department to make up for one's lack of international experience is a mistake. Says Lawrence Lindsey, former governor of the Federal Reserve and White House economic policy advisor under Reagan, "The State Department: while its mission is to represent American interests abroad, cynics often note that its real function is to represent foreign interests to America."[27] Reagan ran into this roadblock when he dared call the Soviet Union "an evil empire"; the political establishment in Washington howled, and of course the apparatchiks in Moscow didn't like it one bit, but the millions of people trapped behind the Iron Curtain loved it.[28] When Reagan wrote a speech draft containing the famous demand, "Mr. Gorbachev, tear down this wall!," the State Department removed the line as offensive. Reagan reinserted it. Several times this charade went back and forth, and in the end, of course, the president said what he wanted to say.

In 1940 Arthur Vandenberg, Robert Taft, and certainly Herbert Hoover had more international experience than Wendell Willkie. Yet Willkie was right, and they were wrong. Willkie's candidacy was propitious for America: it enabled his opponent, Franklin Roosevelt, to stay the pro-international course and ward off the isolationists.

Equally important—and often overlooked—is warding off the war hawks. Sometimes our greatest foreign threats aren't worth fighting over. George Washington was apoplectic when the British started seizing American seamen and putting them to work on British ships, but he knew America couldn't go to war with the one country that provided almost all its trade and credit: He had to make a deal.

Identifying the Greatest Danger

There is a fundamental rule in business, demonstrated in 2012 by the stunning bankruptcy of Kodak, the film company that invented the digital camera in 1975: Think long-term, and do not be wedded to past glories. The same applies to the public sector: programs designed for a simpler era may be out of date due to changing demographics, military threats, and social and economic conditions. If the country is headed down a path where looming threats are obvious, what can be done to correct it? Reagan feared a nuclear Armageddon with no tomorrow; he dared to confront an issue that was never on the 1980 agenda. He was thinking long term, just like in Hollywood where he was one of the few pioneers who accepted the future in embracing television over cinema (a move most actors would abhor as a step down in their career).

Other candidates who showed long-term vision were Washington in establishing the firmament of America, Clinton and Harrison in promoting canals and land grants for westward expansion, and Willkie in defining America's leadership role in the world after World War II. They were men ahead of their time.

Hoover, brilliant though he was, couldn't see beyond the goalposts. Nor could Davis. On the other extreme was Wallace, a man so far ahead of his time he was out of touch with the present, especially in dealing with the Soviet Union.

Any president faced with an intractable problem will be tempted to kick the can down the road, to hope it goes away. It doesn't take a clairvoyant to see that unless drastic changes are made to the budget, the government will handle our mounting federal deficit by having the Fed, using its monopoly power over the currency, print trillions of dollars out of thin air, with disastrous consequences for the value of the dollar and our economic power. Do we want a politician who plays it safe in his quest for reelection, or do we want a leader who dares to tell us the truth—painful though it may be? Where is the George Washington among us who reminds us of our "duties" rather than our "rights"?

. . .

A campaign brochure published in 1852 during the contest between Winfield Scott and Franklin Pierce—unimportant election though it may have been—asks questions of voters that resonate today as we prepare to enter the voting booth:

Which of the two candidates has displayed the greatest abilities? Which had the largest experience? Which has been placed in the most trying situations? And which has exhibited resources equal to every emergency? Which of them entertains the most enlarged and liberal views of national policy? And which will, by his counsels and influence, be most likely to promote measures best adapted to advance the common welfare? Whose opinions are generous, comprehensive, and truly national? And whose are narrow, illiberal, and unbecoming the chief magistrate of a great people? Who will stand at the head of the nation, as Washington did, with a mind to conceive, a heart to embrace, and a hand to execute all that we may justly expect from our admirable frame of government and from the unparalleled resources of the "Ocean-bound Republic"? And who will be the chief of a mere party, executing the petty schemes of such as we are bound together by "the cohesive attraction of the public plunder," and dwarfing the government with the exercise of such functions only as will serve to satiate the voracity of those who throng the doors of the Treasury? The answer to these and similar inquiries will sufficiently Indicate to every honest mind the path of duty. Study well, ponder long, conclude wisely, and act accordingly.[29]

For an interesting exercise we can all relate to, I suggest the following: pick your five most successful friends and ask yourself, "Which one would make the best U.S. president?" You may be surprised: it may be not the one who has made the most money, or achieved the fanciest title, or who is bigger than life, or who happens to be in politics. It may be the Abraham Lincoln one level below fame who has the most balance, integrity, and good judgment. It may be the one who, when everything around him is collapsing, keeps his equanimity and cool. It may be the one whose concerns about the future turn out to be prescient.

Good presidents require thoughtful voters. As they said in 1852, "Study well, ponder long, conclude wisely, and act accordingly."

NOTES

Preface

1. John Adams, "A Dissertation on the Canon and the Feudal Law," *Boston Gazette*, September 30, 1765, National Archives, http://founders.archives.gov /documents/Adams/06-01-02-0052-0006, paragraph 5.

2. The Peter Principle states that people rise to their level of incompetence, after which they fail disastrously.

3. William Dimma, quoted in Taylor and Rosenbach, *Military Leadership*, 56.

4. George Washington, "The Will," in *The Papers of George Washington*, Retirement Series, 4: 494.

5. Goldberg, *Barry Goldwater*, 27.

6. Hale, *The Great American Book of Biography*, 349.

7. Henry Adams, "The Session, 1869–1870," in *The Great Secession Winter of 1860–61 and Other Essays*, 97.

Introduction

1. See Farrand, *The Records of the Federal Convention of 1787*, 1: 99–145.

2. George Will, "Impulse, Meet Experience," *Washington Post*, September 3, 2008.

3. *Federalist 1, 6, 72, 52, 15*.

4. John Dickinson, in Farrand, *The Records of the Federal Convention of 1787*, 1: 123, 145.

5. Benjamin Franklin, in Farrand, *The Records of the Federal Convention of 1787*, 1: 103.

6. Storing, *The Complete Anti-Federalist*, 3: 129.

7. *Federalist 69*, paragraph 2.

8. Novak, *Choosing Presidents*, 23.

9. Bryce, *The American Commonwealth*, 1: 71–72, 74.

10. Wilson, *Documentary History of the Ratification of the Constitution*, 13: 341.

11. Roger Sherman, in Farrand, *The Records of the Federal Convention of 1787*, 1: 99.

12. *Federalist 70*, paragraph 1.

13. Washington, *The Papers of George Washington*, Presidential Series, 2: 322.

1. George Washington, 1789

1. George Washington, letter to Marquis de Lafayette, January 29, 1789, in Washington, *The Papers of George Washington*, Presidential Series, 1: 263.

2. Rodenbough, *Governor Alexander Martin*, 114.

3. Kaminski and McCaughan, *A Great and Good Man*, 95–96.

4. Kaminski and McCaughan, *A Great and Good Man*, 97.

5. Ritter, *Washington as a Businessman*, 82.

6. George Washington, letter to William Gordon, 8 July 1783, in *The Writings of George Washington from the Original Manuscript Sources*, 27: 50.

7. Lodge, *George Washington*, 1: 163.

8. Dalzell and Dalzell, *George Washington's Mount Vernon*, xv.

9. Cincinnatus was a Roman general who was given dictatorial power to raise an army and fight the enemy; after victory was won, he relinquished his power and retired to his farm.

10. Wills, *Cincinnatus*, 15.

11. George Washington, letter to James Madison, March 31, 1787 (image 71), in Washington, *The Papers of George Washington*, Confederation Series, 5: 116.

12. Gouverneur Morris, letter to George Washington, October 30, 1787, in Washington, *The Papers of George Washington*, Confederation Series, 5: 400.

13. George Washington, letter to William Woodford, November 10, 1775, in Washington, *The Writings of George Washington from the Original Manuscript Sources*, 4: 81.

14. Kitman, *George Washington's Expense Account*, 3; Langguth, *Patriots*, 561; Lebergott, *The Americans*, 42. At 98.5 percent depreciation, what cost $100 in 1776 cost $7,000 in 1780.

15. Wills, *Cincinnatus*, 151.

16. Washington, *The Papers of George Washington*, Colonial Series, 1: 26, 119n.

17. Davis, *The Rich*, 187.

18. Unger, *The Unexpected George Washington*, 98.

19. Unger, *The Unexpected George Washington*, 165.

20. George Washington, letter to Marquis de Lafayette, April 28, 1788 (image 88), in Washington, *The Papers of George Washington*, Confederation Series, 6: 245.

21. Washington, *Writings*, 731.

22. Washington, *The Writings of George Washington from the Original Manuscript Sources*, 26: 483–96.

23. Steinberg, *The First Ten*, 23.

24. Kaminski and McCaughan, *A Great and Good Man*, 151.

25. The entire U.S. government had no more than 350 employees. Mount

Vernon had over 400, plus another hundred managing Washington's sixteen thousand acres of landholdings.

26. Adams, *New Letters of Abigail Adams*, 35.

27. George Schultz interview, *Wall Street Journal*, July 14–15, 2012.

28. Beschloss, *Presidential Courage*, 11.

29. Washington's Farewell Address, September 19, 1796, gwpapers.virginia .edu/documents_gw/farewell/transcript.html.

30. Little did he know that this house (which he never saw) would acquire in the early twentieth century the same name as his wife's plantation, the White House. Originally a gray building called the Executive Mansion, it was painted white after being set on fire by the British in the War of 1812.

31. White, *The Federalists*, 35; Jefferson, November 6, 1801, *The Works of Thomas Jefferson*, 9: 310–12.

32. Alden, *George Washington*, 304.

33. Kaminski and McCaughan, *A Great and Good Man*, 88.

34. Eliot, *Four American Leaders*, 43.

2. DeWitt Clinton, 1812

1. Bobbé, *De Witt Clinton*, 100.

2. Siry, *DeWitt Clinton and the American Political Economy*, 61.

3. Stagg, *Mr. Madison's War*, 85.

4. Stagg, *Mr. Madison's War*, 273.

5. Morison, *Harrison Gray Otis*, 262.

6. William G. Morgan, "Origin of the Congressional Caucus," in Buell and Mayer, *Enduring Controversies in Presidential Nominating Politics*, 70.

7. Morgan, "Origin of the Congressional Caucus," 70.

8. Smith, *Clinton's Ditch*, 217.

9. Fox, *The Decline of Aristocracy in the Politics of New York*, 171.

10. Stagg, *Mr. Madison's War*, 117.

11. Raphael, *Mr. President*, 275.

12. Gordon, *Empire of Wealth*, 106.

13. Colden, *Memoir at the Celebration for the Completion of the New York Canals*, paragraph 19 after plate 4.

14. Hosack, *Memoir of DeWitt Clinton*, 257.

15. Clinton, *Memorial, of the Citizens of New York*, 28–41, quoted in Bernstein, *Wedding of the Waters*, 179.

16. Lamb, *History of the City of New York*, 3: 688.

17. Van Buren, *The Autobiography of Martin Van Buren*, 144.

18. Hammond, *The History of Political Parties in the State of New York*, 2: 271–72.

19. Campbell, *The Life and Writings of DeWitt Clinton*, 336, 337, 363.

20. Bernstein, *Wedding of the Waters*, 294; Bobbé, *De Witt Clinton*, 136.

21. Wilson and Davis, *Herndon's Informants*, 476.

3. William Henry Harrison, 1840

1. *Baltimore Republican*, December 11, 1839, quoted in Booth, *Country Life in America*, 161.

2. Gunderson, *The Log Cabin Campaign*, 77.

3. Norton, *Reminiscences of the Log Cabin and Hard Cider Campaign*, 49.

4. Norton, *Reminiscences of the Log Cabin and Hard Cider Campaign*, 375.

5. Norton, *Reminiscences of the Log Cabin and Hard Cider Campaign*, 41.

6. President's Message to Congress, December 18, 1811, http://www.presidency.ucsb.edu/ws/index.php?pid=65925.

7. Cleaves, *Old Tippecanoe*, 312.

8. Jackson, *The Life of William Henry Harrison*, 15–170, 171–77; Hall, *A Memoir of the Public Services of William Henry Harrison*, 7–285, 286–302, 309–23.

9. Moore, *The Contrast*, 2.

10. Norton, *Reminiscences of the Log Cabin and Hard Cider Campaign*, 11.

11. Green, *William Henry Harrison*, 289.

12. Hall, *A Memoir of the Public Services of William Henry Harrison*, 320.

13. Booth, *Country Life in America*, 153.

14. Cleaves, *Old Tippecanoe*, 92.

15. Hildreth, *The People's Presidential Candidate*, 46.

16. Todd and Drake, *Sketches of the Civil and Military Services of William Henry Harrison*, 21.

17. Cleaves, *Old Tippecanoe*, 291.

18. Jackson, *The Life of William Henry Harrison*, 185, 190, 193–94, 197–99; Hall, *A Memoir of the Public Services of William Henry Harrison*, 304–8.

19. Green, *William Henry Harrison*, 295.

20. Green, *William Henry Harrison*, 365.

21. Todd and Drake, *Sketches of the Civil and Military Services of William Henry Harrison*, 159.

22. Green, *William Henry Harrison*, 344.

23. Stoddard, *It Costs to Be President*, 328, 327.

24. Cleaves, *Old Tippecanoe*, 334.

25. Howe, *What Hath God Wrought*, 570.

26. Ellet, *The Court Circles of the Republic*, 289.

27. Howe, *What Hath God Wrought*, 589.

28. Gunderson, *The Log Cabin Campaign*, 273, 400.

29. Quoted in Geoffrey C. Ward, "Presidents, Imperial or Otherwise," *American Heritage*, May/June 1987, 20.

30. A president who dies very early in his first term will have his predecessor and his running mate as fellow presidents in the same year. The three 1841 presidents were Van Buren, Harrison, and Tyler; in 1881 they were Hays, Garfield, and Arthur.

4. Abraham Lincoln, 1860

1. Edwards, *Early Reagan*, 54.
2. Goodwin, *Team of Rivals*, 212.
3. Autobiography written for John L. Scripps, June 1860, in Lincoln, *The Collected Works of Abraham Lincoln*, 4: 65. In this document Lincoln wrote entirely in the third person. The actual quote is "He studied with nobody."
4. Steiner, *An Honest Calling*, 57.
5. "Communication to the People of Sangamo County," March 9, 1832, in Lincoln, *The Collected Works of Abraham Lincoln*, 1: 57.
6. Shenkman, *Presidential Ambition*, 13.
7. Miller, *Plain Speaking*, 158.
8. Goodwin, *Team of Rivals*, 172.
9. Wilson and Davis, *Herndon's Informants*, 479–80.
10. Wilson and Davis, *Herndon's Informants*, 181.
11. Goodwin, *Team of Rivals*, 212.
12. Goodwin, *Team of Rivals*, 186.
13. At the end of the second day of the Republican Convention, held in Chicago, a motion was made to proceed directly to the presidential voting. But the pro-Lincoln convention secretary said the papers for keeping the tally had not yet been prepared, so the voting was put off until the third day. This delay gave Lincoln's supporters an extra evening to work on the other delegates. In the opinion of many, had the voting taken place on the second day as scheduled, Seward would have clinched the nomination.
14. Stoddard, *It Costs to Be President*, 9.
15. Winik, *April 1865*, 241.
16. Fite, *The Presidential Campaign of 1860*, 127.
17. Abraham Lincoln, letter to Albert Hodges, April 4, 1864, in Lincoln, *The Collected Works of Abraham Lincoln*, 7: 281–82.
18. Moore, *Speaking of Washington*, 68.
19. Oates, *Abraham Lincoln*, 128.
20. Donald, *Lincoln*, 289, 301.
21. Donald, *Lincoln*, 15; Donald, *Lincoln Reconsidered*, 131.
22. Lincoln, letter to Albert Hodges.
23. Donald, *Lincoln Reconsidered*, 347.
24. Ann J. Lane, "The Civil War, Reconstruction, and the Afro-American," in Goldstein, *Black Life and Culture in the United States*, 140–41.
25. Lincoln, *The Collected Works of Abraham Lincoln*, 7: 281.
26. Welles, *Diary of Gideon Welles*, 1: 242–43.
27. Franklin, *The Emancipation Proclamation*, 19.
28. Donald, *Lincoln*, 561.
29. This is a famous description by Lincoln's law partner William Hern-

don in a lecture on December 26, 1865, quoted in Wilentz, *The Best American History Essays on Lincoln*, 3.

30. Quoted in Donald, *Lincoln Reconsidered*, 68.

31. Stoddard, *It Costs to Be President*, 20.

32. Quoted in Donald, *Lincoln Reconsidered*, 62.

33. Quoted in Lamb, *Booknotes: Life Stories*, 98.

34. This insight comes from James McPherson, "American Victory, American Defeat," in Boritt, *Why the Confederacy Lost*, 39.

5. Jefferson Davis, 1861

1. Jefferson Davis, letter to Alexander Clayton, January 30, 1861, in Davis, *Papers of Jefferson Davis*, 7:28.

2. *New York Times*, May 1, 1855, quoted in Davis, *Jefferson Davis*, 243.

3. McWhiney, *Cracker Culture*, 51.

4. Davis, *Jefferson Davis, Ex-President of the Confederate States of America*, 1: 163.

5. Kennedy and Kennedy, *Was Jefferson Davis Right?*, 72.

6. W. C. Davis, *Jefferson Davis*, 198.

7. Avary, *Dixie after the War*, 414.

8. Davis, *Life and Reminiscences of Jefferson Davis*, 32–33, 135.

9. Davis, *Life and Reminiscences of Jefferson Davis*, 6.

10. McPherson, *Embattled Rebel*, 20. Numbers are based on the 1860 census.

11. Duyckinck, *National History of the War for the Union*, 118.

12. "Jeff Davis in the White House," Confederate Broadside Poetry Collection, Special Collections and Archives Department, Z. Smith Reynolds Library, Wake Forest University.

13. McClure, *Abraham Lincoln and the Man of War-Times*, 69.

14. Butler, *Autobiography*, 219.

15. Johnson and Buel, *Battles and Leaders of the Civil War*, 1:193.

16. McClellan, *McClellan's Own Story*, 66–67.

17. Johnson and Buel, *Battles and Leaders of the Civil War*, 1: 194–95.

18. Davis, *The Rich*, 367.

19. Robert Toombs, letter to Alexander Stephens, June 21, 1861, in Stephens, *Recollections of Alexander H. Stephens*, 67.

20. Davis, *The Rise and Fall of the Confederate Government*, 2: 549, 423, 570.

21. Stoddard, *It Costs to Be President*, 273–74.

22. James M. McPherson, "American Victory, American Defeat," in Boritt, *Why the Confederacy Lost*, 39.

23. Quoted in Davis, *Life and Reminiscences of Jefferson Davis*, 453.

6. Samuel J. Tilden, 1876

1. Brown, *The Year of the Century*, 56.

2. Bigelow, *The Life of Samuel J. Tilden*, 1: 308–9.

3. Draper, *Great American Lawyers*, 5: 109.

4. Schlesinger, *Running for President*, 1: 330.

5. Barzman, *Madmen and Geniuses*, 77.

6. Holt, *By One Vote*, 100.

7. Bigelow, *The Life of Samuel J. Tilden*, 1: 285.

8. Butterfield, *The American Past*, 220.

9. Stoddard, *It Costs to Be President*, 288.

10. Cornell, *The Life of Hon. Samuel Jones Tilden*, 163–64.

11. Bigelow, *The Life of Samuel J. Tilden*, 1: 220.

12. Bigelow, *The Life of Samuel J. Tilden*, 1: 308.

13. Adams, "The 'Independents' in the Canvass," 306.

14. Quoted in Flick, *Samuel Jones Tilden*, 307–8.

15. Flick, *Samuel Jones Tilden*, 263.

16. Quoted in Adams, "The 'Independents' in the Canvass," 291.

17. Adams, "The 'Independents' in the Canvass," 306–7.

18. Severn, *Samuel J. Tilden and the Stolen Election*, 4.

19. Eckenrode, *Rutherford Hayes*, 142.

20. Entry of September 20, 1876, Diary 1843–1911, 136, John L. Bigelow Papers, Archives and Manuscripts, New York Public Library.

21. Haworth, *The Hayes-Tilden Disputed Presidential Election of 1876*, 44.

22. Nevins, *Abram S. Hewitt*, 332.

23. Flick, *Samuel Jones Tilden*, 351.

24. Nevins, *Abram S. Hewitt*, 330.

25. "The Stoppage of Business," *New York Herald*, November 14, 1876, http://fultonhistory.com/Newspaper%2014/New%20York%20NY%20Herald/New%20York%20NY%20Herald%201876/New%20York%20NY%20Herald%201876%20-%203650.pdf.

26. Eckenrode, *Rutherford Hayes*, 204.

27. Flick, *Samuel Jones Tilden*, 351.

28. Flick, *Samuel Jones Tilden*, 396.

29. Stoddard, *It Costs to Be President*, 255.

30. "Blast from Wendell: The Great Orator Dissects Mr. Hayes and His Advisors," *Boston Globe*, March 27, 1877.

31. Bigelow, *The Life of Samuel J. Tilden*, 2: 74n.

7. William Randolph Hearst, 1904

1. Winkler, *William Randolph Hearst*, 110.

2. Whyte, *The Uncrowned King*, 81.

3. Whyte, *The Uncrowned King*, 24; Swanberg, *Citizen Hearst*, 34.

4. Winkler, *William Randolph Hearst*, 47.

5. Winkler, *William Randolph Hearst*, 62.

6. Winkler, *William Randolph Hearst*, 80, 119.

7. Swanberg, *Citizen Hearst*, 127.

8. Swanberg, *Citizen Hearst*, 196.

9. Whyte, *The Uncrowned King*, 32.

10. Whyte, *The Uncrowned King*, 378, 379.

11. Villard, *Prophets True and False*, 304.

12. Carlson and Bates, *Hearst, Lord of San Simeon*, 150.

13. Nasaw, *The Chief*, 207, 210.

14. Nasaw, *The Chief*, 211.

15. Nasaw, *The Chief*, 213.

16. Carlson and Bates, *Hearst, Lord of San Simeon*, 160.

17. Villard, *Prophets True and False*, 301.

18. Carlson and Bates, *Hearst, Lord of San Simeon*, 162, 229.

8. William Gibbs McAdoo, 1920

1. Morello, *Selling the President*, 4.

2. Johnson, *A History of the American People*, 640.

3. Johnson, *A History of the American People*, 640.

4. Schlesinger, *The Age of Roosevelt*, 29.

5. Neal, *Happy Days Are Here Again*, 122.

6. Neal, *Happy Days Are Here Again*, 130, 126.

7. Walter Lippmann, "Two Leading Democratic Candidates—McAdoo," *National Review*, June 2, 1920.

8. Silber, *When Washington Shut Down Wall Street*, 6.

9. Pietrusza, *1920*, 189, 192.

10. McAdoo, *Crowded Years*, 110, 65. For a fascinating account of McAdoo's Hudson tunnels and railway project, see "Certificate Vignette," http://scri pophily.net/hudmanrail.co.html; Fitzherbert, "William G. McAdoo and the Hudson Tubes."

11. Walter Lippmann, June 20, 1920, column, in Wilson, *Papers of Woodrow Wilson*, 69: 438–39.

12. Woodrow Wilson, letter to Mary Peck (Hulbert), March 15, 1914, in *Papers of Woodrow Wilson*, 29: 346.

13. Fenno, *The President's Cabinet*, 122.

14. Cooper, *Woodrow Wilson*, 511.

15. McAdoo, *Crowded Years*, 443.

16. McAdoo, "The Subway Problem," 3.

17. McAdoo, "The Subway Problem," 445.

18. Broesamle, quoted in Thompson, *Statesmen Who Were Never President*, 6.

19. Bagby, *The Road to Normalcy*, 70.

20. "Murphy Drops Cox, May Go to McAdoo," *New York Times*, June 28, 1920.

21. Burner, *The Politics of Provincialism*, 61; Steel, *Walter Lippmann and the American Century*, 169.

22. Broesamle, *William Gibbs McAdoo*, 167.

23. McAdoo, *Crowded Years*, 178.

24. McAdoo, *Crowded Years*, 45.

25. "McAdoo's Resignation," *Nation*, November 30, 1918.

26. Anthony, *First Ladies*, 354, 401.

27. Cooper, *Woodrow Wilson*, 567.

28. Schlesinger, *Running for President*, 2: 113.

29. Holbrook, *Lost Men of American History*, 329.

30. Broesamle, *William Gibbs McAdoo*, 11.

31. Chase, "William Gibbs McAdoo," 245.

32. Quoted in Broesamle, *William Gibbs McAdoo*, 13.

33. Broesamle, *William Gibbs McAdoo*, 17.

34. McAdoo, *Crowded Years*, 166, 44, 111.

35. U.S. Senate, Finance Committee, *Investigation of Economic Problems: Hearings*, 72nd Congress, 2nd Session, 1933, 1060, 5, 8; "Close to Bottom," *Time*, March 6, 1933.

36. "Close to Bottom," *Time*, March 6, 1933.

9. Herbert Hoover, 1928

1. FDR, letter to Hugh Gibson, January 10, 1920, quoted in Leuchtenburg, *Herbert Hoover*, 47.

2. Wehle, *Hidden Threads of History*, 82–84.

3. Wilson, *Herbert Hoover*, 126.

4. "The Beaver-Man," *Time*, March 26, 1928, 9.

5. Herbert Hoover, Republican nomination acceptance speech, August 11, 1928, in *The New Day*, 16.

6. Hoover, *An American Epic*, vol. 3: *The Relief of Belgium and Northern France*, 443.

7. Burner, *Herbert Hoover*, 111.

8. Allen, *Why Hoover Faces Defeat*, 21.

9. Smith, *The Shattered Dream*, 32.

10. Joslin, *Hoover Off the Record*, 6, 77.

11. Nash, *Understanding Herbert Hoover*, 18.

12. Daniels, *The Wilson Era*, 316–17.

13. Henry F. Pringle, "Hoover: An Enigma Easily Misunderstood," *World's Work* 56 (June 1928): 133–34, quoted in Lloyd, *Aggressive Introvert*, 4.

14. Peel and Donnelly, *The 1928 Campaign*, 105.

15. Barry, *Rising Tide*, 270; Villard, *Prophets True and False*, 25.

16. Lloyd, *Aggressive Introvert*, 71.

17. Joslin, *Hoover Off the Record*, 14.

18. Lloyd, *Aggressive Introvert*, 15.

19. Hoover, *American Individualism*, 9–10.

20. Hoover, *American Individualism*, quoted in Lloyd, *Aggressive Introvert*, 162.

21. Burner, *Herbert Hoover*, 98.

22. Lyons, *Our Unknown Ex-President*, 132.

23. Liggett, *The Rise of Herbert Hoover*, 201–7.

24. Bryson, *One Summer*, 58.

25. Bryson, *One Summer*, 57.

26. "Gallery Four: The Wonder Boy," paragraph 3, Herbert Hoover Presidential Library and Museum, https://hoover.archives.gov/exhibits/Hooverstory/gallery04/index.html.

27. Watson, *As I Knew Them*, 256.

28. Burner, *Herbert Hoover*, 97.

29. Leuchtenburg, *Herbert Hoover*, 39.

30. Wilson, *Herbert Hoover*, 123; Sinclair, *The Available Man*, 125.

31. Daniels, *The Wilson Era*, 318–19.

32. Burner, *Herbert Hoover*, 151; Leuchtenburg, *Herbert Hoover*, 48; Smith, *An Uncommon Man*, 44.

33. Smith, *An Uncommon Man*, 44; Wilson, *Herbert Hoover*, 123.

34. Hoover, Republican nomination acceptance speech.

35. Lester, *On Floods and Photo Ops*, 48.

36. Lloyd, *Aggressive Introvert*, 171; Lyons, *Our Unknown Ex-President*, 27.

37. Roosevelt and Hassett, *The Happy Warrior*, 30.

38. Quoted in Leuchtenburg, *Herbert Hoover*, 77.

39. Smith, *The Shattered Dream*, 57.

40. Colin Seymour, "1927–1933 Chart of Pompous Prognosticators," Gold-Eagle, June 20, 2001, http://www.gold-eagle.com/editorials_01/seymour062001.html.

41. Hoover, *Memoirs*, 3: 195.

42. Sobel, *Herbert Hoover at the Onset of the Great Depression*, 54.

43. Woods, *Meltdown*, 99.

44. Joslin, *Hoover Off the Record*, 10; Lyons, *Our Unknown Ex-President*, 29–30.

45. Wilson, *Herbert Hoover*, 154.

46. Irwin Hoover, *Forty-Two Years in the White House*, 232 (no relation to Herbert Hoover).

47. Smith, *The Shattered Dream*, 239.

48. Wilson, *Herbert Hoover*, 163.

49. Lloyd, *Aggressive Introvert*, 178.

50. Franklin D. Roosevelt, "Four Horsemen" speech, October 25, 1932, in Roosevelt, *Public Papers and Addresses*, 1:831–42.

51. "Hoover Charges Roosevelt 'New Deal' Would Destroy Foundation of Nation," *New York Times*, November 1, 1932.

52. Gies, *Franklin D. Roosevelt*, 101.

53. Wilson, *Herbert Hoover*, 158.

54. Sobel, *Herbert Hoover at the Onset of the Great Depression*, 34.

10. Wendell Willkie, 1940

1. Michael Bechloss, "Before Trump or Fiorina, There Was Wendell Willkie," *New York Times*, August 29, 2015.

2. Moscow, *Roosevelt and Willkie*, 50.

3. Moscow, *Roosevelt and Willkie*, 166.

4. Some sources say it was the number 1, others say it was number 3. The confusion arises from the fact that no source gives the date. Willkie was downsizing this bloated company by getting rid of nonessential, money-losing operations. C&S was the country's largest utility (and losing money) when he took over, and the number 3 (and highly profitable) when he left.

5. Ickes, *The Secret Diary of Harold L. Ickes*, 396.

6. Peters, *Five Days in Philadelphia*, 59.

7. Ickes, *The Secret Diary of Harold L. Ickes*, 92.

8. "Effort Is Started to Block Willkie," *New York Times*, June 20, 1940.

9. Brochure #19, August 15, 1939, in Lilly Library, *An Exhibit*, 9.

10. Willkie, "Government and the Public Utilities," 10.

11. Drummond, "Wendell Willkie," 449.

12. Neal, *Dark Horse*, 144.

13. Walker, introduction to *This Is Wendell Willkie*, 23.

14. Shlaes, *The Forgotten Man*, 61.

15. Barnes, *Willkie*, 120, 148.

16. Walker, introduction to *This Is Wendell Willkie*, 32.

17. Lewis, "The Implausible Wendell Willkie," 233.

18. Alsop, *"I've Seen the Best of It,"* 93.

19. James Flanner, "Rushville's Renowned Son-in-Law," *New Yorker*, October 12, 1940, 28.

20. Raymond Clapper, "GOP's Chance," *Life*, June 24, 1940.

21. "Vandenberg Cites Way to Recovery," *New York Times*, June 6, 1939.

22. "Hoover Urges Nation Shun Moves to Put America into War," *Hartford Courant*, October 1, 1939.

23. "Hoover Demands Armament Policy Protect Civilians," *Los Angeles Times*, October 21, 1939; "We Must Keep Out," *Saturday Evening Post*, October 28, 1939.

24. Wendell Willkie, speech, National Press Club, Washington DC, June 12, 1940, quoted in Barnard, *Wendell Willkie*, 166.

25. Culver and Hyde, *American Dreamer*, 237; Barnes, *Willkie*, 125.

26. Dunn, *1940*, 110.

27. "Wendell Willkie: Would He Be a Sucker to Say Yes?," *Time*, July 31, 1939, 45.

28. Barnes, *Willkie*, 111.

29. Walker, introduction to *This Is Wendell Willkie*, 2.

30. Moscow, *Roosevelt and Willkie*, 59.

31. Rosenman, *Working with Roosevelt*, 167.

32. Culver and Hyde, *American Dreamer*, 134–35.

33. Peters, *Five Days in Philadelphia*, 19; Smith, *Thomas E. Dewey and His Times*, 303.

34. Root, *Persons and Persuasions*, 16.

35. Johnson, *The Republican Party and Wendell Willkie*, 142.

36. Gunther, *Roosevelt in Retrospect*, 311.

37. "Mr. Willkie Checks Out," *Chicago Tribune*, January 18, 1941.

38. *Congressional Record*, October 23, 1941.

39. Willkie, *One World*, 184.

40. Brochure #85, October 26, 1942, in Lilly Library, *An Exhibit*, 19.

41. Simon & Schuster editor, introduction to Willkie, *An American Program*, 2.

42. "Willkie's Book Held 'Imperative,'" *New York Times*, May 7, 1943.

43. Drummond, "Wendell Willkie," 445.

44. Barnes, *Willkie*, 250.

45. Sherwood, *Roosevelt and Hopkins*, 635.

46. "President Is Blunt," *New York Times*, March 30, 1941.

47. "On the Record," *Washington Post*, October 2, 1940; Sherwood, *Roosevelt and Hopkins*, 635; Roosevelt, *My Parents*, 164.

48. "Wendell Lewis Willkie," *Fortune*, May 1937, 204.

11. George C. Marshall, 1944

1. "Man of the Year," *Time*, January 3, 1944.

2. Marshall, *Together*, 158.

3. Roosevelt, *My Parents*, 9.

4. "Official Biographical Sketch," in Marshall, *Together*, 286.

5. "Man of the Year," *Time*, January 3, 1944.

6. Westbrook Pegler, column, *Los Angeles Times*, October 22, 1943.

7. "Democrats Urged to Draft Marshall," *New York Times*, November 27, 1943.

8. *Newsweek*, December 7, 1943.

9. Johnson Hagood, "Soldier," *Saturday Evening Post*, July 15, 1939, 62.

10. Cray, *General of the Army*, 177.

11. Ambrose, *Eisenhower*, 1: 134.

12. Ambrose, *The Supreme Commander*, 104.

13. Acheson, *Sketches from Life of Men I Have Known*, 213.

14. Cray, *General of the Army*, 155.

15. Cray, *General of the Army*, 192.

16. Herman, *Freedom's Forge*, 117. An automobile, by comparison, has fifteen thousand parts.

17. Miller, *Plain Speaking*, 178.

18. Herman, *Freedom's Forge*, 249.

19. George C. Marshall, memorandum to the president, April 24, 1941, in U.S. Congress, *Hearings before the Joint Committee on the Investigation of the Pearl Harbor Attack*, 79th Congress, 2nd Session, 15, 1635 (Washington, DC: U.S. Government Printing Office, 1946). Marshall stated, "Enemy carriers, naval escorts and transports will begin to come under attack at a distance of approximately 750 miles. This attack will increase in intensity until when within 200 miles of the objective, the enemy forces will be subject to attack by all types of bombardment closely supported by our most modern pursuit [planes]."

20. Sherwood, *Roosevelt and Hopkins*, 803.

21. Truman, *Where the Buck Stops*, 372.

22. The question of "highest-ranking" generals is complicated by the fact that five stars did not exist in earlier days. Washington had three stars and Grant and Pershing had four, but all three had a special title, General of the Armies, the highest possible rank at the time. By an act of Congress in 1976 Washington was posthumously awarded a sixth star, with the understanding that no general may ever outrank him.

23. Acheson, *Sketches from Life of Men I Have Known*, 147.

24. Cray, *General of the Army*, 544.

25. Quoted in Acheson, *Sketches from Life of Men I Have Known*, 166.

26. "Marshall Is Dead in Capital at 78," *New York Times*, October 17, 1959.

12. Henry A. Wallace, 1948

1. "Mr. Wallace's Candidacy," *New York Times*, December 30, 1947.

2. Henry A. Wallace Papers, University of Iowa Library, Special Collections.

3. Goulden, *The Best Years*, 350.

4. "Voice of the People?," *Time*, January 12, 1948, 12.

5. James Reston, "The Assistant President," *New York Times Magazine*, October 12, 1941.

6. Stone, *The War Years*, 168.

7. "The Dreamer" by John Boyle O'Reilly (1844–90).

8. Fussell, *The Story of Corn*, 74.

9. Brinkley, *Washington Goes to War*, 17.

10. Obituaries, *Time*, January 3, 1944, 68.

11. Walton, *Henry Wallace, Harry Truman and the Cold War*, 195.

12. Culver and Hyde, *American Dreamer*, 314, 372.

13. Macdonald, *Henry Wallace*, 50.

14. Macdonald, *Henry Wallace*, 23.

15. Macdonald, *Henry Wallace*, 25, 26, 27.

16. Daniels, *The Wilson Era*, 616.

17. Culver and Hyde, *American Dreamer*, 76.

18. Macdonald, *Henry Wallace*, 161.

19. Culver and Hyde, *American Dreamer*, 93.

20. "Wallace Implies Arms Lead to War," *New York Times*, April 21, 1947.

21. "Wallace Asks Talk by Truman, Stalin to Settle Issues," *New York Times*, June 17, 1947.

22. Culver and Hyde, *American Dreamer*, 301.

23. Wallace, *Democracy Reborn*, 52.

24. Fussell, *The Story of Corn*, 86.

25. Quoted in Fussell, *The Story of Corn*, 70.

26. Alsop, *"I've Seen the Best of It,"* 218.

27. Culver and Hyde, *American Dreamer*, 343.

13. Barry Goldwater, 1964

1. Goldwater, *Where I Stand*, 16.
2. Perlstein, *Before the Storm*, 92, 25.
3. "Goldwater Says He'll Run to Give Nation a 'Choice,'" *New York Times*, January 4, 1964; Bell, *Mr. Conservative, Barry Goldwater*, 297; Goldwater, *The Conscience of a Conservative*, 23.
4. Buckley, *Flying High*, 157, 102.
5. "Salesman for a Cause," *Time*, June 23, 1961, 12.
6. Kennedy, *The Enemy Within*, 302.
7. Stewart Alsop, "Can Goldwater Win in '64?," *Saturday Evening Post*, August 24, 1963, 21.
8. Goldberg, *Barry Goldwater*, 28.
9. This is based on $342 million/$16 million. Arizona contributed tax payments of $16 million to the federal treasury and received federal assistance worth $342 million (Goldberg, *Barry Goldwater*, 47).
10. Goldberg, *Barry Goldwater*, 44, 27; Burton Bernstein, "AuH2o," *New Yorker*, April 25, 1988, 49.
11. Goldwater, *With No Apologies*, 74–75.
12. Goldberg, *Barry Goldwater*, 135.
13. Quoted in "Next President? Who Barry Goldwater Is," *U.S. News and World Report*, July 27, 1964, 33–34.
14. Nixon, *RN*, 260.
15. "Goldwater Seeks to End G.O.P. Rift over 'Extremism,'" *New York Times*, August 10, 1964.
16. "The Difficulty of Being Fair to Goldwater," *Life*, September 18, 1964, 94.
17. Goldwater, *The Conscience of a Conservative*, 37.
18. Hanson Baldwin, "Controversy Grows on Who Controls Nuclear Button," *New York Times*, September 27, 1964.
19. White, *The Making of the President, 1964*, 110.
20. Stewart Alsop, *New York Herald Tribune*, June 26, 1964.
21. Rentschler, *Goldwater*, 64.
22. Goldberg, *Liberal Fascism*, 233; ad, *New York Times*, September 12, 1964.
23. Goldberg, *Liberal Fascism*, 232.
24. Rentschler, *Goldwater*, xvii.
25. James Reston, "What Goldwater Lost," *New York Times*, November 4, 1964.
26. Tyrrell, *The Conservative Crack-Up*, 147; Roger Marz, "The Republican Party Has No Future," *New Republic*, December 19, 1964, 11.
27. Quoted in Tyrrell, *The Conservative Crack-Up*, 147.
28. Goldwater, *With No Apologies*, 263–64.
29. Quoted in Rentschler, *Goldwater*, 163.
30. Locher, *Victory on the Potomac*, 10.
31. Locher, *Victory on the Potomac*, 439–40, 444.
32. Edwards, *Goldwater*, 469.

14. Robert F. Kennedy, 1968

1. Clarke, *The Last Campaign*, 21.
2. Kennedy, *To Seek a Newer World*, 230.
3. Schlesinger, *Robert Kennedy and His Times*, 598.
4. Alex Haley interview of Melvin Belli, *Playboy*, June 1965.
5. Gore Vidal, "The Best Man, 1968," *Esquire*, March 1963; see also Gore Vidal interview, *Penthouse*, April 1975.
6. Lasky, *Robert F. Kennedy*, 18.
7. Cordery, *Alice*, 451.
8. Russo and Molton, *Brothers in Arms*, 42.
9. Shannon, *The Heir Apparent*, 43.
10. Shannon, *The Heir Apparent*, 44–45.
11. Laing, *Robert Kennedy*, 72.
12. Schlesinger, *Robert Kennedy and His Times*, 97.
13. Martin, *Jimmy Hoffa's Hot*, 16.
14. Schlesinger, *Robert Kennedy and His Times*, 146.
15. Hugh Sidey, "Brother on the Spot," *Time*, October 10, 1960.
16. Schlesinger, *Robert Kennedy and His Times*, 233.
17. Schlesinger, *Robert Kennedy and His Times*, 532.
18. De Toledano, *R.F.K.*, 179.
19. Stone, *In a Time of Torment*, 18.
20. Laing, *Robert Kennedy*, 22.
21. "The Administration: Remember Not . . . ," *Time*, May 11, 1962, 19.
22. "The Ronnie-Bobby Show," *Newsweek*, May 29, 1967, 26. See Paul Kengor, "The Great Forgotten Debate," *National Review*, May 22, 2007, www.national review.com/articles/220949/great-forgotten-debate-paul-kengor.
23. Halberstam, *The Unfinished Odyssey of Robert Kennedy*, 110.
24. "The Ronnie-Bobby Show," 31.
25. Jules Witcover and Richard M. Cohen, "Where's the Rest of Ronald Reagan?," *Esquire*, March 1976, 153.
26. Lasky, *Robert F. Kennedy*, 119.
27. Pearson, *Diaries*, 524, 564.
28. Hersh, *The Dark Side of Camelot*, 336.
29. Steel, *In Love with Night*, 177; Clarke, *The Last Campaign*, 228.
30. "Kennedy's Inconclusive Victory," *New York Times*, May 8, 1968.
31. Steel, *In Love with Night*, 171.
32. Steel, *In Love with Night*, 193.
33. Gould, *1968*, 47.

15. Ronald Reagan, 1980

1. Dunn, *The Enduring Reagan*, 103. For a complete version of Cutler's remarks, see American Enterprise Institute, "President vs. Congress: Does the Separation of Powers Still Work?," AEI Forums, November 25, 1980, https://www.aei .org/wp-content/uploads/2016/03/AEIForums47.pdf.

2. Garance Franke-Ruta, "The Big House," *Atlantic*, March 2013, http://www.theatlantic.com/magazine/archive/2013/03/the-white-house-list/309225/.

3. Ronald Reagan, "Peace and Security in the 1980s," address to Chicago Council on Foreign Relations, March 17, 1980, 2, http://insidethecoldwar.org/sites/default/files/documents/Address%20to%20Chicago%20Council%20on%20Foreign%20Relations%20Peace%20and%20Security%20in%20the%201980s%20March%2017%2C%201980.pdf.

4. Ronald Reagan, "Acceptance of the Nomination for President," July 17, 1980, CNN, http://www.cnn.com/SPECIALS/2004/reagan/stories/speech.archive/nomination.html.

5. Herman, *Freedom's Forge*, 264.

6. Schaller, *Ronald Reagan*, 20.

7. Reagan and Hubler, *Where's the Rest of Me?*, 174.

8. White and Gill, *Why Reagan Won*, 190.

9. For a fascinating description of Reagan's development and use of shorthand and index cards, see Skinner, *Reagan, in His Own Hand*, xviii–xxii.

10. American Presidency Project, Ronald Reagan, "Remarks at a Wreath-Laying Ceremony at the Lincoln Memorial," February 12, 1981, http://www.presidency.ucsb.edu/ws/?pid=43387.

11. "The Ronnie-Bobby Show," *Newsweek*, May 29, 1967, 26, 31.

12. Skinner, *Reagan, in His Own Hand*, xvii.

13. Reagan and Hubler, *Where's the Rest of Me?*, 40.

14. Reagan and Hubler, *Where's the Rest of Me?*, 20–21.

15. Reagan and Hubler, *Where's the Rest of Me?*, 29.

16. Reagan and Hubler, *Where's the Rest of Me?*, 261.

17. "California: Fast Start," *Time*, August 11, 1967, 17.

18. Paul O'Neil, "The Hottest Candidate in Either Party," *Life*, October 30, 1970, 27–29.

19. Evans, *The Education of Ronald Reagan*, 185.

20. Cannon, *Reagan*, 194.

21. Evans, *The Education of Ronald Reagan*, 195; White and Gill, *Why Reagan Won*, 191.

22. Diggins, *Ronald Reagan*, 146.

23. Hayward, *Greatness*, 41, 175.

24. Deaver, *A Different Drummer*, 77.

25. Hayward, *The Age of Reagan*, xxi.

26. Frank Rich, "What the Donald Shares with the Ronald," *New York*, May 30–June 12, 2016, 36.

27. Adam Clymer, "Ford Cites Economy as Major GOP Issue," *New York Times*, May 20, 1979.

28. Louis Harris gave me this advice about the importance of writing clear, concise memos when I was his assistant in 1975.

29. Schweizer, *Reagan's War*, 91.

30. Evans, *The Education of Ronald Reagan*, 201.

31. Stuckey, *Playing the Game*, 29.

32. Gergen, *Eyewitness to Power*, 189–90.

33. Bruce Bartlett, "Reaganomics Won't Help Us Now," *Week*, February 17, 2012, 42.

34. Ford, *The Writings of Thomas Jefferson*, 7–301.

35. Donald T. Critchlow, *Future Right: Forging a New Republican Majority* (New York: St. Martin's Press, 2016), 129–30.

36. Nicoletta Batini, Giovanni Callegari, and Julia Guerreiro, "An Analysis of U.S. Generational Imbalances: Who Will Pay and How?," International Monetary Fund Working Paper 11/72, April 1, 2011, 24. https://www.imf.org /external/pubs/cat/longres.aspx?sk=24770.0.

37. Reagan, *An American Life*, 257.

38. Lee Edwards, "Ronald Reagan and the Fall of Communism," Heritage Foundation, January 27, 2010, http://www.heritage.org/research/lecture /ronald-reagan-and-the-fall-of-communism.

39. Reagan Foundation, "Ronald Reagan: 'The Westminster Address' behind the Scenes," *Reagan's Country* newsletter, n.d., http://home.reaganfoundation .org/site/DocServer/Westminster_Speech_Essay_June_2012.pdf?docID=853.

40. On Stanislav Petrov, see http://www.brightstarsound.com; David Hoffman, "I Had a Funny Feeling in My Gut," *Washington Post*, February 10, 1999, www.washingtonpost.com/wp-srv/inatl/longterm/coldwar/shatter021099b.htm; Hoffman, *The Dead Hand*, 10–11.

41. Hoffman, *The Dead Hand*, 44.

42. Hoffman, *The Dead Hand*, 44–45. According to FAS, "Enduring National Leadership," NSDD 55, September 14, 1982, "has not been reviewed for release or release has been denied in full." Federation of American Scientists, Intelligence Resource Program, NSDD: National Security Decision Directives, Reagan Administration, http://www.fas.org/irp/offdocs/nsdd/.

43. Hoffman, *The Dead Hand*, 44–45.

44. Ronald Reagan, "Remarks to the National Chamber Foundation," November 17, 1988, Reagan Library, https://reaganlibrary.archives.gov/archives /speeches/1988/111788a.htm.

45. "Why Is This Man So Popular?," *Time*, July 7, 1986.

46. Ann Dowd, "What Managers Can Learn from President Reagan," *Fortune*, September 15, 1986, 40.

47. Reagan, *Reagan: A Life in Letters*, 778.

48. Thomas Jefferson, letter to J. B. Colvin, September 20, 1810, in Jefferson, *The Writings of Thomas Jefferson*, 422.

49. Matlock, *Reagan and Gorbachev*, 326.

50. Joe Gandelman, "Harris Poll Presidential Rankings: Reagan Best President since World War II, Nixon Worst," *Moderate Voice*, February 18, 2012, http://themoderatevoice.com/harris-poll-presidential-rankings-reagan-best -president-since-world-war-ii-nixon-worst/.

51. Anderson, *Revolution*, xxvii–xxviii; Steven Roberts, "Reagan's Final Rating Is Best of Any President since '40s," *New York Times*, January 18, 1989; Reagan's 68 percent was followed by Eisenhower at 59 percent; JFK, 58; Ford, 53; Johnson, 49; Carter, 34; Truman, 31; Nixon, 24.

52. Wallison, *Ronald Reagan*, xiii.

53. Garcia, *Reagan's Comeback*, 15.

54. Kyle Smith, "With Friends Like These . . . ," *New York Post*, September 29, 2013.

55. Schaller, *Ronald Reagan*, 63.

56. Dowd, "What Managers Can Learn from President Reagan," 41.

57. Evans, *The Education of Ronald Reagan*, 220.

Conclusion

1. "Strict Neutrality Demanded by Taft," *New York Times*, May 21, 1940.

2. Isaacson, *Profiles in Leadership*, 90.

3. Reeves, "John F. Kennedy," 104.

4. Newell, *Statesmanship, Character, and Leadership in America*, 112.

5. Harvey Mansfield, "Alexis de Tocqueville's *Democracy in America*," in Lamb, *Booknotes: Stories from American History*, 67.

6. Murray, *Real Education*, 119.

7. Quoted in Gergen, *Eyewitness to Power*, 37–38.

8. McAdoo, *Crowded Years*, 20.

9. Dunn, *1940*, 78, 105.

10. George Washington, letter to Alexander Hamilton, August 26, 1792, in Collins, *Scorpion Tongues*, 27.

11. Diggins, *Ronald Reagan*, 157.

12. Chase, "William Gibbs McAdoo," 365.

13. James Perry, "For the Democrats, Pam's Is the Place for the Elite to Meet," *Wall Street Journal*, October 8, 1981; Deaver, *A Different Drummer*, 112–13.

14. Puryear, *American Generalship*, 340.

15. Two more recent parallels: Lyndon Johnson pushing the 1964 civil rights bill through Congress even though he knew he was delivering the South to the Republicans for the next twenty years; Gerald Ford pardoning Nixon in order to "bring our long national nightmare to an end" even though he knew doing so would cast a dark shadow over his presidency.

16. The quote is from John Freeman Clarke, available at *Goodreads*, http://www.goodreads.com/quotes/910748-a-politician-thinks-of-the-next-election-a-statesman-thinks.

17. Quoted in Schlesinger, *The Cycles of American History*, 287.

18. Stan V. Henkels, *Andrew Jackson and the Bank of the United States: An interesting Bit of History Concerning "Old Hickory,"* pamphlet (N.p.: Gollifax Press, 1928), #10 of 310 copies, Rare Book Collection, New York Public Library.

19. "Quotation #26510 from *Cole's Quotables*," Quotations Page, www.quo
tationspage.com/quote/26510.html.

20. Newell, *Statesmanship, Character, and Leadership in America*, 201.

21. Michael Goodwin, "The LBJ Way," *New York Post*, March 25, 2012.

22. Schweizer, *Reagan's War*, 72.

23. Gergen, *Eyewitness to Power*, 197.

24. Adams, *The Great Secession Winter*, 307.

25. Goleman, "What Makes a Leader?," 14.

26. Daniels, *The Wilson Era*, 559.

27. Lindsey, *What a President Should Know*, 45.

28. I ran into this Eastern European appreciation of freedom when I lived in
Romania in 1994–2007. I encountered many shop signs in Bucharest proclaiming that their goods were of "American quality." Puzzled why they espoused
American quality as opposed to the vaunted German or Japanese quality for
manufacturing automobiles, I was told, "You don't understand: since 1945 we
have been waiting for the return of General Patton's jeeps!"

29. *The Presidency: Winfield Scott—Franklin Pierce, Their Qualifications and
Fitness for High Office*, campaign brochure, privately printed, 1852, New York
Public Library.

BIBLIOGRAPHY

Acheson, Dean. *Sketches from Life of Men I Have Known.* New York: Harper & Row, 1959.

Adams, Abigail. *New Letters of Abigail Adams 1788–1801.* Edited by Stewart Mitchell. Boston: Houghton Mifflin, 1947.

Adams, Henry. *Henry Adams: The Great Secession Winter of 1860–61 and Other Essays.* Edited by George Hochfield. New York: Sagamore Press, 1958.

———. "The 'Independents' in the Canvass." 1876. In *Henry Adams: The Great Secession Winter of 1860–61, and Other Essays,* edited by George Hochfield, 291–332. New York: Sagamore Press, 1958.

Alden, John R. *George Washington: A Biography.* Baton Rouge: Louisiana State University Press, 1984.

Allen, Robert S. *Why Hoover Faces Defeat.* New York: Brewer, Warren & Putnam, 1932.

Alsop, Joseph W. *"I've Seen the Best of It": Memoirs.* New York: Norton, 1992.

Ambrose, Stephen E. *Eisenhower: Soldier, General of the Army, President-Elect, 1890–1952.* New York: Simon & Schuster, 1982.

———. *The Supreme Commander: The War Years of Dwight D. Eisenhower.* Jackson: University Press of Mississippi, 1999.

Anderson, Martin. *Revolution: The Reagan Legacy.* Stanford CA: Hoover Institution Press, 1990.

Anthony, Carl Sferrazza. *First Ladies: The Saga of the Presidents' Wives and Their Power, 1789–1961.* New York: William Morrow, 1990.

Avary, Myrta L. *Dixie after the War.* Boston: Houghton Mifflin, 1937.

Bagby, Wesley M. *The Road to Normalcy: The Presidential Campaign and Election of 1920.* Baltimore: John Hopkins University Press, 1962.

Barnard, Ellsworth. *Wendell Willkie: Fighter for Freedom.* Marquette: Northern Michigan University Press, 1966.

Barnes, Joseph. *Willkie: The Events He Was Part Of, the Ideas He Fought For.* New York: Simon & Schuster, 1952.

Barry, John M. *Rising Tide: The Great Mississippi Flood of 1927 and How It Changed America*. New York: Simon & Schuster, 1998.

Barzman, Sol. *Madmen and Geniuses: The Vice Presidents of the United States*. Chicago: Follett Books, 1974.

Bell, Jack. *Mr. Conservative, Barry Goldwater*. Garden City NY: Doubleday, 1964.

Beran, Michael Knox. *The Last Patrician: Bobby Kennedy and the End of American Aristocracy*. New York: St. Martin's Press, 1998.

Bernstein, Peter. *Wedding of the Waters: The Erie Canal and the Making of a Great Nation*. New York: Norton, 2005.

Beschloss, Michael. *Presidential Courage: Brave Leaders and How They Changed America, 1789–1989*. New York: Simon & Schuster, 2007.

Bickel, Alexander M. "Robert F. Kennedy: The Case against Him for Attorney General." *New Republic* 144, no. 2 (1961): 15.

Bigelow, John L. *The Life of Samuel J. Tilden*. 2 vols. New York: Harper & Bros., 1895.

Bobbé Dorothie. *De Witt Clinton*. 1933. Reprint, New York: G. P. Putnam's Sons, 1968.

Booth, Edward T. *Country Life in America as Lived by Ten Presidents of the United States: John Adams, George Washington, Thomas Jefferson, Andrew Jackson, Martin Van Buren, William Henry Harrison, James Buchanan, Abraham Lincoln, Theodore Roosevelt, Calvin Coolidge*. New York: Knopf, 1947.

Boritt, Gabor S., ed. *Why the Confederacy Lost*. New York: Oxford University Press, 1992.

Brinkley, David. *Washington Goes to War*. New York: Knopf, 1988.

Broesamle, John J. *William Gibbs McAdoo: A Passion for Change, 1863–1917*. Port Washington NY: Kennikat Press, 1973.

Brookhiser, Richard. "The Founder of Gotham's Fortunes," *City Journal* 14, no. 1 (2004), http://www.city-journal.org/html/founder-gotham%E2%80%99s-fortunes-12497.html.

———. "Why Washington Matters." *New York Post*, February 22, 2012, http://nypost.com/2012/02/22/why-washington-matters/.

Brooks, Clayton McClure, ed. *A Legacy of Leadership: Governors and American History*. Philadelphia: University of Pennsylvania Press, 2008.

Brown, Dee. *The Year of the Century: 1876*. New York: Scribner, 1966.

Bryce, James. *The American Commonwealth*. Indianapolis: Liberty Fund, 1995.

Bryson, Bill. *One Summer: America, 1927*. New York: Doubleday, 2013.

Buckley, William F., Jr. *Flying High: Remembering Barry Goldwater*. New York: Basic Books, 2008.

Buell, Emmett H., and William G. Mayer. *Enduring Controversies in Presidential Nominating Politics*. Pittsburgh: University of Pittsburgh Press, 2004.

Burckhardt, Jacob. *Reflections on History*. Indianapolis: Liberty Classics, 1943.

Burner, David. *Herbert Hoover: A Public Life*. New York: Knopf, 1979.

———. *The Politics of Provincialism: The Democratic Party in Transition, 1918–1932.* New York: Knopf, 1976.

Butler, Benjamin F. *The Autobiography and Personal Reminiscences of Major-General B. F. Butler.* New York: A. M. Thayer, 1982.

Butterfield, Alexander. *The American Past: A History of the United States from Concord to Hiroshima, 1775–1945.* 1947. Reprint, New York: Simon & Schuster, 1957.

Campbell, William W. *The Life and Writings of DeWitt Clinton.* New York: Baker and Scribner, 1849. https://archive.org/details/lifewritingsofde00clin.

Cannon, Lou. *Reagan.* New York: G. P. Putnam's Sons, 1982.

Carlson, Oliver, and Ernest Sutherland Bates. *Hearst, Lord of San Simeon.* New York: Viking, 1937.

Chase, Philip M. "William Gibbs McAdoo: The Last Progressive." PhD diss., University of Southern California, 2008.

Chernow, Ron. *Washington: A Life.* New York: Penguin, 2010.

Churchill, Allen. *Park Row.* New York: Rinehart, 1958.

Churchill, Winston S. *The Second World War.* Vol. 4: *The Hinge of Fate.* Boston: Houghton Mifflin, 1950.

Clarke, Thurston. *The Last Campaign: Robert F. Kennedy and 82 Days That Inspired America.* New York: Henry Holt, 2008.

Cleaves, Freeman. *Old Tippecanoe: William Henry Harrison and His Time.* New York: Charles Scribner's Sons, 1939.

Clinton, DeWitt. *Memorial, of the Citizens of New York: In Favour of a Canal Navigation between the Great Western Lakes and the Tide-waters of the Hudson.* Albany NY: Bosford, 1816.

Colden, Cadwallader D. *Memoir at the Celebration for the Completion of the New York Canals.* New York: W. A. Davis, 1825. www.history.rochester.edu/canal/bib/colden/Memoir.html.

Collins, Donald E. *The Death and Resurrection of Jefferson Davis.* Lanham MD: Rowman & Littlefield, 2005.

Collins, Gail. *Scorpion Tongues: Gossip, Celebrity and American Politics.* New York: William Morrow, 1998.

Cooper, John Milton, Jr. *Woodrow Wilson: A Biography.* New York: Knopf, 2009.

Cordery, Stacy A. *Alice: Alice Roosevelt Longworth, from White House Princess to Washington Power Broker.* New York: Viking, 2007.

Cornell, William Mason. *The Life of Hon. Samuel Jones Tilden.* Boston: Lee & Shepard, 1876.

Cornog, Evan. *The Birth of Empire: DeWitt Clinton and the American Experience, 1769–1828.* New York: Oxford University Press, 1998.

Cray, Ed. *General of the Army: George C. Marshall, Soldier and Statesman.* New York: Cooper Square Press, 2000.

Culver, John C., and John Hyde. *American Dreamer: A Life of Henry A. Wallace.* New York: Norton, 2000.

Dalzell, Robert F., Jr., and Lee B. Dalzell. *George Washington's Mount Vernon: At Home in Evolutionary America*. New York: Oxford University Press, 1998.

Daniels, Josephus. *The Wilson Era: Years of War and After, 1917–1923*. Chapel Hill: University of North Carolina Press, 1946.

Davis, Jefferson. *Life and Reminiscences of Jefferson Davis*. Baltimore: R. H. Woodward, 1890.

———. *Papers of Jefferson Davis*. Baton Rouge: Louisiana State University Press, 1971.

———. *The Rise and Fall of the Confederate Government*. 2 vols. New York: D. Appleton, 1881.

Davis, Varina H. *Jefferson Davis, Ex-President of the Confederate States of America: A Memoir by His Wife*. 2 vols. New York: Belford, 1890.

Davis, William. *The Rich: A Study of the Species*. New York: Franklin Watts, 1983.

Davis, William C. *Jefferson Davis: The Man and His Hour*. New York: Harper-Collins, 1991.

Deaver, Michael. *A Different Drummer: My Thirty Years with Ronald Reagan*. New York: HarperCollins, 2001.

De Toledano, Ralph. *R.F.K.: The Man Who Would Be President*. New York: G. P. Putnam's Sons, 1967.

Diggins, John Patrick. *Ronald Reagan: Fate, Freedom, and the Making of History*. New York: Norton, 2007.

Donald, David Herbert. *Lincoln*. New York: Simon & Schuster, 1996.

———. *Lincoln Reconsidered*. New York: Knopf, 2001.

Draper, William, ed. *Great American Lawyers: The Lives and Influences of Judges and Lawyers Who Have Acquired Permanent National Reputation, and Have Developed the Jurisprudence of the United States*. 3 vols. Philadelphia: John C. Winston, 1908.

Drummond, Roscoe. "Wendell Willkie: A Study in Courage." In *The Aspirin Age: 1919–1941*, edited by Isabel Leighton, 444–75. New York: Simon & Schuster, 1949.

Dunn, Charles W., ed. *The Enduring Reagan*. Lexington: University Press of Kentucky, 2009.

Dunn, Susan. *1940: FDR, Willkie, Lindbergh, Hitler—The Election amid the Storm*. New Haven CT: Yale University Press, 2013.

Duyckinck, Evert A. *National History of the War for the Union: Civil, Military and Naval*. Vol. 1 of 3. New York: Johnson, Fry, 1861.

Eckenrode, H. J. *Rutherford Hayes: Statesman of Reunion*. New York: Dodd, Mead, 1930.

Edwards, Anne. *Early Reagan*. New York: William Morrow, 1987.

Edwards, Lee. *Goldwater*. Washington DC: Regnery, 1995.

Eicher, David J. *Dixie Betrayed: How the South Really Lost the Civil War*. New York: Little, Brown, 2006.

Eliot, Charles W. *Four American Leaders*. Boston: American Unitarian Association, 1906.

Ellet, E. F. *The Court Circles of the Republic*. Hartford CT: Hartford Publishing, 1869.

Evans, Thomas W. *The Education of Ronald Reagan: The General Electric Years and the Untold Story of His Conversion to Conservatism*. New York: Columbia University Press, 2006.

Farrand, Max, ed. *The Records of the Federal Convention of 1787*. 4 vols. Revised edition. New Haven CT: Yale University Press, 1937.

Fenno, Richard F., Jr. *The President's Cabinet: An Analysis in the Period from Wilson to Eisenhower*. Cambridge MA: Harvard University Press, 1959.

Fite, Emerson David. *The Presidential Campaign of 1860*. 1911. Reprint, Port Washington NY: Kennikat Press, 1967.

Fitzherbert, Anthony. "William G. McAdoo and the Hudson Tubes." Electric Railroaders Association, June 1964. http://www.nycsubway.org/wiki/The _Public_Be_Pleased:_William_Gibbs_McAdoo_and_the_Hudson_Tubes.

Flick, Alexander C. *Samuel Jones Tilden*. New York: Dodd, Mead, 1939.

Fox, Dixon Ryan. *The Decline of Aristocracy in the Politics of New York*. New York: Longman Green, 1919.

Franklin, John Hope. *The Emancipation Proclamation*. Garden City NY: Doubleday, 1963.

Frommer, Arthur, comp. *Goldwater from A to Z: A Critical Handbook*. New York: Frommer/Pasmantier, 1964.

Fussell, Betty. *The Story of Corn*. New York: Knopf, 1992.

Garcia, Gilbert. *Reagan's Comeback: Four Weeks in Texas That Changed American Politics Forever*. San Antonio TX: Trinity University Press, 2012.

Gergen, David. *Eyewitness to Power: The Essence of Leadership, Nixon to Clinton*. New York: Simon & Schuster, 2000.

Gies, Joseph. *Franklin D. Roosevelt: Portrait of a President*. Garden City NY: Doubleday, 1971.

Goldberg, Jonah. *Liberal Fascism: The Secret History of the American Left from Mussolini to the Politics of Meaning*. New York: Doubleday, 2007.

Goldberg, Robert Alan. *Barry Goldwater*. New Haven CT: Yale University Press, 1998.

Goldstein, Rhoda L., ed. *Black Life and Culture in the United States*. New York: Thomas Y. Crowell, 1971.

Goldwater, Barry. *The Conscience of a Conservative*. Shepherdsville KY: Victor, 1960.

———. *Where I Stand*. New York: McGraw-Hill, 1964.

———. *With No Apologies: The Personal and Political Memoirs of Barry M. Goldwater*. New York: William Morrow, 1979.

Goldwater, Barry, with Jack Casserly. *Goldwater*. New York: Doubleday, 1988.

Goleman, Daniel. "What Makes a Leader?" In *HBR's Ten Must Reads: On Emotional Intelligence*. Cambridge MA: Harvard Business School, 2015.

Goodwin, Doris Kearns. *Team of Rivals: The Political Genius of Abraham Lincoln*. New York: Simon & Schuster, 2005.

Gordon, John Steele. *Empire of Wealth*. New York: HarperCollins, 2006.

Gould, Lewis. *1968: The Election That Shaped America*. Chicago: Ivan R. Dee, 1993.

Goulden, Joseph C. *The Best Years: 1945–1950*. New York: Atheneum, 1976.

Green, James A. *William Henry Harrison: His Life and Times*. Richmond VA: Garrett & Massie, 1941.

Gunderson, Robert Gray. *The Log Cabin Campaign*. Lexington: University of Kentucky Press, 1957.

Gunther, John. *Roosevelt in Retrospect: A Profile in History*. New York: Harper, 1950.

Halberstam, David. *The Unfinished Odyssey of Robert Kennedy*. New York: Random House, 1968.

Hale, Edward Everett. *The Great American Book of Biography: Illustrious Americans, Their Lives and Achievements*. Philadelphia: International Publishing, 1896. https://archive.org/details/greatamericanboo00inte.

Hall, James. *A Memoir of the Public Services of William Henry Harrison*. Philadelphia: Key & Biddle, 1836. https://archive.org/details/memoir ofpublicse00hall.

Hammond, Jabez D. *The History of Political Parties in the State of New York*. 2 vols. Cooperstown NY: H. & E. Phinney, 1846.

Hard, William. *Who's Hoover?* New York: Dodd, Mead, 1928.

Haworth, Paul L. *The Hayes-Tilden Disputed Presidential Election of 1876*. Cleveland OH: Burrows Bros., 1906.

Hayward, Stephen F. *The Age of Reagan: The Fall of the Old Liberal Order, 1964–1980*. Roseville CA: Forum, 2001.

———. *Greatness: Reagan, Churchill and the Making of Extraordinary Leaders*. New York: Crown Forum, 2005.

Hearst, William R. *Selections from the Writings and Speeches of William Randolph Hearst*. Edited by E. F. Tompkins. San Francisco: Privately published, 1948.

Herman, Arthur. *Freedom's Forge: How American Business Produced Victory in World War II*. New York: Random House, 2012.

Hersh, Seymour. *The Dark Side of Camelot*. New York: Little, Brown, 1997.

Hess, Karl. *In a Cause That Will Triumph: The Goldwater Campaign and the Future of Conservatism*. Garden City NY: Doubleday, 1967.

Higginbotham, Don, ed. *George Washington Reconsidered*. Charlottesville: University Press of Virginia, 2001.

Hildreth, Richard. *The People's Presidential Candidate, or The Life of William Henry Harrison of Ohio*. Boston: Weeks, Jordan, 1839.

Hoffman, David E. *The Dead Hand: The Untold Story of the Cold War Arms Race and Its Dangerous Legacy.* New York: Random House, 2009.

Holbrook, Stewart H. *Lost Men of American History.* New York: Macmillan, 1946.

Holt, Michael F. *By One Vote: The Disputed Presidential Election of 1876.* Lawrence: University Press of Kansas, 2008.

Holzer, Harold, ed. *Dear Mr. Lincoln: Letters to the President.* Reading MA: Addison-Wesley, 1993.

Hoover, Herbert. *An American Epic.* 3 vols. Chicago: H. Regnery, 1959.

———. *American Individualism.* Garden City NY: Doubleday Page, 1923.

———. *Memoirs.* Vol. 3: *The Great Depression, 1929–1941.* New York: Macmillan, 1952.

———. *The New Day: Campaign Speeches of Herbert Hoover.* Palo Alto CA: Stanford University Press, 1928.

Hoover, Irwin. *Forty-Two Years in the White House.* Boston: Houghton Mifflin, 1934.

Hosack, David. *Memoir of DeWitt Clinton: With an Appendix, Containing Numerous Documents, Illustrative of the Principal Events of His Life.* New York: J. Seymour, 1829. https://archive.org/details/memoirofdewittcl00hosa.

Howe, Daniel Walker. *What Hath God Wrought: The Transformation of America, 1815–1848.* New York: Oxford University Press, 2009.

Ickes, Harold L. *The Secret Diary of Harold L. Ickes.* Vol. 3: *The Lowering Clouds, 1939–1941.* New York: Simon & Schuster, 1954.

Isaacson, Walter, ed. *Profiles in Leadership: Historians on the Elusive Quality of Greatness.* New York: Norton, 2010.

Jackson, Isaac R. *The Life of William Henry Harrison, the People's Candidate for the Presidency.* Philadelphia: Marshall, Williams & Butler, 1840. https://archive.org/details/lifeofwilliamhenry00jackson.

Jefferson, Thomas. *The Works of Thomas Jefferson.* Edited by Paul Leicester Ford. New York: G. P. Putnam's Sons, 1904–5.

———. *The Writings of Thomas Jefferson.* Edited by Andrew A. Lipscomb and Albert Ellery Burgh. Washington DC: Thomas Jefferson Memorial Association, 1904.

Johnson, Donald Bruce. *The Republican Party and Wendell Willkie.* Urbana: University of Illinois Press, 1960.

Johnson, Paul. *A History of the American People.* New York: HarperCollins, 1997.

Johnson, Robert Underwood, and Clarence Clough Buel, eds. *Battles and Leaders of the Civil War.* 4 vols. 1887–88. Reprint, New York: Thomas Yoseloff, 1956.

Joslin, Theodore G. *Hoover Off the Record.* Garden City NY: Doubleday Doran, 1934.

Kaminski, John P., and Jill Adair McCaughan, eds. *A Great and Good Man: George Washington in the Eyes of His Contemporaries.* Madison WI: Madison House, 1989.

Kengor, Paul. *The Crusader: Ronald Reagan and the Fall of Communism*. New York: Harper Perennial, 2007.

Kennedy, James Ronald, and Walter Donald Kennedy. *Was Jefferson Davis Right?* Gretna LA: Pelican, 1998.

Kennedy, Robert F. *The Enemy Within*. New York: Harper, 1960.

———. *To Seek a Newer World*. New York: Doubleday, 1967.

Kitman, Marvin. *George Washington's Expense Account*. New York: Simon & Schuster, 1970.

Laing, Margaret. *Robert Kennedy*. New York: Coward-McCann, 1968.

Lamb, Brian, comp. *Booknotes: Life Stories. Notable Biographers on the People Who Shaped America*. New York: Three Rivers Press, 1999.

———, comp. *Booknotes: Stories from American History*. New York: Public Affairs, 2001.

Lamb, Martha J. *History of the City of New York: Its Origin, Rise, and Progress*. 3 vols. New York: Valentine's Manual, 1922.

Langguth, A. J. *Patriots: The Men Who Started the American Revolution*. New York: Simon & Schuster, 1988.

Larrabee, Eric. *Commander in Chief: Franklin Delano Roosevelt, His Lieutenants and Their War*. New York: HarperCollins, 1987.

Lasky, Victor. *Robert F. Kennedy: The Myth and the Man*. New York: Trident Press, 1968.

Lebergott, Stanley. *The Americans: An Economic Record*. New York: Norton, 1984.

Lester, Paul Martin. *On Floods and Photo Ops: How Herbert Hoover and George W. Bush Exploited Catastrophes*. Jackson: University Press of Mississippi, 2010.

Leuchtenburg, William E. *Herbert Hoover*. New York: Times Books, 2009.

Lewis, David Levering. "The Implausible Wendell Willkie: Leadership Ahead of Its Time." In *Profiles in Leadership: Historians on the Elusive Quality of Greatness*, edited by Walter Isaacson, 229–59. New York: Norton, 2010.

Liggett, Walter W. *The Rise of Herbert Hoover*. New York: H. K. Fly, 1932.

Lilly Library. *An Exhibit: Wendell Willkie, 1892–1944*. Catalogue. Bloomington IN: Lilly Library, Indiana University, 1980.

Lincoln, Abraham. *The Collected Works of Abraham Lincoln*. 8 vols. Edited by Roy P. Basler. New Brunswick NJ: Rutgers University Press, 1953. http://quod.lib.umich.edu/lincoln/.

Lindsey, Lawrence. *What a President Should Know . . . but Most Learn Too Late: An Insider's View on How to Succeed in the Oval Office*. Lanham MD: Rowman & Littlefield, 2008.

Lloyd, Craig. *Aggressive Introvert: A Study of Herbert Hoover and Public Relations Management, 1912–1932*. Columbus: Ohio State University Press, 1973.

Locher, James R., III. *Victory on the Potomac: The Goldwater-Nichols Act Unifies the Pentagon*. College Station: Texas A&M University Press, 2002.

Lodge, Henry Cabot. *George Washington: The Man*. Boston: Houghton Mifflin, 1898.

Lokos, Lionel. *Hysteria 1964: The Fear Campaign against Barry Goldwater.* New Rochelle NY: Arlington House, 1967.

Lord, Russell. *The Wallaces of Iowa.* Boston: Houghton Mifflin, 1947.

Lucas, Stephen E. *The Quotable George Washington: The Wisdom of an American Patriot.* Madison WI: Madison House, 1999.

Lundberg, Ferdinand. *Imperial Hearst: A Social Biography.* New York: Equinox Corporative Press, 1936.

Lyons, Eugene. *Our Unknown Ex-President: A Portrait of Herbert Hoover.* Garden City NY: Doubleday, 1948.

Macdonald, Dwight. *Henry Wallace: The Man and the Myth.* New York: Vanguard, 1948.

Makey, Herman O. *Wendell Willkie of Elwood.* Elwood IN: National Book, 1940.

Markowitz, Norman D. *The Rise and Fall of the People's Century: Henry A. Wallace and American Liberalism, 1941–1948.* New York: Free Press, 1973.

Marshall, Katherine Tupper. *Together: Annals of an Army Wife.* New York: Tupper and Love, 1946.

Martin, John Bartlow. *Jimmy Hoffa's Hot: A Crest Special.* Greenwich CT: Fawcett, 1959.

Marvel, William. *Mr. Lincoln Goes to War.* Boston: Houghton Mifflin, 2006.

Matlock, Jack F., Jr. *Reagan and Gorbachev: How the Cold War Ended.* New York: Random House, 2004.

McAdoo, W. G. "American Right." Speech. 1917. http://www.firstworldwar.com/audio/americanrights.htm.

———. *Crowded Years: Reminiscences of William G. McAdoo.* Boston: Houghton Mifflin, 1931.

———. "Decent Treatment of the Public by Corporations and Regulation of Monopoly: A Speech . . . before the Chamber of Commerce, Boston, Mass." January 30, 1911. Internet Archive. https://archive.org/stream/xcollection351c1/xcollection351c1_djvu.txt.

———. "The Modern Corporation." Speech. February 7, 1908.

———. *The Relations between Public Corporations and the Public.* New York: Alexander Hamilton Institute, 1910.

———. "The Subway Problem." Speech delivered at the Sixth Annual Dinner under the Auspices of the Board of Trustees of Plymouth Church. Brooklyn, NY. January 19, 1911. http://www.nycsubway.org/wiki/The_Subway_Problem.

McClellan, George B. *McClellan's Own Story: The War for the Union.* London: Sampson, Law, Marston, Searle & Rivington, 1887.

McClure, Alexander. *Abraham Lincoln and Men of War-Times: Some Personal Recollections of War and Politics during the Lincoln Administration.* New York: Times, 1892.

McPherson, James M. *Embattled Rebel: Jefferson Davis and the Confederate Civil War.* New York: Penguin, 2014.

McWhiney, Grady. *Cracker Culture: Celtic Ways in the Old South*. Tuscaloosa: University of Alabama Press, 1988.

Miller, Merle. *Plain Speaking: An Oral Biography of Harry S. Truman*. New York: Berkley, 1974.

Moore, Jacob Bailey. *The Contrast, or Plain Reasons Why William Henry Harrison Should Be Elected President of the United States, and Why Martin Van Buren Should Not Be ReElected*. New York: J. P. Griffing, 1840.

Moore, John L. *Speaking of Washington: Facts, Firsts, and Folklore*. Washington DC: Congressional Quarterly, 1993.

Morello, John A. *Selling the President, 1920: Albert D. Lasker, Advertising, and the Election of Warren G. Harding*. Westport CT: Praeger, 2001.

Morison, Samuel Eliot. *Harrison Gray Otis, 1765–1848: The Urbane Federalist*. Boston: Houghton Mifflin, 1969.

Moscow, Warren. *Roosevelt and Willkie*. Englewood Cliffs NJ: Prentice-Hall, 1968.

Murray, Charles. *Real Education*. New York: Crown, 2008.

Nasaw, David. *The Chief: The Life of William Randolph Hearst*. Boston: Houghton Mifflin, 2000.

Nash, Lee, ed. *Understanding Herbert Hoover: Ten Perspectives*. Stanford CA: Hoover Institution Press, 1987.

Neal, Steve. *Dark Horse: A Biography of Wendell Willkie*. Garden City NY: Doubleday, 1984.

———. *Happy Days Are Here Again: The 1932 Democratic Convention, the Emergence of FDR—and How America Was Changed Forever*. New York: William Morrow, 2004.

Nelson, John T., II. "General George C. Marshall: Strategic Leadership and the Challenges of Reconstituting the Army, 1939–1941." 1993. http://.strategic studiesinstitute.army.mil/pubs/display.cfm?PubID=358.

Nevins, Allan. *Abram S. Hewitt: With Some Account of Peter Cooper*. New York: Harper & Bros., 1935.

Newell, Terry. *Statesmanship, Character, and Leadership in America*. New York: Palgrave Macmillan, 2012.

Nixon, Richard M. *RN: The Memoirs of Richard Nixon*. New York: Grosset and Dunlap, 1978.

Noonan, Peggy. *When Character Was King: A Story of Ronald Reagan*. New York: Viking, 2001.

Norton, A. Banning. *Reminiscences of the Log Cabin and Hard Cider Campaign*. Mount Vernon OH: A. B. Norton, 1888.

Novak, Michael. *Choosing Presidents: Symbols of Political Leadership*. New Brunswick NJ: Transaction, 1992.

Novak, Robert D. *The Agony of the GOP 1964*. New York: Macmillan, 1965.

Oates, Stephen B. *Abraham Lincoln: The Man behind the Myths*. New York: Harper & Row, 1984.

Papers of Abraham Lincoln. www.papersofabrahamlincoln.org.

Parmet, Herbert S., and Marie B. Hecht. *Never Again: A President Runs for a Third Term*. New York: Macmillan, 1968.

Payne, Robert. *The Marshall Story: A Biography of General George C. Marshall*. New York: Prentice-Hall, 1951.

Pearson, Drew. *Washington Merry-Go-Round: The Drew Pearson Diaries, 1960–1969*. Lincoln NE: Potomac, 2015.

Peel, Roy V., and Thomas C. Donnelly. *The 1928 Campaign: An Analysis*. New York: Richard R. Smith, 1931.

Perlstein, Rick. *Before the Storm: Barry Goldwater and the Unmaking of the American Consensus*. New York: Hill and Wang, 2001.

Peters, Charles. *Five Days in Philadelphia: The Amazing "We Want Willkie!" Convention of 1940 and How It Freed FDR to Save the Western World*. New York: Public Affairs, 2005.

Pietrusza, David. *1920: The Year of Six Presidents*. New York: Carroll & Graf, 2007.

Procter, Ben. *William Randolph Hearst: The Early Years, 1863–1910*. Oxford: Oxford University Press, 1998.

———. *William Randolph Hearst: Final Edition, 1911–1951*. Oxford: Oxford University Press, 2007.

Puryear, Edgar F., Jr. *American Generalship: Character Is Everything. The Art of Command*. New York: Presidio, 2000.

Raphael, Ray. *Mr. President: How and Why the Founders Created a Chief Executive*. New York: Knopf, 2012.

Reagan, Ronald. *An American Life: The Autobiography*. New York: Simon & Schuster, 1990.

———. *Reagan: A Life in Letters*. Edited by Kiron Skinner, Annelise Anderson, and Martin Anderson. New York: Free Press, 2003.

Reagan, Ronald, and Richard G. Hubler. *Where's the Rest of Me?* New York: Duell, Sloan and Pearce, 1965.

Reeves, Richard. "John F. Kennedy." In *Character Above All: Ten Presidents from FDR to Bush*, edited by Robert A. Wilson, 82–104. New York: Simon & Schuster, 1995.

Rentschler, William H. *Goldwater: A Tribute to a Twentieth-Century Political Icon*. Lincolnwood IL: Contemporary Books, 2000.

Renwick, James. *A Discourse on the Character and Public Services of DeWitt Clinton*. New York: Carvill, 1829.

———. *Life of DeWitt Clinton*. New York: Harper & Brothers, 1840. http://babel.hathitrust.org/cgi/pt?id=loc.ark:/13960/t37084m7x;view=1up;seq=9.

Ritter, Halsted L. *Washington as a Businessman*. New York: Sears, 1931.

Roberts, Andrew. *Masters and Commanders: How Four Titans Won the War in the West, 1941–1945*. New York: Harper Perennial, 2010.

Rodenbough, Charles D. *Governor Alexander Martin: Biography of a North Carolina Revolutionary War Statesman*. Jefferson NC: McFarland, 2004.

Roosevelt, Elliott, with James Brough. *A Rendezvous with Destiny: The Roosevelts of the White House.* New York: G. P. Putnam's Sons, 1975.

Roosevelt, Franklin D. *The Public Papers and Addresses of Franklin D. Roosevelt. Volume 1: The Genesis of the New Deal, 1928–1932.* New York: Random House, 1938.

Roosevelt, Franklin D., and William D. Hassett. *The Happy Warrior, Alfred E. Smith: A Study of a Public Servant.* Boston: Houghton Mifflin, 1928.

Roosevelt, James. *My Parents: A Differing View.* New York: Playboy Press, 1976.

Root, Oren. *Persons and Persuasions.* New York: Norton, 1974.

Rosenman, Sam. *Working with Roosevelt.* New York: Harper & Bros., 1952.

Russo, Gus, and Stephen Molton. *Brothers in Arms: The Kennedys, the Castros, and the Politics of Murder.* New York: Bloomsbury, 2008.

Schaller, Michael. *Ronald Reagan.* New York: Oxford University Press, 2011.

Schapsmeier, Edward L., and Frederick H. Schapsmeier. *Henry A. Wallace of Iowa: The Agrarian Years, 1910–1940.* Ames: Iowa State University Press, 1970.

Schlafly, Phyllis. *A Choice Not an Echo.* Alton IL: Pere Marquette Press, 1964.

Schlesinger, Arthur M., Jr. *The Age of Roosevelt.* Vol. 1: *The Crisis of the Old Order 1919–1933.* 1957. Reprint, New York: Mariner, 2003.

———. *The Cycles of American History.* New York: Houghton Mifflin, 1986.

———. *Robert Kennedy and His Times.* Boston: Houghton Mifflin, 1978.

———, ed. *Running for President: The Candidates and Their Images.* 2 vols. New York: Simon & Schuster, 1994.

Schweizer, Peter. *Reagan's War: The Epic Story of His Forty-Year Struggle and Final Triumph over Communism.* New York: Doubleday, 2002.

Scully, Frank. *Rogues' Gallery: Profiles of My Eminent Contemporaries.* Hollywood: Murray & Gee, 1943.

Severn, Bill. *Samuel J. Tilden and the Stolen Election.* New York: Ives Washburn, 1968.

Shadegg, Stephen. *Barry Goldwater: Freedom Is His Flight Plan.* New York: Fleet, 1962.

Shannon, William V. *The Heir Apparent: Robert Kennedy and the Struggle for Power.* New York: Macmillan, 1967.

Shenkman, Richard. *Presidential Ambition: Gaining Power at Any Cost.* New York: Harper Perennial, 2000.

Sherwood, Robert E. *Roosevelt and Hopkins: An Intimate History.* New York: Harper & Bros., 1948.

Shlaes, Amity. *The Forgotten Man: A New History of the Great Depression.* New York: HarperCollins, 2007.

Silber, William. *When Washington Shut Down Wall Street: The Great Financial Crisis of 1914 and the Origins of America's Monetary Supremacy.* Princeton NJ: Princeton University Press, 2007.

Sinclair, Andrew. *The Available Man: The Life behind the Masks of Warren Gamaliel Harding.* New York: Macmillan, 1965.

Siry, Steven E. *DeWitt Clinton and the American Political Economy: Sectionalism, Politics and the Republican Ideology, 1787–1828.* New York: Peter Lang, 1990.

Skinner, Kiron K., Annelise Anderson, and Martin Anderson, eds. *Reagan, in His Own Hand: The Writings of Ronald Reagan That Reveal His Revolutionary Vision for America.* New York: Free Press, 2001.

Smith, Gene. *The Shattered Dream: Herbert Hoover and the Great Depression.* New York: William Morrow, 1970.

Smith, Richard Norton. *Thomas E. Dewey and His Times.* New York: Simon & Schuster, 1982.

———. *An Uncommon Man: The Triumph of Herbert Hoover.* New York: Simon & Schuster, 1984.

Smith, Robert H. *Clinton's Ditch: The Erie Canal–1825.* Del Mar CA: C Books, 2002.

Smith, Theodore C. *The Wars between England and America.* New York: Henry Holt, 1914.

Sobel, Robert. *Herbert Hoover at the Onset of the Great Depression, 1929–1930.* Philadelphia: J. B. Lippincott, 1975.

Southwick, Leslie H. *Presidential Also-Rans and Running Mates, 1788–1980.* Jefferson NC: McFarland, 1984.

Sproat, John G. *The Best Men: Liberal Reformers in the Gilded Age.* New York: Oxford University Press, 1968.

Stagg, J. C. A. *Mr. Madison's War: Politics, Diplomacy, and Warfare in the Early American Republic, 1783–1830.* Princeton NJ: Princeton University Press, 1983.

Steel, Ronald. *In Love with Night: The American Romance with Robert Kennedy.* New York: Simon & Schuster, 2000.

———. *Walter Lippmann and the American Century.* Boston: Atlantic Monthly Press, 1980.

Stein, Jean, and George Plimpton. *American Journey: The Times of Robert Kennedy.* New York: Harcourt Brace Jovanovich, 1970.

Steinberg, Alfred. *The First Ten: The Founding Presidents and Their Administrations.* Garden City NY: Doubleday, 1967.

Steiner, Mark E. *An Honest Calling: The Law Practice of Abraham Lincoln.* DeKalb: Northern Illinois University Press, 2006.

Stephens, Alexander H. *Recollections of Alexander H. Stephens: His Diary Kept When a Prisoner at Fort Warren, Boston Harbour, 1865.* Edited by Myrta L. Avary. New York: Doubleday, Page, 1910.

Stoddard, Henry L. *It Costs to Be President.* New York: Harper & Bros., 1938.

Stone, I. F. *In a Time of Torment: 1961–1967.* Boston: Little, Brown, 1967.

———. *The War Years, 1938–1945.* Boston: Little, Brown, 1988.

Stone, Irving. "Samuel J. Tilden." In *They Also Ran: The Story of the Men Who Were Defeated for the Presidency.* 1943. Reprint, Garden City NY: Doubleday, 1966.

Storing, Herbert J., ed. *The Complete Anti-Federalist*. Chicago: University of Chicago Press, 1981.

Stuckey, Mary E. *Playing the Game: The Presidential Rhetoric of Ronald Reagan*. New York: Praeger, 1990.

Swanberg, W. A. *Citizen Hearst: A Biography of William Randolph Hearst*. New York: Scribner, 1961.

Szasz, Ferenc Morton. *Abraham Lincoln and Robert Burns: Connected Lives and Legends*. Carbondale: Southern Illinois University Press, 2008.

Taylor, Robert L., and William E. Rosenbach. *Military Leadership: In Pursuit of Excellence*. Boulder CO: Westview Press, 1992.

Tebbel, John William. *The Life and Good Times of William Randolph Hearst*. New York: E. P. Dutton, 1952.

Thomas, Evan. *The War Lovers: Roosevelt, Lodge, Hearst, and the Rush to Empire, 1898*. Boston: Little, Brown, 2010.

Thompson, Kenneth, ed. *Statesmen Who Were Never President*. Vol. 3. Lanham MD: University Press of America, 1997.

Todd, Charles Stewart, and Benjamin Drake. *Sketches of the Civil and Military Services of William Henry Harrison*. 1840. Reprint, New York: Arno Press, 1975.

Truman, Harry S. *Where the Buck Stops: The Personal and Private Writings of Harry S. Truman*. Edited by Margaret Truman. New York: Warner Books, 1989.

Tyrrell, R. Emmett, Jr. *The Conservative Crack-Up*. New York: Simon and Schuster, 1992.

Unger, Debi, and Irwin Unger. *George Marshall: A Biography*. New York: HarperCollins, 2014.

Unger, Harlow Giles. *The Unexpected George Washington: His Private Life*. Hoboken NJ: John Wiley & Sons, 2006.

Van Buren, Martin. *The Autobiography of Martin Van Buren*. Edited by John C. Fitzpatrick. 1920. Reprint, New York: De Capo Press, 1973.

Villard, Oswald Garrison. *Prophets True and False*. New York: Knopf, 1928.

Von Damm, Helene. *Sincerely, Ronald Reagan*. Ottawa IL: Green Hill, 1976.

Walker, Stanley. Introduction to *This Is Wendell Willkie: A Collection of Speeches and Writings on Present-Day Issues*, by Wendell L. Willkie, 1–37. New York: Dodd, Mead, 1940.

Wallace, Henry A. *Democracy Reborn*. Edited by Russell Lord. New York: Reynal & Hitchcock, 1944.

Wallison, Peter J. *Ronald Reagan: The Power of Conviction and the Success of His Presidency*. Boulder CO: Westview Press, 2003.

Walton, Richard J. *Henry Wallace, Harry Truman and the Cold War*. New York: Viking, 1976.

Ward, Geoffrey C. "Presidents, Imperial or Otherwise." *American Heritage* 38, no. 4 (1987): 20.

Washington, George. *George Washington's Rules of Civility and Decent Behaviour in Company and Conversation.* Edited by Charles Moore. Cambridge M A: Printed for Houghton Mifflin Company by the Riverside Press, 1926.

———. *The Papers of George Washington.* Edited by W. W. Abbot and Dorothy Twohig. Charlottesville: University Press of Virginia, 1997.

———. *Washington on Washington.* Edited by Paul Zall. Lexington: University Press of Kentucky, 2003.

———. *Writings.* Edited by John Rhodehamel. New York: Library of America, 1997.

———. *The Writings of George Washington from the Original Manuscript Sources, 1745–1799.* Edited by John C. Fitzpatrick. Washington D C: U.S. Government Printing Office, 1931–44. https://archive.org/details/writingsofgeorge27wash

Watson, James E. *As I Knew Them: Memoirs of James Watson, Former United States Senator from Indiana.* Indianapolis N Y: Bobbs-Merrill, 1936.

Weedon, Ann. *Hearst: Counterfeit American.* New York: American League against War and Fascism, 1936.

Wehle, Louis B. *Hidden Threads of History: Wilson through Roosevelt.* New York: Macmillan, 1953.

Welles, Gideon. *Diary of Gideon Welles.* Boston: Houghton Mifflin, 1911.

White, F. Clifton, and William J. Gill. *Why Reagan Won: A Narrative History of the Conservative Movement 1964–1981.* Chicago: Regnery Gateway, 1981.

White, Leonard D. *The Federalists: A Study in Administrative History.* New York: Macmillan, 1948.

White, Theodore H. *The Making of the President, 1964.* New York: Atheneum, 1965.

Whiting, Justin R. *Wendell L. Willkie, 1892–1944: Courageous Pioneer of the Utility Industry.* New York: Newcomen Society in North America, 1950.

Whyte, Kenneth. *The Uncrowned King: The Sensational Rise of William Randolph Hearst.* Berkeley C A: Counterpoint, 2009.

Wilentz, Sean, ed. *The Best American History Essays on Lincoln.* New York: Palgrave Macmillan, 2009.

Willkie, Wendell. *An American Program.* New York: Simon & Schuster, 1944.

———. "Government and the Public Utilities." Address at a joint meeting of Economic Club of New York and Harvard Business School Club. Privately printed, January 21, 1935.

———. *One World.* New York: Simon & Schuster, 1943.

Wills, Garry. *Cincinnatus: George Washington and the Enlightenment.* Garden City N Y: Doubleday, 1984.

Wilson, Douglas, and Rodney Davis, eds. *Herndon's Informants: Letters, Interviews, and Statements about Abraham Lincoln.* Urbana: University of Illinois Press, 1998.

Wilson, James. *Documentary History of the Ratification of the Constitution.* Edited by Merrill Jensen et al. Madison: Wisconsin Historical Society Press, 1976.

Wilson, Joan Hoff. *Herbert Hoover: Forgotten Progressive*. Boston: Little, Brown, 1975.

Wilson, Woodrow. *Papers of Woodrow Wilson*. 69 vols. Edited by Arthur S. Link. Princeton NJ: Princeton University Press, 1966–94.

Winik, Jay. *April 1865: The Month That Saved America*. New York: Harper Perennial, 2006.

Winkler, John K. *William Randolph Hearst: A New Appraisal*. New York: Hastings House, 1955.

Woods, Thomas E., Jr. *Meltdown: A Free-Market Look at Why the Stock Market Collapsed, the Economy Tanked, and Government Bailouts Will Make Things Worse*. Washington DC: Regnery, 2009.

ILLUSTRATION CREDITS